Fiscal Policy in Economic and Monetary Union

Fiscal Policy in Economic and Monetary Union

Theory, Evidence and Institutions

Marco Buti

Director of the Economies of the Member States, European Commission

Daniele Franco

Director, Public Finance Division, Research Department, Bank of Italy

Edward Elgar

Cheltenham, UK • Northampton, MA, USA

Published by
Edward Elgar Publishing Limited
Glensanda House
Montpellier Parade
Cheltenham
Glos GL50 1UA
UK

Edward Elgar Publishing, Inc.
136 West Street
Suite 202
Northampton
Massachusetts 01060
USA

This book has been printed on demand to keep the title in print.

A catalogue record for this book
is available from the British Library

Library of Congress Cataloguing in Publication Data
Buti, Marco.
Fiscal policy in EMU : theory, evidence, and institutions / Marco Buti, Daniele Franco.
p. cm.
Includes bibliographical references.
1. Fiscal policy—European Union countries. 2. Monetary policy—European Union countries. 3. Economic and Monetary Union. 4. European Union countries—Economic integration. I. Franco, Daniele, 1953– II. Title.

HJ1000.B88 2006
332.4'566'094—dc22 2005044221

ISBN 1 84542 017 9 (cased)

Contents

Figures

Tables

Foreword

European Monetary Union (EMU) is an ambitious endeavour and a new historical development. Many countries have given up their own monetary and exchange rate policy and have delegated responsibility to the newly created European Central Bank. Fiscal policy has remained a national responsibility. This creates a new policy framework with new incentives and constraints.

Monetary Union became operational in 1999. In 2002 coins and banknotes were introduced in 12 countries. The common monetary policy has rapidly consolidated and the euro has become part of the European way of life.

The success of the euro contrasts with the problematic developments concerning the fiscal policy framework that was expected to complement and support the common currency. Several countries have deficits in excess of the agreed limits. Procedures have been modified according to countries' pressures. Fiscal rules are widely criticized while reform proposals abound. The endpoint of these development is very much uncertain.

In the debate on Europe's Economic and Monetary Union, fiscal policy has occupied a special place since the beginning. The Maastricht fiscal policy criteria and the Stability and Growth Pact are probably the most contentious building blocks of EMU's institutional architecture. They have aroused heated controversies between academic economists, policy makers and informed observers at large. Positions have often been extreme: those who see the Pact as a fundamentally flawed piece of accounting arithmetic that would not stand the test of reality are opposed by others who view it as an untouchable building block of EMU without which the whole construct of the single currency would crumble.

As EMU's fiscal rules undergo the first severe shock of the severe slowdown of the beginning of the 2000s and an uncertain economic recovery, the radicalism of the debate is far from abating. Europe is still searching for its fiscal soul: 'the Stability Pact is dead, long live the Pact'.

We have been involved in the policy debate concerning European fiscal rules since the mid-1990s. We have long supported the need for rules in the EMU framework. The developments of the last decade have taught us that the implementation of rules is in no way an easy task. Economic problems and political considerations frequently conflict with the required fiscal behaviour.

We have also been taught that there are no miracle solutions to the European fiscal policy dilemmas: the difficult trade-offs between rules and flexibility and between common objectives and national interests will stay with us.

The rules introduced in the 1990s may not be perfect, but no alternative solution has emerged as clearly superior. Better national budgetary procedures, tighter coordination at the European level, greater fiscal transparency and more effective market-based fiscal discipline can all contribute to ensuring a sound fiscal policy framework. But common fiscal rules still represent the main pillar of EMU. Improving their design and implementation while maintaining simplicity and transparency is the main challenge ahead.

It is clear that the EU fiscal rules are not set in stone. While many proposals of reform have been put forward, the mainstream debate revolves around the technical and political issues dealt with in this book: from the nature of the 3 per cent of GDP deficit ceiling to setting the appropriate medium-term budgetary targets, from the role of fiscal policy in cyclical stabilization to the long term sustainability of public finances, from the contribution of public finances to potential growth to statistical governance. These are also the main issues that have been debated in European fora which culminated with the reform of the Stability and Growth Pact in spring 2005. Such chapters are discussed in a Postscript at the end of the volume.

This book is about the origins, the rationale, the problems and the prospects of the European fiscal policy framework. It aims at providing the reader with a roadmap to understand the evolution of the debate on fiscal policy in EMU. Our basic premise is that one cannot fully understand EMU's fiscal rules without placing them in a historical perspective and abstracting from the uniqueness of EMU where sovereign countries retain a large degree of fiscal independence while monetary policy is entrusted to an independent central bank with the overriding mission of maintaining price stability. Hence any relevant analysis of fiscal policy in EMU has to uncover its historical roots, develop a theory of supranational fiscal rules and devote particular attention to its institutional architecture.

The book brings together in a structured fashion work that we have done since 1998. It includes both analytical and policy-oriented studies. Several chapters have been adapted, in particular by dropping clearly outdated sections. Although each chapter is self-contained, we trust that the final outcome will be more than the sum of the individual parts. The completion of this book would have not been possible without the contribution of several people. We are particularly grateful to our coauthors who graciously allowed us to reproduce our joint papers here: Mike Artis, Fabrizio Balassone, Anne Brunila, Sylvester Eijffinger, Mario Nava, Paul van den

Noord, Hedwig Ongena, Werner Roeger, Jan in't Veld and Stefania Zotteri. Their continuous intellectual stimulus and friendship over all these years has been paramount in our endeavour.

Several chapters were originally published in different journals: Chapters 2 and 11 in *Oxford Review of Economic Policy*, Chapters 3, 5 and 9 in *Journal of Common Market Studies*, Chapter 4 in *Empirica*, Chapter 6 in *Fiscal Studies*, and Chapter 8 in *Journal of Public Finance and Public Choice*. We thank the editors of those journals for their permission to use this material.

We are also indebted to Vittorio Gargaro and Renzo Pin who provided excellent editorial support. Finally, the assistance of Luke Adams was instrumental for the rapid publication of the book.

1. EMU's fiscal rules in a historical perspective*

1. INTRODUCTION

Fiscal sustainability is a central tenet of European Monetary Union (EMU); it is a pre-condition for financial and monetary stability. Budgetary flexibility is needed for stabilization policy; it has become more important in EMU as member states can no longer rely on a monetary policy tailored to meet national needs nor on exchange rate adjustments. EMU fiscal rules have been designed with the goal to ensure that national policies keep a sound fiscal stance while allowing sufficient margins for budgetary flexibility in bad times.

The Stability and Growth Pact (SGP) commits EMU member states to a medium-term objective of budgetary position close to balance or in surplus. The main rationale for such a target is that its attainment will allow member states to deal with normal cyclical fluctuations while keeping the government deficit within the value of 3 per cent of GDP set in the Treaty of Maastricht.[1] Compliance with this threshold, and with the 60 per cent ceiling for the debt to GDP ratio, will prevent the public finances of EMU member states from taking unsustainable paths.

In this chapter we try to assess to what extent the issue facing the founders of EMU was a new one in the field of public finance and to what extent the solution chosen can be regarded as innovative. To this end, in the second section we review the literature on budgetary rules from its very beginning to the years immediately before the Treaty of Maastricht. The review is largely based on quotations drawn from economists and policy makers. On the basis of this review, in the third section we argue that the bulk of EMU fiscal regulation does not qualify as innovative; however, the interaction between the multinational nature of EMU and the lack of a federal political authority (a truly innovative feature) shaped the solution chosen. The highly decentralized setting of fiscal policy in EMU gave prominence to moral hazard issues and EMU fiscal

*Fabrizio Balassone and Daniele Franco, 'EMU Fiscal Rules: A New Answer to an Old Question?', Banca d'Italia, proceedings of the workshop on Fiscal Rules, 2002.

rules, while drawing heavily on ideas that are central to the long-lasting debate on fiscal rules, are innovative in the way in which different approaches are blended and complemented by innovative and pragmatic choices.

2. THE BALANCED BUDGET RULE AND ITS AMENDMENTS

Mankind has always displayed a certain degree of awareness of the potential negative effects of excessive borrowing. Exhortation to sound fiscal behaviour can be found as early as in the Bible: 'And thou shalt lend unto many nations, but thou shalt not borrow' (Deuteronomy 15:6).

Several centuries later, as Hansen (1941, p. 110) reminds us:

> Scholastic theologicians, like Thomas Aquinas, were bitterly opposed to loans . . . Political philosophers of the early modern period continued to regard the prior accumulation of treasures as superior to borrowing . . . [For] Jean Bodin . . . emergencies should be met by accumulated hoards, and only war provided justification for extraordinary levies or loans. Thomas Hobbes was more realistic . . . [allowing] the monarch [to resort] occasionally even to the public credit . . . [but] Adam Smith reverted to the older tradition . . . Hume likewise wrote . . . [that] to mortgage the public revenues . . . [is] a practice that appears ruinous.

Burkhead (1954) notes that there is a common body of doctrine that may be characterized as the classical view of debt and deficits that goes from Smith to Mill. These writers recognized that there are productive uses to which borrowed resources may be put; however, they feared that unproductive use was more likely and strongly opposed deficit finance when giving policy advice. They noted that interest payments would pose a burden on future taxpayers, but their main concern was the loss of wealth borne when the deficit was incurred in the first place.

Smith opposed an unbalanced budget on the grounds that government borrowing would deprive society of resources which could be invested more productively. He also noted that beyond a certain threshold, debt inevitably leads to national bankruptcy.

Say argued that the possibility of borrowing allows governments

> to conceive gigantic projects that lead sometimes to disgrace, sometimes to glory, but always to a state of financial exhaustion; to make war themselves and stir up others to do the like; to subsidize every mercenary agent and deal in the blood and the consciences of mankind; making capital which should be the fruit of industry and virtue, the prize of ambition, pride, and wickedness.[2]

Ricardo refers to the debt as 'one of the most terrible scourges which was ever invented to afflict a nation',[3] as 'a system which tends to make us less thrifty, to blind us to our real situation'. He feared that the citizen initially 'deludes himself with the belief, that he is as rich as before' and then, faced with the taxes levied to pay for the debt, is tempted 'to remove himself and his capital to another country, where he will be exempted from such burdens'.[4]

In short, for a long time the only budgetary rule was that of a balanced budget. This rule was probably based on an analogy between government and family finance drawn when the budget of the state was the budget of a monarch and was separate from the finances of his subjects. The precept was therefore to avoid living beyond one's means: 'As Adam Smith put it, "what is prudence in the conduct of every private family, can scarcely be folly in that of a great kingdom" '[5] or, following Dickens' Mr Micawber: 'if a man had twenty pounds a year for his income, and spent nineteen pounds nineteen shillings and sixpence, he would be happy, but . . . if he spent twenty pounds he would be miserable'.[6]

In the second part of the nineteenth century, the precept of a balanced budget still found widespread endorsement. Ursula Hicks notes that 'Gladstonian budgeting is inextricably bound up with the theory of the ever-balanced (or even over-balanced) budget' (1953, p. 25) and quotes the following statement by Lowe, a disciple of Gladstone: 'I would define a Chancellor of the Exchequer as an animal who ought to have a surplus; if under extraordinary conditions he has not a surplus he fails to fulfil the very end and object of his being' (p. 25).[7]

Deficit and debt drew less attention from economists. For instance, as Burkhead (1954) notes, Marshall's *Principles* devote no attention to these issues. Noticeably, Puviani (1903) devotes most of his analysis of fiscal illusion to public expenditure and revenue. While he notes that politicians may prefer borrowing to extraordinary levies because citizens underestimate future interest burdens, this argument remains relatively unimportant in his analysis of the methods employed by governments to influence citizens' perception of fiscal policy.

The consensus on the balanced budget is witnessed by Pigou's 1929 writing:

> in normal times the main part of a government's revenue is required to meet regular expenditure that recurs year after year. There can be no question that in a well-ordered state all such expenditure will be provided for out of taxation, and not by borrowing. To meet it by borrowing . . . would involve an ever-growing government debt and a corresponding ever-growing obligation of interest. . . . The national credit would suffer heavy damage; . . . This thesis is universally accepted. (1929, p. 233)

Even after the Keynesian revolution the virtue of a balanced budget kept being praised. Truman's 1951 *Economic Report of the President* stated that 'we should make it the first principle of economic and fiscal policy in these times to maintain a balanced budget, and to finance the cost of national defence on a "pay-as-we-go" basis'.

As Schumacher noted in 1944, the precepts of sound public finance were grounded in the opinion that the economy is self-equilibrating:[8]

> The logical corollary of orthodox economics is orthodox finance. If it is believed that all factors of production are normally and inevitably utilised by private business, it follows that the state can obtain the use of such factors only by preventing private business from using them. . . . From this it follows that the first principle of 'sound' public finance is that the budget should be balanced. (p. 86)

Almost 70 years later than Pigou, Buchanan echoes his words: 'the first century and one-half of our national political history did, indeed, embody a norm of budget balance. This rule was not written in the constitution document, as such, but rather it was part of an accepted set of attitudes about how government should, and must, carry on its fiscal affairs' (1997, p. 119).

However, even in family finance borrowing is not necessarily evil. Even classical advocates of the balanced budget were aware of the necessity of allowing borrowing in certain circumstances and of its usefulness in others. Therefore economists have had a hard job in trying to specify in what circumstances exceptions to the balanced budget rule were to be allowed, caught between the Scylla of missed opportunities as a consequence of the constraint and the Charybdis of waste and instability caused by its removal.

The need for exceptions as well as the need for tight rules to deal with them was clearly recognized by Pigou (1929). He deemed it to be plain that when

> non-remunerative government expenditures *on a wholly abnormal scale* have to be undertaken, as in combating the consequences of an earthquake or to meet an imminent threat of war . . . to collect what is required, and required at a very short notice in these conditions, through the machinery of taxation is politically and administratively impracticable. (p. 39; emphasis added)

He also argued that concerning 'government expenditure devoted to producing capital equipment . . . *the fruits of which will subsequently be sold to purchasers for fees* . . . it is generally agreed that the required funds ought to be raised by loans. . . . Upon this matter . . . there is no room for controversy' (p. 36; emphasis added). Finally, he notes that 'since changes in taxation always involve disturbance, to keep the rates of taxation as nearly as possible constant from year to year . . . it may be desirable . . . to arrange a budget so that good and bad years make up for one another, *a deficit in one balancing a surplus in another*' (p. 35; emphasis added).

2.1 Ordinary vs. Extraordinary Finance

One first exception was thus found in the distinction between ordinary and extraordinary finance: the former dealt with recurrent expenditures, to be financed by recurrent revenues so as to avoid the depletion of non-renewable assets; the latter dealt with one-off outlays to be backed also by borrowed funds. Also the rationale for this exception was found by way of analogy to family finance. De Viti de Marco (1934) points out that 'if an individual has to face an expense which he reckons to exceed his annual income . . . he will either have to sell his assets or raise a loan' (p. 390; our translation) and applies the same line of reasoning to public finances.[9]

De Viti de Marco is very much aware of classification problems as the extraordinariness of an outlay is a matter for subjective assessment both at the individual and at the collective level: 'this subjective element does not allow to define a rigorous and objective rule that draws the line . . . between ordinary and extraordinary finance' (1953, p. 390, our translation). Margins for moral hazard and opportunistic behaviour arise as 'the distinction between "ordinary" and "extraordinary" receipts and expenditure is admittedly not clear-cut, depending ultimately on the judgement of the classifying authority as to whether the receipts and expenditure in question are to continue indefinitely in the future' (United Nations, 1951, p. 61).

While extreme cases were easily identified (on the one hand, interest outlays and salaries; on the other, the cost of a war), in some cases it is not straightforward to see what is ordinary and what is not. 'It is impossible to define *ex ante* what is an extraordinary outlay. Building a school may be an extraordinary effort for a small town, an ordinary one for a big city' (Einaudi, 1948, p. 318; our translation). Ultimately,

> there is no great technical difficulty in producing for a series of years budgets which are balanced at the end of the year to the nearest penny . . . Perhaps half a dozen financial writers in the country would understand from the published accounts what was happening, but I doubt if any one of the half dozen is capable of making the position clear to the public.[10]

National experiences did not differ much. 'In the case of France, the extraordinary budget was proverbially the dumping place for all expenditures which could not be balanced by tax receipts' (Hansen, 1941, p. 199). In 1945 Keynes notes that in the United Kingdom

> the present criterion leads to meaningless anomalies. A new G.P.O. is charged 'below', a new Somerset House 'above'. A Capital contribution to school buildings is 'above' in the Exchequer Accounts and is paid for out of Revenues, and is 'below' in the Local Authority Accounts and is paid for out of loans. The cost of a road is 'above', of a railway 'below'. And so on.[11]

In Canada, although not always realised even by Canadians, a budgetary distinction between ordinary and capital expenditures has been made ever since the confederation in 1867. The official reports show surpluses in fifty of the sixty-six years following 1867; but if the accounting were made on the United States basis, surpluses would appear in only fifteen of the sixty-six years (Hansen, 1941, p. 199).[12]

2.2 The Double Budget

The double budget is a refinement of the ordinary/extraordinary distinction which reduces the degree of arbitrariness of the decision concerning which expenditures can be deficit-financed. The budget is split into a current and a capital account. While the former must be balanced or in surplus, the latter can run a deficit (the so-called *golden rule*) and thus the cost of durables can be spread over all the financial years in which they will be in use rather than charging them entirely to one year. It can be a powerful instrument in overcoming liquidity constraints and fostering economic development structurally.

Arguments along these lines can be found earlier than the dual budget debate per se. The productive character of a large part of public outlays was noted by German scholars in the second part of the nineteenth century. They also argued that government can borrow to finance undertakings that are expected to improve the income of future generations (Cohn, 1895). Bastable (1927) argues that 'non-economic (i.e. non-remunerative) expenditure is primarily to be met out of income, and, unless it can be so dealt with, ought not to be incurred . . . [and] . . . that borrowing should hardly ever be adopted except for strictly economic expenditure, and then only when the extension of the state domain is clearly advisable' (pp. 670–71).

The usefulness of a dual budget has been long debated.[13] It is still an unsettled issue, which has been tackled in different ways in different countries and at different times. Sweden introduced the dual budget in 1937 and suppressed it in 1980.

First of all, the distinction between current and capital items retains a certain degree of ambiguity which can be used opportunistically. 'The classification procedures which are to be followed in separating "current" and "capital" transactions are among the most controversial and difficult questions in budgetary procedure, especially in view of the frequent abuses of so-called "capital budgets" in hiding deficits which otherwise would have become apparent' (United Nations, 1951, p. 11).

According to Lindbeck (1968), this distinction 'facilitated tactical political manoeuvres and hampered the fiscal policy debate for many years [in Sweden] by focusing it on complicated bookkeeping issues understood by very few and of very little economic relevance' (p. 34).

In principle, one can distinguish between durable goods producing a direct revenue, durable goods producing an indirect revenue as, respectively, investments by publicly owned enterprises and public infrastructures that reduce the costs borne by private producers and/or consumers, and durable goods with pure consumption functions. It may be argued that the latter should be excluded from the capital account as they do not affect growth and thus do not imply a future financial benefit for the public sector; therefore they worsen the sector's net worth.

In practice, however, the divide between the second and the third category is very unclear. In the case of infrastructures, for example, there is the issue of the treatment of expenditures determined by the attempt to reduce the impact on the environment. If the overall costs increase should these expenditures be considered as producing an indirect revenue or as pure consumption? If for this reason we include in the capital account all durables, we end up creating a distortion in allocation only based on duration, rather than on contribution to growth, thus 'the analogy with private accounting may be conductive to an irrational preference for capital expenditures over current expenditures' (Goode and Birnbaum, 1955, p. 1).[14]

Clearly there are current expenditures, such as those increasing human capital, that can give a relevant contribution to growth as 'indirect revenue need not come through a durable good' (Steve, 1972, p. 164; our translation). If one is not careful about the expenditures to be included in the capital section, the dual budget may result 'in a preference for expenditures on physical assets rather than greater spending for intangibles such as health or education' (Colm and Wagner, 1963, p. 125). Thus, 'the need for a return, either in the limited financial sense or in the broader context of the social return, is a view that needs to be applied over a wider spectrum of public expenditures and not confined to capital budget only' (Premchand, 1983, p. 296).

However, the inclusion in the capital account (which can be financed through debt) of all expenditures contributing to human capital would imply high levels of deficits and pose serious problems of classification.[15]

One should also take into account that a part of expenditures replaces existing capital.

Furthermore, the possibility to borrow, without strict limits, in order to finance investments can lower the attention paid when evaluating the costs and benefits of each project. In a way, with the double budget the analogy between government and private finance moves from the household to the business sector where the distinction between current and capital budget is customary. But the analogy between public sector accounts and those of private enterprises overlooks the absence of mechanisms that would penalize the public body investing in low revenue projects.

2.3 Stabilization Policy

Another attempt at justifying deviations from the balanced budget rule came from Keynesian theory where the budget plays a crucial role in cushioning the effects of cyclical downswings in the economy compensating for insufficient private demand. Therefore a balanced budget was no longer to be achieved in each financial year but to be attained over the whole length of the economic cycle.

On 5 April 1933 Keynes wrote in *The Times*: 'The next budget should be divided into two parts, one of which shall include those items of expenditure which it would be proper to treat as loan-expenditure in the present circumstances.' Later he sharpens the distinction between the government's own current expenditure and a capital budget to provide for sufficient national investment. In 1942 he writes: 'I should aim at having a surplus on the ordinary budget, which would be transferred to the Capital Budget, thus gradually replacing dead-weight debt by productive or semi-productive debt . . . I should not aim at attempting to compensate cyclical fluctuations by means of the ordinary budget, I should leave this duty to the capital budget.'[16]

Fiscal policy in Sweden and in the USA moved along these lines.[17] In 1937 Sweden reformed its budget rules and abandoned the annual balancing. In Lindbeck's account, the Swedish reform was based on the idea that 'in normal times the capital budget should be financed by loans whereas the current budget should be financed by taxes. In boom periods the current budget should, however, be overbalanced, hence part of the capital budget would be financed by taxes; in recession the current budget should be underbalanced, hence partly financed by loans' (1968, p. 33).

Hansen explains how in the USA,

> President Roosevelt . . . divided federal expenditures into 'ordinary' and 'extraordinary'. The former relate to the 'operating expenditure for the normal

> and continuing functions of government' . . . [and] . . . should be met out of current revenues' . . . He expressed the hope that in times of prosperity current revenues would so far exceed ordinary expenditures as to produce 'a surplus that can be applied against the public debt' . . . The extraordinary expenditures, which are concerned with loans, capital expenditure and relief of need, he deemed to be sufficiently flexible in character as to permit their contraction and expansion as a 'partial offset for the rise and fall in the national income'. (1941, p. 219)

However, the idea of balancing the government accounts over the course of the business cycle had an exceptionally brief life span. Blinder and Solow (1974) point out that while it 'had considerable appeal . . . in the immediate post-Keynesian years, when the balanced budget was [still] influential, it is almost never discussed nowadays' (p. 37). It was the turn of functional finance to take the lead: 'Functional finance rejects completely the traditional doctrines of "sound finance" and the principle of trying to balance the budget over the solar year or any other arbitrary period . . . government fiscal policy . . . shall all be undertaken with an eye only to the results of these actions on the economy' (Lerner, 1943, p. 41). And Hansen noted that 'if one adopts wholeheartedly the principle that government financial operations should be regarded exclusively as instruments of economic and public policy, the concept of a balanced budget, however defined, can play no role in the determination of that policy' (1941, p. 188).

The way in which these ideas were first met is exemplified in the following passage by Chamberlain in 1933:[18] 'If I were to pretend I could lay out a programme under which what I borrowed this year would be met by a surplus at the end of three years, everyone would soon perceive that I was only resorting to the rather transparent device of making an unbalanced budget look respectable.'[19]

It was also pointed out that

> the requirement of a balanced budget was and still is the simplest and clearest rule to impose 'fiscal discipline' and to hold government functions and expenditure to a minimum . . . Even an avowedly counter-cyclical policy is believed to give rise to an upward trend in expenditures that might not otherwise occur. The expenditures undertaken to counteract a depression are unlikely to be discounted in the succeeding boom. If the boom is countered at all, the measures taken will be credit restriction or increased taxation. (Smithies, 1960)

The obstacles posed by politics to a symmetric and timely reaction of the budget to cyclical developments were stressed. Agreement over the appropriate budgetary items to use may take too long; it may prove difficult to reduce expenditures once they have been increased. Drees (1955) and Steve (1972) provide early discussions of the relevance of the balance of powers between the Parliament and the government and of the relationship between the government and its parliamentary majority: budgetary rules cannot be evaluated per se but need to be set in the overall institutional context.

Among the remedies suggested to the political problem described, an enhanced reliance on automatic stabilizers and the so-called formula flexibility were suggested. The latter consisted in the introduction of a predetermined relationship between tax rates (or benefits levels) and the level of economic activity.[20]

But support in favour of functional finance was strong.

> Even if stability in the budget has something to recommend it, stability in the economy is surely better . . . Who makes the rule? Who decides when to abide to it and when to countermand it? Furthermore, within the framework of a political democracy, the case for taking stabilisation policy out of the hands of politicians is an uneasy one: into whose hands shall it be placed? . . . No budgetary rule can be provided with a solid intellectual foundation. This will hardly be new to economists. The best that can be said for rules is that some of them may be better than incompetently managed discretionary policy. (Blinder and Solow, 1974, pp. 43 and 45)

This view was broadly accepted in some public finance textbooks.[21]

Along the same lines, though less aggressively, Steve (1972) notes that 'budgetary policy cannot be reduced to simple rules, it should take into account the overall effects of the budget on private demand components and national income' (p. 170; our translation).[22]

The stagflation in the 1970s; the difficulties concerning the estimate of the actual impact of budget changes on the economy; the risks of fine tuning given the lags between the decision to change the budget and its implementation; the development of theoretical models questioning the possibility for the government to influence the level of government activity all contributed to a decline of interest in the theory of functional finance.

Advocates of the balanced budget regained the fore. 'The balanced-budget principle played a crucial role in holding the pre-Keynesian fiscal constitution together, and constraining the otherwise inherent biases of that system to over-expenditure and deficit finance. Once the balanced-budget had been bowled over by the Keynesian revolution, those biases were unleashed' (Buchanan *et al.*, 1978, p. 47).[23] And politicians praised again the virtues of balanced budgets:

> At one time, it was regarded as the hallmark of good government to maintain a balanced-budget; to ensure that, in time of peace, Government spending was fully financed by revenues from taxation, with no need for Government borrowing. Over the years, this simple and beneficent rule was increasingly disregarded . . . And I have balanced the budget. (Nigel Lawson, Budget Statement, 1988)

The recent policy debate has largely recognized that in normal circumstances automatic stabilizers ought to be allowed to operate freely.[24] On the contrary, discretionary fiscal action is generally considered problematic in view of irreversibility and timing problems and of the uncertainty about its effects.[25]

3. EMU FISCAL RULES: A NEW ANSWER TO AN OLD QUESTION?

European Monetary Union represents a new historical development. For the first time a number of sovereign countries have adopted a common currency while retaining independent fiscal policies. The need for fiscal rules complementing monetary union has been at the core of the debate on EMU since the early 1990s.[26]

Some arguments were put forward against the introduction of fiscal rules at the European level. It was noted that fiscal rules may have costs in terms of stabilization policies and may hamper the achievement of allocative and distributive objectives. It was also noted that excessively stringent rules may be counter-productive. If the Pact leads to an unduly tight fiscal stance in one or more countries, pressure may mount on the European Central Bank (ECB) to deliver a monetary offsetting.[27] Otherwise, the credibility of the Pact may be endangered.[28]

However, the prevailing view in the policy debate was clearly in favour of the introduction of formal rules. It was argued that procedural or fiscal rules are necessary because the factors that in recent decades have determined fiscal profligacy in several countries have not disappeared. Moreover, the multinational dimension of EMU is likely to increase the need for such rules.

Stark (2001) describes the genesis and the rationale of the Stability and Growth Pact;[29] he stresses how in Europe, up to the early 1990s, lax fiscal policy

> occurred although it is indisputable that unsound fiscal policy practices have adverse effects on price stability, growth and employment: large deficits and large public debt place constraints on the ability of a country . . . to act during different stages of the business cycle . . .; the state's absorption of resources which would otherwise have found their way into private investments results in higher long term interest rates . . .; . . . a stifling government debt ratio impair(s) the overall efficiency of an economy and create(s) risks to price stability . . .; these problems are especially pronounced in monetary union since . . . the policy of a single country might have adverse consequences for all the other participating countries.

These arguments combine the two main strands of opinion about the budgetary balance: the one stressing the importance of stabilization policies and budgetary flexibility and the other maintaining that unbalanced budgets imply distortions in the allocation of resources.

It was also pointed out that, without strong rules, the legal independence of the ECB may turn out to be an empty shell because of pressure by high-debt countries for *ex ante* bail-out (refraining from raising interest rates in conditions of inflationary tensions) or *ex post* bail-out (debt relief through unanticipated inflation). EMU can induce unilateral fiscal expansions since governments may feel less inclined to preserve fiscal rectitude, as they individually face a less steep interest rate schedule in a monetary union than under flexible exchange rates.

The debate on fiscal rules in EMU was grounded on the wider debate that took place in the 1990s about the role of fiscal institutions and procedures in shaping budgetary outcomes.[30] While certain political configurations, such as weak coalition governments, have been recognized as conducive to budgetary misbehaviour or to hampering attempts to redress the budgetary situation,[31] inadequate budgetary institutions and procedures may also contribute to a lack of fiscal discipline.[32]

In this context, institutional reforms in the fiscal domain have been discussed and introduced in several countries. As noted by Beetsma (2001), these reforms come in two main categories: (a) the introduction of procedural rules conducive to a responsible fiscal behaviour and (b) the introduction of a fiscal rule, that is, a permanent constraint on domestic fiscal policy in terms of an indicator of the overall fiscal performance (budget balance, borrowing, debt, reserves) of central and/or local government.

In national experiences, both types of measures have proved to be effective tools in containing political biases in fiscal policy-making and in achieving and sustaining fiscal discipline. In a multinational context, the adoption of harmonized tight budgetary procedures may lead to fundamental problems from the point of view of national sovereignty (Beetsma, 2001). Moreover, institutional reforms are more difficult to monitor centrally, compared with numerical targets. The latter are also simpler to evaluate and easier to grasp by public opinion and policy makers. In the end a clear consensus emerged about the introduction of common numerical rules and an elaborated multilateral surveillance mechanism.[33]

The fiscal framework of EMU was developed gradually. The Treaty of Maastricht in 1992 set the fiscal criteria to be met for joining Monetary Union. The Stability and Growth Pact (SGP), adopted by the European Council in Amsterdam in June 1997, developed these criteria with a view to permanently restraining deficit and debt levels while allowing room for fiscal stabilization. The Pact also strengthened the monitoring procedures complementing the quantitative rules.

3.1 A Description[34]

As we have anticipated in the introduction, EMU fiscal rules have been designed with the goal to ensure that national policies keep a sound fiscal stance while allowing sufficient margins for budgetary flexibility in bad times.

The Treaty of Maastricht stated that budget deficits cannot be larger than 3 per cent of GDP unless (a) there are exceptional circumstances, such as deep recessions, (b) they remain close to 3 per cent, (c) the excess only lasts for a limited period of time.[35] If the deficit exceeds the 3 per cent limit when the above three conditions are not met, the deficit is deemed 'excessive' and it sets off a procedure intended to force corrective measures by the deviating country. If such measures are not taken the Treaty foresees monetary sanctions which increase as situations of excessive deficit persist.

The Stability and Growth Pact specified what is meant by 'exceptional' and 'limited period' in the clauses allowing a deficit greater than 3 per cent of GDP not to be considered 'excessive'. A recession is considered exceptional if real GDP diminishes by 2 per cent. Milder recession (where the reduction in real GDP is at least 0.75 per cent) may also be considered exceptional if, for example, it is abrupt. The excess above 3 per cent must be reabsorbed as soon as the 'exceptional circumstances' allowing it are over.

The Pact also specified that each country should aim for a medium-term objective of a budgetary position 'close to balance or in surplus'. According to the guidelines provided by the European Council, the choice of the medium-term target should take into account both the budgetary risks of recessions and those linked to fluctuations of other economic factors (e.g. interest rates). Countries with debt ratios above 60 per cent of GDP should also take into account the need to decrease such ratios, at a satisfactory pace, towards the threshold. Moreover, an increase in the debt ratio during recessions should be avoided.[36] Finally, other risk factors, such as the effects of demographic trends, ought to be taken into account.[37]

According to the European Council, compliance with the Pact should be assessed considering the cyclical position of the economy. In practice, EMU fiscal rules require that each member state choose a budgetary target in cyclically adjusted terms and let automatic stabilizers or discretionary action operate symmetrically around it. The lower this budget balance with respect to the 3 per cent threshold, the wider the margins for counter-cyclical policy without running the risk of an excessive deficit.

Each member state must submit its budgetary targets officially in multi-year budgetary documents (stability programmes); these documents are updated annually and are subject to a review by the European Commission aimed at assessing their consistency with EMU fiscal rules.

Overall, the approach taken by the EU can be characterized as less flexible than the solutions adopted in some federally structured countries:[38]

1. the rules are defined on the basis of established numerical parameters;
2. *ex post* compliance with the parameters is required each year; overshoots must be rapidly dealt with;
3. margins of flexibility are envisaged only in connection with exceptional cyclical events (established *ex ante* as a decline in GDP) or in any case events beyond the governments' control;
4. no special provision is made for investment expenditure;
5. monitoring procedures are envisaged, whereby peer pressure is strengthened by the European Council's power to make formal representations to governments of the need to adopt corrective measures during the year and by the application of preestablished monetary sanctions.

3.2 A New Answer to an Old Question?

With European Monetary Union the need for fiscal rules arises in a multinational context for the first time. The review in the previous section shows how the arrangements adopted are deeply embedded in the long-lasting debate on budgetary rules. The novel features of EMU guided the choice between alternative solutions and required the introduction of some innovations.

The need to reconcile fiscal soundness and budgetary flexibility led to different approaches being combined:

- Setting a predetermined upper bound for the deficit is a new pragmatic solution;[39]
- Balancing the budget over the cycle is a precept derived from the Keynesian approach. In 1951 a report by the United Nations, commenting on the 1937 Swedish reform, points out that 'while counter-cyclical budgeting introduced an element of flexibility in the fiscal policy of Government, the concept of "financial soundness" has been retained' (p. 69);

- Prudence when fixing the average target to be achieved over the cycle ('close to balance or in surplus') has a classical flavour. In 1927 Bastable argued that 'the safest rule for practice is that which lays down the expedience of estimating for a moderate surplus, by which the possibility of a deficit will be reduced to a minimum' (p. 611).

The stress on fiscal soundness motivates the rejection of a dual budget approach and of any distinction between ordinary and extraordinary finance. However, pragmatism called for the allowance of margins for exceptional circumstances, this rests on the idea that 'in some circumstances, indeed, a balanced budget is a pedantic luxury, which a community, hard pressed by sudden and exceptional misfortune, can ill afford' (Dalton *et al.*, 1934, p. 12).

A broadly balanced budget, like that required by the SGP, may negatively affect the public investment level; this effect can be especially relevant during the transition to the low debt levels consistent with the chosen structural balance. The double burden determined by this transition can be assimilated to that arising from the transition from a pay-as-you-go to a funded pension system. However, besides the criticism of the double budget system examined in the previous sections, in the context of EMU the golden rule would be an obstacle to deficit and debt reduction. In particular, given the ratio of public investment as a percentage of GDP, the long-run equilibrium level of government debt could be very high, especially in an environment of low inflation. This could imply that the debt ratio would rise in low-debt countries, while in high-debt countries there would be a very slow pace of debt reabsorption. The golden rule would also meet with practical difficulties, such as the evaluation of amortization, and would make the multilateral surveillance process more complex by providing leeway for opportunistic behaviour. Governments would have an incentive to classify current expenditure as capital spending.[40]

The asymmetry in EMU between the monetary regime, with the single currency and a single monetary authority, and the political landscape, lacking an authority of federal rank, gave prominence to moral hazard issues. It is probably at the root of the rejection of both the dual budget and the distinction between ordinary and extra-ordinary finance. It motivated the adoption of a detailed multilateral surveillance procedure and the introduction of a predetermined limit for the annual deficit in a framework that envisages the targeting of a balanced budget over the cycle.[41]

EMU may be termed a 'radical federation', where in the absence of fiscal rules member states enjoy absolute autonomy in matters of public expenditure and taxation and recourse to debt. In this context, the stability of monetary and financial conditions represents a public good to which all local governments contribute by maintaining sustainable budget positions. There is an incentive for each local government to exploit the benefits accruing from the discipline of others without itself complying with the rules. This creates a double cost for the other entities: the free-rider's excessive indebtedness can put pressure on interest rates to rise; it can also result in bankruptcies requiring bail-outs.[42]

The need for monitoring was felt also in earlier days. For instance, Durrell (1917) argues that: 'the public and the Parliament should be satisfied that . . . there is some authority which . . . will give timely warning if that expenditure or those obligations are either outrunning the revenue provided for the year or engaging the nation too deeply in the future' (p. 242). However the monitoring procedure adopted for EMU is novel with respect to its scale, complexity and tightness.

Until now the chosen mix of approaches has been successful in securing a reduction in budget deficits and debt across EMU member states. It remains to be seen whether it will also be successful in maintaining fiscal discipline once at regime. Unfavourable economic developments will test EMU's fiscal constitution and the issue of legitimacy of rules in a democracy pointed out by Blinder and Solow may come to the fore again.

Fiscal rules can be successfully implemented over a long period of time only if public opinion considers them a valuable contribution to policy-making. In the words of Bastable (1927):

> it but remains to again lay emphasis on the fact that good finance cannot be attained without intelligent care on the part of the citizens. The rules of budgetary legislation are serviceable in keeping administration within limits; but prudent expenditure, productive and equitable taxation, and due equilibrium between income and outlay will only be found where responsibility is enforced by the public opinion of an active and enlightened community. (p. 761)

2. The Maastricht Treaty and the Stability and Growth Pact*

1. INTRODUCTION

The European Economy and Monetary Union (EMU) is built on solid fiscal discipline requirements. The Stability and Growth Pact (SGP), which aims to uphold fiscal discipline once in EMU, demands that member states achieve a budgetary position which allows them to respect the Treaty's deficit criterion, even during periods of unfavourable growth. The SGP makes it clear that the 3 per cent of GDP reference value can be breached only temporarily and in exceptional circumstances. The waivers foreseen in the SGP are subject to such stringent conditions that the 3 per cent of GDP threshold becomes *de facto* a strict upper limit for the deficit, which EMU members will want to avoid breaching in order not to be put into excessive deficit and risk incurring sanctions.

Countries participating in the euro area need to attain a sound fiscal position to face the budgetary consequences of adverse economic developments without having to resort to pro-cyclical behaviour. As spelled out in the Resolution of the European Council on the SGP, 'adherence to the objective of sound budgetary positions close to balance or in surplus will allow all member states to deal with normal cyclical fluctuations while keeping the government deficit within the value of 3 per cent of GDP'. Fiscal discipline and flexibility are thus the main principles governing budgetary policy in EMU. Fiscal discipline strengthens the credibility of monetary policy, while flexibility is required to deal with country-specific shocks (European Commission, 1990).

The Pact focuses exclusively on the budget balance as the main operational variable to establish and maintain budgetary discipline. Such exclusive attention to the deficit sparked criticism in the policy debate, where it was stressed that the risks of instability in EMU are more likely to be related to the high levels of outstanding debt than to overshooting the deficit threshold.

* Marco Buti, Daniele Franco and Hedwig Ongena, 'Fiscal Discipline and Flexibility in EMU, The Implementation of the Stability and Growth Pact', *Oxford Review of Economic Policy*, 1998, 14(3): 81–97.

Several questions have been raised since the SGP's adoption in June 1997. What is a medium-term budgetary position of 'close to balance or in surplus'; how quickly should the highly indebted countries reduce their debt ratio towards the 60 per cent of GDP reference point; how should overall budgetary behaviour change to comply with the Pact; will fiscal flexibility be hindered? These questions are examined in this chapter. The chapter takes the institutional set-up of the Pact as given and explores its implications for the behaviour of budgetary authorities.

The second section of the chapter provides a brief overview of the Maastricht fiscal rules and recalls the debate on the initial proposal for a '*Stability Pact for Europe*' by the German Finance Minister, Theo Waigel. The main provisions of the Stability and Growth Pact are also examined in this section as well as the rationale for a common commitment to ensure fiscal discipline in EMU. The third section analyses the ongoing debate on the Pact's implementation and its impact on budgetary policy-making in EMU. The fourth section addresses some of the open policy issues related to the implementation of the Pact.

2. ENSURING FISCAL DISCIPLINE IN EMU

2.1 Fiscal Discipline in the Maastricht Treaty

The requirements of achieving fiscal discipline to join the single currency and of maintaining it once in EMU are at the core of the Maastricht Treaty. Article 104 of the Treaty states that, in EMU, '*Member states shall avoid excessive government deficits*'.

Compliance with the Treaty's fiscal discipline requirement is assessed, *inter alia*, on the basis of the behaviour of the government budget deficit in relation to the reference value of 3 per cent of GDP and by the evolution of the government debt ratio with respect to the 60 per cent of GDP threshold. The deficit criterion is satisfied when the government deficit ratio remains below the 3 per cent of GDP threshold or has fallen substantially and continuously and comes close to that level.

The Treaty allows the 3 per cent ceiling to be exceeded without causing an excessive deficit, but only under a highly restrictive set of conditions. The original cause of the rise of the deficit above the 3 per cent ceiling must be 'exceptional', the deficit must, in any case, remain close to this threshold, and must return promptly below it once the initial driving force is over. The range of events not giving rise to an excessive deficit depends on the degree of restriction with which these conditions are interpreted but the Treaty does not provide any further indications to guide this interpretation.

The government debt ratio has to remain below 60 per cent of GDP or has to be on a clearly downward path towards that level. Government debt is defined as gross debt at nominal value outstanding at the end of the year and consolidated between and within the sectors of general government. Data availability and definitional problems as well as the fact that financial instability concerns are usually linked to gross rather than net debt motivated this choice.

When a country is subject to a Council decision on the existence of an excessive deficit, a procedure aimed at correcting this situation is initiated. This procedure includes several steps involving increasing pressure on the member state through recommendations and notice to take effective measures to reduce the deficit. If such correction does not take place, the Maastricht Treaty foresees that sanctions may be applied to EMU members. Among the sanctions cited in the Treaty are non-interest bearing deposits and fines. The Treaty, however, leaves a certain discretion to the Council on the application and the content of these sanctions and does not set time limits on the various steps of the procedure.

2.2 The Initial Waigel Proposal

A proposal for a 'Stability Pact for Europe' was put forward by the German Finance Minister, Theo Waigel, in November 1995. While clearly stating that no renegotiation of the Maastricht criteria for participation in EMU was envisaged, Waigel's Pact presented a number of proposals to make fiscal prudence watertight in EMU. In order to achieve this, member states were supposed to enter a voluntary commitment encompassing the following elements:

- setting a medium-term goal of 1 per cent of GDP in 'normal' economic conditions, thereby providing a safety margin of 2 percentage points of GDP above this target so that the 3 per cent of GDP deficit limit would not be breached even in economically unfavourable periods;
- granting exceptions to observance of the 3 per cent limit only in extreme circumstances, such as an annual fall in real GDP by at least 2 per cent or a decrease in GDP during four quarters in a row;
- failure to comply with the 3 per cent of GDP threshold would automatically trigger pecuniary sanctions, in the form of non-interest bearing deposits of 0.25 per cent of GDP for each point or share of a point of the budget deficit above the 3 per cent ceiling. This deposit was to be transformed into a fine if an excessive deficit still existed two years later.

Other elements of the proposal envisaged a further reduction of the government debt ratio to well below the reference value of 60 per cent of GDP, a limitation of the share of the government sector in the economy by keeping the rate of growth of government expenditure below that of nominal GDP and the creation of a 'Stability Council', composed of the member states participating in EMU, which would supervise the strict application of the Stability Pact.

While the aim of ensuring that budgetary discipline would not be only an entry criterion but a permanent feature of EMU was widely shared, a number of these provisions were not retained. The automaticity of sanctions was deemed to go beyond the provisions of the Treaty, which left a degree of discretion to the European Commission and Ecofin Council in this respect. The additional constraint on government debt was considered unnecessary because a sustained budget balance below the 3 per cent of GDP reference value would automatically imply a progressive fall of the government debt ratio to well below the 60 per cent of GDP reference point.

A uniform target of 1 per cent of GDP was deemed not to take sufficient account of country-specific requirements and was considered neither necessary nor sufficient to guarantee respect of the 3 per cent ceiling. In addition, the lack of any flexibility on the 'exceptionality' clause concerning the severity of recessions was considered too harsh. Finally, reducing the share of the government sector in the economy, while probably desirable for purely efficiency reasons, was not accepted as a general rule. The freedom of each country to decide on the split between private and government sector activities – in conformity with the so-called subsidiarity principle – and the lack of evident cross-country spill-overs led to this choice.

2.3 After the Negotiations: The Stability and Growth Pact

Negotiations on the Pact were conducted during 1996 and the first half of 1997. The politically difficult issue of the 'exceptional' conditions under which a breach of the 3 per cent threshold was allowed were settled at the European Council in Dublin in December 1996.

The final package, adopted by the European Council in Amsterdam in June 1997, included a Council Regulation on strengthening the surveillance of budgetary positions – the preventive arm of the Pact – and one on speeding up and clarifying the implementation of the excessive deficit procedure – the dissuasive arm. These two legal texts were complemented by two European Council resolutions: the first on the commitments by all the actors to move swiftly in the event of fiscal misbehaviour, and the second on growth and employment.

The core elements of the Stability and Growth Pact include:

- Pursuing country-specific 'medium-term objectives of budgetary positions close to balance or in surplus', so as to allow member states to respect the 3 per cent ceiling even during economic downturns.
- Defining the meaning of the 'exceptionality' condition. This condition recognizes that, in the event of a harsh and persistent recession, the budgetary room for manoeuvre between close-to-balance and a deficit of 3 per cent of GDP may not be sufficient to cushion the negative effects of the shock on economic activity. In particular, this can be called on if the deficit overshooting takes place in the presence of a severe economic downturn.
  The latter is considered 'exceptional' if there is an annual fall of real GDP of at least 2 per cent. An annual fall of GDP of less than 2 per cent could nevertheless be considered exceptional in the light of further supporting evidence, such as the abruptness of the downturn or the accumulated loss of output relative to past trends. In any event, in evaluating whether the economic downturn is severe, the member states will, as a rule, take an annual fall in real GDP of at least 0.75 per cent as a reference point.
- Defining the meaning of the 'temporariness' condition. The excess of the deficit over 3 per cent of GDP will be considered temporary and thus allowed by the Pact only insofar as the 'exceptional' conditions mentioned above persist. Therefore, the deficit has to move back below the 3 per cent threshold in the year following that during which these 'exceptional' circumstances occurred.
- Specifying the scale of sanctions in the event of persistent excessive deficits. The amount of the non-interest bearing deposit in the first year of application of the sanctions is composed of a fixed component equal to 0.2 per cent of GDP and a variable component equal to one-tenth of the difference between the deficit and the 3 per cent reference value. A ceiling of 0.5 per cent of GDP is set. In each subsequent year, until the excessive deficit decision is abrogated, only the variable component will be applied. As a rule, a deposit is to be converted into a fine after two years if the excessive deficit persists. If no action is taken to correct the excessive deficit, sanctions can be imposed within the calendar year in which the decision on the existence of the excessive deficit is taken.
- Speeding up the excessive deficit procedure. In order to avoid the imposition of sanctions, the member state which has been put into excessive deficit needs to take immediate action and complete correction of the deficit in the year following the identification of the

excessive deficit. Thus, in order to avoid sanctions, the member state concerned should bring back its deficit below the reference value two years after the occurrence of an excessive deficit and one year after its identification, unless special circumstances are given. The Pact does not specify what these special circumstances are but it seems to be widely accepted that this clause could be relied on in case of protracted or very severe recessions.

The Pact does not define the meaning of the 'closeness' condition. So far, there has been no case of a member state having a deficit above but sufficiently close to the 3 per cent of GDP reference point for it to be put out of excessive deficit. A *de facto* interpretation of the 'closeness' condition based on the abrogation of the excessive deficit decision is thus not available either. As the Pact has given a sufficiently stringent interpretation of the 'exceptionality' and 'temporariness' conditions, a broader definition of the 'closeness' condition would not produce significantly different results with respect to the decision on the existence of an excessive deficit (Buti *et al.*, 1997).

Under the early-warning mechanism of the Pact, member states participating in the euro zone will have to submit stability programmes, while those not participating in EMU will have to present convergence programmes. The key feature of both types of programmes is the specification of the national medium-term budgetary objectives. The Council will regularly examine both sets of programmes. The Council can issue a recommendation under Article 99(4) of the Treaty urging the member state concerned to take adjustment measures, should significant slippage from the targets set in the programmes be identified.

The Pact applies to all EU countries but it stops short of imposing sanctions on the non-EMU members. It can be expected, however, that peer pressure and concern about being declared in excessive deficit would also exert discipline on the latter group.

2.4 Was There a Need to Supplement Maastricht?

Given the Maastricht fiscal rules – which, in the eyes of many scholars and policy makers already appear very strict – why did EU countries feel obliged to undertake a further commitment on budgetary discipline?

As explicitly stated in the initial proposal by Theo Waigel, clarifying and tightening up the Treaty provisions on the excessive deficit procedure was the main objective of the Pact. Several reasons for a Stability Pact in EMU have been put forward in the debate. These arguments boil down to three, not mutually exclusive, explanations. A formal commitment to a tight interpretation of the excessive deficit procedure of the Treaty would be helpful in:

- Tying the hands of politicians to *counter a domestic deficit bias* (Beetsma and Uhlig, 1999). The Pact can be interpreted as a 'commitment technology' to ensure fiscal prudence, since governments may feel less inclined to preserve fiscal rectitude, as they individually face a less steep interest rate schedule in a monetary union than under flexible exchange rates. The Maastricht public finance rules – specific numerical targets, with a precise calendar to achieve them – provided a strong incentive to pursue budgetary consolidation in the run-up to EMU. The credible threat of exclusion from the first wave of countries moving to the euro was considered a heavy penalty, especially for member states traditionally on the frontline of European integration. However, once in EMU, incentives to pursue budgetary retrenchment may weaken substantially as an equivalently powerful penalty – expulsion from the euro zone – is not foreseen by the Treaty. The 'temptation' to relax budgetary efforts may be further increased by the need to draw breath after the sharp acceleration in consolidation in 1997 and a need to move to the 'next stage' of policy-making in which governments care more about growth and employment than financial rigour. Some commentators (for example, Eichengreen and Wyplosz, 1998) have argued that such a shift in priorities may be beneficial as it would allow governments in the euro area to tackle the real problems hampering the functioning of EMU, namely the structural rigidities of European labour markets. The Pact, by increasing multilateral surveillance on budgetary developments, speeding up the excessive deficit procedure and specifying the application and type of sanctions, aims at countering such opportunistic behaviour.
- Achieving a *balanced policy mix* at the outset of EMU. From a short-term perspective, a common drive towards further fiscal adjustment will create the conditions to allow the European Central Bank (ECB) to deliver the desirable offsetting monetary response. As pointed out by Allsopp and Vines (1996, p. 99), '[o]nly if all [countries] act together will the monetary offset to fiscal tightening be likely to eventuate. Thus, participating governments will not only want to commit themselves, they will want to impose commitment on others as well'. Without such a common undertaking, the likelihood of an over-restrictive monetary stance would increase, also in view of the credibility-building strategy of the newly created ECB.
- Underpinning the *credibility of the single monetary authority* (Ackrill and Garrat, 1997; Artis and Winkler, 1997; Eichengreen and Wyplosz,

1998). Without strong fiscal rules, the legal independence of the ECB may turn out to be an empty shell because of pressure by high-debt countries for *ex ante* bail-out (refraining from raising interest rates in conditions of inflationary tensions) or *ex post* bail-out (debt relief through unanticipated inflation). As stated by McKinnon (1997, p. 228), 'once each European finance minister no longer has the central-bank support for debt management [. . .], very high nominal debts would become unsustainable unless the capital markets could see some tightly specified program for debt reduction already in place'. The SGP aims to fulfil this role.

3. CHANGES IN BUDGETARY BEHAVIOUR TO COMPLY WITH THE PACT

3.1 What is 'Close to Balance or in Surplus'?[43]

As stated earlier, member states should set their medium-term budgetary positions in such a way that they allow the provisions of the Stability and Growth Pact to be respected. Under a neutral discretionary policy, member states would have to aim for a budgetary position which allows the automatic stabilizers to operate fully without breaching the 3 per cent of GDP ceiling. The budgetary position targeted by the member states in 'normal' economic conditions corresponds to the budget balance corrected for the influence of cyclical fluctuations in economic activity.

If countries want to pursue an active counter-cyclical budgetary policy in addition to letting the automatic stabilizers play, a supplementary safety margin around the medium-term budgetary positions would need to be ensured. Additional room for manoeuvre would be created by setting the budgetary targets at a more ambitious level than would be the case if no such active budgetary policy was pursued. An additional safety margin may also be required to cope with unforeseen variability arising from factors such as unexplained tax shortfalls, more rapid expansion of spending on entitlement programmes than expected, and so on.

Unlike the numerical rules of the Maastricht Treaty – which set a common upper limit for the government deficit for all member states – the Pact introduces an element of country-specificity. The Pact *de facto* relies on the concept of the cyclically adjusted budget balance, a measure considered by several commentators as a more appropriate policy target than the actual deficit. As pointed out by Artis and Winkler (1997, p. 40), 'the 3 per cent ceiling on the actual deficit induces behaviour not much different from a target on structural deficits. The main difference is that countries can choose their target structural deficit for themselves, i.e., the optimal size of their "cushion" depending on their own preferences'.

In identifying a 'safe' medium-term budgetary position, the size and volatility of the budget's cyclical component need to be examined. These are determined by the size and volatility of cyclical fluctuations in output as well as by the sensitivity of the budget to the cycle.

It is still uncertain what effect the move to the EMU regime will have on the cyclical behaviour of the EU economies. As country-specific policy-induced shocks are likely to decrease in EMU, it can be expected that cyclical variations will be reduced and will become more similar between member states (European Commission, 1998b). However, as monetary policy in EMU will be geared towards the economic conditions prevailing in the EMU as a whole and since budgetary policy will remain less effective in the more open economies of the smaller member states, the economies of the smaller peripheral member states could still exhibit more pronounced variability than those of the large countries.

It is also unclear whether the sensitivity of budget balances to the cycle will change significantly once in EMU. While the ongoing reduction in the weight of the government sector in the economy may reduce the budget's cyclical sensitivity, such an effect will not take place overnight. Estimates by the Commission services indicate that, among the EMU countries, the highest budgetary sensitivity to the cycle is found in the Netherlands and Finland (0.8). All the other EMU countries have a sensitivity between 0.4 and 0.6. Outside EMU, Sweden has the highest sensitivity (0.9). Budgetary receipts are much more sensitive to cyclical fluctuations in economic activity than expenditure, owing to the importance of the tax share in the economy and to the progressivity of the tax system. Divergences in the cyclical sensitivity of revenue among member states are due to differences in tax rates and tax structures. Government transfers to households to cover costs related to unemployment are the only spending category which is deemed to react automatically to cyclical variations on the expenditure side. Other categories of government spending are considered to remain unaffected. Depending on the transfer system in place, the cyclical sensitivity of government spending may also vary significantly among member states.

If it is assumed that, in line with historical experience, the largest negative output gap that could occur once member states are in EMU amounts to 4 per cent of trend GDP[44] and that the sensitivity of the budget to the cycle will remain broadly unchanged in the coming years, then most of the countries would have to aim for an underlying budgetary position of between 0 and 1 per cent of GDP. The Netherlands and, outside EMU, Sweden, whose budgets have a higher sensitivity to the cycle, would need a small surplus.[45]

While all countries entering EMU will have to respect the close-to-balance rule, it can be argued that, in addition, high-debt countries should ensure a sufficiently fast reduction in their debt ratio. As discussed later, low-debt EMU members as well as, possibly, the ECB may have strong incentives to push for a high speed of debt reduction. Such additional conditions may require that the high-debt member states would have to go beyond the budgetary targets these countries would need to simply satisfy the deficit criterion.

Finally, while the need to establish sufficient room for manoeuvre to allow automatic stabilizers to work is an important concern in setting medium-term targets, other elements also play a role. For instance, a more ambitious budgetary position may be required to face the budget burden of future demographic developments. As shown by Franco and Munzi (1999), over the 1997–2030 period, the ageing population may increase the share to GDP of primary expenditure by, for example, around 6 to 7 percentage points in Finland and Germany, 5 to 5.5 points in Belgium, 4 to 5 points in Italy and the Netherlands, 2 to 4 points in Sweden and 1 to 3 points in Spain.[46]

3.2 The Evolution of the Debt Ratio during Recessions

The SGP focuses exclusively on government deficit and does not address the issue of government debt. The concern of ensuring the controllability of the target variable was at the root of this choice. From a theoretical standpoint, a deficit rule is important to underpin the 'functional', as opposed to the 'legal', independence of the central bank: as argued by Canzoneri and Diba (1996), without a credible deficit criterion, the central bank would not be able to keep control of the price level, which would have to adjust in order to ensure public finance solvency.

As discussed, if the 'right' medium-term target is pursued, the 3 per cent deficit threshold will always be respected, unless the negative shock to the budget has features of true exceptionality. In such a case, presumably, the exceptions granted by the Pact will be triggered. Therefore, while *ex ante* optimization is sufficient to prevent breaching the deficit rule, it may not be enough to keep the debt from rising during harsh recessions. This may be the case, in particular, for low-debt countries, that is, countries whose debt ratio exceeds the 60 per cent threshold but remains not far above it. The negative contribution of nominal GDP growth to the change in the debt ratio is lower the lower the level of the debt ratio. At very low rates of nominal GDP growth, this contribution diminishes and becomes insufficient to offset the debt-increasing effect of the deficit, even if the latter remains low. As a result, the debt ratio starts to increase. Therefore, it will be more difficult for low-debt countries to prevent their debt ratio from rising during periods of economic slowdown than for high-debt countries. For the low-debt countries, even strict observance of the deficit criterion may not be sufficient in the event of a severe recession to keep their debt ratio on a downward path.[47]

It is unlikely that countries having joined EMU with a relatively high stock of debt will initially be confronted with a debt ratio which starts rising again during periods of slow growth. As long as nominal GDP growth remains positive, the contribution of GDP growth to the decline in the debt ratio is likely to be sufficient to offset the debt-increasing effect of the deficit in these countries. As these highly indebted countries move to a position with a lower debt ratio, they could encounter the same type of problem.

Will a member state whose deficit remains below the 3 per cent of GDP threshold but whose debt ratio starts increasing during a recession be put in a situation of excessive deficit, and will such a member state be subject to sanctions? Up to now there is no precedent of a country being put into excessive deficit because of a violation of the debt criterion alone. There are no special provisions in the Treaty – as is the case for the deficit – allowing for an exceptional rise in the debt ratio during severe economic slowdowns. It is also not clear whether sanctions would be applied if a decision on the existence of an excessive deficit was taken in such a situation. The sanctions spelled out in the Pact only apply when the excessive deficit results from non-compliance with the deficit criterion. As with other issues, the Council will have to make a decision on a case-by-case basis, using the discretion allowed by the Treaty.

Member states will only be confronted with these problems during a transitory period when their debt ratio is still above the 60 per cent of GDP reference value. Once they have brought their debt ratio below this threshold and are operating at 'cruising speed', only the deficit criterion will be binding since no constraint is imposed by the Treaty as long as the debt ratio remains below the 60 per cent of GDP threshold.

3.3 Budgetary Behaviour Over the Cycle

How would member states' budgetary behaviour have to change in order to comply with the requirements of the Pact? Would the Pact have helped member states to avoid past policy mistakes?

Figure 2.1 presents an illustration of budgetary behaviour that is compatible with the SGP. In this graph, the overall budget balance and its cyclical and discretionary components are pictured against the output gap. Here it is assumed that the government maintains a balanced budget position when the output gap is zero. The graph is drawn by assuming a neutral

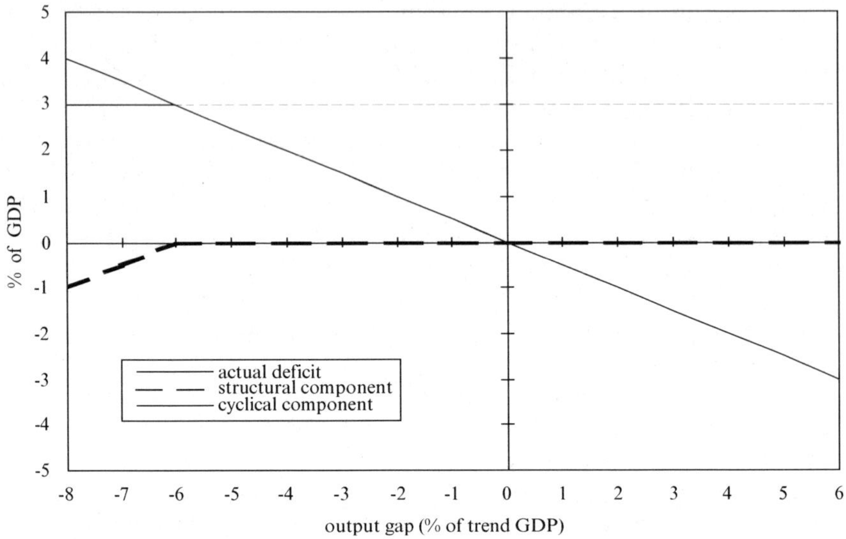

Figure 2.1 Stylized budgetary behaviour over the cycle

discretionary policy and a cyclical sensitivity of the budget of 0.5, which is commonly estimated as the average for the EMU countries in 1997.

Under the assumption of a 'normal' growth of nominal GDP of 4.5 per cent, a balanced budget would allow a debt of 100 per cent of GDP to be brought down below the 60 per cent reference value in about 12 years.

How does the actual budgetary behaviour of EU countries compare to that sketched out in Figure 2.1?

In Figure 2.2, the actual and cyclically adjusted balances for high- and low-debt EU countries are set out against their output gaps over the period 1970–90, that is, the period before fiscal consolidation was undertaken in the run-up to EMU. A country is classified as belonging to either the high-debt or low-debt group depending on whether its government debt was situated above or below the EU average during each year of the 1970–90 period.[48]

Figure 2.2 shows that low-debt countries seem to have incorporated *ante litteram* the logic of the Pact. In particular, they have kept their budgets close to a balanced position during periods of 'normal' economic conditions. Moreover, these countries conducted a broadly neutral discretionary policy in 'good' periods, thereby letting automatic stabilizers work and eventually moving into surplus. Finally, they did not allow their budgets to get out of hand during periods of economic slowdown but instead capped their overall deficit at 3 per cent of GDP during such periods.

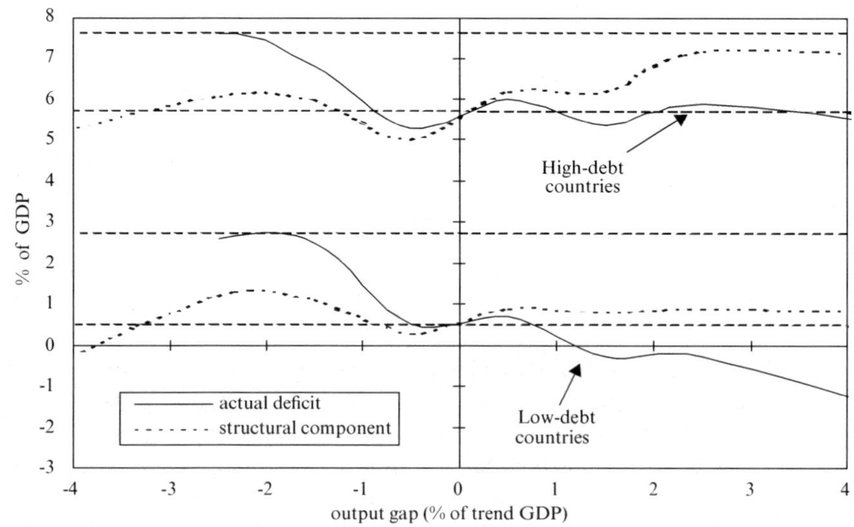

Note: Based on pooled for EU member states.

Source: European Commission.

Figure 2.2 Output gap and budget deficit in high- and low-debt EU countries, 1970–90

The high-debt countries, on the contrary, were a long way from the type of budgetary behaviour implied by the Pact. These countries maintained deficits of around 6 per cent of GDP during periods of 'normal' economic growth and kept their deficits unchanged at this level even during expansionary periods with positive output gaps, by leading pro-cyclical discretionary policies. Part of the gap in the overall deficit between high-debt and low-debt countries is of course explained by the difference in the interest burden. However, qualitatively similar conclusions are obtained when the analysis is carried out in terms of the net-of-interest (primary) balance.

4. LIVING WITH THE PACT: POLICY ISSUES[49]

4.1 Different Preferences on the Pace of Fiscal Consolidation?

While basically agreeing on the need to lead prudent fiscal policies, EMU members may have a different attitude towards the pace of further fiscal consolidation. The simple model of the Barro-Gordon type in Box 2.1, which builds on De Grauwe (1996), helps illustrate such potential problems.

Incentives to slow down the efforts of budgetary adjustment may be strong in high-debt countries, which have in recent years attained historically high levels of primary surpluses. Therefore, the objective of a speedy convergence towards the 60 per cent debt level may run into difficulties. On the contrary, low-debt countries may be interested in a fast reabsorption of the debt in order to bring the debt below the 60 per cent ceiling and thus be let off the 'debt hook'. They are also interested in fast debt reduction by high-debt countries in order to lessen risks of financial instability and bail-out pressures.

Not only may member states have different preferences for the pace for debt reduction in the early years of EMU, but the game is made more complex by the presence of the newly created ECB. Indeed, the end result may well depend on the position of the single monetary authority. The latter may be torn between two conflicting objectives: allowing for a 'reasonable' speed of debt reduction so as to prevent high-debt countries to run against their '*maximum politically feasible primary surplus*' (as defined by Blanchard, 1984), thereby pressing for an inflation rate incompatible with the price stability mandate of the ECB, and pushing for a speedy decline in the stocks of debt to tune down possible risks of financial instability and reduce the pressure for *ex ante* bail-out. On balance, the latter concern is likely to prevail also because, in the ECB's view, the 'maximum politically feasible primary surplus' – and, consequently, the related speed of debt reduction – may be higher than that which the government itself is ready to accept.

In perspective, such conflicts may well be heightened by the budgetary effects of factors like the ageing of population and tax competition. (See Box 2.1.)

BOX 2.1 POLITICAL FEASIBILITY OF BUDGETARY RETRENCHMENT

Let us start from a simplified interpretation of the Maastricht debt rule:

$$b \leq \gamma\,(60 - b) \tag{2.1}$$

where b is the debt to GDP ratio and γ is the agreed minimum speed of reduction of the debt towards the 60 per cent reference value. If (2.1) is satisfied, the debt will be considered as '*sufficiently diminishing and approaching the reference value at a satisfactory pace*' (article 104c(2) of the Treaty).

Given the familiar expression of the government budget constraint:

$$\dot{b} = -s + [(r + \pi^e) - (y + \pi)]\, b - (y + \pi)\, m \qquad (2.2)$$

where s is the primary surplus, r is the real rate of interest, π is the inflation rate, y is real GDP growth and m is the inverse of money velocity, we can derive the short run and long run conditions (in the latter case, inflation expectations are realized) for which the above debt rule is satisfied. If the government dislikes both inflation and primary surpluses (and minimizes a quadratic loss function of the usual type), it is easy to show that the equilibrium values of the primary surplus, s^*, and of inflation, π^*, are a positive function of the initial debt stock, b, and of the speed of debt convergence, γ.

The short run and long run equilibrium conditions are pictured in Figure 2.3, which presents the cases of a low- and a high-debt country. The line depicting the short run condition is less steep than the long one and it is flatter the higher the stock of debt.[50]

The higher the level of debt, the higher is the likelihood that the required primary surplus exceeds its 'maximum politically feasible' level. In such a case, the rate of inflation will have to be higher (point B in Figure 2.3). This, however, may well violate another political feasibility condition, namely that of price stability in EMU. Therefore, a high-debt country may fall outside the politically feasible area ($0s_{MAX}A\pi_{MAX}$): once pushed against its maximum politically feasible primary surplus, a country may require too high an inflation rate thereby violating also the price stability condition. Under such conditions, if the ECB holds its position, the country in question may press strongly for a more gradual convergence towards the debt target: a lower γ would reduce both equilibrium values of primary surplus and inflation.

Summing up, this simple model points to two important conclusions: it helps explain the reluctance by low inflation countries and the (conservative) central bank to allow high-debt countries into the monetary union; it signals that if the latter, in spite of this resistance, become members of the monetary union, then maintaining low inflation may require a not-too-fast pace of debt consolidation.

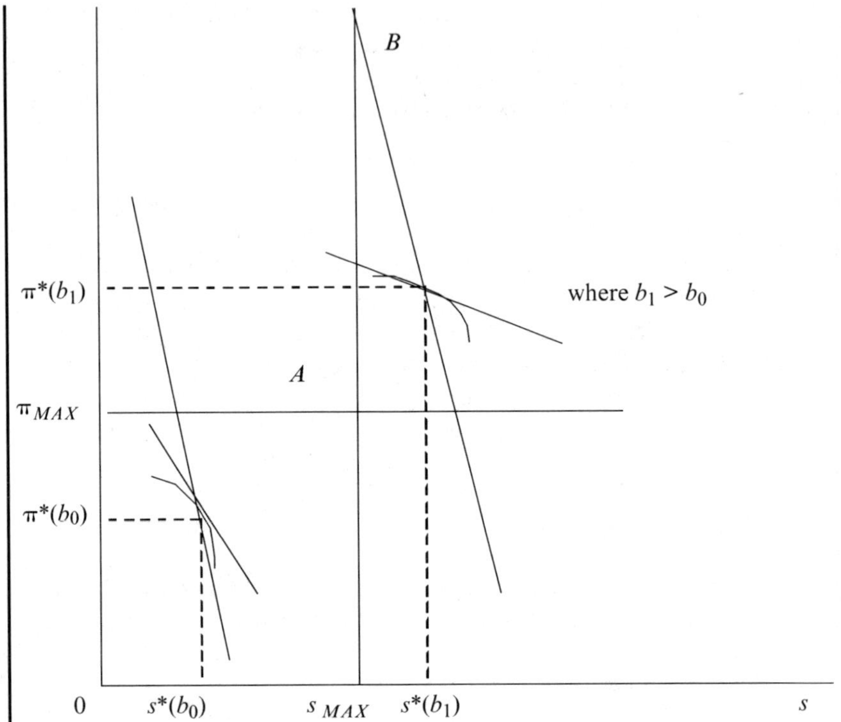

Figure 2.3 Different consolidation preferences in EMU

4.2 WILL THE PACT LIMIT THE FLEXIBILITY OF FISCAL POLICY?

It is widely recognized that forsaking the nominal exchange rate as an adjustment tool increases the role of fiscal policy in stabilizing the cycle. As spelled out before, the Pact stipulates that, during periods of economic slowdown, the budget can go into deficit but should still remain below the 3 per cent threshold.

Does a 3 per cent ceiling, as argued by some (for example, Eichengreen, 1996; Eichengreen and Wyplosz, 1998), necessarily reduce the flexibility of fiscal policies?

If EMU members optimize *ex ante* by setting a suitable target for their structural balance and let automatic stabilizers work in both 'good' and 'bad' periods, the 3 per cent constraint of the Pact will not bite. Once the steady state of a budgetary position 'close to balance or in surplus' is reached, the margins around this target should provide sufficient leeway for the automatic stabilizers to operate fully. Thus, contrary to strict balanced-budget rules such as those enforced in several US states, the Pact allows the automatic stabilizers to operate and in this way to contribute to the stabilization of cyclical fluctuations in economic activity.

Furthermore, it can be argued that achieving sound budgetary positions, as required by the Pact, is a pre-condition to 'free' fiscal policies from the burden of high public finance imbalances, which hampered their use for stabilization purposes. Fiscal laxity does not buy more effective stabilization. On the contrary, over the past decades, the high-debt countries have increasingly lost the room for their automatic stabilizers to operate.

Empirical evidence underpins such conclusion. As shown in Buti *et al.* (1997) (see also Chapter 3, section 2), during periods of severe recession (defined as entailing a fall in real GDP by at least 0.75 per cent), countries with deficit and debt ratios above the EU average were forced to tighten their fiscal stance by reducing their structural primary deficits by 1.2 percentage points of GDP. Retrenchment policies aimed at preventing a worsening of the budgetary situation were adopted especially during protracted recession episodes. On the contrary, member states with low fiscal imbalances undertook relaxation policies by increasing their structural primary deficits by 0.8 percentage points on average. Inspection of Figure 2.2 lends support to such a conclusion. The area under the actual deficit curve for negative output gaps is almost twice as large in the case of low-debt countries as for high-debt countries. This seems to indicate that the latter used only half the room for manoeuvre for cyclical stabilization during recessions compared to that available to the low-debt countries.

Therefore, the potential conflict between discipline and flexibility would only occur during the transition period when budget balances were still relatively close to the 3 per cent threshold. In the event of a recession during the early years of EMU, pro-cyclical fiscal policies would have to be implemented to prevent countries from moving into excessive deficit. This would be undesirable not only from the standpoint of stabilization, but could also increase pressure on the ECB for a much laxer monetary stance to offset the unduly restrictive fiscal policy. However, despite these costs, such a one-time pro-cyclical action during the transition period might be necessary to keep the government budget on track and to safeguard fiscal discipline.

4.3 Will Government Investment be Reduced?[51]

The obligation for member states under the Pact to maintain budgetary positions which are close to balance or in surplus implies that governments will have to fund the bulk of capital expenditure out of current revenues.

Debt finance will no longer be available to smooth the burden of investment projects over the generations of taxpayers receiving the services of the investment goods. The choice between tax and deficit financing of government investment thus affects the distribution of welfare across generations.

Assuming a smooth flow of government investment in any period, the difference between tax and deficit finance concerns only the welfare of the generations alive when the flow starts: under tax finance they pay for projects from which they will only partly benefit. However, if the smooth-flow hypothesis is dropped, every time a large public project is implemented, the generation whose taxes are financing it will suffer a loss to the benefit of future generations.

The transition from debt to tax financing of government investment is likely to exert an additional negative effect on investment decisions. During the transition period, current generations will have to pay fully for new projects while also paying the interest due on debts incurred in the past. Because of these interest expenditures on the accumulated debt, for any given level of government investment a balanced budget entails a larger gap between tax revenues and current government expenditure for services and transfers to the present generation. The opportunity cost of funds devoted to investment is thus higher. As a result, there may be a significant risk of a squeeze in government investment. The issues arising in this context are analogous to those arising during the transition from funded to pay-as-you-go pension systems.

Unless complete altruism between the different generations and a smooth flow of investment are assumed – in which case tax and debt financing of government investment are equivalent in the steady state – a bias towards current expenditure will be present. As a result, tax financing may reduce government investment, with undesirable effects on growth and employment.

The Treaty implicitly refers to the notion of a 'golden rule' by stating that in its report initiating the excessive deficit procedure, the Commission needs to take into account 'whether the government deficit exceeds government investment expenditure'. There is evidence that government investment remains higher under a 'golden rule' than under stringent balanced-budget restrictions. Poterba (1995) examined the institutional variation across US states and suggests that government investment may be lower under a deficit ceiling than under a 'golden rule'. He finds that US states that maintain separate budgets for capital and current expenditures tend to spend more on public capital than states using unified budgets. He also finds that states that borrow to finance investment have a higher level of both capital and current expenditures than states that do not. However, it can be questioned whether a fully fledged 'golden rule' allowing EMU members to run deficits up to the amount of their investment expenditure would have represented a feasible alternative to the balanced-budget obligation of the Pact.

A satisfactory implementation of such a rule raises several difficulties. Since the 'golden rule' is implicitly based on a dual budget system, that is, on splitting the budget into a current and a capital section, governments would have strong incentives to classify current expenditure as capital spending. As a result, budgetary positions would become even more difficult to monitor than is currently the case. Moreover, as stressed by Buiter *et al.* (1993), to the extent that the full social returns of public investment are not appropriated by the government, excessive borrowing may arise. Finally, the division of the budget into current and capital accounts tends to reduce budgetary flexibility and hamper the conduct of stabilization policies. In the EMU budgetary framework, the 'golden rule' may thus be inconsistent with the achievement of the twin objectives of ensuring sufficient room for stabilization policies and attaining a sound fiscal stance.

There are several ways to minimize the negative effects of the loss of intertemporal smoothing of investment decisions: the selection process for investment projects could be improved, the share of resources devoted to current primary spending should be controlled tightly as increases in current spending would further reduce the scope for government investment and a safeguard clause could also be introduced in the budgetary process to ensure that expenditure cuts are not concentrated on capital outlays. Moreover, the currently ongoing shift towards the private financing and operation of public infrastructure investments is likely to continue in coming years and should partially counter-balance the reduction of government investment expenditure.

3. Medium-term fiscal targets*

1. INTRODUCTION

The Maastricht Treaty introduced convergence requirements on fiscal policy as a condition of eligibility for membership of Economic and Monetary Union (EMU). These requirements were spelled out in terms of 'reference values' for the deficit-to-GDP ratio and the debt-to-GDP ratio (3 per cent of GDP and 60 per cent of GDP) with 'forgiveness clauses' to accommodate deviations from these values.

The Stability and Growth Pact (SGP) demands that the countries of the European Union (EU) aim for 'medium-term objectives of budgetary positions close to balance or in surplus'. The Pact can be seen as strengthening the procedures introduced by the Maastricht Treaty, at least in relation to the deficit criterion. Its objective is to ensure that respect for fiscal prudence, as embodied in the fiscal criteria, applies not only in the run up to monetary union but also within it, that is once participation in the euro area has been achieved and the threat of exclusion dissolved.

The aim of this chapter is to provide the policy maker with a roadmap in implementing this important clause of the Pact. We ask how to set the medium-term fiscal targets having in mind the need to strengthen the credibility of EMU fiscal discipline, the objective of restoring room for manoeuvre for cyclical stabilization in EMU, and the long-term sustainability of public finances. In short, the task is to show how to set a medium-term fiscal target which is 'roughly right'.

The Maastricht deficit criterion pertains to the actual value of the unadjusted, interest-inclusive deficit. The choice of the actual deficit is dictated by the legal exigencies of the focal position the deficit occupies in the Maastricht Treaty. This means that the definition chosen had to be as free as possible from methodological ambiguities. However, there are good reasons for thinking that a better description of the 'thrust' of fiscal policy is to be found in the concept of the structural balance, a point that has been made with particular reference to the provisions of the Stability Pact by, for

*Michael J. Artis and Marco Buti, '"Close to Balance or In Surplus" – A Policy Maker's Guide to the Implementation of the Stability and Growth Pact', *Journal of Common Market Studies*, 2000, 38(4): 563–92.

example, Eichengreen (1997). As the medium-term budget target can be seen as a cyclically adjusted position, the Pact represents an 'economics-friendly' innovation compared to the Treaty.

In his proposal for a 'Stability Pact for Europe' in November 1995, the German Finance Minister, Theo Waigel, proposed to set a medium-term goal of 1 per cent deficit of GDP, thereby providing a safety margin of 2 percentage points of GDP. During the negotiations on the Pact, however, it emerged that a uniform safety margin was not appropriate given the different sensitivity of the budget balance to the economic cycle and the different cyclical behaviour across EU countries. In particular, a budget surplus was felt to be appropriate in the case of Nordic countries. Some governments (Sweden) also insisted on mentioning a surplus target explicitly as they had already announced such an objective in their programme and risked a backlash in public opinion in the event of a 'looser' European clause. The compromise was a call for budgetary positions of 'close to balance or in surplus'.

However, no precise definition is given of this concept. Several factors have been highlighted in the debate.[52] First, the influence of fluctuations in economic growth on the government's budget needs to be considered. This is clearly spelled out in the Resolution of the European Council on the Stability and Growth Pact, which states that 'adherence to the objective of sound budgetary positions close to balance or in surplus will allow all member states to deal with normal cyclical fluctuations while keeping the government deficit within the value of 3 per cent of GDP'. A supplementary safety margin may need to be ensured in the case of countries having a 'taste' for active counter-cyclical budgetary policy working on top of the automatic stabilizers. Second, a safety margin around the medium-term budgetary positions may be required to cope with unforeseen variability in the budget balance arising from non-cyclical factors such as unexplained tax shortfalls, interest rate shocks, and so on. Finally, there is the issue as to whether the medium-term targets should encompass directly the need to prepare for the future fiscal burden of population ageing.

The chapter analyses the factors influencing the setting of fiscal targets and provides initial evidence on how to quantify them. In doing so, the basic assumption is made that member countries will treat the prospect of infringing the 3 per cent deficit ratio as one to be strictly avoided. We recognize that political pressure could weaken the application of the SGP, but confine our analysis to situations where the sanctions are fully credible.

After a brief section where we argue that fiscal discipline is a precondition for the use of fiscal policy for stabilization purposes, we illustrate in the third section the economic mechanisms at work through a simple model which examines the interplay between the national fiscal authorities and the supranational monetary authority. This section goes on to present the currently available estimates for the cyclical safety margin which would allow countries to respect the deficit ceiling in economic downturns while letting automatic stabilizers work freely. It also provides a tentative quantification of unforeseen fiscal developments which, if sizeable, may also be a source of risk. The fourth section examines the consistency between the close to balance provision and the long-term sustainability of public finances. As a first step in computing a long-run safety margin, it presents a tentative quantification of the required structural balance to pre-empt the budgetary consequences of future demographic developments. The final section concludes.

2. FISCAL DISCIPLINE AS A PRE-CONDITION FOR FISCAL FLEXIBILITY

The goal of fiscal prudence is translated within the framework of the Pact into a commitment by EU countries to aim for a budgetary position providing a large enough safety margin so that the 3 per cent of GDP deficit criterion will not be breached in the event of recessions.

Does the requirement for fiscal prudence embodied in the Maastricht criteria and the Pact hamper fiscal stabilization? If so, the loss of monetary independence compounded by constrained fiscal policies may lead to a sub-optimal degree of stabilization especially in the event of country-specific shocks. During the initial years of EMU, before budgetary targets have been achieved, cyclical stabilization may be restricted because of the closeness of initial deficits to the 3 per cent ceiling (Allsopp and Vines, 1996, and Eichengreen and Wyplosz, 1998). Indeed, as already pointed out by Buti *et al.* (1997, p. 362), 'in the event of a severe recession during the early years of EMU, since several countries will still have deficits in the 2 to 3 per cent of GDP range, they risk moving into excessive deficit, unless they take a pro-cyclical budgetary stance'.

Beyond this transition period, however, no contradiction exists between fiscal discipline and fiscal flexibility. To the contrary, the Stability and Growth Pact can be interpreted as a commitment device to recover room for manoeuvre for fiscal policy to sustain the cycle. Indeed, sound budgetary positions in 'normal' times may be important for the effective use of fiscal policy for stabilization purposes in periods of cyclical slowdown. This conclusion is based on two related sets of considerations: the effectiveness of fiscal expansions under conditions of 'fiscal stress', on the one hand, and the actual behaviour of fiscal authorities in cyclical slowdowns, on the other hand.

According to a recent literature, the traditional Keynesian effects of fiscal policies may be reversed in conditions of considerable imbalances in the public finances. The unsustainability threat arising from a fiscal expansion when public debt is high or rapidly growing may imply substantial premia in interest rates to cover for explicit or implicit default risks. This may crowd out investment, thereby offsetting the direct effect of the budgetary boost. On the consumption side, 'when debt reaches extreme values current generations of consumers know that they will be alive when the next stabilization programme is implemented. A fiscal deficit can have a contractionary effect on consumer spending in these situations' (Sutherland, 1997).[53]

Empirical evidence in favour of non-Keynesian effects in the presence of high fiscal imbalances is found by Perotti (1999). In a panel regression on 20 OECD countries, this study finds that the effects of spending shocks on private consumption are positive in normal circumstances, but that the opposite holds in situations of fiscal stress. The point estimates for the EU countries during 1971–93 indicate that smoothing through the government deficit is higher for low deficit countries. However, this does not hold for the OECD group, leading the authors to conclude that there is no evidence of a relation between the size of the deficit and the amount of consumption smoothing it provides. Alesina and Ardagna (1998) and Giavazzi *et al.* (1998) also find no strong evidence that high or increasing debt ratios are associated with non-Keynesian effects.

As the empirical evidence is mixed, it may be useful to look at the actual behaviour of governments during periods of slowdown. The use of fiscal policy (or lack thereof) could be taken as an indication of its perceived *ex ante* effectiveness to support demand. Buti *et al.* (1997) have examined the behaviour of the fiscal authorities in EU countries in severe recession episodes over the period 1960–97. Severe recessions are those defined as involving a drop in real GDP of 0.75 per cent or more, which would potentially trigger the 'exceptionality clause' under the Pact (see Chapter 2). As shown in Table 3.1, countries with low debt and deficits have in fact responded to such severe shocks via fiscal policy much more than countries with highly unbalanced public finances.

Member states with high deficit and debt ratios tightened their fiscal stance and reduced their structural primary deficit by 1.2 percentage points of GDP on average during severe recession episodes. Fiscal retrenchment policies aimed at preventing a worsening of the budgetary situation were adopted especially during protracted recession periods. On the contrary, countries with relatively lower deficit and debt ratios undertook 'prudent' fiscal relaxation policies by supplementing their automatic stabilizers with an increase in their structural primary deficits of 0.8 percentage points of GDP.[54]

Table 3.1 Comparison of budgetary reactions to severe recessions starting from different pre-recession budgetary situations, 1961–97

Pre-recession budgetary situation	Cumulative change between year before recession and last year of the recession (average over episodes)			
	actual deficit	*of which*: primary deficit	structural deficit	*of which:* structural primary deficit
Member states with deficit and debt ratios above the EU average	1.9	−0.4	1.1	−1.2
Member states with deficit and debt ratios below the EU average	5.1	1.4	4.4	0.8
Average over all episodes	3.6	0.5	2.8	−0.1

Source: Buti *et al.* (1997).

That fiscal discipline and fiscal flexibility are in mutual support is suggested by the observation that countries with strong built-in stabilizers, which produce large swings in the deficit over the cycle, have managed to maintain their average stock of debt within reasonable boundaries. This is illustrated in Figure 3.1. On the *x*-axis is depicted the change in the public debt ratio during positive output gaps over the past three decades, as estimated by the European Commission. Clearly, a large majority of EU countries continued to accumulate debt even in periods of above-trend growth, providing *prima facie* evidence that they did not follow 'tax-smoothing'. On the *y*-axis, the graph shows the degree of stabilization provided by automatic stabilizers as estimated by the Commission services' QUEST model. The smoothing effect of the automatic stabilizers was computed as the difference in output changes following a private consumption shock under a scenario in which the stabilizers are free to work and an alternative scenario in which the stabilizers were prevented from operating via discretionary counterbalancing measures (Buti and Sapir, 1998). Although only suggestive, the negative correlation shown in the graph underpins the view that strong fiscal discipline in 'good times' goes hand in hand with fiscal stabilization in 'bad times'.

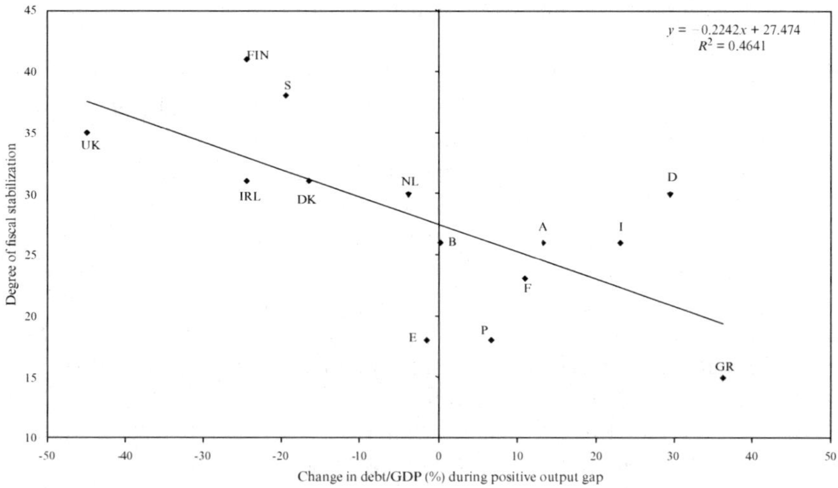

Source: Buti and Sapir (1998) and own calculations.

Figure 3.1 Stabilization and public debt accumulation

3. RESPECTING THE DEFICIT CEILING

3.1 An Illustrative Model

The approach underlying the Pact is that EMU countries select an appropriate structural budgetary position and then let the automatic stabilizers work freely. This target should be sufficiently ambitious to withstand cyclical fluctuations without exceeding the 3 per cent deficit ceiling. Throughout this chapter, in line with the Maastricht institutional framework, it is assumed that the overriding concern of fiscal authorities is to prevent the budget deficit from exceeding a given ceiling even in bad circumstances while allowing the built-in stabilizers to operate fully. Hence, as argued by, for example, Eichengreen and Wyplosz (1998) and confirmed by the concrete experience so far with the application of the Pact, it is assumed that the 3 per cent 'limit' is regarded as a 'hard' ceiling.

The safety room under the deficit ceiling depends on several factors. In order to explore the mechanisms at work, we lay out a simple model which illustrates various channels influencing the choice of the medium-term fiscal target. The model is formally presented in Annex 1. We look at a single country within a monetary union. The model encompasses a demand (IS) equation and a supply (Phillips curve) equation of standard type determining the value of the output gap and inflation. The policy rules are very simple:

- National fiscal authorities set a target for the cyclically adjusted balance and then let automatic stabilizers work. This formulation implies that, when interest rates move, there occurs an internal compensation between the interest burden and the primary balance so as to keep the structural balance constant. Therefore, even if there is no active Keynesian fiscal policy, some discretionary adjustments within the budget do take place. While playing a role implicitly within the structural balance, the stock of public debt explicitly enters the IS equation via the fiscal impulse variable, which is assumed to be the inflation adjusted budget balance.
- The monetary authority follows a Taylor rule, taking into account the average inflation and output gap in the currency area.[55] Given the fact that the monetary authorities do not target an unemployment rate below the NAIRU, the model does not exhibit the Barro–Gordon inflation bias. Provided that the coefficient of inflation is sufficiently high, this formulation appears to be consistent with the primary statutory duty of the ECB to ensure price stability.

The interactions within the monetary union arise via the behaviour of the central bank and trade linkages between the member countries (the currency union as a whole is assumed to be a closed economy). These two channels are influenced by the type of shocks hitting the countries. In order to simplify the analysis, two extreme categories of shocks are considered:

1. 'Pure symmetric' shocks. Since we disregard the asymmetric responses to symmetric disturbances arising from different transmission mechanisms (e.g. industry structure, degree of labour market flexibility, etc.), these shocks affect the member countries in an identical manner and the countries' external balance does not change. Hence, beside the automatic fiscal stabilizers, only the monetary smoothing channel is at work.
2. 'Pure asymmetric' shocks in which a shock hitting the domestic country is fully offset by an identical shock of the opposite sign affecting the other member countries. As the average output gap and inflation of the currency area do not change, the interest rate does not move and only the balance of payments operates in smoothing output.

The medium-term budgetary target is computed on the basis of the 'worst possible' shocks affecting the economy. These shocks, by feeding through the economy and interacting with the monetary and fiscal behaviour, give rise to large, negative output gaps. The initial deficit position has to be sufficiently low to accommodate such adverse circumstances without exceeding the nominal deficit ceiling. To be on the safe side the most binding cases across different types of shocks are retained.

As shown in Annex 1, the fiscal target is influenced by the structural features of the model and the assumed reaction function of the central bank. Crucially, the way in which these elements affect the fiscal target depends on the most binding shock and its synchronicity across frontiers. The general conclusions derived formally in Annex 1 are summarized hereafter.

In the case of *demand shocks*, a country which is in tune with the rest of the currency area (hence is affected mainly by symmetric disturbances) can select a less (more) ambitious budgetary target if monetary smoothing is stronger (weaker) than the balance of payments smoothing. This is likely to be the case of a large country, which is less affected by the external balance and, by influencing the monetary union average, can more likely trigger a favourable monetary response. On the opposite side of the spectrum, a small country with a cycle 'out of synch' with the rest of the currency area will have to face the perverse effect of monetary policy while benefiting from the rise in net exports. Germany and Ireland today appear to approximate those two cases. Countries with a high debt can choose less ambitious targets because the lower inflation causes a fall in the inflation tax, thereby limiting the deterioration of the output gap. For identical levels of debt, the inflation tax goes down more in the asymmetric country because its inflation rate is allowed to fall without intervention by the central bank. Notice also that countries with a more flexible labour market (that is a higher coefficient of the inflation surprise in the Phillips curve) need to select a more ambitious budgetary target because the fall in inflation brings about a larger fall in the output gap. Again, this effect is higher in the case of asymmetric shocks.

In the case of *supply shocks*, a rise in inflation goes hand in hand with a negative output gap. The fiscal target is influenced by the degree of conservatism of the central bank. If the shock is symmetric, a 'hard-nosed' central bank will react to the rise in inflation with a pro-cyclical rise in interest rates, which leads to an even larger negative output gap. Hence, in order to let automatic stabilizers work fully without breaching the deficit criterion, the fiscal target has to be more ambitious. If the shock is asymmetric, the net smoothing effect brought about by the external balance depends on the relative importance of the income effect (positive) and the competitiveness effect (negative).[56] All in all, a small country 'out of synch' with the average cycle of the currency area can choose a less ambitious budgetary target. Due to a rise in the inflation tax, countries with a high stock of debt have to set more ambitious fiscal targets. However, given the already high interest burden, these countries may hit their 'maximum politically feasible primary surplus' (Blanchard, 1984), thereby running up against a 'political feasibility constraint'. An increase in the degree of 'conservatism' of the central bank entails a lower decrease in the medium-term target in high-debt countries than in low-debt countries. This is because under a more conservative central bank inflation will rise by less. Therefore, countries with a higher stock of debt will experience a lower increase in the inflation tax. Contrary to the case of demand shocks, countries with a more flexible labour market can select a less ambitious fiscal target.

Fiscal shocks cover essentially unexpected tax shortfalls or unforeseen expenditures, including interest rate shocks to the extent that the change in the interest burden is not fully offset by an opposite move in the structural primary balance. While demand or supply shocks are likely to be the 'binding' shocks, adverse fiscal shocks can play a role if the country wants to be on the safe side by creating an additional safety margin under the deficit ceiling. This additional safety margin is higher the higher the budgetary sensitivity to the cycle.

The main conclusion of this discussion is that the degree of ambition of the medium-term target is influenced by the type of 'most binding' shock (either supply or demand shock), the size of the country (which affects the degree of symmetry of the shocks) and the public finance variables (stock of debt, cyclical sensitivity of the budget, 'pure' fiscal shocks). The behaviour of the central bank also has an important role. Given the reaction function of the central bank, under the assumption of a 'hard-nosed' central banker, large countries (affecting the monetary union average) should fear more negative supply shocks, while in the case of small, de-synchronized countries negative demand shocks are more likely to bite.

3.2 Estimates of the 'Worst' Cyclical Component

To identify a 'safe' budgetary position allowing the deficit to be kept below 3 per cent of GDP, the influence of all factors contributing to the volatility of the budget balance needs to be examined. Many of these aspects are likely to change in the new EMU framework.

Size, origin and synchronicity of the shocks will affect the size and volatility of cyclical fluctuations in output. While EMU will entail changes it is not clear in what direction these will run. In the longer run, it might be expected that cyclical variations will become more synchronized between EMU members. Given the stability-oriented macroeconomic framework of EMU, country-specific, policy-induced shocks are likely to decrease in the euro area. Furthermore, trade integration may spread shocks more uniformly across frontiers and higher competition in product markets will reduce the risk of wage setting shocks (Buti and Sapir, 1998). As argued in the previous section, sound macroeconomic conditions will also increase the smoothing effectiveness of stabilization policies. The extent of these convergence-promoting effects is not known, however, and trade-induced patterns of industrial specialization may change in a direction that promotes some divergence. However, in the shorter run, different economic structures as well as lack of full availability of stabilization instruments may work in the opposite direction. Furthermore, what is relevant for the present analysis is not the impact of the new EMU framework on the 'normal' cyclical profile of EMU members, but the exposure of these economies to important economic shocks giving rise to 'large' output gaps.

It is also unclear whether the sensitivity of budget balances to the cycle will change significantly once in EMU. Even in the event that the ongoing reforms of the tax system – in particular of corporate taxes and social security contributions – and of transfer payments to the unemployed lead to a reduction of the budget's cyclical sensitivity, such an effect will not take place overnight. It can therefore be assumed that the sensitivity of the budget to the cycle will not change much in the coming years.

As discussed in the previous section, the exact nature of the ECB's monetary strategy is bound to play an important role. In relation to the pre-ERM era, of course, countries are giving up the possibility of using their own monetary policy actions to stabilize their economies; however, compared to the ERM period, (non-German) countries can expect a proportionate weight in ECB decisions which they did not have in the Bundesbank's policy.

All in all, EMU is 'too young' to allow us to identify as yet the direction of change. Given these uncertainties, we have resorted to an analysis of the past cyclical history of EU member countries. To give some quantified indications, illustrative country-specific 'minimal benchmarks' have been calculated on the basis of estimates for the largest possible cyclical component that occurred in the past.

The basis for the estimates, which are detailed in Table 3.3, is conveyed in Figure 3.2. Here the level of output (Y) is measured along the horizontal axis, the budget surplus (s) and deficit (d) ratios along the vertical. The schedule $d'd'$ represents a country's 'fiscal programme'. The value of output corresponding to the natural rate of unemployment is designated as Y_f. The corresponding level of the deficit, d_s, given by the schedule $d'd'$, is the structural deficit associated with the fiscal programme. The slope of the $d'd'$ schedule corresponds to the estimates of the budget sensitivity to output gap changes which are computed by all three of the leading international economic policy advisory organizations – the OECD, IMF and EC.

Table 3.2 Ensuring an adequate cyclical safety margin

Member states	Sensitivity of budget balance to the cycle (1)	Mid-point of range of budgetary positions (government deficit, % of GDP) (2)
Countries participating in the euro area:		
Belgium	0.6	1.0
Germany	0.5	1.1
Greece	0.4	1.4
Spain	0.6	0.4
France	0.5	1.5
Ireland	0.5	0.9
Italy	0.5	1.2
Luxembourg	0.6	0.0
Netherlands	0.8	0.1
Austria	0.5	1.3
Portugal	0.5	0.6
Finland	0.7	−1.3
Euro area	0.5	1.0
Countries not participating in the euro area:		
Denmark	0.7	0.7
Sweden	0.9	−0.8
United Kingdom	0.7	0.1
EUR15	0.6	0.8

Notes:
(1) The figures come from the European Commission.
(2) The mid-point figures shown are computed from the range implied by three alternative assumptions about the output gap. The first of these is the unweighted average of the largest negative output gaps in EU member states which, over the period 1960–98, was 4 per cent of GDP. The second is the largest negative output gap that has been recorded in each member state over the period 1960–97. The third is the average volatility of the output gap in each member state, as measured by two times its standard deviation. For each country, the two extrème cases of these three alternatives have been retained as the bounds for the range for budgetary positions which would allow member states to let the automatic stabilizers operate fully without running the risk that the deficit exceeds the 3 per cent of GDP threshold. The mid-point of this range is then taken as a first approximation for the country-specific benchmark.

Source: European Commission.

The values used here are those produced by the European Commission and are shown in the first column of Table 3.2. The calculation of the 'safe' structural deficit is the one that ensures that at the lowest level of output foreseen (Y_{min}), the fiscal programme and its associated

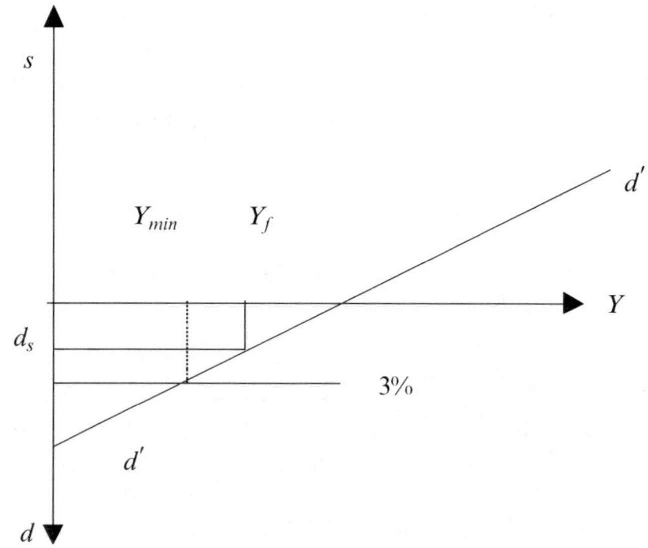

Figure 3.2 Finding the safe medium-term (structural) deficit

structural deficit do not produce a current deficit in excess of 3 per cent of GDP. As drawn, the fiscal programme $d'd'$ and its associated structural surplus are just adequate in this respect. A fiscal programme displaced downwards from that shown would run the risk of producing a deficit in excess of 3 per cent in the event that the 'worst case' output gap should be realized.

Clearly, the selection of that 'worst case' is critically important to the calculation of the 'safe' structural deficit. The footnote (2) to Table 3.2 indicates that what was done here, in fact, was to take three possible values for Y_{min} and to choose as the safe figure the mid-point of the range of the two most conservative structural deficit figures.

These calculations permit the computation of the so-called 'minimal benchmarks' (European Commission, 1999a). As shown in Table 3.2, assuming that the cyclical behaviour of EU economies does not change with the advent of EMU, Belgium, Denmark, Spain, Ireland, Luxembourg, the Netherlands, Portugal and the United Kingdom will have to aim for a structural budgetary deficit of between 0 and 1 per cent of GDP in order to keep the budget balance within the 3 per cent of GDP reference value. Germany, Greece, France, Italy and Austria could aim for a deficit even slightly above 1 per cent of GDP. Sweden and Finland would have to aim for a surplus as their budgets have a high sensitivity to the cycle and their economies have in the past shown a high degree of volatility.[57]

3.3 Coping with Unforeseen Budgetary Developments

The risk of exceeding the 3 per cent ceiling is not only related to the cyclical component of the budget, but also to unforeseen fiscal developments not directly linked to the working of built-in stabilizers. Unexpected tax shortfalls, higher-than-projected spending commitments or interest rate shocks can push up the deficit and represent a further source of fiscal instability. Figure 3.3 illustrates the point. The graph is identical to Figure 3.2 except in allowing that a fiscal shock might displace $d'd'$ to a position like that indicated by the schedule $d''d''$. In that event, as can be seen, the previously 'safe' structural deficit could result in an infringement of the SGP.

In order to disentangle this erratic component from other budgetary developments a promising approach involves the comparison between fiscal forecasts and out-turns, a strand of research recently developed by Artis and Marcellino (1999). Table 3.3 presents a summary of descriptive statistics of the fiscal forecast record of the EU member countries, drawing on data in Keereman (1999).

The forecasts for which the descriptive error statistics are quoted are those generated in the spring of year *t* for year *t* – so-called 'current year forecasts' – and are forecasts for the fiscal deficit as a percentage of GDP.

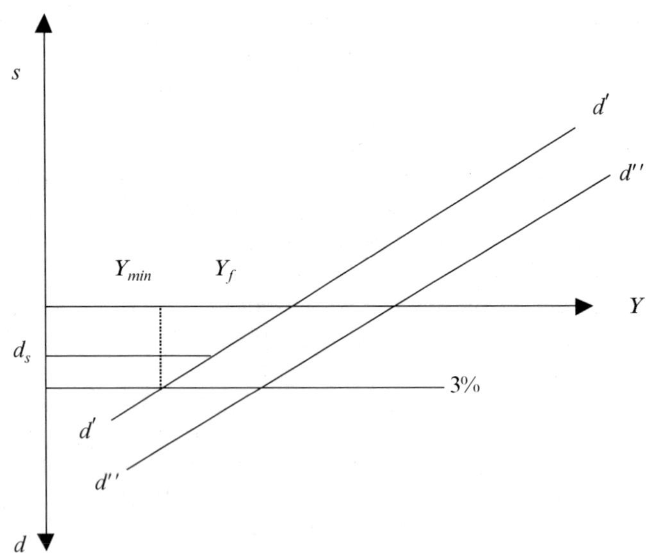

Figure 3.3 Finding the safe medium-term (structural) deficit: the incidence of 'pure' fiscal shocks

Table 3.3 Overall fiscal forecast accuracy (% of GDP)

Country	Mean error	Mean absolute error	Root mean squared error
Belgium	−0.2	0.4	0.6
Denmark	−0.1	0.9	1.2
Germany	0.2	0.8	1.0
Greece	−0.5	2.0	2.4
Spain	−0.3	0.1	1.3
France	0.1	0.7	1.0
Ireland	0.2	1.4	1.9
Italy	−0.2	1.1	1.5
Luxembourg	0.6	1.7	2.0
Netherlands	0.3	0.9	1.1
Portugal	0.6	1.0	1.0
UK	−0.2	0.7	1.0

Note: Sample periods vary; they are: Belgium 1971–97; Denmark 1977–97; Germany 1969–97; Greece 1982–97; Spain 1986–97; France 1969–97; Ireland 1974–97; Italy 1969–97; Luxembourg 1974–97; Netherlands 1969–97; Portugal 1986–97; UK 1973–97; EU 1969–97.

Data source: Keereman (1999).

The table gives the mean, the mean absolute error and the root mean square error. The mean errors are generally very low – with the exception of Portugal and Luxembourg none exceeds 0.5 per cent of GDP. However, it can be seen from the figures of mean absolute error that the low means in some cases are due to large offsetting errors, Greece being a notable example. The RMSE figures thus generally lie between 1 and 2 per cent of GDP.

At first sight, this might seem to indicate that a cautious participant in the SGP might have to allow (i.e. subtract) a margin of 2 to 4 per cent of GDP in calculating a safe deficit figure to aim for. However, it is well known (see, e.g., Artis and Marcellino, 1999, Table 5) that a prime source of fiscal forecast error lies in mistaken output growth projections. It would be in line with the previous calculations set out in this chapter to allow for this source of error.

Formally, the expected and the actual budget deficits as a share of GDP can be written as follows:

$$d^e = d_s^e - \alpha Y^e \tag{3.1}$$

$$d = (d_s^e + \varepsilon) - \alpha Y \tag{3.2}$$

Table 3.4 Statistics on the 'fiscal shock' component

Country	Mean (% of GDP)	Variance	75% quartile (% of GDP)	Mean of positive deviations (% of GDP)	Correlation with output growth
Belgium	0.1	0.58	0.5	0.3	0.91
Denmark	−0.3	0.74	0.3	0.3	0.75
Germany	0.4	1.45	1.4	0.7	0.67
Greece	−0.2	6.10	1.0	0.9	0.23
Spain	−0.1	2.75	0.9	0.6	0.98
France	−0.1	0.72	0.3	0.3	0.74
Ireland	1.6	3.16	2.6	1.9	0.73
Italy	0.1	0.46	0.6	0.4	0.27
Luxemb'g	0.6	5.09	2.0	1.2	0.25
N'lands	0.6	0.78	1.2	0.8	0.67
Portugal	0.6	2.00	1.6	1.0	0.54
UK	−0.0	1.30	0.5	0.4	0.92
EU	0.1	0.48	0.8	0.4	0.89

Note: The sample period is 1986–97.

Data source: Keereman (1999).

where d is the budget deficit, d_s is the cyclically adjusted deficit, Y is the output gap, α is the cyclical sensitivity of the budget and ε is the erratic fiscal shock. The superscript e indicates expected values. The total forecast error is given by the forecast error on the discretionary component, ε, and the error on the cyclical component of the budget. Under the assumption that trend growth does not change over the forecast period, the forecast error on the output gap corresponds to the forecast error on real GDP growth and we can derive the expression of the erratic component in the budget:

$$\varepsilon = d - d^e + \alpha(y - y^e) \tag{3.3}$$

As shown in equation (3.3), in order to gauge the size of the erratic component in the budget, the effect of the GDP growth forecast error has to be netted out. By applying the figures of the cyclical sensitivity of the budget shown in Table 3.2 to these errors, we can estimate the 'pure' erratic component in the deficit. The results are set out in Table 3.4.

The early part of the sample period underlying Table 3.3 features some extraordinary fiscal forecast errors for some countries and represents a volatile high-inflation era in which some very large fiscal swings also occurred. Probably, the conditions prevailing in the later years are more relevant for our assessment. The data shown in Table 3.4 accordingly pertain to the period 1986–97. The first two columns show the overall mean and variance of the 'pure' fiscal shock component. As can be seen, for the most part these are relatively small. Our concern, however, is with upside risks on the deficit, since we try to quantify what allowance, if any, countries should make in setting their deficit target to prevent 'pure fiscal error' from triggering the onset of the sanctions procedure in the Pact. Accordingly, Table 3.4 presents the 75 per cent quartile which indicates the largest value of three-quarters of all observations. Some of the values are large and, in two countries (Ireland and Luxembourg) are 2 percentage points of GDP or higher. In three other countries (Netherlands, Germany and Portugal) deviations are larger than non-negligible, but it does not appear that large positive deficit shocks occurred in periods of low growth, when the cyclical component in the budget deficit is also large. In all other countries the 75 per cent quartile lies between 0.3 and 1 per cent of GDP.

Given the fact that some of these large deviations occurred in the early years of the sample, 'extreme' values may not be representative of 'bad' risks in the current situation. Accordingly, the last column of Table 3.4 shows the mean of positive deviations. With the exception of two countries (Ireland and Luxembourg), the average deviations lie in the 0.3 to 1 per cent range.

An additional reason for not focusing on outlier values is the fact that large positive shocks do not seem likely to occur when the deficit is already large for cyclical reasons. The last column of the table shows the correlation between the actual growth rate of output and the pure fiscal shock; the positive association indicated there suggests that positive deficit shocks tend to coincide with periods of high growth. The consistency of this positive correlation between ε and output growth may be felt to be somewhat puzzling. One explanation could be related to forecast error on the interest burden: as interest rates in forecast exercises are often set in a 'quasi-technical' manner (i.e. small or no change is projected over the forecast period), while severe recessions (booms) are usually associated with monetary relaxation (tightening), the forecast interest burden tends to be systematically biased.[58]

Moreover, our approach implies that the forecast error on the discretionary component, ε, is due fully to unexpected, erratic developments or measurement errors. However, in the case of countries having frequently adopted within-year budgetary measures (such as Italy), our results may overestimate the 'pure' erratic component. To the extent that pro-cyclical budgetary measures tend to occur in episodes of above-average or below-average growth, a positive correlation between the 'erratic' component and output growth may result. This explanation is consistent with the results in Buti *et al.* (1997) who find that discretionary fiscal policies have generally been 'prudent' in periods of severe recessions and that pro-cyclical fiscal policies were enacted in 'good times'.

Summing up, while further research is required to disentangle the various factors behind the results in Table 3.4, we are inclined to conclude that the additional margin for fiscal shocks to be allowed for in the computation of 'safe' structural deficits would be relatively small. Additional room for manoeuvre of between 0.5 and 1 per cent – broadly corresponding to the average range in Table 3.4 – would seem appropriate for a risk-averse policy maker.

4. STRUCTURAL BALANCE AND LONG RUN SUSTAINABILITY OF PUBLIC FINANCES

4.1 Government Solvency and Population Ageing[59]

The Pact does not mention the debt criterion and has been firmly criticized for this omission (see Pisani-Ferry, 1996, for an early criticism). The criticism gains particular force from the idea that the externality prompting the need for the Pact is the risk of contagion from 'debt runs'. In their study of the solvency of EU government finances, Artis and Marcellino (1998) find that in general there is a tendency for debt/GDP ratios to stabilize at a positive value (not at zero). The absence of explosive behaviour is reassuring. But the market's belief in the government's ability actually to repay its debt is based on the government's ability to tax and on its ability to pay off debt in its own currency. In the context of EMU an individual country can no longer implicitly promise to pay off its own debt in its own money. The European Central Bank is expressly forbidden from conniving in any such activity. McKinnon (1994) has thus correctly emphasized that the transition to EMU is something of a regime change. The presumption is that debt/GDP ratios which were satisfactory in the previous regime may no longer be so in the new one. It thus seems desirable that fiscal policy should be so framed as to reduce debt/GDP ratios. The medium-term target of close to balance, or surplus – since the balance is interest-inclusive – necessarily implies a potential trend reduction in debt/GDP ratios and stabilization 'in steady state' at modest or, possibly, negative levels.[60]

The literature on government solvency implies that the future stream of spending and revenue is accounted for. Demographic developments and, in particular, the ageing of populations are increasingly pointed at as an important factor affecting future spending commitments.

There exist a number of studies which attempt to quantify the budgetary impact of the ageing of populations. Many projections translate, in a mechanical fashion, existing estimates of age-related public expenditures to future demographic profiles. Using common assumptions on productivity, unemployment and growth rates, and assuming 'no policy change', an OECD study (Roseweare *et al.*, 1996), estimated primary balances between 1995 and 2030. A common U-shaped pattern is evident. Favourable demographic trends (growing labour force, large baby-boom cohort in high income earning years) initially result in improving budget balances prior to a rapid deterioration after 2010, when the baby boom generation will retire.

A study by the European Commission (Franco and Munzi, 1999) integrated the results of pension expenditure projections carried out by national authorities with mechanical estimates of the effects of demographic changes on the other main age-related expenditure items (such as health care, education and family allowances) for a number of member states. In the resultant budgetary projection for a subset of euro-area countries, the share of total primary expenditure to GDP over the period 2000 to 2030 is estimated to increase by almost 6 percentage points in Germany, by approximately 5 percentage points in Belgium, Italy and the Netherlands, and by 1 percentage point in Spain. Under unchanged policies, present primary surpluses would be eroded over time and the debt-to-GDP ratio, while declining initially, would undergo unsustainable increases in some member states.

4.2 A Fiscal Strategy of 'Internal Budgetary Compensation'?

While the analysis of the appropriate medium-term target for fiscal policy focuses on the 'institutional' requirement not to breach the 3 per cent deficit ceiling, considerations related to the future burden on the budget of population ageing may come into play. For instance, in its assessment of the stability programmes, the Council invited Germany to prepare for the future burden on the budget of demographic developments. Spain and Finland were also advised to take measures to address the problem of population ageing.

Clearly, the way forward implies tackling the problem at source, by reforming welfare programmes most sensitive to the impact of ageing. Without such structural reforms, the ageing of populations will have a sizeable negative impact on GDP and employment in the long run (McMorrow and Roeger, 1999). However, since bold reforms in such areas are politically difficult, it has been suggested that a strategy of 'internal budgetary compensation' may help to pre-empt the fiscal consequences of ageing: fiscal targets which entail a fall in the stock of public debt would lead to a

Table 3.5 Internal budgetary offsetting: rise in spending and required budget balance (% of GDP)

	2000–10		2010–20		2020–30		'Minimal benchmarks'
	A	*d*	*A*	*d*	*A*	*d*	
Belgium	1.5	−1.4	2.0	0.6	1.5	1.0	−1.0
Germany	1.4	0.4	1.0	0.5	3.2	5.6	−1.1
Italy	1.3	−1.8	1.6	−0.3	2.1	1.7	−1.2
Spain	0.6	−1.3	0.9	−0.3	1.2	0.9	−0.4
Netherlands	0.9	−0.5	1.3	0.9	2.4	4.0	−0.1

Notes: A = Increase in spending due to ageing (Franco and Munzi, 1999); d and 'minimal benchmarks' = surplus (+) or deficit (−); Interest rate − growth rate differential = 2%.

reduction in the interest burden. In turn, this could offset, at least partly, the budgetary impact of demographic developments. Such a strategy would *de facto* amount to pre-funding the ageing problem.

Given a number of simplifying assumptions, the level of the budget balance which would allow the budgetary impact of ageing to be offset via a reduction in the interest burden can be computed. Annex 2 sets out the arithmetic of the calculations. In the exercise below, we posit 'full offsetting' within each decade between 2000 and 2030. This means that, for each decade, we compute the constant budget balance which would bring about a reduction in interest payments matching exactly the rise in government spending over the same period, as estimated by Franco and Munzi (1999).[61] The results are presented in Table 3.5.

Table 3.5 shows the expected increase in public spending due to ageing, A, and the budget balance, d, which, if maintained over the period, brings about a fall in interest payments by the end of the period matching exactly the rise in spending. The last column shows the 'minimal benchmarks' already discussed in the previous section.

As shown in Annex 2, and confirmed by inspection of Table 3.5, the initial level of debt plays an important role, alongside the 'intensity' of the projected ageing impact on public finances. Sticking to their 'minimal benchmarks' would allow high-debt countries to compensate, at least partly, the higher spending due to ageing. As shown in the table, the required budget deficit in Belgium and Italy to fully offset the ageing impact over the period 2000–10 (1.4 and 1.8 per cent of GDP, respectively) is higher than the 'minimal benchmarks' computed in the previous section. However, even in the case of these countries, such a deficit level would fall short of full offsetting over a longer time period.

Compared with Italy and Belgium, low-debt countries would require much higher budget surpluses to generate similar savings. This point is clearly illustrated by the case of Germany, which is expected to undergo similar budgetary pressures as Belgium and Italy in the 2000–10 period, but would require a considerably higher adjustment, given its lower potential for interest savings. Given the relatively low expected increase in spending, Spain and the Netherlands would achieve full compensation in the first decade by sticking to their 'minimal benchmarks'.

As the ageing impact gathers pace in the future, the 'full-offsetting' budget balance becomes considerably more ambitious. As shown in the table, the required fiscal improvement would bring the budget balance beyond the minimal benchmarks for all the countries in the sample in the period 2000–20. The gap becomes particularly large in countries with a relatively low debt such as Germany and the Netherlands. Even in the case of high-debt countries, if the reduction in the interest burden has to cover the whole effect of ageing, the adjustment needs to be sizeable. For instance, Belgium and Italy would have to go well beyond the minimal benchmarks and accept a sustained correction bringing the medium-term target to a surplus of over 1 per cent of GDP.

In sum, 'myopic' behaviour aiming at making room for the budgetary impact of ageing as and when the spending pressure materializes, implies relatively unambitious budget balances in the early years, but would require growing budget surpluses in the future, going well beyond 'close to balance' targets. Hence, postponing the adjustment makes pre-funding increasingly unattractive. On the contrary, front loading, by entailing a fast reduction in the stock of debt, would allow budgetary efforts to be distributed more evenly over time.

While a pre-emptive budgetary strategy may be appealing, 'full' pre-funding aiming at covering the whole impact of ageing via a lower interest burden may not be politically feasible, nor economically desirable. Ambitious budgetary targets – in the form of a strict adherence to the 'close to balance' target of the SGP – will help in facing the budgetary pressure of ageing with a lower public debt, but will not relieve policy makers of responsibility for tackling the ageing problem head on by reforming pension and health care systems.

5. CONCLUSIONS

This chapter examined an important aspect in the implementation of fiscal policy in EMU, namely that of choosing a medium-term budgetary target consistent with the provisions of the Stability and Growth Pact.

Via this choice, attention is shifting from the nominal, uniform 3 per cent deficit ceiling – two features of the EMU set-up often criticized in academic debate – to cyclically adjusted, country-specific targets.

The available estimates of the structural budgetary positions encompassing a sufficient cyclical safety margin point to a target between 0 and 1 per cent of GDP for most of the EU countries, and a surplus for the Nordic countries which, traditionally, have experienced a larger cyclical component in their budgets. The three large countries in the euro area would need to achieve a structural deficit of at least 1 per cent of GDP.

The empirical evidence in this chapter helps to qualify these indications. We provide some evidence on the erratic component in the budget deficit which, if sizeable, may also be a source of risk. The additional safety margin to cover for such risks – of the order of 0.5 to 1 per cent of GDP – would bring most countries of the euro area towards a balanced budget or a small surplus. In a longer term perspective, such targets would help countries to face the demographic shock with a lower stock of public debt.

ANNEX 1 SETTING THE MEDIUM-TERM FISCAL TARGET: AN ILLUSTRATIVE MODEL

The model is for a member country of a monetary union composed of two identical countries. The rest of the world is omitted. The model encompasses a demand (IS type) equation and a supply equation, determining the level of the output gap, y (per cent trend GDP), and inflation, π:

$$y^D = \phi_0 + \phi_1(d - \pi b) - \phi_2(i - \pi^e) + \varepsilon_1 - \phi_3(\pi - \pi_f) - \phi_4(y - y_f) \qquad (3A1.1)$$

$$Y^S = \omega(\pi - \pi^e) + \varepsilon_2 \qquad (3A1.2)$$

where d is the budget deficit (per cent of GDP), i is the nominal interest rate, b is the stock of public debt (per cent of GDP), ε_1 is demand shock and ε_2 is a supply shock. The superscript e indicates expected variables, the subscript f the other country in the monetary union. The fiscal impulse in the IS equation is the inflation-adjusted budget balance $(d - \pi b)$. According to the fiscal rule, the government sets the level of the structural balance, d_s, and lets the automatic stabilizers work:

$$d = d_s - \alpha y + \varepsilon_3 \qquad (3A1.3)$$

where α is the cyclical sensitivity of the budget and ε_3 is the fiscal shock. The nominal deficit d should not exceed a deficit ceiling: $d \leq \bar{d}$.

The central bank follows a monetary rule *à la* Taylor:

$$i = i^* + \beta(\bar{\pi} - \pi^*) + (c - \beta)\bar{y} \qquad (3A1.4)$$

where π^* is the inflation target, i^* is the equilibrium nominal interest rate compatible with the inflation target π^*, and β is the degree of 'conservatism' of the monetary authorities. In this formulation, c indicates the degree of 'activism' of the central bank ($c > \beta$). A positive, large, value of β indicates a 'hard-nosed' central bank. The central bank targets *average* inflation rate and the *average* output gap of the monetary union.

Under rational expectations, the model can be solved for the output gap. The general solution is the following:

$$y = \frac{1}{\Omega}\{\omega\varepsilon_1 - [\phi_2(c + \beta)\gamma + \phi_3 - \phi_1 b]\varepsilon_2 - \omega\phi_1\varepsilon_3 + B(\pi_f - \pi_f^e) + C(y_f - y_f^e)\} \qquad (3A1.5)$$

where:

$$\Omega = \omega[1 + \phi_1\alpha + \phi_2(c - \beta) + \phi_4] + \phi_2(c + \beta)0.5 + \phi_3 + \phi_1 b > 0$$
$$B = \phi_2(c + \beta)0.5 - \phi_3$$
$$C = \phi_2(c - \beta)0.5 - \phi_4$$

In order to obtain a definite solution, we need to make assumptions about the type of shocks affecting the monetary union. Under the extreme cases of 'pure symmetric' and 'pure asymmetric' shocks, the solution is immediate because we do not need to model explicitly the behaviour of inflation and output gap in the rest of the union. Under *pure symmetry* the external trade effects vanish:

$$y = \frac{1}{\Omega_s}\{\omega\varepsilon_1 + [\phi_2(c + \beta) - \phi_1 b]\varepsilon_2 - \omega\phi_1\varepsilon_3\} \quad (3A1.6)$$

where: $\Omega_s = \omega[1 + \phi_1\alpha + \phi_2(c - \beta)] + \phi_2(c + \beta) + \phi_1 b$,

Under *pure asymmetry*, $\bar{\pi}$ and $\bar{y}$ do not change (hence i remains fixed):

$$y = \frac{1}{\Omega_A}[\omega(\varepsilon_1 + \phi_1\varepsilon_3) + 2(\phi_3 + \phi_1 b)\varepsilon_2] \quad (3A1.7)$$

where $\Omega_A = 2\{\omega[0.5(1 + \phi_1\alpha) + \phi_4] + \phi_3 + \phi_1 b\}$.

The structural budget balance is set so as to have $d = \hat{d}$ for *maximum* adverse shocks $(\hat{\varepsilon}_1, \hat{\varepsilon}_2, \hat{\varepsilon}_3)$. Under pure symmetry and asymmetry, we obtain, respectively:

$$\hat{d}_s = \hat{d} - \frac{\alpha}{\Omega_s}[\omega\hat{\varepsilon}_1 + \phi_2(c + \beta)\hat{\varepsilon}_2] + \frac{\omega[1 + \phi_2(c - \beta)] + \phi_2(c + \beta)}{\Omega_s}\hat{\varepsilon}_3 \quad (3A1.8)$$

$$\hat{d}_s = \hat{d} - \frac{\alpha}{\Omega_A}(\omega\hat{\varepsilon}_1 + 2\phi_3\hat{\varepsilon}_2) + 2\left[\frac{\omega(0.5 + \phi_4) + \phi_3}{\Omega_A}\right]\hat{\varepsilon}_3 \quad (3A1.9)$$

The effects of different values of structural parameters and policy preferences are discussed in the text.

ANNEX 2 PRE-EMPTING THE BUDGETARY IMPACT OF AGEING

A strategy of internal budgetary compensation between higher spending in ageing related programmes and lower interest burden can be formalized as follows:

$$i[b(0) - b(T)] = A \tag{3A2.1}$$

where i is the exogenously given nominal interest rate, $b(t)$ is the level of debt (at the beginning and at the end of the decade) and A is the higher spending due to ageing between 0 and T.

By replacing in (3A2.1) the expression for public debt accumulation and solving for the budget deficit, d^*, we find

$$d^* = b(0)(y + \pi) - \frac{A(y + \pi)}{i[1 - e^{-(y+\pi)T}]} \tag{3A2.2}$$

where $y + \pi$ is the nominal GDP growth (assumed constant).

Clearly, the required budget deficit is a positive function of the level of debt, $b(0)$ and a negative function of the ageing impact, A. In Table 3.5 the level of debt in $t = 0$ is that attained at the end of 2000 for the 2000–10 calculations; in subsequent periods the initial stock of debt is that attained at the end of the previous decade by maintaining the budget balance at its required 'equilibrium' level.

4. Cyclical stabilization*

1. INTRODUCTION

The policy assignment and institutional arrangements of EMU are based on a widespread consensus that monetary policy should take care of stabilization in the event of symmetric shocks while the smoothing of asymmetric shocks and diverging cyclical conditions falls to national fiscal policy as the single monetary policy responds only to area-wide price developments. The feasibility of this policy assignment rests of course on the assumption that fiscal policy is an effective stabilization tool.

Recent academic literature assessing the functioning of the rule-based fiscal framework of EMU draws largely on the presumption that fiscal policy is indeed a useful stabilization instrument.[62] This implies a turnaround in the views concerning the potency of fiscal policy interventions in smoothing cyclical fluctuations. Since the collapse of the Keynesian consensus in the second half of the 1970s, fiscal stabilization has become increasingly unpopular among academics and policy makers. While the real effects of fiscal policy were called into question in Barro's (1974) seminal paper on Ricardian equivalence, Sargent and Wallace (1981) revealed 'fiscal roots' of high inflation in the form of debt monetization in the event of persistent budgetary imbalances.[63] Reflecting these underpinnings, the task of short-term stabilization was left to monetary policy, whereas fiscal policy should be geared to medium-term structural issues and long-term sustainability of public finances.

While the potential usefulness of fiscal stabilization is being reconsidered, the 'heritage' of the debate in the 1980s casts a strong scepticism over the use of discretionary fiscal action to fine tune the economy. Political economy arguments and institutional constraints also militate against using fiscal policy to fine tune the business cycle (European Commission, 2002a). Therefore, the overall set of fiscal rules in EMU relies on the working of automatic stabilizers (i.e. the cyclically induced changes in axes and expenditures) as the main tool for fiscal stabilization once member countries have achieved their medium-term fiscal positions of 'close to

*Anne Brunila, Marco Buti and Jon In't Veld, 'Fiscal Policy in Europe: How Effective are Automatic Stabilizers?', *Empirica*, 2003, 30: 1–24.

balance or in surplus' according to the Stability and Growth Pact. As discussed in the previous chapter, adhering to the medium-term budgetary target allows enough breathing space for the automatic stabilizers to work freely without breaching the 3 per cent of GDP deficit threshold. While exceptions to this rule can be envisaged, the underlying policy behaviour is more akin to 'tax smoothing' than to active fiscal management. Moreover, this non-discretionary approach should, at least in principle, guarantee that the behaviour of the actual budget balance is always counter-cyclical and hence contributes to economic stability.

Considering the criticisms raised against fiscal activism, rule-based fiscal policy relying on the working of automatic stabilizers provides clearly several advantages. State-contingent tax revenues and expenditures (basically unemployment-related expenditure) cushion economic fluctuations practically with no information and implementation lags. Moreover, the impact lag of automatic stabilizers is generally considered to be relatively short. In principle, if automatic stabilizers are allowed to operate symmetrically over the cycle, they do not contribute to structural deterioration in budgetary positions.

Once it is recognized that using discretionary fiscal policy should be the exception rather than the rule in EMU, crucial questions arise from the point of view of stabilization. Is the size of current automatic stabilizers sufficient? Would the sole working of automatic stabilizers produce an appropriate fiscal stance both at the national and euro area level given the single monetary policy? Are automatic stabilizers always stabilizing?

While these questions are very important from a policy-making perspective, the aim of our chapter is more modest. We focus on the role and effectiveness of automatic fiscal stabilizers in EU countries with a particular emphasis on the issue of national cyclical stabilization. The next section analyses the working of automatic stabilizers in a simple aggregate demand–aggregate supply (AD–AS) model. The third section reviews recent empirical evidence on the size of automatic stabilizers in EU countries. The fourth and fifth sections present simulations of the effectiveness of automatic stabilizers with the European Commission model QUEST under various types of shocks. The final section concludes.

2. THE SIMPLE ECONOMICS OF AUTOMATIC STABILIZERS

In general, automatic stabilizers tend to increase with the size of the government sector, the progressivity of the tax system, the relative share of taxation of cyclically sensitive tax bases, the generosity of unemployment benefit systems and the sensitivity of unemployment to fluctuations in output.[64] Among country-specific factors, the openness of the economy and the flexibility of the labour, product and financial markets have a significant impact on the smoothing capacity of automatic stabilizers. Moreover, different shocks affect the budget in a different way depending on their degree of 'tax intensity' (see below). Of course, in reality it is often difficult to identify the type of shock hitting the economy and whether it is temporary or permanent without a considerable delay, and in most cases shocks have a demand as well as a supply dimension. Conceptually, however, this distinction is useful.

The effect of automatic stabilizers on output and inflation under different types of shocks is explored through a simple aggregate demand/supply model of a country in a monetary union:[65]

$$y^d = \phi_1(d - \pi b) - \phi_2(i - \pi^e) - \phi_3(y - \varepsilon_d^X) + \varepsilon_d^C + \varepsilon_d^I \tag{4.1}$$

$$y^s = \omega(\pi - \pi^e) + \varepsilon_s \tag{4.2}$$

Equation (4.1) is an IS-type schedule where aggregate demand, y^d, depends on the inflation-adjusted budget deficit, $d - \pi b$ (where b is the stock of public debt and π is the inflation rate),[66] the real interest rate $(i - \pi^e)$, a private consumption shock, ε_d^C, and private investment shock, ε_d^I. The external current account also affects output. It depends on the domestic output gap, y, and a shock to foreign output, ε_d^X.[67]

Equation (4.2) is a Lucas–Phillips supply function where aggregate supply, y^s, depends on the inflation expectation error, $\pi - \pi^e$, and a supply shock, ε_s. The slope of the supply curve, ω, captures the degree of real wage rigidity.[68]

All shocks are country-specific. Demand shocks are temporary, while supply shocks can be temporary or permanent (in the latter case they affect potential output). All variables but the stock of public debt are expressed as changes from baseline. By positing that fiscal authorities pursue a neutral discretionary policy and simply let automatic stabilizers operate freely, the budget deficit is reduced to its cyclical component:

$$d = -(\alpha y + \alpha_C \varepsilon_d^C + \alpha_I \varepsilon_d^I + \alpha_X \phi_3 \varepsilon_d^X) \tag{4.3}$$

The three demand shocks have a direct effect on the budget (α_C, α_I, α_X) and an indirect effect (α) via their impact on disposable income.[69] The direct effect is a function of the respective 'tax intensity': hence α_C is larger than α_I or α_X because of the effect of private consumption shocks to receipts from indirect taxes.

It is assumed that monetary authorities set the interest rate i according to a simple Taylor rule:

$$i = \lambda(\pi + \beta y) \tag{4.4}$$

where β is the relative preference of monetary authorities between output and inflation, and λ captures the impact of the developments in the domestic economy on currency area variables: hence the larger the country, the higher λ.[70] It is assumed that the equilibrium level of the interest rate (not shown here) ensures that inflation is on target in the medium run (i.e. when shocks are zero). Under these behavioural rules,[71] the model can be solved for y and π:

$$y = \frac{1}{\mu}\{\omega[(1-\phi_1\alpha_c)\varepsilon_d^C + (1-\phi_1\alpha_I)\varepsilon_d^I + \phi_3(1-\phi_1\alpha_X)\varepsilon_d^X] + (\phi_1 b + \lambda\phi_2)\varepsilon_s\} \tag{4.5}$$

$$\pi = \frac{1}{\mu}[(1-\phi_1\alpha_c)\varepsilon_d^C + (1-\phi_1\alpha_I)\varepsilon_d^I + \phi_3(1-\phi_1\alpha_X)\varepsilon_d^X - (1+\phi_1\alpha+\lambda\phi_2\beta)\varepsilon_s] \tag{4.6}$$

where $\mu = \omega(1+\phi_1\alpha+\phi_2\lambda\beta+\phi_3)+\phi_1 b+\lambda\phi_2$.

Clearly, a higher sensitivity of the budget deficit to shocks (higher α_is) helps stabilizing both output and inflation in the case of temporary demand shocks. Higher openness of the economy (i.e. higher ϕ_3) helps to smooth domestic demand shocks through import leakage but increases a country's exposure to a foreign country's output shocks. A higher stock of public debt has a stabilizing effect under demand shocks as higher inflation reduces the real value of debt and hence consumption, while it reinforces the effects of supply shocks. A higher ω (i.e. a flatter supply function) helps to smooth supply shocks but is destabilizing under demand shocks. The impact of a higher ϕ_1 on output in the event of supply shocks is ambiguous, the reason being that the higher direct effect tends to be compensated by the effect of inflation on the real value of the debt. Under the assumption that the central bank is inflation-conservative, however, a higher ϕ_1 implies higher output stabilization also in the case of supply shocks.[72] A higher λ has an ambiguous effect on output in the case of supply shocks. However, unlike the previous case, under normal values of the parameters, a higher λ is output-destabilizing.[73]

Figure 4.1 illustrates the effect on output and inflation of a positive consumption and investment shock under high and low automatic stabilizers.

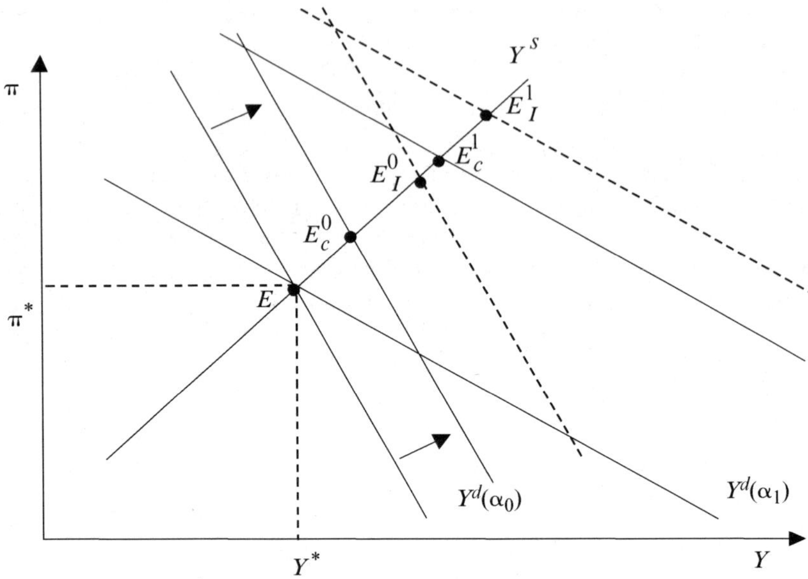

Figure 4.1 *Demand shock*

A higher budget sensitivity α implies a lower (absolute) coefficient of π – that is a higher (negative) slope – and a lower shift to the right of y^d in the event of a positive demand shock. The shift in the demand schedule depends not only on α but also on the shock-specific budgetary elasticities α_i: it is smaller in the case of a consumption shock than in the case of an investment (or an export) shock. As Figure 4.1 shows, if prior to the shock, output was at its potential level and inflation was on target, higher automatic stabilizers entail a smaller output gap and a smaller deviation of inflation from target after the shock. The degree of output and inflation stabilization is larger in the case of a consumption shock than in the case of a shock to investment (or exports).

In the case of a *temporary* supply shock (i.e. a shock that does not affect potential output), equations (4.5) and (4.6) show that high automatic stabilizers reduce the output variability, but imply a higher deviation of π from target. The effect of different size of automatic stabilizers in the event of a negative supply shock is illustrated in Figure 4.2. If the supply shock is *permanent* (i.e. potential output changes by the size of the shock ε_s), the expression of the 'new' output gap can be derived from (4.5) and is the following:

$$y - \varepsilon_s = -\frac{\varepsilon_s}{\mu}[\omega(1 + \alpha\phi_1 + \phi_3 + \lambda\phi_2\beta)] \tag{4.7}$$

$$\pi = -\frac{\varepsilon_s}{\mu}[1 + \alpha\phi_1 + \phi_3 + \lambda\phi_2\beta] \tag{4.8}$$

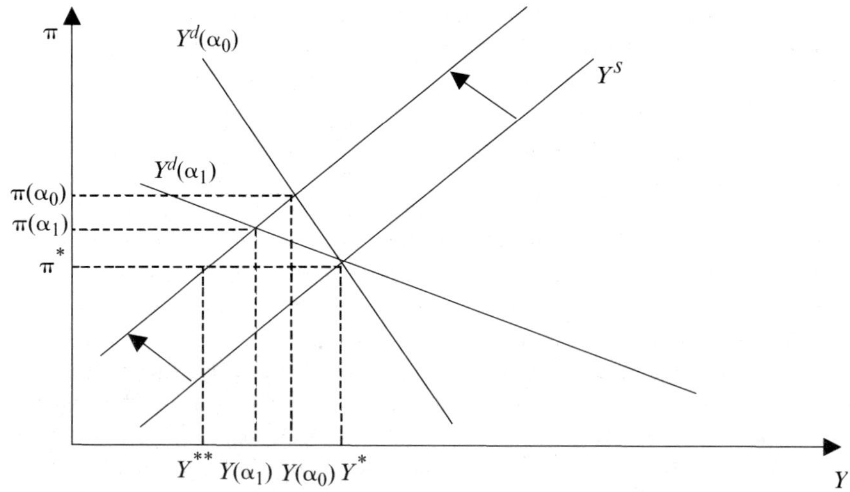

Figure 4.2 Supply shock

A higher value of α increases the gap around the *new* potential output and, as a consequence, is both inflation- and output-destabilizing. This result is illustrated in Figure 4.2 which shows that, in the case of a permanent negative supply shock, higher automatic stabilizers are destabilizing for both output and inflation. Notice also that, if inflation is the only concern of the central bank, perfect inflation stabilization ($\pi = \pi^*$ at each point in time) implies also perfect output stabilization in the event of a permanent supply shock (i.e. output jumps directly from the old to the new potential level).

3. EMPIRICAL EVIDENCE ON THE DEGREE OF FISCAL STABILIZATION

Having discussed the working of automatic stabilizers in theory, this section focuses on the existing empirical evidence on their smoothing power. How effective are automatic stabilizers in EU countries?

In general, the measurement of the stabilizing power of fiscal variables involves two channels. The first one is related to the sensitivity of government revenue and expenditure components to economic fluctuations. In an economic downturn, tax receipts will be lower as the respective tax bases are negatively affected, while on the expenditure side unemployment benefits will increase in line with unemployment. The opposite will occur in an upturn. The second channel is related to the dampening effect of these cyclically induced changes in budgetary components. Estimating the smoothing power of automatic stabilizers is particularly challenging due to the complex interactions between fiscal variables, types of the shocks and reactions of the private sector.

Most empirical studies investigating the impact of automatic stabilizers on economic activity are based on large macroeconometric model simulations. The appeal of using models is in their ability to account for many of the influences and interactions between the key economic variables. The results obtained are, however, model-specific and depend on the assumptions made on the accompanying monetary and exchange rate policies. As the simulations produce a range of estimates conditional on the imposed structure of the model and the underlying assumptions, the measurement of the smoothing capacity of automatic stabilizers is by no means uncontroversial. This is important to acknowledge when assessing the results.

On the basis of recent studies, what cyclical smoothing can be expected from 'pure' automatic stabilization? Table 4.1 presents the results

Table 4.1 Degree of stabilization provided by automatic stabilizers (%)

	INTERLINK(1)	NiGEM(2)
Belgium	22	5
Germany	31	18
Greece	14	–
Spain	17	13
France	14	7
Ireland	10	7
Italy	23	5
Netherlands	36	6
Austria	7	12
Portugal	–	10
Finland	58	7
Euro area	–	11
Denmark	–	–
Sweden	26	–
UK	30	–

Notes:
(1) 1-RMSD (Root mean square deviations) of the gap in the 1990s.
(2) 1-RMSD of GDP growth.

Source: European Commission (2001a).

of analyses with two well-known macroeconometric models: INTERLINK of the OECD (Van den Noord, 2000) and NiGEM of the National Institute of Economic and Social Research (Barrell and Pina, 2000).

The OECD finds on average a smoothing effectiveness between 25 and 30 per cent for the euro area, that is, automatic stabilizers smooth on average 25 to 30 per cent of the output gap. As to the country-specific results, the simulations indicate that Finland and the Netherlands, with their large budgetary automatic stabilizers, obtain the highest degree of output stabilization, while the degree of stabilization is significantly lower in Austria, France, Greece and Spain. The countries outside the euro area show a relatively high degree of cyclical smoothing.

The analysis with NiGEM (which only considers euro area countries) points to considerably smaller effects, in the range of 5 to 18 per cent, with the euro area at 11 per cent. Germany shows the highest dampening effects while, surprisingly, Finland features one of the lowest (just 7 per cent). The lower stabilizing effect appears to be due to the fact that the simulations do not just focus on demand disturbances, and in particular shocks to private consumption for which automatic stabilizers are most powerful, but consider multiple sources of uncertainty and so arrive at a lower average stabilizing effect.[74]

Inspired by the recent empirical literature on monetary policy as well as the new institutional policy framework of EMU, a small but growing body of literature on the effects of fiscal policy based on a framework of vector autoregressions (the VAR estimation techniques) has started to emerge.[75] By estimating the short- and long-term fiscal multipliers[76] these studies seek to extract the impact of various fiscal policy instruments on economic activity. The results are in general in line with Keynesian thinking as regards to the sign of the multipliers. However, in most cases short-term fiscal multipliers turn out to be significantly lower than predicted by the Keynesian framework or by model simulations. Consequently, even sizeable fiscal expansions may produce only a modest impact on economic activity.

4. AUTOMATIC STABILIZERS IN PRACTICE: QUEST MODEL SIMULATIONS

4.1 Simulation Strategy

This section presents the framework of analysis when estimating the size of automatic stabilizers in EU countries with the European Commission's quarterly macroeconomic model QUEST. The analysis distinguishes between three types of demand shocks – a shock to private consumption, private investment and export demand – and a supply shock to labour productivity.

For any quantitative assessment of the smoothing capacity of automatic fiscal stabilizers, a benchmark regime has to be defined in which the budgetary impact of economic fluctuations is exactly offset by changes in other components of the budget and with which a comparison can be made. But results are sensitive to which budget items adjust to keep the overall fiscal balance fixed. Some studies define the benchmark regime as one in which tax revenues for some selected categories (and sometimes also selected expenditure items) are kept constant and the impact of economic fluctuations is implicitly offset by changes in tax rates. Here a more general approach is considered in which the impact of economic fluctuations on the budget is offset by across-the-board changes in all other budget items, such that the overall fiscal balance is kept constant. Hence, the quantitative assessment of automatic stabilizers in this chapter involves two steps: first the impact of economic fluctuations on the budget is estimated, and this is then combined with the average effect of fiscal policy changes on economic activity in the model to provide an estimate of the smoothing capacity of automatic stabilizers.[77]

The QUEST model can be characterized as a modern version of the neoclassical-Keynesian synthesis. Behavioural equations in the model are based on intertemporal optimization of households and firms with forward-looking expectations. Prices adjust sluggishly and the nominal wage response is delayed because of overlapping wage contracts. The model has Keynesian features in the short run, but the effectiveness of fiscal policy is more limited than in the textbook Keynesian model because of intertemporal budget constraints imposed in the model.[78]

As already pointed out, fiscal multipliers associated with various policy actions are not independent of the assumptions underlying the simulations. Both the size and sign of the output effects of the budgetary measures depend *inter alia* on the assumptions made on the monetary policy response, formation of private sector expectations, price and wage flexibility, functioning of labour market institutions and the response of other fiscal variables to simulated budgetary policy changes.

Fiscal policy in the QUEST model operates basically through two standard channels in the short run: via the direct aggregate demand channel and through the interest and exchange rate channel. The extent of crowding out through induced changes in interest rates and the exchange rate affects the size of fiscal multipliers but in general, does not change their sign. In response to fiscal expansions interest rates tend to rise and with flexible exchange rates, higher domestic interest rates by attracting capital inflows tend to appreciate the exchange rate.

More specifically, it is assumed that the ECB follows a targeting rule which puts a high weight on (expected) inflation and a low weight on output, and hence interest rates increase in response to fiscal shocks that raise inflationary pressures in the euro area. Denmark with a narrow fluctuation band vis-à-vis the euro, is assumed to follow the ECB interest rate policy, while Sweden and the UK are assumed to follow an independent monetary policy. Therefore, in the case of a negative demand shock, this implies that the central bank increases money supply as output contracts in order to closely meet a baseline inflation target. The fact that monetary policy is allowed to function as another stabilizing mechanism in the simulations and interacts with the operation of the automatic fiscal stabilizers has an important bearing for the results.[79]

Consumption and saving in the model are based on a forward-looking optimizing model of life-cycle behaviour. The main variables determining consumption are lifetime income (i.e. human wealth, consisting of the current income and the expected discounted future net income stream) and financial wealth. In addition, it is assumed that a fraction of households are liquidity constrained and in consequence their consumption is determined by current disposable income.[80]

Furthermore, when interpreting the results of the simulations, it is important to note that the model contains a tax policy rule that stabilizes the debt to GDP ratio in the medium term. In the simulations this reaction function is turned off during the first years (the deficit and debt to GDP ratios rise in the first years). As it is assumed that fiscal stabilizers operate symmetrically over the cycle, the temporary shocks are reversed in following years such that there is no structural deterioration in budgetary positions, but the tax policy rule is turned on in the medium term so that lump-sum taxes are increased gradually to stabilize the debt to GDP ratio.

Simulations involve three steps, as follows:

1. The sensitivity of the budget balance to the cycle is obtained by simulating the impact of a shock of 1 per cent of real GDP on government revenues and expenditures. Simulations are run separately for the three types of demand shocks and one supply shock, each scaled to equal 1 per cent of real GDP. All shocks are asymmetric individual country shocks, that is, one country at the time is affected by a negative disturbance that reduces GDP in the first year by 1 per cent relative to baseline.[81]
2. The impact of an expansionary fiscal shock of 1 per cent of real GDP on economic activity is derived to calculate the short-term fiscal multipliers associated with temporary changes in government expenditures and revenues.

3. The smoothing capacity of automatic stabilizers is computed by using the estimated budgetary sensitivities and fiscal multipliers. It should be noted that the results are sensitive to the type of assumptions made regarding the hypothetical benchmark scenario where automatic fiscal stabilizers are not allowed to operate.[82]

The first two steps are discussed in the following text, while the final one is presented in the next section.

4.2 Sensitivity of the Budget to Economic Fluctuations

The modelling of tax revenues is crucial for the assessment of the operation of the automatic budget stabilizers. The QUEST model distinguishes between labour income tax (inclusive of social security contributions), corporate profit tax and consumption tax (VAT). These taxes are modelled proportionally, that is, for each category the tax revenue has a unitary elasticity with respect to its respective tax base.[83] For instance, for corporate profit tax, this implies that tax revenues are proportional to profits, and the cyclical sensitivity of corporate tax revenues depends on the sensitivity of profits to output fluctuations. As was argued in the second section, this in turn depends on the origin of the shock.

The sensitivity of income tax revenues (including social security contributions) to output fluctuations reflects the sensitivity of employment and wages to output shocks. Indirect tax revenues depend on fluctuations in consumption. A consumption shock has a direct impact on VAT revenue, while investment and export shocks only have an indirect effect. As will become clear, the origin of the shock has very important implications for the magnitude of the cyclical sensitivity of the tax revenues.

Concerning government expenditure, it is common practice to focus on unemployment-related expenditure as an automatic stabilizer. As different types of shocks to output have different effects on unemployment, transfers related to unemployment benefits will fluctuate in proportion to the impact on unemployment. While other expenditure categories also tend to fluctuate with the cycle, often in a pro-cyclical fashion, this is considered here as non-automatic and discretionary, although the distinction may be somewhat artificial and controversial.[84] For this exercise, it is assumed that these other expenditure categories do not react to cyclical swings, and they are thus kept fixed at their base levels. Although this may not be a good description of the real behaviour of fiscal authorities, it allows one to concentrate on the operation of 'pure' automatic stabilizers.

Table 4.2 reports the estimated budgetary sensitivities under various shocks to the economy, all scaled to equal 1 per cent of GDP. These

Table 4.2 Sensitivity of the budget under various shocks

	Consumption shock	Investment shock	Export shock	Productivity shock
Belgium	0.57	0.17	0.27	0.07
Germany	0.65	0.19	0.27	0.16
Greece	0.87	0.20	0.27	0.1
Spain	0.77	0.18	0.25	0.09
France	0.80	0.21	0.30	0.12
Ireland	0.50	0.10	0.17	0.03
Italy	0.68	0.22	0.30	0.23
Netherlands	0.59	0.15	0.23	0.08
Austria	0.61	0.17	0.26	0.09
Portugal	0.82	0.17	0.26	0.13
Finland	0.77	0.16	0.25	0.03
Euro area average	0.70	0.19	0.28	0.14
Standard deviation	0.12	0.03	0.04	0.06
Denmark	0.67	0.18	0.28	0.06
Sweden	0.77	0.16	0.25	0.29
UK	0.60	0.18	0.27	0.28

measure the changes in the deficit to GDP ratios that are the result of these shocks. The budget sensitivity is particularly large under private consumption shocks. The deficit to GDP ratio rises by between 0.5 and 0.9 percentage points (in Ireland and Greece, respectively), as tax revenues, and in particular indirect taxes, are directly affected by this shock. Shocks to private investment and export demand have a smaller impact on the budget than consumption shocks, less than half the size, as no tax category is directly affected by this type of disturbance. Also technology shocks have a lower impact on the budget deficit.

The widely used OECD estimates for budget sensitivity to cyclical fluctuations (see Van den Noord, 2000) produce an overall responsiveness of the budget deficit to the changes in the output gap that averages around 0.5 for the EU and varies between 0.3 for Austria and 0.8 for Denmark. While such estimates have the advantage that the elasticity of the budget to the cycle can be summarized into a single statistic, the drawback is that they hide some very crucial differences in the impact of various shocks on the budgetary position. The results are also sensitive to the period chosen.

The simulations presented here clearly show that the cyclical sensitivity of the budget depends crucially on the origin of the shock. If variations in

GDP are primarily driven by consumption shocks then the cyclical sensitivity of the budget is much higher than when they are primarily driven by investment or export shocks. Not surprisingly, a foreign demand shock, like the Asian crisis in 1997–98, has a much smaller effect on the deficit than a shock to domestic consumption, as the latter directly affects VAT returns.[85]

While direct comparison of these shock-specific elasticity estimates with the average elasticities reported by the OECD is not straightforward, the overall size of the cyclical sensitivity of the budget balance is broadly similar.[86] However, the country-specific ranking is different and varies between the shocks. Under consumption shocks the cyclical sensitivity of the budget varies considerably more across euro area countries than under the other shocks. This is partly a reflection of differences in effective tax rates on consumption in the model, which is low in Spain and much higher in nordic countries (Martinez-Mongay, 2000). Countries with higher overall tax rates display a higher budget sensitivity but what is particularly important for the consumption shock is the share of indirect tax in total tax revenues, which is high in, for example, Portugal.

4.3 Short-term Fiscal Multipliers

As budgetary components have different effects on aggregate demand and supply, in order to obtain a measure of the short-term impact of budgetary changes on real GDP (i.e. the short-term fiscal multipliers), various categories of government revenue and expenditure were shocked separately. Short-term expenditure multipliers are derived from a shock in which government expenditures are increased by 1 per cent of (baseline) GDP. On the expenditure side, a distinction is made between government purchases of goods and services, government investment, transfers to households and government employment. Short-term revenue multipliers are produced by reducing labour tax, corporate profit tax and value added tax by 1 per cent of (baseline) GDP. As the focus is on automatic stabilizers, assumed to operate symmetrically over the cycle, the fiscal shocks are all temporary shocks lasting two years, but reversed in the following year.[87]

The effectiveness to stimulate economic activity by higher government expenditure is relatively modest, because a large part of the fiscal expansion is crowded out or leaks abroad through higher imports. This outcome is due to several effects. First of all, private consumption falls in response to higher government expenditure. Higher real interest rates triggered by expansionary fiscal policy make saving more attractive and induce forward-looking consumers to reduce consumption. A rise in interest rates also has negative wealth effects, as it increases the rate at which expected future income is discounted. Moreover, although liquidity constrained consumers increase their consumption as they see their disposable income rise, permanent income consumers anticipate the temporary nature of the fiscal expansion (which is later reversed), and permanent income is not much affected.

The second channel through which a fiscal expansion crowds out private spending is private investment. While profitability is boosted by the fiscal expansion in the short run, the rise in real interest rates offsets this positive effect and net effect on private investment is generally small (positive or negative).

As to the specific simulation results, the short-term fiscal multipliers associated with various expenditure categories for each EU member state are reported in Figure 4.3.

According to the simulations the impact of a 1 per cent of GDP increase in government outlays varies significantly across spending categories and over time, but the pattern is roughly the same in all countries. The first-year impact of all spending categories is positive, although in most cases small. The notable exception is government employment, which has a multiplier close to unity in all countries.[88] However, the strong positive impact of higher government employment is only temporary and in the event of more persistent or even permanent shocks, it would be crowded out in the medium term through its effect on private sector wages (higher public employment reduces overall unemployment and leads to higher wage demands, which have a negative effect on private sector employment and output).

The short-term impact of government purchases of goods and services as well as government investment is somewhat smaller than that for employment, the multipliers being in the range of 0.5–0.7. In case of more persistent shocks, the expansionary effect of higher government purchases would fade away rapidly over the medium term, whereas that of government investment would have a more lasting impact by raising public capital stock and potential output. The smallest expansionary effect in all countries is achieved through a temporary increase in higher government transfer payments, most of which is saved.

Figure 4.4 reports the short-term multipliers associated with reductions in labour income tax, corporate profit tax and value added tax by 1 per cent of (baseline) GDP. In general, the simulations suggest that the impact of temporary labour and corporate income tax cuts on output is small because the intertemporal optimizing behaviour of economic agents smooth away most of it.[89] Over the medium term the impact of a tax cut would gain strength as distortionary effects of taxation are reduced.

A reduction in labour income taxes has a direct demand effect through its impact on disposable income and a positive supply-side effect through increased employment. The principal reason why the short-term impact

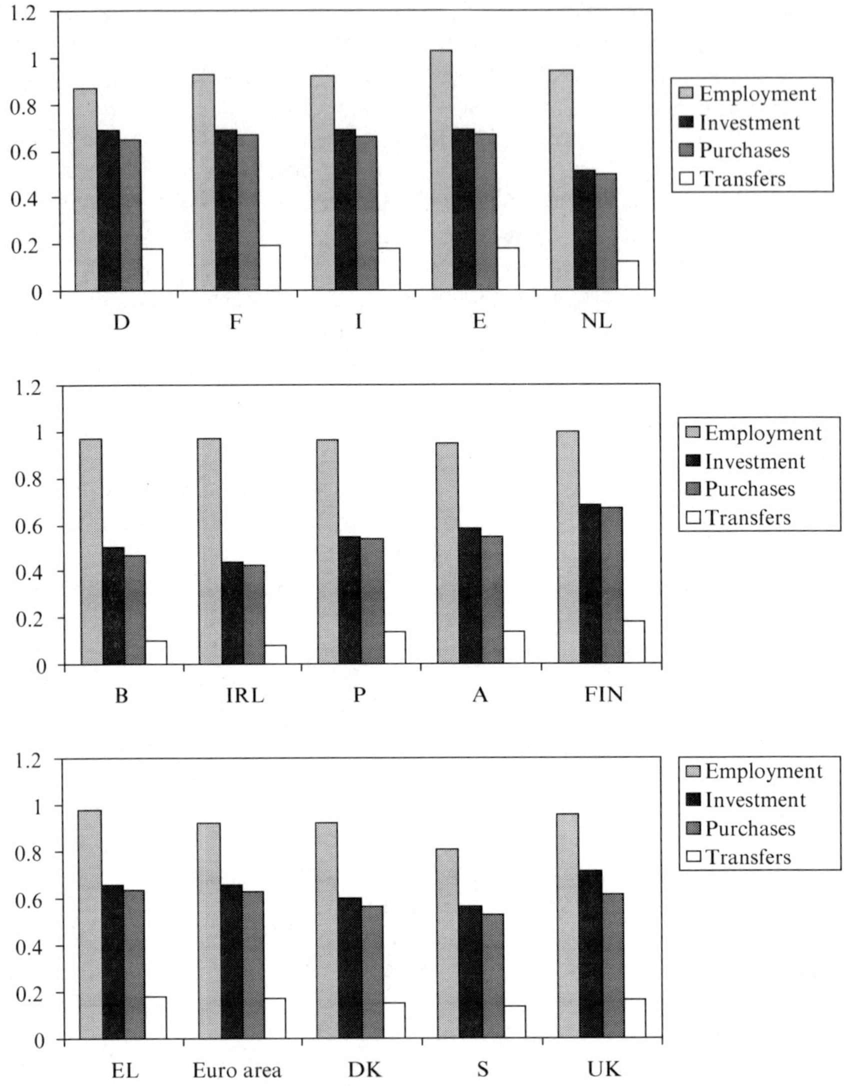

Figure 4.3 Short-term expenditure multipliers: the impact on GDP of an increase in government expenditure by 1 per cent of GDP

of lower labour income taxes remains very small is that consumers smooth the temporary tax cut over a large number of periods, while supply-side effects, by fostering labour demand, would only start to feed in with a lag. This positive supply-side effect is also associated with a depreciation of the

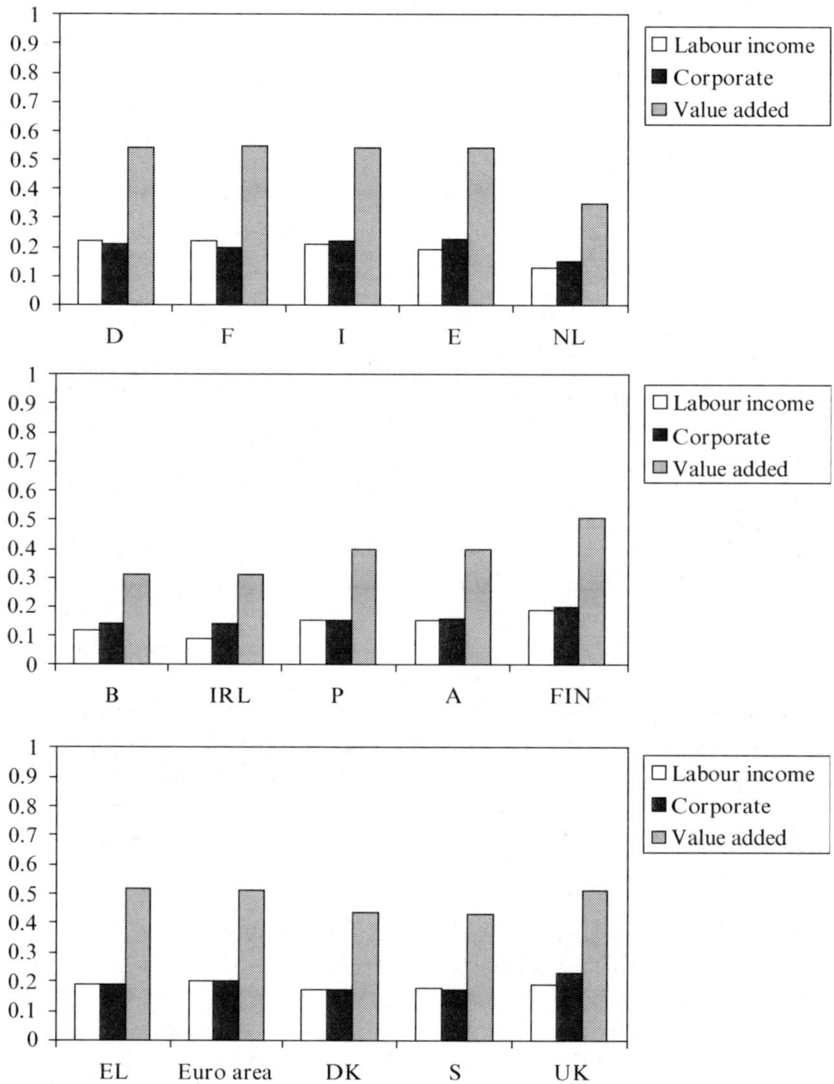

Figure 4.4 Short-term tax multipliers: the impact on GDP of a decrease in taxes by 1 per cent of GDP

real exchange rate which boosts demand further, especially in small open economies in EMU.

The employment response to a change in labour taxation differs per country, but tends to be higher in the continental European countries than in the Scandinavian and Anglo-Saxon countries. These country-specific differences arise, *inter alia*, from varying lags in the labour demand and different labour market institutions.[90] It should also be noted that to some extent monetary policy with independent inflation targeting in Sweden and the UK has an important bearing on the simulation results. In these two countries a larger part of fiscal expansion is crowded out through higher interest rates because monetary policy reacts more to domestic inflationary pressures than is the case in the euro area countries, where monetary policy reacts only to area-wide inflation.

A reduction in corporate taxes has a direct demand impact through its effect on current profits, but as the tax cut is reversed in the medium term the positive impact remains small. A reduction in value added tax boosts consumer spending in the short term, as forward looking consumers front-load their spending to the current year in anticipation of higher indirect taxes again in following years. However, a large proportion of the positive impact is crowded out through higher interest rates or, for the smaller more open economies, leaks abroad via higher imports. As interest rates rise to contain inflationary pressures stemming from higher consumer spending, private investment is also crowded out.

As a very broad characterization, the results therefore indicate that in the short run, the impact of fiscal policy is larger on the expenditure side than on the tax side.

However, it should be borne in mind that this conclusion holds for temporary fiscal policy. In the case of longer lasting more persistent fiscal policy actions, the impact from the expenditure side would fade out in the medium term (due to crowding out effects) while on the tax side the impact increases over time as supply-side effects become more important.[91]

5. SMOOTHING POWER OF AUTOMATIC STABILIZERS UNDER VARIOUS SHOCKS

To obtain an estimate for the smoothing power of automatic stabilizers, the cyclically induced change in the budget balance is multiplied by the weighted average of the short-term revenue and expenditure multipliers. Following the differences in the estimated sensitivity of the budget to cyclical fluctuation, the simulations suggest that the degree of smoothing provided by automatic stabilizers varies significantly under various types of shocks and across countries. What matters is not only government size as such, but the relative size of cyclically sensitive budget items.

The highest degree of stabilization is provided under a shock to private consumption – which is very 'tax-rich' – and the lowest under an investment shock. The results for export demand shocks are generally close to those under private investment shocks. Under supply shocks the smoothing effectiveness is relatively low.

The estimations of the smoothing impact of automatic stabilizers for individual EU countries are presented in Figure 4.5. The results indicate

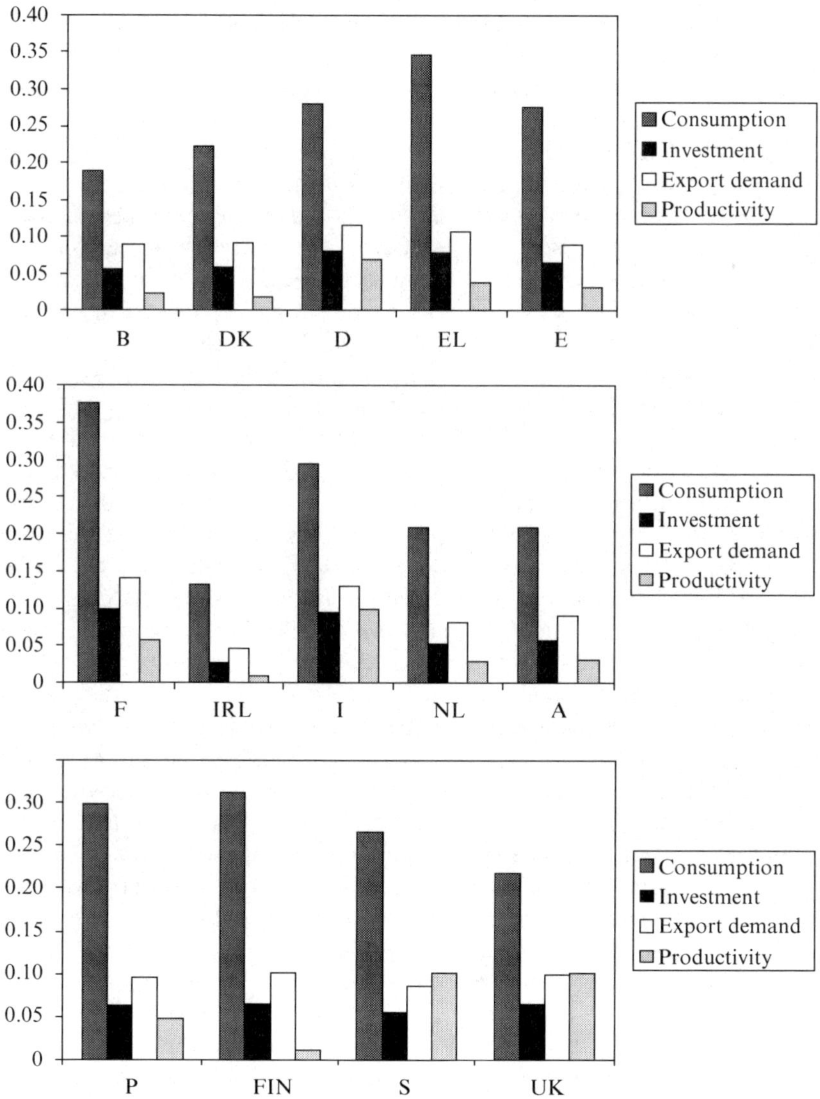

Figure 4.5 Smoothing power of automatic stabilizers

that, in the case of a *private consumption shock*, automatic stabilizers smooth over 30 per cent of GDP fluctuations in France, Finland and Greece, while in Belgium and Ireland the smoothing impact of automatic stabilizers is less than 20 per cent.

As pointed out, the smoothing impact of automatic stabilizers depends to a large extent on the cyclical sensitivity of the budget: the larger the cyclical sensitivity of the budget the higher the stabilization provided by automatic stabilizers. In the case of a consumption shock, an important factor behind the differences across countries is the structure of taxes: automatic stabilization is larger in countries with a relatively high share of tax revenues coming from indirect taxes as they are directly affected by a consumption shock. However, the 'efficiency' of automatic stabilizers – that is, the smoothing impact of a given change in the budget balance – is not the same across the countries. For instance, a worsening of the budget deficit by 0.77 percentage points of GDP under a negative consumption shock both in Finland and Spain has a large smoothing impact in Finland (over 30 per cent) compared with Spain (less than 30 per cent).

In the case of a *private investment shock*, the power of automatic stabilizers is considerably lower. Differences across countries largely reflect differences in the sensitivity of the budget to this shock but the variation is small. The same holds for an *export demand shock*. The highest stabilization is derived in France (10 and 14 per cent, respectively), and the lowest is in Ireland (3 and 5 per cent). The more open economies have a relatively low impact multiplier for expenditure shocks in the model and this implies a lower smoothing capacity of the stabilizers. Ireland also displays a lower budget sensitivity to this particular shock, reflecting a higher reliance on indirect taxation, and achieves a lower degree of smoothing.

While automatic stabilizers have a desirable impact under demand shocks, the dampening effect provided by tax and welfare systems may be less desirable under supply shocks if the shock is permanent, as it delays the adjustment of output to its new potential. As pointed out in the second section, in the event of a negative supply shock, there also arises the issue of potential conflict between fiscal and monetary authorities as output goes down while inflation accelerates. In the case of large countries within the euro area, monetary authorities will respond by raising interest rates to offset the inflationary impact of the shock, and this will have a negative effect on GDP. Clearly, the larger the stabilizers the stronger the reaction of the central bank. In the case of small euro area countries, the monetary response will be very limited and, as a result, inflation will rise in the country concerned. Again, large automatic stabilization will entail further negative consequences on competitiveness.

The empirical relevance of these theoretical concerns is still under-researched as, more generally, is the role of automatic stabilizers in the event of supply shocks. In order to explore this issue, we have simulated a negative shock to labour productivity which lasts for two years. As shown in Figure 4.5, the average degree of stabilization provided by automatic stabilizers is modest in all EU countries. Again, Ireland appears to have the smallest smoothing capacity for this particular shock, as it is a small open economy and relies more on indirect taxes, which are not directly affected by this type of shock. Overall the differences across countries are small, ranging from 1 per cent in Ireland, and Finland to 10 per cent in Italy, Sweden and the UK. Shocks in the larger countries are accompanied by a larger monetary tightening, given their weight in the ECB reaction function, which increases the negative impact on their budgetary positions. The highest sensitivity of the budget is found in Sweden and the UK, which have an independent monetary policy.

These results are comforting as 'too much' stabilization may be harmful in the event of a long-lasting shock as it could lead to potential conflicts with monetary authorities, negative competitiveness effects and a slowdown of structural change: in other words the low smoothing effect shown by the simulations may actually be a good thing.[92]

6. CONCLUSIONS

This chapter has addressed the issue of the role and effectiveness of automatic stabilizers in EU countries. Fiscal stabilization is desirable in the case of a demand shock because it allows the smoothing of both output and inflation. Our results show that automatic stabilizers are quite effective in the case of shocks to private consumption, while they are less effective in the case of shocks to investment or external demand. In the latter case, within-EMU real exchange rate adjustment via inflation differentials may supplement fiscal stabilization.

In the case of a temporary supply shock such as a short-term surge in the oil price affecting the whole euro area or a large country, a conflict may arise between monetary and fiscal policy as inflation and output move in opposite directions. Interest rates may have to be raised to keep inflation in check while automatic stabilizers tend to limit the output loss. Nevertheless, some degree of output smoothing via automatic stabilizers may be desirable since the adverse effect on inflation is necessarily short-lived. If the supply shock only hits a small economy in the euro area, the common monetary policy does not react and fiscal stabilization helps smooth output, but aggravates inflationary pressures at the national level thereby leading to a loss of competitiveness.

In the event of permanent supply shocks which change the output potential of the economy (e.g. a lasting change in productivity due to technological innovation, long-lasting real wage gap, evolving degree of competition on the product markets, permanent shift in the terms of trade), output smoothing may not be the optimal response. Ideally, in the event of a permanent shock, the economy should adjust to a new equilibrium level, and fiscal stabilization may slow down the inevitable structural adjustment. In contrast, public finances (i.e. tax and welfare systems) that are conducive to real labour market flexibility and resource reallocation foster the adjustment of the new structural conditions of the economy.

In sum, automatic stabilizers are useful to stabilize output in the case of temporary shocks, although in the case of supply shocks output stabilization may come at the cost of temporarily higher inflation. However, in the case of permanent (mainly supply) shocks, high automatic stabilizers may delay the inevitable structural adjustment and, if they are symmetric, imply a stronger response by the monetary authorities.

Our analysis does not pretend to provide definite answers to the issue of cyclical stabilization in EMU. First of all, the degree of smoothing provided by automatic stabilization may change over time. EMU as such may increase the stabilization efficiency of fiscal policy by dampening interest and exchange rate responses to changes in fiscal policy in individual member countries. Also structural reforms may lead to lower fiscal stabilization if they entail a reduction in progressivity of tax systems and less generous unemployment benefits. This trade-off is however not self-evident in terms of overall adjustment capacity of the economy, since tax and spending reforms should also increase flexibility in factor markets and thereby reduce the need for traditional fiscal stabilization.

A related issue is whether the degree of stabilization provided by the current set of automatic stabilizers is sufficient or appropriate with respect to national and area-wide needs in the euro area. Automatic stabilizers have not in general been designed with cyclical considerations in mind and certainly not in view of the monetary union, but rather are the outcome of the working of tax and welfare systems, themselves the expression of social and political preferences regarding income redistribution and social insurance.

5. Interactions between monetary and fiscal policies*

1. INTRODUCTION

The completion of Economic and Monetary Union (EMU) – based on the mandate given to the European Central Bank (ECB) to maintain price stability and guidelines for the conduct of national fiscal policies – has prompted renewed interest in the interplay between monetary and fiscal policies (Buti, 2003a).

The traditional Optimal Currency Areas literature pointed out long ago that, in a monetary union, fiscal policy has to play a more important role in cyclical stabilization given the loss of national monetary independence. This is particularly the case if shocks are not perfectly correlated across frontiers. Fiscal flexibility, together with budgetary discipline and coordination, has come to be seen as a central pillar of fiscal policy in a currency area (European Commission, 1990). The Stability and Growth Pact (SGP) has been the operational response of EU countries to the quest for budgetary discipline in EMU.

Recent theoretical and empirical developments have shed new light on the 'old' issue of the interactions between monetary and fiscal authorities. The theoretical literature reviewed here looks at the rationale for budgetary constraints but rarely embodies explicitly EMU and SGP-relevant rules in budgetary behaviour. While a number of studies, like for example those of Aarle *et al.* (2000), Bennett and Loayza (2000) and Leitmo (2000), encompass a cost of 'fiscal policy activism', to our knowledge, no paper encompasses the 3 per cent plus 'close-to-balance' rule of the SGP, which would ensure budgetary prudence while leaving room for manoeuvre for fiscal stabilization. The empirical literature, while providing interesting insights, lacks theoretical foundations and, as such, is of limited usefulness in understanding the reaction function of monetary and fiscal authorities and, especially, in anticipating the type of interactions which will prevail in EMU. As we argue here, strategic substitutability and

* Buti, M., Roeger, W. and J. in't Veld, 'Stabilising Output and Inflation: Policy Conflicts and Coordination under a Stability Pact', *Journal of Common Market Studies*, 2001, 39(5): 801–28.

complementarity between the two policies – and their interpretation in terms of 'conflict' or 'cooperation' – depend crucially on the typology of shocks hitting the economy and on the objective functions of monetary and fiscal authorities. In the case of demand shocks we find that cooperation only gives limited benefits, while in the case of supply shocks, which drive output and inflation into opposite directions, cooperation is welfare improving.

This chapter provides a simple analytical setting for assessing the interactions of monetary and fiscal authorities when the latter are subject to upper limits on the budget deficit. A particular emphasis is put on the design of stabilization policies.

The structure of the chapter is as follows. In the second section we provide a short survey of the existing literature. The third section presents a simple model of monetary and fiscal behaviour capturing some of the main features of the Maastricht institutional framework. The solution of the game between monetary and fiscal authorities under non-cooperation and cooperation is provided in the fourth and fifth sections respectively. The sixth section presents some numerical simulations with the Commission Services' QUEST model on the quantitative relevance of the theoretical findings. The final section provides a summing up of the main results and discusses some policy implications.

2. LITERATURE REVIEW

At the theoretical level, much work has been devoted to the rationale for fiscal constraints in a monetary union. A formal model of the SGP is provided by Beetsma and Uhlig (1999) (see also Beetsma, 2001). In a two-period model of a monetary union, myopic governments who know that they may be replaced at the beginning of the second period issue more debt than a social planner would do. This would constrain monetary policy in the second period. This effect is magnified in a monetary union because the adverse impact on the common monetary policy is diluted. As a result, the incentive to restrain public debt accumulation is reduced and we end up with an overburdened monetary policy. Hence, a pact limiting public debt accumulation increases welfare in a monetary union.

However, Chari and Kehoe (1998) argue that the desirability of imposing fiscal constraints crucially depends on the ability of the single monetary authority to commit to its future policies. There are gains from imposing budgetary constraints only to the extent that monetary policy cannot commit. This conclusion is 'consistent with the view that the framers of the treaty thought that it is extremely difficult to commit monetary policy and therefore wisely included debt constraints as an integral part of the treaty' (Chari and Kehoe, 1998; p. 2).

The degree of commitment by the central bank affects the design of stabilization policies in a monetary union. If the central bank is 'strong', fiscal constraints are damaging because they limit the room for manoeuvre by fiscal authorities in responding to shocks. This result is emphasized by Cooper and Kempf (2000). These authors conclude that if shocks are highly correlated across countries and the central bank is strongly committed to price stability, then a fiscally constrained monetary union dominates the outcome with multiple currencies. Instead, under idiosyncratic shocks, moving to a fiscally constrained monetary union would be welfare-reducing: 'if the set of policy instruments open to fiscal authorities is sufficiently restricted, then monetary union may not increase welfare. Despite having commitment power, the central bank lacks the tools to stabilize in the presence of country specific shocks that are not perfectly correlated' (Cooper and Kempf, 2000; p. 27).

The conclusion that a monetary union with a strong central bank and no limits on fiscal policies is optimal has been questioned. Recent contributions have pointed out that the 'strength' or 'weakness' of the central bank is not exogenous to the behaviour of fiscal authorities.

The so-called Fiscal Theory of the Price Level (FTPL) has highlighted that, if government solvency is not guaranteed, monetary policy will not be able to control the price level. In order to ensure stability, fiscal policy has to react sufficiently strongly to a rise in the interest rate in the event of inflationary pressures by increasing the primary surplus. In other words, monetary policy aiming at keeping inflation in check – as the ECB is mandated to behave – has to go hand in hand with a fiscal policy obeying a solvency constraint.[93] Once the FTPL is applied to the EMU institutional set up, however, seemingly different conclusions are drawn. While Sims (1999) considers the Maastricht plus SGP rules insufficient to rule out FTPL's doom scenario, Canzoneri and Diba (2001) conclude that the SGP appears far too strict from the point of view of guaranteeing fiscal solvency. The latter authors, in particular, call for shifting the attention from actual to cyclically adjusted budget balances in assessing the compliance of EMU members with budgetary prudence so as not to hamper fiscal stabilization.

The ability of budgetary authorities to affect monetary commitment is also explored in a number of recent papers by Dixit and Lambertini (see Dixit and Lambertini, 2000a, b, c; and Dixit, 2000). In a game theoretic framework, monetary and fiscal authorities minimize a quadratic loss function in inflation and output, but final targets and the weight attributed to them vary (typically the central bank is assumed to be more inflation-conservative). These authors conclude that fiscal discretion 'destroys monetary commitment' and, as such, may justify rules imposed on budgetary behaviour. But imposing rules is not sufficient per se: another important conclusion by Dixit and Lambertini is that if final targets differ (e.g. the central bank is an inflation hawk and the fiscal authority aims at pushing output beyond its natural level), a race between monetary and fiscal policy would lead to equilibrium levels of output and inflation far away from the preferred choices. Hence, agreement on the final targets between monetary and fiscal authorities is paramount in leading to a Nash equilibrium which is close to the authorities' preferred choices.

Hence, agreement on the final targets between monetary and fiscal authorities is paramount in leading to a final situation which is close to the authorities' preferred choices, even without formal cooperation.

The importance of the difference in objectives of monetary and fiscal authorities is also stressed by Demertzis *et al.* (1999) and Hughes Hallett and Viegi (2000) who find that, if the two authorities pursue their separate goals independently, a conflict arises. From a political economy viewpoint, the authors point out that the establishment of a conservative central bank – strongly biased in favour of price stability – may increase the chances of left-of-centre governments – mainly output-concerned – being elected. This divergence of preferences would heighten the monetary and fiscal conflicts and, by the same token, increase the gains from coordination.

Quite unrelated to this theoretical development, an empirical literature has addressed in recent years the issue of how monetary and fiscal authorities 'actually' behave. In a seminal paper, Jacques Mélitz uses pooled data for 19 OECD countries, including 14 EU members (except Luxembourg) for the period 1960 until 1995 (Mélitz, 1997b). He finds that monetary and fiscal policy tend to move in opposite directions. In his definition, the two policies are 'strategic substitutes': looser fiscal policy promotes tighter monetary policy, while tighter monetary policy triggers an expansionary fiscal policy. In other words, the 'Sargent and Wallace' scenario of a sustained fiscal boost eventually triggering monetary relaxation is not confirmed by the data. As the author points out in a more recent paper, '[t]his negative interaction should be interpreted as saying that tightening (easing) of one instrument means less tightening (easing) of the other. Both instruments may still concurrently be tight (or easy, as the case may be)' (Mélitz, 2000, p. 16).

Evidence of strategic substitutability is also found in Wyplosz (1999): the central bank raises the interest rate when the deficit increases. In other words, '[b]oth [authorities] attempt to keep inflation in check and to conduct counter-cyclical policies, but each does less when the other moves in the same direction' (Wyplosz, 1999, p. 43). The result that fiscal policy tends to relax when monetary conditions become tighter is confirmed by Von Hagen *et al.* (2000) for a panel of 20 OECD countries from 1973 to 1989. These authors, however, find that monetary conditions react positively to a tighter fiscal policy, which implies that the reaction of monetary policy to fiscal policy has the opposite sign from the reaction of fiscal policy to monetary policy.

To what extent has the EMU project influenced the reaction function of monetary and fiscal authorities? Von Hagen *et al.* (2000), find evidence of a 'Maastricht effect' in the 1990s in the EU: 'on average in the EMU member states, fiscal policy in the 1990s was less reactive to cyclical fluctuations of output and changes in monetary policy than it was in earlier times' (Von Hagen *et al.*, 2001, p .58). A recent report by the European Commission (2000a), argues that monetary policy has, on average, loosened since the beginning of the 1990s (albeit starting from a very tight position), thereby supporting the budgetary retrenchment by EU countries to meet the Maastricht criteria for joining EMU.[94] Hence, in Mélitz's definition, monetary and fiscal policies have been strategic substitutes in the last decade in most EU countries.[95]

3. A SIMPLE MODEL OF MONETARY AND FISCAL POLICY INTERACTIONS

The Maastricht Treaty and secondary legislation provide a clear assignment of objectives to monetary and fiscal authorities in EMU.

The primary task of the ECB is to maintain price stability. In order to achieve this, the single monetary authority is entrusted with both 'goal' and 'instrument' independence. To the extent that price stability is not jeopardized, the ECB is called on to support the general economic policies of the Community.

The SGP is the backbone of fiscal policy in EMU. As discussed in Chapter 2, the Pact can be seen as strengthening the procedures introduced by the Maastricht Treaty, at least in relation to the deficit criterion. It demands that the countries of the European Union (EU) aim for 'medium-term objectives of budgetary positions close to balance or in surplus'. This objective is believed to ensure budgetary discipline while preserving sufficient room for manoeuvre for fiscal stabilization without infringing the 3 per cent of GDP deficit ceiling.

The model outlined next, which builds on that presented in the previous chapters, aims at capturing in simplified fashion some of the main features of the Maastricht monetary and fiscal architecture, namely the objectives of price stability and fiscal prudence. The model consists of a standard demand-(IS) equation and a supply-(Phillips curve) equation of standard type determining the value of output, y, and inflation, π:

$$y^D = \phi_1 d - \phi_2(i - \pi^e) + \varepsilon_1 \tag{5.1}$$

$$y^S = \omega(\pi - \pi^e) + \varepsilon_2 \tag{5.2}$$

where d is the budget deficit, i is the nominal interest rate, ε_1 is a demand shock and ε_2 is a supply shock. The superscript ^{e} indicates expected variables. Aggregate demand, equation (5.1), is negatively affected by the expected real interest rate via the usual consumption and investment response. Government deficits exert a positive effect on aggregate demand, that is, Ricardian equivalence does not hold fully (except for $\phi_1 = 0$). Following the standard Lucas specification, surprise inflation can temporarily increase output above the natural rate because of nominal rigidities and/or imperfect information. The coefficient ω in (5.2) can be interpreted as the degree of labour market flexibility: a high ω implies that an inflation surprise, by lowering real wages, entails a strong rise in supply; on the contrary, a low ω implies that real wages are rigid and supply responds little to unexpected inflation. The rest of the world is omitted.

The budget deficit is defined as follows:

$$d = d_s - \alpha y \tag{5.3}$$

where d_s is the cyclically adjusted balance and α is the cyclical sensitivity of the budget.[96] The budget deficit d should not exceed a given ceiling: $d \leq \bar{d}$. By replacing (5.3) in (5.1) and solving for y and π, we obtain:

$$y = \frac{1}{1 + \phi_1 \alpha}[\phi_1 d_s - \phi_2(i - \pi^e) + \varepsilon_1] \tag{5.4}$$

$$\pi = \frac{1}{\omega(1 + \phi_1 \alpha)}(\phi_1 d_s - \phi_2 i + \varepsilon_1) - \frac{\varepsilon_2}{\omega} + \left[1 + \frac{\phi_2}{\omega(1 + \phi_1 \alpha)}\right]\pi^e \tag{5.5}$$

The policy rules specify the setting of d_s by fiscal authorities[97] and i by the central bank.

Fiscal authorities choose d_s to minimize the following loss function:

$$L(FP) = (d_s - d_s')^2 + \theta(y - y')^2 \tag{5.6}$$

Equation (5.6) indicates that the government cares about output and would like to deviate as little as possible from the medium term target d_s' which is consistent with the 'close to balance' rule of the SGP. In other words, fiscal authorities have a preferred output target but, given the constraints imposed by the Pact, policy activism to achieve it is costly.

A crucial choice concerns the preferred output gap: if the fiscal authority simply aims at stabilizing the business cycle, y' will be equal to zero. A strict interpretation of the SGP provisions (see Chapter 2) would imply setting a sufficiently ambitious budgetary target and just letting automatic stabilizers work. This implies $\phi = 0$. Instead, if the government aims for a level of output higher than the natural level (i.e. an unemployment below the natural rate), y' is positive. This formulation seems to us more consistent with actual preferences and institutional arrangements than models in the Barro–Gordon tradition which attribute to the central bank the willingness to reduce the unemployment rate below its natural level via surprise inflation.[98]

The choice of the medium-term target d_s' is dictated by the need to avoid exceeding the deficit ceiling. The basic assumption underlying this behaviour is that member countries treat the prospect of infringing the deficit ceiling as one to be strictly avoided.[99] The monetary authority aims at maintaining price stability. It is also assumed that the central bank faces a cost in changing the interest rate. This is consistent with the assumption that, as supported by recent evidence, the central bank smooths out the interest rate.[100] As a consequence, it minimizes the following loss function:

$$L(CB) = \pi^2 + \beta(i - i_0)^2 \tag{5.7}$$

where i_0 is the interest rate prevailing at the start of the period. In equation (5.7), without loss of generality, the inflation target has been set to zero.

The lack of an output stabilization term in $L(CB)$ simplifies the algebra but does not change the results qualitatively if we maintain that inflation stabilization has substantially higher weight than output stabilization in the central bank preferences.

A justification for interest rate smoothing is that, in the case of conflict between inflation and output stabilization, the central bank moves slowly towards the required interest rate level. In this case, the smoothing term in (5.7) can be seen partly as a way to take care of output stabilization by the central bank.[101] It will be shown later that interest rate smoothing is crucial to maintain a role for fiscal stabilization in the case of demand shocks.

Equation (5.7) attempts to capture an inherently dynamic behaviour such as interest rate smoothing within an atemporal setting. Our formulation implies that, at each point in time, if the inflation rate is off target, the interest rate is changed to close the gap, but only partly. Hence, following a shock, the interest rate converges gradually towards a value that is consistent with the inflation target. What we look at next is a situation in which the adjustment has been completed and the interest rate has reached its equilibrium level. We show that this equilibrium level depends on the preferences of the fiscal authorities. What we examine in the following sections is the reaction of monetary and fiscal variables to shocks starting from a position of long run equilibrium. Given the demand and supply equations and the behavioural rules of fiscal and monetary authorities, the Nash and the cooperative solutions commonly used in game theory are presented in the next two sections respectively.

4. NASH EQUILIBRIUM

The Nash equilibrium describes the solution under non-cooperation, when each authority minimizes its own loss function, taking the reaction of the other authority as given, thereby disregarding the spill-overs onto one's policy actions arising from the other party's behaviour. Minimization of (5.6) gives the following expression for d_s:

$$d_s = \frac{(1+\phi_1\alpha)[(1+\phi_1\alpha)d'_s + \theta\phi_1 y'] + \theta\phi_1[\phi_2(i-\pi^e) - \varepsilon_1]}{(1+\phi_1\alpha)^2 + \theta\phi_1^2} \tag{5.8}$$

The structural budget balance is raised when monetary policy tightens, while it reacts negatively to a rise in expected inflation and to positive demand shocks.

Solving the central bank's minimization problem gives the following expression of i:

$$i = \frac{i_0\beta\omega^2(1+\phi_1\alpha)^2 + \phi_2\{\phi_1 d_s + \pi^e[\phi_2 + \omega(1+\phi_1\alpha)] + \varepsilon_1 - (1+\phi_1\alpha)\varepsilon_2\}}{\beta\omega^2(1+\phi_1\alpha)^2 + \phi_2^2} \tag{5.9}$$

An expansionary fiscal policy leads to monetary tightening. The interest rate is increased in the event of a positive demand shock and is reduced in the event of a positive supply shock. The opposite holds in the case of negative shocks.[102]

The interplay between monetary and fiscal behaviour is illustrated in Figure 5.1 which illustrates the reaction functions in the policy instruments space. Both reaction functions are positively sloped but FP is steeper than CB.[103]

The Nash equilibrium is determined by the intersection of the two reaction functions. Since the central bank does not pursue an output objective,

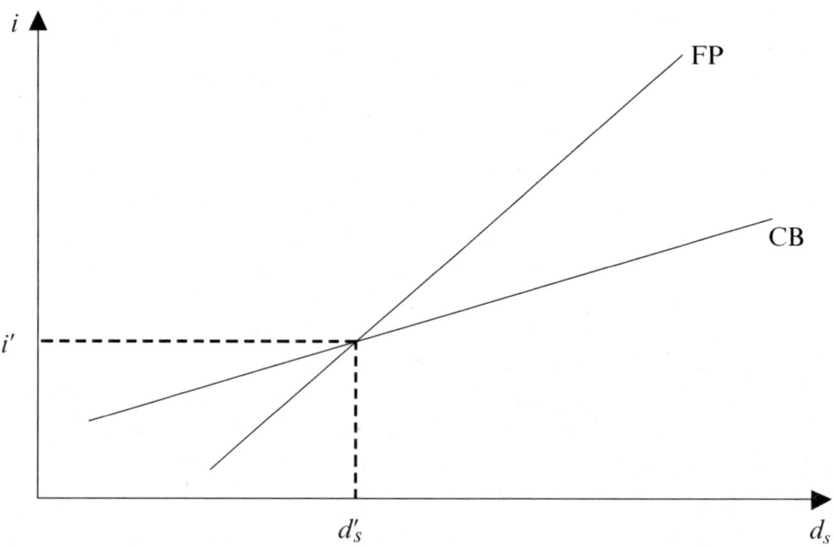

Figure 5.1 *FP and CB's reaction functions*

it does not face a dilemma between output and inflation. Hence, in equilibrium it can always meet its inflation target provided that it sets the appropriate interest rate. The equilibrium interest rate, i', is obtained from equation (5.8), under the assumption of no shocks and $\pi^e = \pi = 0$:

$$i' = \frac{\phi_1}{\phi_2}\left(d_s' + \frac{\theta\phi_1 y'}{1 + \phi_1\alpha}\right) \tag{5.10}$$

where the term in brackets is the level of the budget deficit prevailing in equilibrium. In the absence of shocks, the central bank meets the inflation target while there exists a 'deficit bias' if $y' > 0$. The intuition behind this result is similar to that of the classic Barro–Gordon inflation bias for monetary policy: fiscal authorities keep stimulating demand in an attempt to push output beyond its natural level until the cost of further increasing the deficit brings it too far from target. Clearly, a Maastricht-type ceiling reduces the equilibrium budget deficit via a lower structural target (d_s'). It is easy to show that, if the budget deficit does not enter $L(FP)$, the system is unstable as the government keeps stimulating the economy (while being always frustrated in equilibrium). From this perspective, the SGP help to anchoring the system and prevent a 'passive' fiscal policy from bringing about the FTPL insolvency scenario.[104]

The authorities' reaction functions shift in response to shocks. In the case of a negative demand shock (such as a fall in private consumption), FP moves to the right and CB shifts down. The new equilibrium is a lower interest rate while the change in the budget deficit is ambiguous. However, under normal values of the parameters, one may expect a rise in the budget deficit. In the case of a supply shock (such as an oil price rise), monetary and fiscal policies move in the opposite direction: the interest rate goes up to keep inflation under control and, as a response, the budget deficit expands to prop up output. The new equilibrium is characterized by a higher interest rate and a higher budget deficit. Hence, the likelihood of the budget deficit exceeding the target and shifting fiscal policy into the constrained regime is higher under supply shocks.

In order to obtain the expression of the output gap and inflation in the event of demand and supply shocks, we cross substitute from (5.8) and (5.9) and, after replacing i' from (5.10), we plug the solution for d_s and i in (5.4) and (5.5). Under rational expectations, we obtain:

$$y = \frac{\beta\omega^2(1+\phi_1\alpha)\varepsilon_1 + \phi_2^2\varepsilon_2}{\phi_2^2 + \beta\omega^2[(1+\phi_1\alpha)^2 + \theta\phi_1^2]} \tag{5.11}$$

$$\pi = \frac{\beta\omega\{(1+\phi_1\alpha)\varepsilon_1 - [(1+\phi_1\alpha)^2 + \theta\phi_1^2]\varepsilon_2\}}{\phi_2^2 + \beta\omega^2[(1+\phi_1\alpha)^2 + \theta\phi_1^2]} \tag{5.12}$$

Equations (5.11) and (5.12) show the fundamental role played by interest rate smoothing. If, contrary to the assumption above, β is set equal to zero, all demand-side parameters disappear from the solution. This implies that the central bank can offset perfectly any demand shock. The intuition is straightforward: as the output gap and inflation move in the same direction, the central bank faces no dilemma and, via a sufficiently strong response of interest rates, is able to close the output gap and preserve at the same time its inflation target. If β is positive, the central bank faces a cost in changing the interest rate. Hence, demand shocks are not fully smoothed and fiscal stabilization comes back into play. Under $\beta = 0$, supply shocks feed through unsmoothed while the inflation target is always met.[105]

The impact of structural parameters and policy preferences on the output gap and inflation are summarized in Table 5.1. A positive (negative) sign indicates that a rise in the variable leads to an amplification (smoothening) of the shock.

The sign of the partial derivatives is as expected. In particular, a high degree of interest rate smoothing – implying a low response of monetary policy to shocks – is destabilizing in the case of demand shocks while it is output-stabilizing and inflation-destabilizing in the case of supply shocks. A high preference for output stabilization by fiscal authorities helps to

Table 5.1 Influence of policy parameters and preferences on y *and* π

		ϕ_1	ϕ_2	α	θ	β
ε_1	y	+/−	−	+/−	−	+
	π	+/−	−	+/−	−	+
ε_2	y	−	+	−	−	−
	π	+	−	+	+	+

stabilize output and inflation in the event of demand shocks, but is inflation-destabilizing in the case of supply shocks.

As shown in Table 5.1, high automatic stabilizers (α) and high effectiveness of fiscal policy (ϕ_1) may not lead to overall higher stabilization in the case of demand shocks. This seemingly counterintuitive result occurs if monetary policy is very effective. In such a case, the combination of a higher response by the budget deficit and a lower reaction by the interest rate (due to interest rate smoothing), may imply a lower overall degree of stabilization. While theoretically interesting, under normal values of the parameters, higher budgetary stabilizers and a more effective fiscal policy can be expected to lead to higher output stabilization.

These results help to highlight the preference of each authority for the behaviour of the other authority.[106] The central bank would like to see higher fiscal stabilization in the event of demand shocks because that will allow it to achieve lower deviations of inflation from target for given changes in the interest rate (or, conversely, attain the same degree of inflation stabilization with a smaller variation of the interest rate from its equilibrium level). On the contrary, monetary authorities would prefer lower fiscal stabilization in the event of supply shocks because that will result in lower changes in inflation and interest rates. The preference of fiscal authorities on monetary behaviour depends on the assumptions on the target level of the output gap. If the government pursues 'pure' output stabilization (i.e. $y' = 0$), it would like to see high monetary stabilization in the case of demand shocks (i.e. high ϕ_2 and low β) and low monetary stabilization in the case of supply shocks.

Hence, each authority would like the other to do *more* in the case of demand shocks and *less* in the case of supply shocks.[107]

5. COOPERATIVE EQUILIBRIUM

Under cooperation, both authorities collaborate to achieve their respective objectives, thereby taking into account the spill-overs arising from each other's behaviour. Formally, in the cooperative solution the two policy instruments, d_s and i, are chosen so as to minimize a joint loss function which combines the respective preferences of fiscal and monetary authorities:

$$FPCB = \eta[(d_s - d_s')^2 + \theta(y - y')^2] + (1 - \eta)[\pi^2 + \beta(i - i')^2] \quad (5.13)$$

where $0 \leq \eta \leq 1$ gives the 'bargaining power' of the two policy authorities: a large (small) η indicates a strong (weak) fiscal authority.

Given the cumbersome algebra, we illustrate the main results under simplifying assumptions on a number of parameters. An important result is that, if fiscal policy pursues 'pure' output stabilization (i.e. $y' = 0$), under no shocks the Nash and the cooperative equilibria are the same (namely $y = \pi = 0$). However, if the government targets a positive output gap ($y' > 0$), the equilibrium solution is characterized by a 'deficit bias' *and* an 'inflation bias'. Under the assumption $\phi_1 = \beta = 0$, the expression of the inflation bias is the following:

$$\pi = \frac{y'\omega\eta\theta}{\phi_2(1 - \eta)} \quad (5.14)$$

Clearly, the inflation bias is a positive function of the bargaining power of the fiscal authority and the output gap target. The reason is that, via the combined loss function, the central bank encompasses the fiscal policy target of a positive output gap. Therefore, as in the classic Barro–Gordon result, the central bank stimulates the economy until the (temporary) output gains would be offset by the additional costs of a further rise in inflation (and, in the general case, by the cost of shifting the interest rate away from its equilibrium value).[108]

What conclusions can be drawn on the incentives of monetary and fiscal authorities to cooperate? Clearly, if the government aims at attaining a positive output gap, there is no incentive for an inflation-conservative central bank – as the ECB is mandated to be – to engage in cooperation because it would have to accept an inflation bias in equilibrium. Notice however that, in general, there is a trade-off between the inflation and the deficit bias because the use of the interest rate to stimulate demand would partly take the place of the rise in the deficit. To the extent that, under non-cooperation, a high deficit bias leads to an unsustainable accumulation of public debt, the central bank would face an unpalatable choice between higher inflation now (to reduce the deficit bias) and (debt monetization and hence) higher inflation in the future.

If the government pursues 'pure' cyclical smoothing, under no shocks, the Nash equilibrium and the cooperative equilibrium both imply $y = 0$

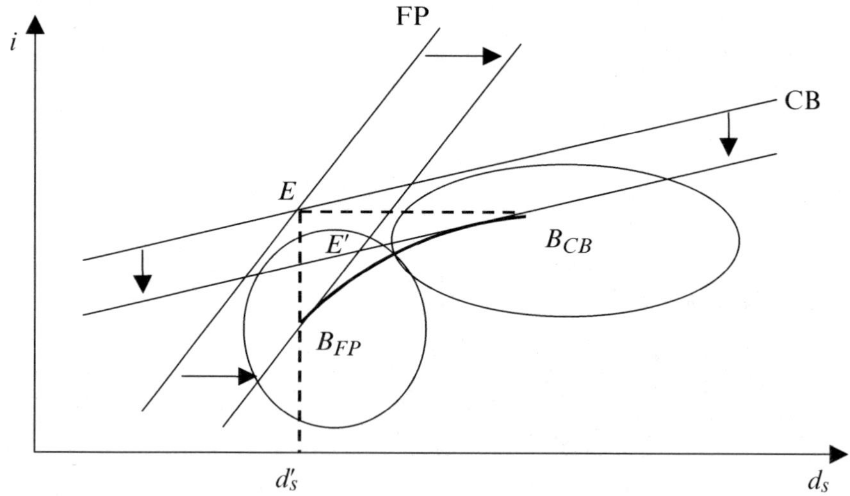

Figure 5.2 Negative demand shock

and $\pi = 0$. Hence the incentives for cooperation depend on welfare gains and losses in response to shocks.

Under demand shocks, as both policies move in the same direction the gains from cooperation are ambiguous. This is illustrated in Figure 5.2 which pictures the policy reactions to a negative demand shock. Both policies are expansionary and the new Nash equilibrium is E'. The points where the two authorities are individually better off in terms of minimization of their respective loss functions – referred to in the literature as Bliss points – are B_{FP} and B_{CB}: ideally, as discussed before, each authority would prefer the whole stabilization to be borne by the other authority. The line between the two Bliss points is the contract coordination line. As shown in the figure, E' is very close to such a line, indicating that any gain from coordination for both authorities, even if positive, is necessarily minor and could even be negative if the coordination process involves 'transaction costs'.

In the case of supply shocks, since under Nash the two policy instruments move in opposite directions, there are unambiguous gains from cooperation. This can be easily understood since, in the non-cooperative solution, part of the change in the interest rate occurs in order to offset the change in the opposite direction in the budget deficit. This result is illustrated in Figure 5.3 which shows the policy reactions to a negative supply shock. The additional change in the interest rate, *K*, is given by the difference between the new interest rate following the supply shock and the

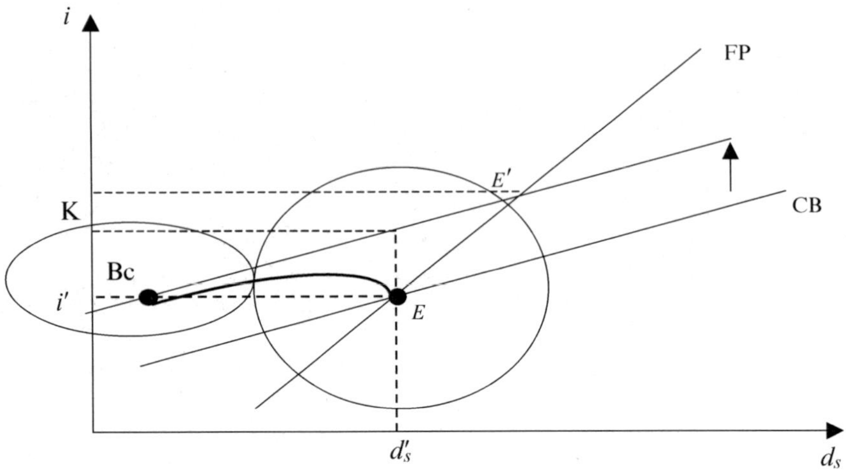

Figure 5.3 Negative supply shock

interest rate that would have resulted from a change in the structural deficit (i.e. by keeping d_s unchanged in equation (5.9)):

$$K = -\frac{\phi_1^2 \phi_2 \varepsilon_2}{(1+\phi_1\alpha)\{\phi_2^2 + \beta\omega^2[(1+\phi_1\alpha)^2 + \theta\phi_1^2]\}} \tag{5.15}$$

Given the policy preferences of the central bank, the latter would like fiscal policy to turn restrictive to keep inflation under control. Conversely, the government would like to see no change in the interest rate so that all the shock will feed through into higher inflation.[109] Instead, under no cooperation, each authority moves in the opposite direction to that hoped for by the other authority. As shown in Figure 5.3, the degree of output and inflation stabilization implied by non-cooperation could be achieved at lower values of both policy instruments.[110] Given interest rate smoothing in $L(CB)$ and the deficit target in $L(FP)$, this implies a welfare gain for both authorities. Cooperation also implies a lower likelihood to shift in the fiscally constrained regime.

6. ILLUSTRATION OF POLICY INTERACTIONS WITH THE QUEST MODEL

This section attempts to provide some quantitative evidence on some of the effects derived in the third and fourth sections. We use a two-country version of the DG ECFIN's QUEST model to capture the quantitative importance of fiscal–monetary policy interactions. The model can be characterized as a modern version of a neoclassical Keynesian synthesis model, with the behavioural equations of households and firms derived from explicit dynamic optimization problems subject to budget constraints and adjustment costs. Monetary policy is effective because of sluggish price adjustment in the goods market due to price adjustment costs of monopolistically competitive firms (see, for example Rotemberg, 1982, 1996 and Hairault and Portier, 1993) and the nominal wage response is delayed because of overlapping one year contracts.[111]

Both the fiscal authorities and the monetary authorities set their policy instruments to minimize their respective loss functions. As the empirical model used here is a dynamic one, the focus is on the impact responses of the shocks, to stay close to the theoretical analysis above. This implies that both the fiscal authorities as well as the monetary authorities face a high rate of time preference, optimize their respective responses over the short run and discount the medium- to long-term effects more heavily. Another difference from the theoretical model is that here the policy response of the monetary authorities is not formulated in terms of interest rates but in terms of the money supply. This is inconsequential since both instruments are linked via a stable money demand equation in the model. The instrument for the fiscal authorities is government expenditure g.

6.1 Non-cooperation

Given the dynamic complexity as well as non-linearity of the model it is impossible to derive explicit decision rules for monetary and fiscal policy. The general form of the rules over which we optimize is given by equations (5.16) and (5.17) and optimization requires selecting parameters such that the fiscal and monetary policy objective functions are minimized.[112] The underlying utility function corresponds to the specification in the theoretical section. In particular we assume that fiscal policy does not care about inflation and monetary policy puts zero weight on output stabilization. Also, in order to mimic as closely as possible the stabilization motive of both policy makers, we assume a high discount rate:

$$m_t = m_{t-1} + c_2\varepsilon_1 + c_3\varepsilon_2 \tag{5.16}$$

$$g_t = \bar{g} - f_1(b - b_0) - f_2\Delta b + f_3\varepsilon_1 + f_4\varepsilon_2 \tag{5.17}$$

Given the standard money demand equation in the model, this rule can be rewritten in terms of an interest rate rule as follows:

$$\Delta i_t = \frac{1}{\varphi}(\Delta y_t + \Delta\pi_t) - c_2\varepsilon_{1t} - c_3\varepsilon_{2t} \tag{5.16a}$$

where φ denotes the semi-interest elasticity of real balances with respect to nominal interest rates. As can be seen from this expression, the optimal rule comes close to a Taylor rule formulated in first differences and with equal weights given to both output growth deviations from trend[113] and inflation. However, according to the optimal rule the central bank takes into account the source of the shock. In the case of a positive/negative demand shock it will increase/lower interest rates more than implied by changes in GDP and inflation while in the case of a positive/negative supply shock monetary policy will be less/more restrictive than implied by the Taylor rule.

For the demand and supply shocks we assume that the demand shock is a temporary shock to consumption, *ex ante* 1 per cent of GDP in the first quarter, which is phased out in the following quarters. The supply shock is a persistent technology shock, of similar magnitude of 1 per cent of GDP. Since a persistent technology shock leads to a new long run level of potential GDP, the question therefore arises whether fiscal policy[114] should target the historic or future potential output. We assume in this analysis that fiscal policy targets the historic level of potential output. Given the high discount rate, the government is mainly interested in short run stabilization. An immediate move towards the new potential output target would be counterintuitive, since the short run perspective of the government would force fiscal policy to adjust output strongly towards the new level. This would be inconsistent with the notion that the output gap term in the utility function represents an output smoothing motive for fiscal policy. Finally it must be noted that for less persistent supply shocks the first year response of the model economy would not differ qualitatively from a permanent shock. In the case without a deficit constraint, the following monetary and fiscal reaction functions can be obtained for the Nash equilibrium, given the specifications of the loss functions and the types of shocks considered here:

$$g_t = \bar{g} - 0.04(b - b_0) - 0.05\Delta b - 0.3\varepsilon_1 - 3.0\varepsilon_2 \tag{5.18}$$

$$m_t = m_{t-1} - 0.000125\varepsilon_1 + 0.025\varepsilon_2 \tag{5.19}$$

Figures 5.4 and 5.5 illustrate the fiscal and monetary reaction functions under negative demand and supply shocks respectively and Table 5.2 gives the corresponding welfare losses for both authorities under the Nash solution.

The response parameter for a demand shock is negative. In the case of a negative consumption shock, $\varepsilon_1 < 0$, the fiscal authorities respond by raising expenditure to boost output. The monetary authorities respond by offsetting the deflationary impact of this shock and raise the money supply and reduce interest rates, which will also stimulate domestic demand. Thus,

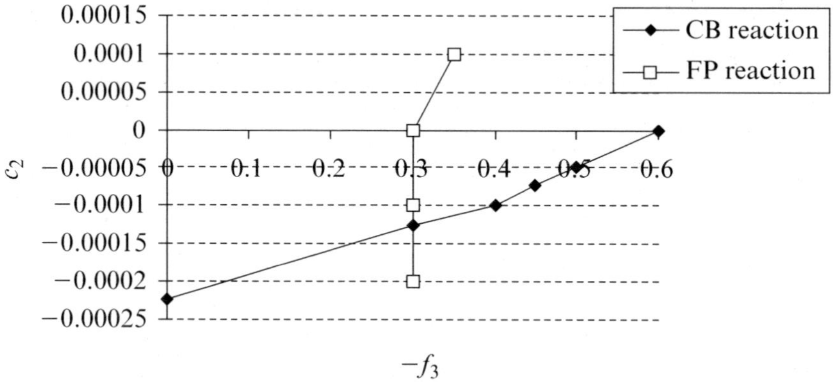

Figure 5.4 Optimal policy responses – negative demand shock

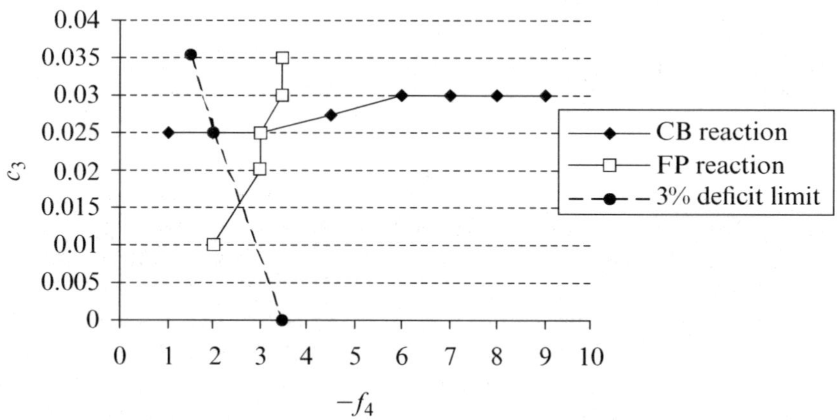

Note:
Monetary reaction function: $m_t = m_{t-1} + c_2\varepsilon_1 + c_3\varepsilon_2$.
Fiscal reaction function: $g_t = \bar{g} - f_1(b - b_0) - f_2\Delta b + f_3\varepsilon_1 + f_4\varepsilon_2$.

Figure 5.5 Optimal policy responses – negative supply shock

under demand shocks, both policies move in the same direction and if one authority does more, the other has to do less. This is illustrated in Figure 5.4, which depicts the optimal settings of the respective response parameters for the monetary and fiscal authorities under this particular shock. On the vertical axis, the size of the monetary reaction is given, where a smaller negative value represents a smaller monetary expansion or higher interest rates. The horizontal axis gives the absolute value of the fiscal

Table 5.2 Non-cooperative policy responses under negative supply and demand shocks

	Negative supply shock (1% of GDP)		Negative demand shock (1% of GDP)	
Nash optimal response:				
Fiscal policy parameter	$f_4 = -3.0$		$f_3 = -0.30$	
Monetary policy parameter	$c_3 = 0.025$		$c_2 = -0.000125$	
	FP: 47.40755	CB: 0.06552	FP: 0.01081	CB: 0.00029
Effect on:				
GDP	−1.40		0	
Inflation	0.14		0	
Deficit	3.8		0.11	

Note:
Monetary reaction function: $m_t = m_{t-1} + c_2\varepsilon_1 + c_3\varepsilon_2$.
Fiscal reaction function: $g_t = \bar{g} - f_1(b - b_0) - f_2\Delta b + f_3\varepsilon_1 + f_4\varepsilon_2$.

response parameter and a larger parameter implies a larger increase in government expenditure and a larger deficit. If the response of the fiscal authorities becomes stronger and they raise expenditure by more, the monetary authorities can reduce the size of the monetary loosening. Thus, in Figure 5.4, the CB reaction function is upward sloping. If the central bank reacts more strongly to the negative demand shock and raises the money supply by more, that will help to prop up output again and the fiscal authorities will have to do less. Thus the FP reaction curve is also upward sloping. The FP reaction curve is steeper than the CB curve, consistent with the analysis in the fourth section (see Note 103).

In the case of a negative supply shock, $\varepsilon_2 < 0$, monetary and fiscal policies go in opposite directions. The response parameter for a supply shock is positive in the monetary reaction function. Monetary policy contracts to offset the inflationary impact of this negative technology shock and the central bank raises interest rates. The fiscal authorities respond by increasing government expenditure to prop up output (i.e. a negative coefficient). The policy responses now move output and inflation in opposite directions. The CB reaction reduces output even further and fiscal policy responds by raising expenditure even more. Hence in Figure 5.5 the FP reaction curve is upward sloping. If the fiscal authorities react more strongly and increase expenditure, then the monetary authorities will react to the additional inflationary pressure by further monetary tightening. Thus the CB curve is also upward sloping. The Nash solution is then determined by the intersection of the CB and FP reaction curves. The policy parameters and their corresponding welfare losses are given in Table 5.2.

In the case of a demand shock, fiscal and monetary authorities are able to stabilize output and inflation. The rise in the deficit remains small and well within the limits of the SGP. However, under the particular supply shock given here, the Nash equilibrium in this optimization game with this inflation-conservative central bank that stabilizes inflation immediately implies a large response by the fiscal authorities. The optimal fiscal response in this setting would mean that the deficit would exceed the SGP limit of 3 per cent. The 3 per cent deficit limit under this shock implies the fiscal response parameter could not exceed the range of 2–3.5.[115]

Cooperation

Under demand shocks, monetary and fiscal policies move in the same direction and from the theoretical analysis it is not unambiguously evident whether both parties would gain from cooperation. It was shown earlier that the fiscal and monetary authorities are able to stabilize output and inflation in this scenario and the respective welfare losses are relatively small. With the deficit entering the FP loss function, a larger fiscal policy response increases the fiscal welfare losses and no improvement relative to the Nash solution can be achieved where both parties would be better off.

When there is a negative supply shock, both parties are unambiguously better off under cooperation. Policies move in opposite directions and part of the monetary tightening occurs in order to offset the effects of the fiscal expansion and vice versa. Thus both authorities can gain from reacting less. When the fiscal authorities reduce the size of the expansion and the central bank tightens less, both FP and CB are better off. In Figure 5.5, there is a whole region below and to the left of the Nash outcome where both FP and CB gain from coordination. The example given in Table 5.3

Table 5.3 Example of welfare improving policy coordination under negative supply shock

Fiscal policy parameter	$f_4 = -1.0$	
Monetary policy parameter	$c_3 = 0.02$	
	FP: 39.96268	CB: 0.04230
Effect on:		
GDP	−1.35	
Inflation	0.16	
Deficit	1.51	

raises the deficit to 1.5 per cent of GDP. Both CB and FP benefit from coordination, but relative to the Nash outcome, the gain for CB is largest as the fiscal response is reduced by most. It is important to bear in mind that these results of positive gains from coordination hold only under these specific scenarios. It is assumed in this exercise that fiscal authorities do not target an output level beyond the natural level and no inflation bias arises.

7. CONCLUSIONS

This chapter has looked at the interactions between monetary and fiscal authorities, when fiscal policy is constrained by upper limits on the budget deficits, as in EMU. Conflicts between monetary and fiscal policy arise when the central bank's objective function differs from that of fiscal authorities. This is generally assumed in the literature. In particular it is assumed that the fiscal authority has less incentive to stabilize inflation, while inflation stabilization is the most important goal of the central bank. Also, different degrees of output stabilization as well as different output targets can be consistent with the objectives of both authorities. Here it has been assumed that the central bank adheres to strict inflation control and attaches zero weight to output stabilization, but that it also tries to smooth nominal interest rates. The latter element is introduced since, first, there is sufficient empirical evidence in its favour and, second, it restricts the power of monetary policy with respect to neutralizing demand shocks and allows for more interesting policy interactions.

For fiscal policy it is assumed that the government does not care about inflation but only about output stabilization (around a level which can be higher than the natural rate). The SGP introduces an additional constraint on fiscal policy. This constraint is introduced in the model via the objective function which penalizes deficits that deviate from the 'close-to-balance' target of the SGP.

Within this theoretical framework, we analysed how parameters of fiscal and monetary policies and the preferences of the central bank affect the response of output and inflation to shocks. The main results of the theoretical analysis are summarized hereafter.

Under *non-cooperation*, demand shocks affect output and inflation only insofar as the central bank smooths the interest rate. The central bank prefers high fiscal stabilization under demand shocks and low fiscal stabilization under supply shocks; conversely, the government would like to see low interest rate smoothing under demand shocks and high smoothing under supply shocks. Given the move of policies in opposite directions, under negative supply shocks there is a higher likelihood of hitting the deficit ceiling. If fiscal authorities target a positive output gap, there is a 'deficit bias' in equilibrium. However, under non-cooperation, since the central bank does not aim at pushing output beyond its natural level, there is no 'inflation bias'.

Under *cooperation*, if fiscal authorities pursue a positive output gap, there is in equilibrium an 'inflation bias' and a 'deficit bias', though the latter is lower than under Nash. If the government only pursues 'pure' cyclical stabilization, the gains from cooperation are ambiguous and necessarily small under demand shocks, but there are positive gains from coordination under supply shocks. This implies that, provided that the objective of the government is output stabilization around its natural level, policy coordination may be looked at as insurance against future shocks.

Our simulations with the QUEST model lend support to these theoretical predictions. It is shown that the Nash solution, under a sufficiently severe negative supply shock, implies a violation of the deficit threshold. The simulations also confirm that there are positive gains from coordinating the policy response to supply shocks.

These results help to shed light on a number of issue which have been raised in the academic and policy debate. It has been shown that the *substitutability* or *complementarity* between monetary and fiscal policies crucially depends on the type of shocks hitting the economy. In the event of supply shocks, the two policies move in opposite direction: a loosening (tightening) of fiscal policy goes hand in hand with a tightening (loosening) of monetary policy. Hence there is a clear conflict between the two arms of macroeconomic policy. The empirical observation, however, of policy substitutability does not necessarily imply a conflict. For instance, as mentioned before, a relaxation of monetary policy during periods of budgetary consolidation – as in the EU during the 1990s – may actually be 'implicit' coordination: by helping to cushion the output losses due to the budgetary retrenchment, the expansionary monetary policy facilitates the task of the fiscal authorities. Under demand shocks, both policies move in the same direction, but if one does more, the other does less. In this case, there exists a sort of 'distributional' conflict between monetary and fiscal authorities on how to share the burden of stabilization.

Our results may provide a rationale for the traditional central banks' aversion for *ex ante* coordination of macroeconomic policies. This reluctance was expressed forcefully by Otmar Issing, chief economist of the ECB (Issing, 2000, p. 1): '[N]ot much can be expected from attempts to coordinate these macroeconomic policies *ex ante* [. . .]. On the contrary, such attempts give rise to the risk of confusing the specific roles, mandates and responsibilities of the policies in question.' And later (p. 2): 'if there is already an *efficient* initial assignment of responsibilities in place, which does take into account the individual policy makers' objectives and actions, calls for policy coordination [. . .] would not be necessary. To put it simply, an efficient initial assignment of objectives and responsibilities will largely substitute the need for coordinated policies later on.'

As shown earlier, if fiscal authorities target an output beyond the natural level, under cooperation an inflation bias will arise in equilibrium. This is likely to put off any incentive for policy coordination by an inflation-conservative central bank, whatever the possible gains from it in responding to shocks. However, if budgetary authorities only pursue cyclical stabilization, the Nash and the cooperative solutions are identical under zero shocks and no deficit or inflation biases arise in equilibrium. Therefore, the possible benefits of coordination have to be assessed by looking at the response to shocks under Nash and cooperation. Our analysis points to gains from coordinating monetary and fiscal policies in response to shocks. If policy coordination is viewed as insurance against future shocks, there seems to be good case for entering into a contract between monetary and fiscal authorities to provide an optimal response to shocks.

Obviously, this conclusion does not consider other factors such as the existence of 'transactions' costs of implementing coordination or the fact that supply shocks – especially if long-lasting – should be dealt with via structural reforms and microeconomic adjustment rather than macroeconomic stabilization. Arguably, the central bank's reluctance to engage in coordination is justified by 'suspicion' about the real objectives of fiscal authorities. Hence, 'soft coordination' helping to understand each other's targets, identify the type of shocks, and achieve a common view on the output gap, would certainly be beneficial.[116]

The analysis in this chapter is subject to obvious limitations. First of all, as the analysis encompasses only one fiscal authority, one should be cautious in deriving direct policy conclusions for EMU. Beetsma *et al.* (2001) extend this model to a framework with two fiscal authorities and analyse policy interactions in a monetary union. Another limitation is the extremely simplified structure of the model and policy preferences. We look at an atemporal equilibrium and do not explore the dynamics of the response to shocks or to changes in policy preferences. For instance, an intertemporal trade-off may arise between inflation bias and deficit bias. Also, choosing the interest-inclusive budget balance – instead of the primary balance – as a control variable has cut off an important channel of policy interactions. Finally in the empirical section, the way in which the reaction functions of monetary and fiscal authorities have been derived deserves further investigation.

6. Public investment*

1. INTRODUCTION

The slowdown in actual and potential growth in the early years of EMU raises worries and doubts concerning the fiscal rules set in the Treaty of Maastricht and in the Stability and Growth Pact. It has been argued that these rules may represent an excessively binding constraint for appropriate counter-cyclical action and that the attempt to reach rapidly a budget position 'close to balance or in surplus' may worsen the slowdown. The risk that the rules may permanently reduce the public sector's contribution to capital accumulation has also been pointed out.

In this framework the adoption of a *golden rule* has been suggested. The rule would exclude investment spending from the computation of the fiscal parameters relevant to the Excessive Deficits Procedure.[117] In the opinion of those supporting the amendment, this would allow EU member states to loosen their fiscal stance while positively affecting long run growth: debt finance would thus not harm future generations.

Underlying the debate there are several issues. It is important to separate problems concerning the current economic situation from those concerning the design of the EMU's fiscal constitution *per se*. The solution to the potential conflict between the objective of moving towards a close to balance position and the need to avoid a worsening of short-term economic prospects may not require changes to the rules set in the Treaty and in the Pact. Furthermore, the risk that a revision of the rules could harm the credibility of the commitment to fiscal sustainability, which in turn may prevent the adoption of the appropriate policy mix, must be taken into account.

Also the need to allow more room for counter-cyclical budgetary action and the need to increase public investment should be dealt with separately. As to the public sector's contribution to capital accumulation, one cannot simply assume that an increase in public investment spending is always superior to a cut in taxes, an increase in current outlays for human capital formation or a reduction in the deficit.

* Fabrizio Balassone and Daniele Franco, 'Public Investment, the Stability Pact and the Golden Rule', *Fiscal Studies*, 2000, 21(2): 207–29.

Finally, it is necessary to evaluate whether the *golden rule* is consistent with the objectives underlying present European fiscal rules. These rules aim at reducing the risk that unbalanced budgets in some member states may harm other members of the Union, and even endanger EMU, through financial instability and inflationary pressures. The rules also aim at allowing countries to adopt the appropriate policy mix when dealing with both symmetric and asymmetric shocks. The reduction of deficits and debts, necessary for reaching both objectives, may find an obstacle in the *golden rule* depending on the way the rule is implemented.

Starting from the recent debate, this chapter tackles two issues: (1) the implications of the Pact for public investment, (2) the pros and cons of introducing a *golden rule* in EMU's fiscal framework, given the objectives of low public debts and adequate margins for stabilization policy. The analysis suggests that the rules set in the Treaty and in the Pact may negatively influence public investment. However, the *golden rule*, although intuitively appealing, does not seem to be an appropriate solution to the problem.

The chapter is organized as follows. The next section examines the implications of a balanced budget for public investment both in the long run, when the debt reaches the new equilibrium level, and during the transition towards such equilibrium. The third section reviews the empirical evidence on the link between fiscal consolidations and reductions in public investment. The fourth section reviews the literature on the effects of public investment on growth in order to assess the possible consequences of a reduction in investment spending. The fifth section highlights the difficulty in reconciling different specifications of the *golden rule* with EMU's fiscal framework, and the sixth section summarizes the main conclusions.

2. THE STABILITY AND GROWTH PACT AND PUBLIC INVESTMENT

The achievement of budget positions 'close to balance or in surplus' implies that most capital expenditure will have to be funded from current revenues. Hence it will no longer be possible to spread the cost of an investment project over all the generations of taxpayers who benefit from it. This has two main implications which are analysed below:

1. there is a disincentive to undertake large projects producing deferred benefits and entailing a significant gap between current revenues and current expenditures;
2. the disincentive will be stronger while the deficit is being reduced:[118] the above mentioned gap will grow if the flow of investment stays

unchanged; it will remain larger than the initial level until the decline in interest expenditure induced by the reduction of the debt equals the decline in the deficit.

Concerning the first consequence, in Balassone and Franco (1999) we show how the introduction of a deficit ceiling can imply a reduction in investment in a two-period model where a policy maker with a finite horizon maximizes disposable income and the latter is positively affected by investment with a lag. The finite horizon suggests a political economy interpretation of the result. Without a ceiling, the policy maker, who cares about economic performance only when he or she is in power, can run deficits and invest in the first period without reducing disposable income. With a ceiling, investment will reduce disposable income in the first period, and the policy maker invests less.

However, the introduction of a ceiling implies a reduction of investment also in the case of a benevolent planner aiming at maximizing social welfare. In Barro (1979), given an expenditure profile, the efficiency loss caused by distortionary taxation is minimized if the tax rate is constant (*tax-smoothing*). If a budget constraint is introduced, indivisible investment projects may have welfare costs (the tax profile is no longer smooth); if the expenditure profile is not given, these costs may induce a reduction in investment.

Finally, since investments produce deferred benefits, the means of financing them (tax rather than debt) also affect intergenerational equity. Tax financing implies a welfare loss for the current generation and favours future ones: the former fully pays for a project whose benefits will partly accrue to the latter. When a budget constraint is introduced, it is then possible that voters will prefer a reduction in capital expenditure to an increase in taxes or a reduction in current outlays (from which they fully benefit). The disincentive would mainly apply to projects with very uneven cost distributions. With an homogeneous expenditure flow the difference between tax and debt financing is limited:[119] only those generations living when the earliest projects are undertaken suffer a loss under tax finance; future generations will have to pay more or less the same, be it to finance interest on past debt (while new projects are financed via new debts) or to finance new projects (while past ones have already been paid for by past generations).

The transition to a lower deficit level is equivalent to an expenditure peak. If the flow of investment is unchanged, current generations will have to pay part of the new projects (the whole if the budget is balanced) while also paying interest on debts: taxes will have to be raised or current expenditures cut. For these generations the transition would be less burdensome if the level of investment (producing deferred benefits) was reduced, so that a smaller tax increase (or current outlays reduction) would be needed.[120]

The problem can easily be seen with reference to the budget constraint:

$$T+B=G=C_p+I(D)+K \quad \Rightarrow \quad T-C_p=K+I(D)-B \qquad (6.1)$$

where T is taxes, B the deficit, G overall outlays (made up by interest I, other current outlays C_p, and investment K). The burden for current generations is $T-C_p$, since they give up resources (T) in excess of the transfers and services that they receive (C_p). This burden is compensated by the flow of services produced by investment projects which were undertaken in the past and financed by deficit. The burden is a positive function of interest payments (and hence of past debt, D) and of present investment spending; it is reduced by the deficit, so that the transition to a lower deficit implies an increase in the burden, which is higher the higher are K and D; *ceteris paribus* it will be higher in those countries where deficit finance has also been used to pay for current expenditures.

The double burden issue is exemplified in Figure 6.1, which is drawn assuming both nominal GDP growth rate and nominal interest rate at 5 per cent, and an initial debt to GDP ratio at 60 per cent of GDP. The initial deficit ratio is 3 per cent of GDP; thereafter a balanced budget is attained. Three phases can be separated:

1. The first, labelled 'steady state before the Pact', is a situation in which the overall deficit is constant at 3 per cent of GDP; this implies

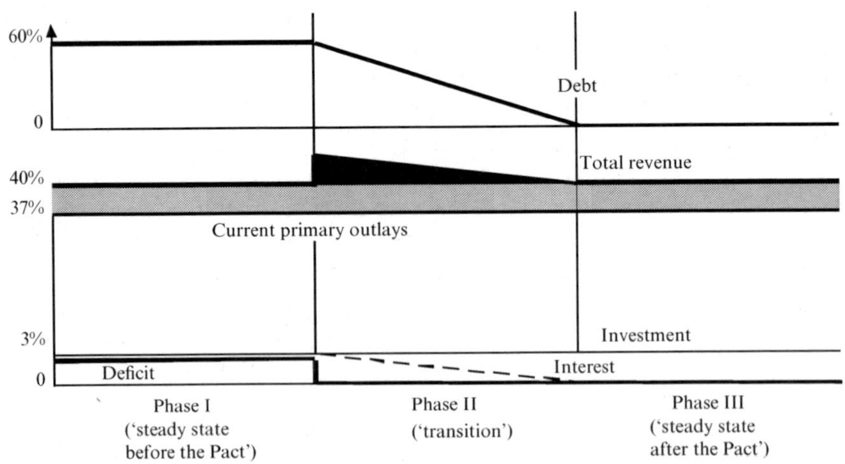

Figure 6.1 The burden of transition

a balanced primary budget and a constant debt to GDP ratio. The primary balance is assumed to result from a 40 per cent revenue to GDP ratio, a 37 per cent current primary expenditure ratio and a 3 per cent capital expenditure ratio. There is a 3 per cent of GDP gap between revenues and current primary expenditures (the light-shaded area) which is assumed to be balanced by the flow of services produced by past public investments.

2. The second phase ('transition'), opens with the abrupt reduction of the deficit to zero. This is obtained via an increase of 3 percentage points of GDP in the revenue ratio (a reduction in current primary outlays would have the same effect).[121] The gap between revenues and current primary outlays doubles. As the debt ratio gradually declines, so do interest expenditures and the revenue ratio can slowly move back to 40 per cent. The additional burden induced by the reduction of the deficit during the transition phase corresponds to the dark triangle.
3. The third phase ('steady state after the Pact'), begins when the debt ratio and interest expenditures are nil. The gap between revenues and current primary outlays is back to 3 per cent, balanced again by the flow of services produced by past investments.

The problems involved in the transition from deficit to tax financing of public investment are similar to those involved in the transition from a pay-as-you-go to a funded pension scheme.[122] In both cases the burden on current generations depends on the speed of the transition and on the stock of debt. In countries where a shift to funded schemes is underway, the burdens determined by the two transitions will be summed.

3. FISCAL CONSOLIDATION AND PUBLIC INVESTMENT REDUCTION: THE EMPIRICAL EVIDENCE

The link between fiscal consolidation and cuts in capital spending is confirmed by the experience of EU countries during the run up to EMU. In 1992, the year of the Treaty, the deficit ratio exceeded 3 per cent in nine countries. In 1997, for all these countries but Greece the ratio was at or below the threshold; all had reduced the investment to GDP ratio; all but Greece and the Netherlands had lowered the investment to primary outlays ratio (Table 6.1). Over the same period investment ratios to GDP and primary outlays increased in three of the six countries that met the deficit criterion in 1992.

Table 6.1 Deficit and public investment in EU countries, 1992–97 (ESA79 data)

	Deficit (% of GDP)		Investment (% of GDP)		Investment (% primary outlays)	
	1992	1997	1992	1997	1992	1997
Italy	9.6	2.7	3.0	2.4	6.8	5.7
France	3.9	3.0	3.5	3.1	6.9	6.1
Germany	2.6	2.7	2.8	1.9	6.1	4.3
UK	6.2	1.9	2.1	1.1	5.2	3.0
Spain	3.8	2.6	4.1	3.1	9.7	7.9
Belgium	6.9	2.1	1.5	1.4	3.4	3.2
Denmark	2.1	−0.7	1.7	1.8	3.2	3.4
Greece	12.8	4.0	3.5	3.3	10.1	10.2
Eire	2.5	−0.9	2.0	2.2	5.9	7.1
Luxembourg	−0.8	−1.7	5.4	4.9	n.d.	n.d.
Netherlands	3.9	1.4	2.1	1.9	4.2	4.2
Portugal	3.0	2.5	3.8	4.3	10.7	10.9
Austria	2.0	2.5	3.3	2.6	6.9	5.3
Finland	5.9	0.9	3.5	2.7	6.0	5.5
Sweden	7.7	0.8	2.7	2.4	4.3	4.2

It must be said that in some countries the reduction of investment may reflect the privatization process or changes in the classification of public utilities and other units (from the general government to the private sector); for Austria the latter factor accounts for half of the reduction between 1993 and 1997. In the UK the use of *public finance initiatives* (involving private capital in the realization of projects of public interest) may explain about one-third of the reduction in public investment expenditure between 1993 and 1997. The contribution from sales of public real estate, which is recorded as negative investment outlays by general government, appears less relevant.

Similar evidence emerges when considering data from the last two decades. Between 1980 and 1997, we identify 32 episodes of lasting and significant budget consolidation in EU countries: in 25 cases the ratio of investments to GDP decreased; in 23 the ratio of investment to primary outlays decreased (Table 6.2).[123]

With the exception of Greece, Portugal and Spain which, however, benefited from particular conditions (e.g. EU support for infrastructure development), the ratio of investment to GDP and primary outlays decreased in the EU between the first half of the 1980s and the 1995–97

Table 6.2 Deficit reduction and changes in public investment: EU countries, 1980–97 (ESA79 data)

Country	Period	Deficit improvement	Changes in ratios invest./GDP	inv./primary exp.
Italy	1985–89	2.5	−0.4	−0.9
	1990–97	8.4	−0.9	−1.7
France	1985–89	1.7	0.2	0.8
	1994–97	2.8	−0.1	−0.1
Germany	1981–85	2.5	−0.6	−1.4
UK	1984–89	4.9	−0.3	0.0
	1993–97	6.0	−0.8	−1.7
Spain	1985–87	3.8	−0.3	−0.4
	1995–97	4.7	−0.7	−1.2
Belgium	1983–85	2.6	−0.8	−1.2
	1986–90	3.7	−1.0	−1.7
	1993–97	5.0	−0.2	−0.4
Denmark	1982–86	12.5	−0.8	−1.7
	1994–97	3.5	0	0.3
Greece	1985–87	2.0	−1.0	−2.4
	1995–97	6.3	0	0.7
Eire	1982–84	3.8	−1.2	−2.4
	1985–89	8.9	−2.0	−3.5
	1995–97	3.1	0	0.4
Netherlands	1982–85	3.0	−0.6	−0.8
	1995–97	2.6	−0.1	0.0
Portugal	1985–89	4.1	0.6	1.8
	1993–97	3.6	0.3	0.3
Austria	1983–85	1.5	−0.2	−0.6
	1987–90	1.8	−0.2	−0.1
	1995–97	2.7	−0.2	−0.2
Finland	1983–86	2.4	−0.5	−1.6
	1987–89	5.3	−0.7	−1.1
	1993–97	7.1	−0.1	0.6
Sweden	1982–84	4.1	−0.5	−1.0
	1985–87	8.0	−0.5	−0.1
	1993–97	11.4	1.3	−0.9

period. With the exception of Greece, the larger reductions occurred in high debt countries (Belgium, Ireland and Italy), where the investment to GDP ratio declined from an average of 3.7 per cent in 1980–84 to 2.3 per cent in 1995–97; at the same time the deficit to GDP ratio decreased from 9.8 to 4.2 per cent. In the rest of the EU, while the deficit decreased from

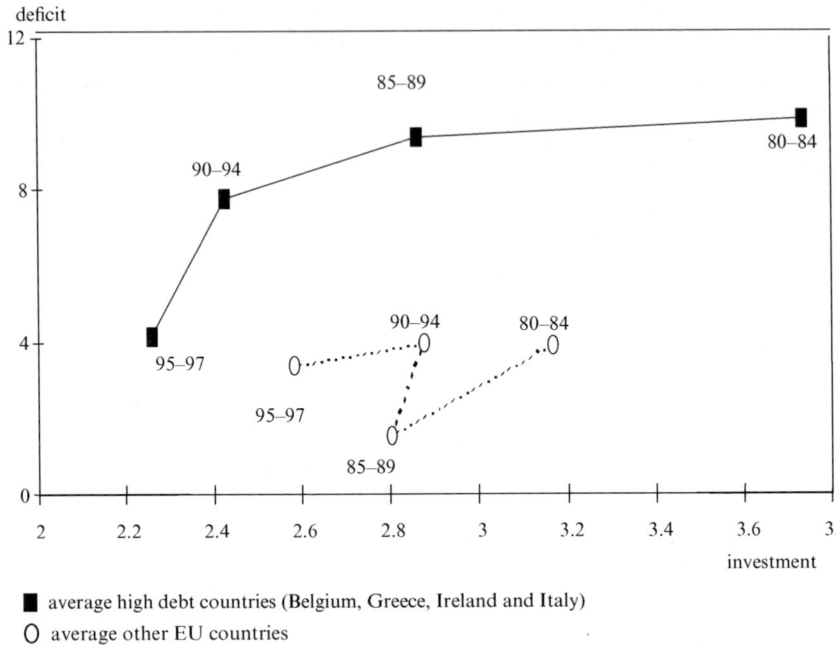

Figure 6.2 *Investment and deficit in EU countries (% GDP) (ESA79 average over 1980–84; 1985–89; 1990–94; 1995–97)*

3.9 to 3.4 per cent of GDP, investment was reduced from 3.2 to 2.6 per cent (Figure 6.2). A similar picture emerges for the investment to primary outlays ratios (Figure 6.3). The growth of deficit and investment in low debt countries in the first half of the 1990s may reflect expansionary policies implemented in response to a cyclical downswing: this opportunity was not available to countries where fiscal consolidation was still under way. During the 1990s, the investment to GDP ratio in high debt countries was significantly lower than in low debt countries.

4. THE EFFECTS OF A REDUCTION IN PUBLIC INVESTMENT EXPENDITURE

The reduction in public investment is a problem if, as implicitly assumed in the previous sections, it reduces the productive and growth potential of the economy. However, the empirical evidence on the effects of public investment is not unequivocal.[124]

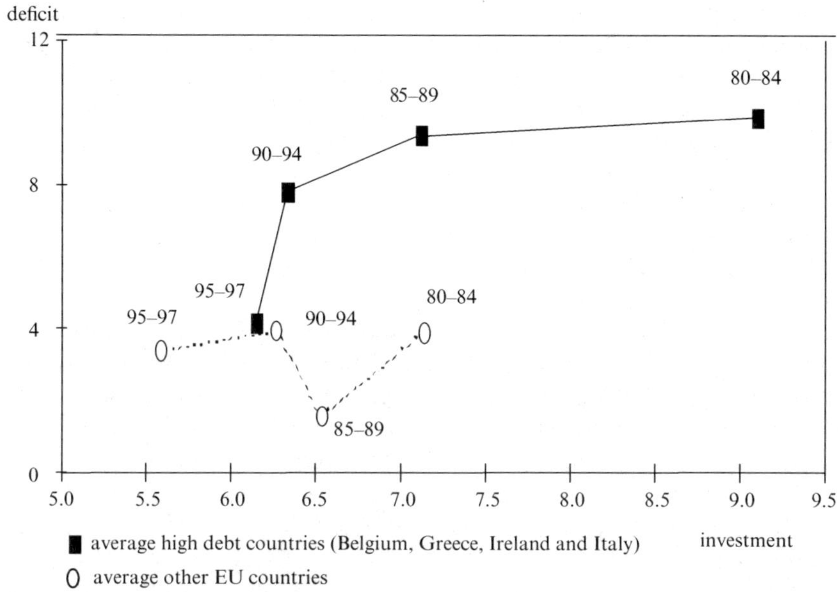

Figure 6.3 Deficit (% GDP) and investment (% primary expenditure) in EU countries (ESA79 average over 1980–84; 1985–89; 1990–94; 1995–97)

Various techniques have been used to measure the impact of public capital. Direct estimation of a production function dates back to Mera (1973) and Ratner (1983).[125] Using this approach Aschauer (1989) revived the debate. He found that non-military public capital is a significant input to a national production function for the US and that the implied marginal product of public capital is high; he argued that the slowdown in public capital growth in the US during the 1970s and the 1980s explains the decline in productivity growth that occurred over the same period. Aschauer's work spurred a literature aimed at refining his method and results (see the reviews in Eberts, 1990; Munnel, 1992 and Gramlich, 1994). Many studies initially confirmed (in sign if not in value) Aschauer's results also using US state-level panel data. However, subsequent efforts have found that when controlling for state fixed-effects the positive infrastructure–output link found in OLS and random effects models disappears (Holtz-Eakin, 1994; Garcia-Milá *et al.*, 1996; Kelejian and Robinson, 1997); similar results have been obtained by Evans and Karras (1994) using a panel of seven OECD countries.[126]

The statistical measurement of the effect of public capital on private production encounters several problems: the causality direction is difficult to assess, there is potential endogeneity of inputs and outputs, time-series may not be stationary, the proper treatment of fixed and random effects is an unsettled issue, the measurement of the stock of public capital or of the net addition to the stock generated by the annual flow of public investment is often inadequate (see the review in Hurst, 1994).

To this effect, the Italian experience clearly indicates that the ratio of investment to GDP is not a good indicator of variations in the stock of public capital: the Italian ratio has long been among the highest in western countries without improving Italy's relative position in terms of infrastructures.[127] Besides the obvious issue of amortization, the result may also reflect improper management or any other source of inefficiency. Furthermore a large part of the infrastructures presumably affecting productivity and growth is not included among general government investment as the institutions responsible for such infrastructures are not part of the general government (this is frequently the case for energy, telecommunications and railways).

Hence, while there is a consensus that private-sector production of goods and services depends crucially on an adequate infrastructure of roads, electricity, telecommunications, water and other similar facilities, the public investment to GDP ratio cannot be the sole indicator of year-to-year changes in the stock of public capital.

The problem of efficiency of public investment is also stressed by Girard *et al.* (1994, 1995) who argue that 'the different quality of investment has played a significant role in the different economic growth experiences of the EU, Japan and USA' (1995, p. 731) and by Girard and Hurst (1994), who argue that sub-optimal public capital stock is consistent with too high a rate of public capital accumulation, that is, 'that there is some maximum rate at which viable projects can be prepared' (p. 13).[128]

5. WHICH 'GOLDEN RULE' FOR EMU?

The usefulness of a dual budget has been long debated, since the 1930s, when a dual budget was proposed in order to foster the acceptance of using public debt to finance investment. It is still an unsettled issue, which has been tackled in different ways in different countries and at different times.[129] Sweden, for example, introduced the dual budget in 1937 and suppressed it in 1980.

The separation of current and capital operations is attractive for various respects; one of its main advantages is perhaps the possibility to spread the costs of durables over the years during which they will be used. However, it has been noted that it is necessary to be more precise about which expenditures should be included in the capital account otherwise the dual budget would result 'in a preference for expenditures on physical assets rather than greater spending for intangibles such as health or education' (Colm and Wagner, 1963, p. 125). Clearly there are current expenditures, such as those increasing human capital, that can give a relevant contribution to growth.[130] Moreover, the possibility to borrow, without strict limits, in order to finance investments can lower the attention paid when evaluating the costs and benefits of each project. Contrary to what happens in the private sector, there would be no mechanism to penalize public institutions investing in low revenue projects.

Besides taking into account the aspects specific to the *golden rule*, the proposal to introduce such a rule into EMU's fiscal framework must be evaluated with regard to its consistency with the objectives of EMU's fiscal rules and to its impact on the effectiveness of the surveillance procedure set to safeguard their enforcement. The reference values and targets defined in the Maastricht Treaty and in the Stability and Growth Pact do not distinguish between current and capital outlays. The latter are only mentioned among the other relevant factors for evaluating excessive deficits (art. 104(3)); investment expenditure must be specified in the Convergence Programmes that each member state will submit annually to the Council and the European Commission.

The objectives of the Treaty and the Pact are a sound fiscal stance (to this end quantitative limits are set for the deficit and the debt to GDP ratios) and sufficient room for counter-cyclical action (to this end, given the above mentioned limits, a medium-term target of a budget position close to balance or in surplus is set).

As discussed in Chapter 3, such a medium-term target is to be obtained 'over the cycle'; in other words, it may be thought of as applying to structural budgets around which automatic stabilizers will be operating and, if necessary, discretionary interventions will be made. The lower this budget balance with respect to the 3 per cent threshold, the wider the margins for counter-cyclical policy. The actual value set by each country for the medium-term target depends on three elements: the size of foreseeable recessions; the elasticity of the budget to the cycle; and the size of discretionary interventions that may be needed to supplement automatic stabilizers.[131] Countries with debt ratios above 60 per cent of GDP should also take into account the need to decrease the ratio, at a satisfactory pace, towards the threshold. Moreover, an increase in the debt ratio during recessions should be avoided.[132]

As shown in Chapter 3, in most EU countries a cyclically adjusted budget between 0 and 1 per cent of GDP would allow full operation of automatic stabilizers with no risk of breaching the 3 per cent threshold.

Countries with cycles of lower amplitude and lower budget elasticity could stay closer to the upper part of this 'safety zone'.

A stylized version of the EMU fiscal constitution can be drawn as follows: the reference parameter is general government deficit (DEF); the parameter is subject to an upper ceiling (3 per cent of GDP) and to a medium-term objective of a position close to balance or in surplus (to allow stabilization policy without breaching the upper ceiling):

$$\begin{aligned} (DEF/GDP)_t &\leq 0.03 && \forall t \\ (DEF_s/GDP)_t &\in (0.00, 0.01) && \forall t \end{aligned} \qquad (6.2)$$

where DEF_s is the structural deficit, and the medium-term objective of a position of close to balance or in surplus is operationalized in terms of the 'safety zone' defined above.

This characterization allows us to distinguish three ways to introduce the *golden rule*: (1) changing the reference parameter; (2) changing the upper limit; and (3) changing the medium term objective. For each option both the kind of investment outlays considered and the time span to which one refers need to be specified.

The implications of the three types of reform can be explained by looking at solutions already adopted in some countries or proposed in the debate:

1. The proposal made by Modigliani *et al.* (1998), suggesting the use of a deficit net of net investment, represents a reform of the first type.
2. In Germany (art. 115 of the Constitution), yearly deficits are allowed up to the level of gross investment in the federal budget (this includes items which differ from those considered in national accounts);[133] the adoption of this solution at EMU level would represent a reform of the second type.
3. In the UK public borrowing cannot exceed the level of net investment over the cycle (HM Treasury, 1997); the adoption of this solution for EMU member countries would represent a reform of the third type.

To evaluate the consistency of each solution with the objectives of the Treaty and the Pact it is useful to refer to the graphs in Figures 6.4a–6.4d, where the effects of each proposal on the structural deficit and on the margins for stabilization policy are stylized. The curves show the level of the balance; they are traced assuming 4 per cent difference in GDP between the position at the top of the upswing and the position at the bottom of the downswing (this is assumed to be sufficient for stabilization purposes). The straight lines show the limits set to the deficit. Figure 6.4a depicts the

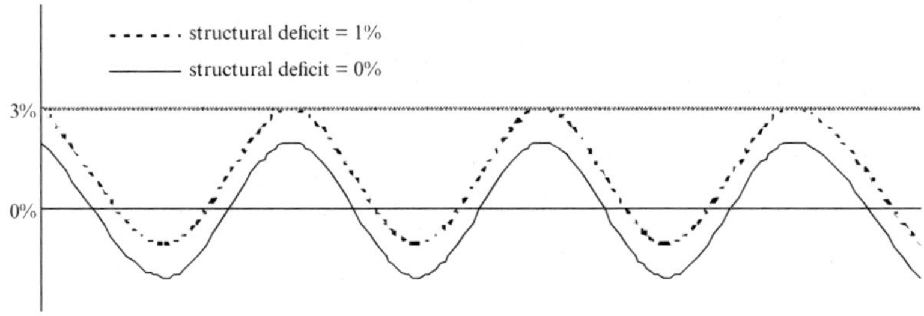

Figure 6.4a The Stability Pact

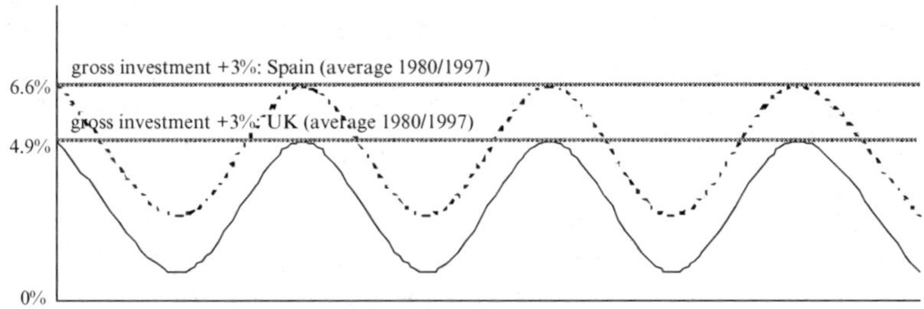

Figure 6.4b Excluding gross investment

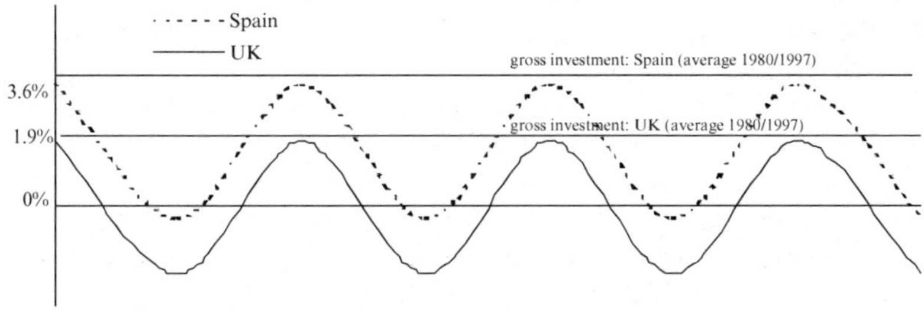

Figure 6.4c Golden rule – *German model*

present situation. The two curves refer to a balanced structural budget and a 1 per cent structural deficit. To simplify the analysis in the next subsections reference is made only to the latter situation.

Changing the reference parameter as proposed by Modigliani *et al.* the conditions in (6.2) would change into:

$$\begin{aligned}&\{[DEF-(INV-AMM)]/GDP\}_t \leq 0.03 \quad \forall t\\&\{[DEF_s-(INV-AMM)]/GDP\}_t = 0.01 \quad \forall t\end{aligned} \qquad (6.3)$$

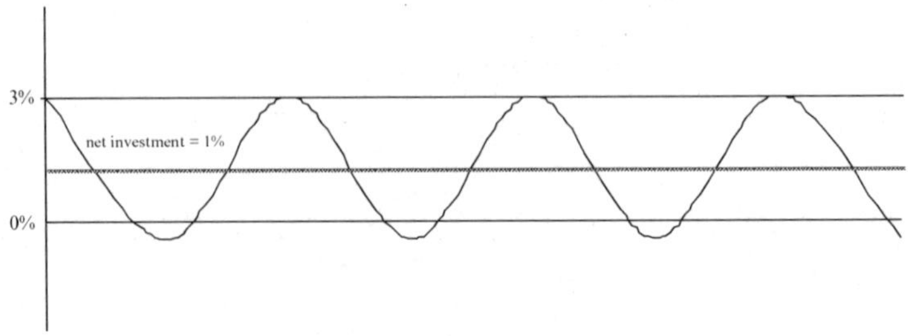

Figure 6.4d Golden rule – *UK model*

where *INV* and *AMM* stand for gross investment and amortization respectively. These conditions amount to an increase in the upper limit and the medium-term objective presently set for the overall deficit. The increase depends on the country's level of net investment. In fact, (6.3) can be rewritten as:

$$\begin{aligned} (DEF/GDP)_t &\leq \{0.03 + [(INV - AMM)/GDP]_t\} \quad \forall t \\ (DEF_s/GDP)_t &= 0.01 + [(INV - AMM)/GDP]_t \quad \forall t \end{aligned} \qquad (6.3')$$

The margins for counter-cyclical action are unchanged with respect to (6.2). However, this proposal would determine an increase in the structural deficit which, for high enough values of net investment, may be incompatible with the reduction of debt.

Reference to net investment is what a proper application of the dual budget requires. It has the merit of making the deficit level conditional on the level of that part of expenditures that actually can increase a country's productive potential.[134] However, it also poses some problems for evaluation: (a) amortization would have to be evaluated item by item with high administrative costs; (b) this would be complicated by the fact that public infrastructures have multiple functions and no market value. Furthermore, the margins for opportunistic behaviour may widen.[135] These problems are all the more relevant for the multilateral surveillance procedure.

The use of gross investment would not be in line with the correct application of a double budget but would avoid the above mentioned difficulties. The elements for the computation of the modified reference parameter (overall deficit and gross investment) are already available and communicated to the EU by member states within the Excessive deficits procedure.[136] There would not be extra administrative costs and the leeway for opportunistic behaviour would be less pronounced.[137] However, the monitoring of results during the year would become more difficult.[138]

The constraints in (6.3′) would change to:

$$\begin{aligned}&(DEF/GDP)_t \leq [0.03 + (INV/GDP)_t] \quad \forall t\\&(DEF_s/GDP)_t = 0.01 + (INV/GDP)_t \quad \forall t\end{aligned} \tag{6.3″}$$

In this case, if gross investment remain at the levels recorded on average over the last two decades, the resulting structural deficit would not be consistent with the objective of a sound fiscal stance. In Figure 6.4b two lines are traced, corresponding to the limits to the overall deficit resulting from the minimum and maximum value of the gross investment to GDP ratio recorded on average in the 1980–97 period in EU countries (respectively 1.9 per cent in the UK and 3.6 per cent in Spain). The structural deficit would lie between 1.9 and 4.6 per cent of GDP (considering fluctuation margins respectively equal to 3 and 2 percentage points).[139] Such values, given the present low inflation environment, would only be consistent with the limit set for the debt ratio (60 per cent of GDP) under sustained real growth rates; for a country with a structural deficit of 3 per cent and a debt ratio of 60 per cent, growth rates higher than 5 per cent would be required. For Italy, a nominal growth rate of 4.5 per cent and structural deficit of 3 per cent would imply a debt ratio still at 100 per cent in the year 2010.

The German model would meet difficulties similar to those already mentioned from the point of view of multilateral surveillance (again, gross investment is used). The constraints in (6.2) would change to

$$\begin{aligned}&(DEF/GDP)_t \leq (INV/GDP)_t \quad \forall t\\&(DEF_s/GDP)_t = (INV/GDP)_t - 0.02 \quad \forall t\end{aligned} \tag{6.4}$$

where, as in (6.3′), it is assumed that the change in the upper ceiling of the reference parameter also determines a change in the medium-term objective allowing stabilization policy without breaching the upper limit (the margins are left unaltered at 2 per cent).

As for the consistency with the objectives of the Treaty and the Pact, if the same level of expenditure experienced in the past were to prevail in the future, this solution would not imply a significant change with respect to the present situation for most EU member states. On average between 1980 and 1997 the ratio of gross investment to GDP in EU countries was slightly below 3 per cent; only in a few countries and for very limited periods of time did it go above 4 per cent; so, in order to have sufficient margins for countercyclical action, most countries would have to target a structural balance between 0 and 1 per cent of GDP. In Figure 6.4c two examples are depicted concerning the countries with the lowest and the highest gross investment to GDP ratio in the EU (again the fluctuation margins are set to 2 per cent of GDP).

The UK model refers to results over the cycle; thus it appears to be better suited to be consistent with the objectives of soundness and flexibility of the budget. Adopting this model in EMU would imply the following constraints:

$$\begin{aligned}(DEF/GDP)_t &\leq [(INV-AMM)/GDP]_a + 0.02 \quad \forall t\\ (DEF_s/GDP)_t &\leq [(INV-AMM)/GDP]_a \quad \forall t\end{aligned} \tag{6.5}$$

where the upper ceiling on the reference parameter has been defined so as to leave the fluctuation margins for the budget unaltered and $[(INV-AMM)/GDP]_a$ is the average level of the net investment to GDP ratio over the cycle.

The actual determination of the reference period (the length of the cycle) may encounter some difficulties on both theoretical and practical grounds. It also adds to the complexity of the multilateral surveillance process. As already mentioned, additional problems stem from the reference to net investment. Depending on the level of net investment, the medium-term target consistent with the UK model may or may not fall in the 'safety zone'.[140] In the first case, the UK model would only differ from the present situation in that a structural deficit could only be incurred if net investment were underway; it would leave unaltered both the margins for stabilization policy and the safeguard of a structural budget consistent with a sustainable debt level. In the second case, both objectives could be compromised. Considering the investment undertaken by EU countries between 1980 and 1997, the structural deficit would lie between $(1.9-x)$ and $(3.6-x)$, where $x=AMM/GDP$; these levels are lower than those allowed by the proposal in Modigliani *et al.* $(1.9-x;\ 4.6-x)$, but they could still be inconsistent with a reduction of the debt ratio.[141] Furthermore, if the 3 per cent threshold for the overall deficit is kept (Figure 6.4d), net investment larger than 1 per cent would imply shrinking margins for stabilization policy.

In conclusion, the adoption of the *golden rule* cannot significantly change the policy options open to EU countries without conflicting with the objective of a sound fiscal stance and without making the multilateral surveillance process more complex.[142]

6. CONCLUSIONS

The Maastricht Treaty defines the soundness of public finances as a necessary condition for the success of EMU and sets quantitative limits to deficit and debt in EU member countries. The centralization of monetary policy and the impossibility of using the exchange rate as a policy instrument make fiscal policy all the more important. Indeed, fiscal policy together with structural policy becomes the main instrument of national economic policy. Fiscal policy must deal with asymmetric shocks and with situations in which the national cycle diverges from that of the Union as a whole. This requires sufficient margins of fluctuation for the budget. In order to avoid that flexibility conflicting with soundness, a structural budget close to balance is called for.

This arrangement is not without problems: (a) the transition to a balanced budget can have negative effects on conjunctural developments; (b) the long process of debt reduction brings significant costs in terms of primary surpluses to current generations; and (c) there is limited scope to using debt in order to finance investment and this in turn can determine a reduction in investment.

The first problem is undoubtedly relevant. In the event of extremely unfavourable conjunctural developments, prudent tuning of the transition may be considered. It should be noted that in several countries the interest to GDP ratio tends to decrease as the reduction in interest rates affects the average cost of debt and as the debt ratio itself declines, making the needed effort in terms of primary surplus less demanding.

The effect of the transition to a balanced budget could be lessened by increasing the degree of competition and of flexibility in product and factor markets. A loosening of the rules designed to govern the system after the transition does not seem necessary; it may damage the credibility of the commitment to sustainable public finances; monetary policy may be called to take a restrictive stance. Moreover, the *golden rule* does not help during downswings: investment decisions only translate into actual expenditure with a significant delay.

The second problem cannot be avoided. The burden in terms of primary surplus is the price to pay to gain budget flexibility and soundness. In some countries the reduction of the debt can break the vicious cycle between high debt and high interest rates which has conditioned economic policy in recent years (for Italy see Sartor, 1998). Furthermore, it allows margins for counter-cyclical action, avoiding the risk that an expansionary policy may be perceived as a threat to sustainability.[143] Finally, it permits tackling, from a sounder financial position, the coming phase of intense ageing and compensating with lower interest payments the ensuing increase in expenditure (see, e.g., Franco and Munzi, 1999). If the introduction of the *golden rule* implied a reduction in primary surpluses, it could endanger the objectives of soundness and flexibility set for government budgets.

Previous sections have explained how the third problem evolves: a broadly balanced budget reduces the possibility of spreading investment costs over the generations benefiting from investment and can negatively affect the investment level. This effect can be especially relevant during the transition to the low debt levels consistent with the chosen structural balance. The reduction in deficit recorded in EU countries in recent years benefited from cuts in investment spending; in relative terms these cuts have often been higher than the corresponding cuts in other items. The problem may be more serious for countries and regions with a lower stock of public capital. However, a reduction in investment as measured in the general government accounts should not be too worrisome since this is not the most appropriate measure of change in public capital.

Should a *golden rule* be introduced into EMU fiscal framework to avoid the reduction in investment? The analysis here points to a negative answer. Some of the solutions proposed may be an obstacle to deficit and debt reduction, others meet practical difficulties, such as the evaluation of amortization. Generally, leeway for opportunistic behaviour would increase and the surveillance of outcomes and trends would be more complex.

Perhaps it is better to search for different solutions. While an exhaustive list is certainly not the aim of this chapter, some ideas can be put forward. At the national level, one may consider safeguard clauses to avoid fiscal consolidation efforts translating into investment cuts. The adoption of the UK model at the national level may be a useful self-discipline mechanism warranting a minimum level of investment; if the mechanism has no relevance at EU level, no surveillance problem will arise. In adopting this model, the actual use of the margins for a structural deficit allowed by the EU fiscal constitution will become conditional on the realization of infrastructure. As noted in the fifth section, in order to avoid excessive reduction of the margins for counter-cyclical action and to make sure that EU fiscal rules are not breached, the structural deficit should not be above 1 per cent of GDP; this is a modest amount which should also limit the relevance of the conceptual problems posed by the double budget system.

In order to ensure a larger flow of resources available for public investment, other measures are necessary. For example, especially for smaller projects, the decentralization of investment decisions and financing may help to reduce the disincentive for projects with deferred benefits. At the local community level intergenerational altruism may be stronger and people may be more willing to bear a larger gap between taxes and immediate benefits. More generally, private capital will have to be involved in funding projects of public interest. Most infrastructure networks are already the responsibility of institutions and firms outside the general government.

7. Long-term sustainability*

1. INTRODUCTION

While the intuition is clear (a sustainable policy must ultimately avoid bankruptcy), the analytical and operational definition of sustainability is not straightforward. The theory has proposed different conditions for sustainability (from a non ever-rising tax rate to an intertemporal discounted budget constraint);[144] furthermore, the problem has always been dealt with in a partial equilibrium framework where the interactions between the budget and the economy are not fully taken into account. In practice difficulties arise with regard to the statistical definition of the main variables to be used for the assessment of sustainability (is it gross or net debt to be relevant, how should the deficit be measured?); moreover, as sustainability is a forward-looking concept, long-term projections are needed and these are necessarily subject to wide margins of error.

Yet sustainability is a central tenet of the Maastricht Treaty. Article 109(1) makes a sound government financial position an explicit criterion for a country's eligibility to join EMU. The fiscal rules set out in the Treaty and subsequently integrated by the Stability and Growth Pact require budget positions close to balance or in surplus in the medium term, deficits lower than 3 per cent of GDP and the reduction of debt to GDP ratios below 60 per cent. Compliance with these rules, which aims at combining fiscal discipline and flexibility, clearly excludes divergent and unsustainable fiscal dynamics.[145]

Although the choice of the actual parameters is somewhat arbitrary,[146] the pragmatic approach taken by the Treaty and the SGP is justified by the difficulty to firmly base on theoretical grounds any benchmark against which to assess sustainability. EMU rules can be said to provide applied economists with the benchmark the theory has not produced. In a sense, EMU rules have also reduced uncertainty concerning the statistical definition of the main variables to be used for the assessment of sustainability: European legislation refers to statistical protocols for the definition of 'debt' and 'deficit'.

* Franco Balassone and Daniele Franco, 'Assessing Fiscal Sustainability: A Review of Methods with a View to EMU', Banca d'Italia, *Fiscal Sustainability*, 2000: 22–60.

Prospective compliance with EMU rules can thus be assessed using techniques developed for the analysis of sustainability on the basis of data whose definition is no longer subject to debate. As the accuracy of such prospective assessments is crucial both for policy evaluation and for the feasibility of timely corrective intervention, it seems a worthwhile exercise to re-examine the pros and cons of different assessment methods proposed in the literature: while EMU's rules provide a reference for the definition of sustainability and of the variables relevant to its assessment, the problems related to the partial equilibrium nature of the analysis and to the use of long-term projections are left for the economists to tackle.

The need for accurate indicators is presently made compelling by such issues as the unfavourable demographic trends facing most EU countries, the sensitivity to macroeconomic shocks of the large stocks of government liabilities still outstanding in some countries, and the risk that the process of economic integration may trigger tax competition and degradation.

The purpose of this chapter is to review the literature on fiscal sustainability in order to examine the comparative advantages and disadvantages of different methodologies and indicators and to highlight the areas in which more effort is needed. The next section focuses on the theoretical definition of sustainability, while the third section is concerned with statistical issues. The fourth to seventh sections review the literature on assessment methods grouping studies into two main strands: (a) those testing for the sustainability of past policies (fourth section); and (b) those assessing prospective fiscal stances. Among the latter a distinction is drawn between works based on standard national accounting concepts (fifth section) and generational accounting exercises (sixth section). The seventh section summarizes the main findings and concludes.

2. DEFINING SUSTAINABILITY

For a long time the issue of sustainability has been addressed only in terms of the effects of public debt on the economy. According to Hume, public debt was likely to lead to injurious tax increases in the short term and possibly to default in the long term. Smith also considered that debt financing would lead to default. The consensus view was that debt financing was to be used only in exceptional circumstances, such as wars.[147]

Initially the analysis focused on the comparison between tax and deficit finance of public expenditure. The main issues concerning the hypothesis of debt neutrality (i.e. the equivalence of deficit and tax finance with respect to capital accumulation) and the intergenerational distribution of its burden were tackled by Ricardo.[148] Against debt neutrality he argued that, due to fiscal illusion (i.e. the inability of agents to correctly anticipate future taxes needed to finance the debt), debt induces a smaller reduction of consumption than taxes do; hence the former exerts a comparatively negative effect on capital accumulation. According to Ricardo the cost of debt is borne when resources are used and therefore falls onto current generations. In his writings, there is only one channel through which future generations may be burdened by the debt, that is the negative effects of debt finance on capital stock.

Between the end of the nineteenth and the beginning of the twentieth century, the 'Italian school' of public finance explored further the conditions needed for debt neutrality to hold: Pantaleoni and Borgatta focused on the role of bequests; De Viti De Marco on financial markets imperfections; Griziotti on agents' time horizons; Puviani on bounded rationality and fiscal illusion.[149] The neutrality hypothesis came to the fore again much later with Barro's (1974) contribution, which put it into a fully formalized framework and highlighted the relevance of intergenerational altruism as an alternative hypothesis to the one concerning infinite time horizons.

The issue of the generational distribution of the burden of the debt was also debated for a long time. The position originally held by Ricardo, that the cost of debt is borne when resources are used, was taken up in the 1940s by the so-called 'real resources view'. According to the supporters of this view the burden of the debt is borne by current generations as they pay the opportunity cost of financing it. The future servicing and repayment of the debt will only entail transfers from the general tax payers to the bondholders, and as long as the debt is internally held this does not alter the overall volume of resources available (the 'we owe the debt to ourselves' argument; see, e.g., Lerner, 1943 and Chase, 1943).

Supporters of the 'real resource view' generally recognized the relevance of the effects of debt finance on the rate of capital accumulation, and agreed that if these effects are negative then future generations may be said to be burdened by the debt in the sense that they receive a lower capital stock. On the other hand, they pointed out that this does not necessarily imply a reduced degree of Pareto efficiency. Moreover, they highlighted the need to consider the use to which resources are put by the public sector: if public expenditure translates into capital accumulation then the rates of return to private and public use of available resources need to be compared.[150]

The 'real resource view' developed in the context of the gradual diffusion of Keynesian theory, according to which markets are generally unable to ensure full employment of available resources. Debt finance is therefore necessary to provide the proper level of aggregate demand 'when private investment is insufficient to absorb intended savings over a relatively long period of time' (Domar, 1944, p. 798).[151]

The legitimacy of debt finance for public investment (the 'golden rule') was increasingly recognized. During the 1930s, the introduction of the dual budget was proposed and hotly debated.[152] Sweden, for example, introduced the dual budget in 1937. The separation of current and capital operations was considered attractive since it spreads the costs of durables over the years during which they will be used and emphasizes the effects of each budgetary operation on the net worth of the public sector. In the same vein, Article 115 of the German Constitution allows yearly deficits up to the level of gross investment in the federal budget.[153]

Debt finance met opposition with respect to the dead-weight loss due to the larger taxes needed later to service and repay the debt. Contrary to this view, it was pointed out that 'public debt need not be repaid . . . [as] . . . the debt is refunded' (Musgrave and Musgrave, 1984, pp. 688–9)[154] and that 'the phrase "burden of the debt", if it has any meaning, evidently refers to the tax rate (or rates) which must be imposed to finance the service charges, and that the *tax rate* will rise is far from evident' (Domar, 1944, p. 798).

At this stage the issue of debt sustainability was essentially specified in its main respects. The question was: are there limits to debt accumulation in the sense that its effects on accumulation and growth may determine an unbearable burden (as measured by the implied tax rate)? The answer requires the specification of the equation governing the dynamics of the debt to GDP ratio as a function of budgetary policy (tax, interest and primary expenditure ratios) and of its effects on macro parameters such as the rate of interest and the rate of growth. Unfortunately there was not (and there still is not) an agreed theory of the interactions between the public budget and the economy.

The only choice was (and still is) to use a partial equilibrium framework, assuming that both the interest rate and the growth rate are exogenous to fiscal policy. The partial equilibrium nature of the exercise implies that the possible effects of growing debt on interest rates and growth are overlooked.[155] The analysis is driven back to the crucial issue of the traditional debate on the burden of the debt: its effects on accumulation and growth.

This framework was first used by Domar (1944) to answer concerns that 'continuous government borrowing results in an ever rising public debt, the servicing of which will require higher and higher taxes; and that the latter will eventually destroy our economy or result in outright repudiation of the debt' (p. 799). Domar showed that a constant overall deficit to GDP ratio ensures convergence of both the debt to GDP ratio and the interest to GDP ratio to finite values. Consequently, also, taxes needed to service interest payments converge to a finite value as a share of GDP.

Formally, let d be the debt to GDP ratio, b the deficit to GDP ratio, τ the tax to GDP ratio set equal to the ratio of interest payments to GDP, γ the rate of growth of GDP and ρ the rate of interest, then:

$$d_t = [1/(1+\gamma)]d_{t-1} + b \tag{7.1}$$

$$d_t = d_0(1+\gamma)^{-t} + b\sum_{i=1}^{t}(1+\gamma)^{-(t-i)} \tag{7.2}$$

$$\lim_{t\to\infty} d_t = b\,(1+\gamma)/\gamma \tag{7.3}$$

$$\lim_{t\to\infty} \tau_t = \lim_{t\to\infty} \rho[d_{t-1}/(1+\gamma)] = b\,(\rho/\gamma) \tag{7.4}$$

The partial equilibrium nature of the model does not allow the definition of a sufficient condition for sustainability. Whether the levels to which the debt and tax ratios converge according to (7.3) and (7.4) can be sustained depends on their effects on ρ and γ. The assessment must be made outside the model. However, a necessary condition for sustainability can be defined: an ever-growing tax ratio cannot be sustainable. Equation (7.4) shows that this requires the debt to GDP ratio to converge to a finite value.[156]

The debate on sustainability took a new twist in the 1980s, in connection with the growth of the public sector and the unfavourable demographic trends. It was spurred by estimates pointing to substantial prospective increases in public expenditure.[157] The development of large welfare systems implied large-scale implicit liabilities whose amount is related to the age structure of the population. The additional tax burden required to finance expected expenditure increases became the primary concern. The cost of implicit liabilities would in several countries dwarf that of the public debt. In evaluating public finance sustainability it was no longer sufficient to examine the tax rate implications of a constant deficit, à la Domar. It became necessary to estimate the future deficit path implied by current policies.

However, from a formal point of view, Domar's definition of sustainability was still acceptable. Buiter (1985) defined a sustainable policy as one capable of keeping the ratio of public sector net worth to output at its current level. Blanchard *et al.* (1990) proposed two necessary conditions for sustainability: (1) 'that the ratio of debt to GNP eventually converges back to its initial level' (p. 11); and (2) that 'the present discounted value of the ratio of primary deficits to GNP . . . is equal to the negative of the current level of debt to GNP' (p. 12).

The second condition can be derived as follows. Let us rewrite equation (7.1), splitting the deficit between the primary balance (p_t) and interest payments:

$$d_t = [(1+\rho)/(1+\gamma)]\, d_{t-1} + p_t \tag{7.5}$$

According to (7.5) the debt ratio at any time is given by:

$$d_T = [(1+\rho)/(1+\gamma)]^T d_0 + \sum_{t=1}^{T} \{p_t[(1+\rho)/(1+\gamma)]^{(T-t)}\} \tag{7.6}$$

Discounting (7.6) to time zero we have:

$$[(1+\rho)/(1+\gamma)]^{-T} d_T = d_0 + \sum_{t=1}^{T} \{p_t[(1+\rho)/(1+\gamma)]^{(-t)}\} \tag{7.7}$$

and taking the limit for $T \to \infty$

$$\lim_{T\to\infty} [(1+\rho)/(1+\gamma)]^{-T} d_T = d_0 + \lim_{T\to\infty} \sum_{t=1}^{T} \{p_t[(1+\rho)/(1+\gamma)]^{(-t)}\} \tag{7.8}$$

Finally, assuming that the discounted value of the debt ratio tends to zero, that is:

$$\lim_{T\to\infty} [(1+\rho)/(1+\gamma)]^{-T} d_T = 0 \tag{7.9}$$

we have the required condition:

$$\lim_{T\to\infty} \sum_{t=1}^{T} \{p_t[(1+\rho)/(1+\gamma)]^{(-t)}\} = -d_0 \tag{7.10}$$

Blanchard *et al.* (1990) treat the two conditions as equivalent (pp. 11–12). However, as the authors acknowledge (p. 14), there is a difference: the necessary requirement for the second definition, that is, the convergence to zero of the discounted value of the debt ratio (equation (7.9)), is consistent with the undiscounted debt ratio converging to its initial value, converging to any other finite value, or diverging though at a rate lower than the difference between the interest rate and the rate of growth of GDP. So, while the first condition implies the second, the latter is necessary but insufficient for the first to apply.

With respect to the necessary condition for sustainability used in Domar's paper (convergence of the undiscounted debt ratio to a finite value), the first definition in Blanchard *et al.* is tighter; but this is at a cost of arbitrariness. As we have already noted, Domar's model cannot specify the maximum sustainable debt level and Blanchard *et al.* do acknowledge that 'the justification for the ratio to eventually return to its initial level, as opposed say to zero, or to a higher but stable level, is, however, much less evident' (p. 11).[158]

On the contrary, the second definition is looser than Domar's: an ever-growing undiscounted debt ratio is allowed. As the authors explain, 'this is because of discounting, which implies that things far in the future do not matter much for today' (p. 14). However, as pointed out by Artis and Marcellino (1998), 'this suggests that both quantities should be analysed and not only the discounted one' (p. 6).

All three conditions have been employed in empirical studies on sustainability, so it is not always clear that different authors are talking about the same thing when they try to assess the 'sustainability' of public finances. The absence of a clear-cut theoretical benchmark to assess sustainability has often favoured the use of ad hoc definitions such as that of Buiter (1985) and the first one proposed by Blanchard *et al.* (1990). The problem also became evident in the definition of EMU's fiscal rules.

The Treaty of Maastricht (Article 109j(1)) requires 'the sustainability of the government financial position' for a country's eligibility to EMU. Article 104c(2) defines the criteria to evaluate sustainability by means of reference values for deficit and debt to GDP ratios. The annexed Protocol on excessive deficits specifies such values respectively as 3 and 60 per cent. A pragmatic approach to the issue was therefore taken. Sustainability is defined as non-violation of arbitrarily predefined parametric standards.

The Stability and Growth Pact has introduced the medium-term target of a position close to balance or in surplus, thus tightening the deficit rule while also trying to reconcile it with the possibility of counter-cyclical fiscal policy. In this context the issue arises of the actual definition of the 'medium-term position close to balance or in surplus' which allows compliance with the 3 per cent ceiling during cyclical downturns (see, e.g., Buti *et al.*, 1997 and 1998, and OECD, 1998, and Chapter 3). The equilibrium value of the debt ratio will depend on the actual numerical realization of the medium term close to balance or in surplus position.

The deficit ceiling is reminiscent of the constant deficit assumption analysed by Domar (1944). Apparently conscious of the partial equilibrium nature of Domar's results, the debt ceiling avoids convergence at high levels of debt.[159] For policy evaluation, we may see EMU fiscal rules as providing applied economists with that unique benchmark that the theory has not produced.

3. DEFINING VARIABLES

General Issues

The identification of the empirical counterparts to variables appearing in the equations of the previous section is also a relevant issue. It is closely related to the definition of sustainability adopted.

First of all, the sector of reference should be defined. In principle, the definition should include all the public bodies whose financial behaviour ultimately has an impact on central government accounts. In practice, there is a large grey area, regarding, in particular, public enterprises. As to the debt, one has to choose between gross and net measures, face values and market prices, nominal and real values. The definition of sustainability adopted is especially relevant to the choice between gross and net measures. The tax rate on which Domar (1944) focuses his analysis refers to the additional revenue needed to pay interest on debt with respect to a situation in which no debt is issued. In this case the appropriate measure of debt would appear to correspond to gross interest bearing liabilities. If reference is made to the intertemporal discounted budget constraint, all liabilities should be considered. The debt measure could be either net or gross of assets as long as the deficit measure is defined accordingly (i.e. as resulting from non-financial transactions only in the first case or as resulting from non-financial transactions plus transactions in assets in the second).

As the assets owned by government can be sold to repay the debt, a net debt measure may perhaps constitute a clearer benchmark (although the issue of the degree of liquidity of government assets should also be taken into account). However, data on assets are often regarded as unreliable, especially those on non-interest bearing assets, so that on practical grounds one may opt for a gross measure of debt.[160]

The issue of valuation can be addressed from different points of view. For governments, market valuation is not the relevant measure. It refers to the sum the government would be asked to pay if it were to buy back its debt before it falls due, but the government has no obligation to do so. In evaluating its solvency, therefore, the relevant price is the one to be paid when liabilities fall due. For investors, the market value of government liabilities matters only in so far as they intend to sell or buy such liabilities on the market. However, in evaluating government solvency, investors should also look at redemption values. Furthermore, reference to market values makes the debt measure extremely volatile.[161]

Finally real values or ratios to GDP seem appropriate if the ultimate objective of the analysis is to measure the bearability of the tax cost induced by the debt.

Once the choice concerning the debt measure is made, the deficit must be measured accordingly, so that equation (7.1) holds. *Ex post* this poses no special problems: the deficit can simply be computed as the first difference of debt. *Ex ante*, however, information on the items determining the deficit is needed to produce forecasts.

The most detailed deficit data are those from national accounts. From the point of view of its financing, the national accounts deficit represents the difference between transactions in assets and transactions in liabilities: conceptually it corresponds to changes in net debt measures.[162] However, these deficit figures are not fully consistent with nominal net debt dynamics; they need to be corrected to take into account three factors: (1) exchange rate fluctuations affect the whole stock of foreign currency denominated assets and liabilities (they determine a change in net debt) but are not reflected in the deficit as this is only concerned with actual transactions; (2) different accounting conventions are adopted for recording the effect of transactions on stocks and on flows with respect to liabilities not issued at par and to liabilities denominated in foreign currency;[163] and (3) sales/acquisitions of assets affect the net debt stock according to the nominal (book) value of the assets, while they enter the deficit according to their market value (the price paid).

The methodological choices adopted in studies assessing sustainability are by no means homogeneous. Both net and gross debt measures have been used and sometimes also mixed solutions have been adopted. Both market and face valuation of liabilities have been taken into consideration.

Pension Liabilities

In recent years a number of studies have estimated the liabilities of public pay-as-you-go (PAYG) pension schemes[164] and have argued that these liabilities should be taken into account when evaluating the state and the perspectives of public finances.[165] It has been claimed that 'the strains that higher dependency ratios will impose on budget policies can be seen by examining the present value of future net liabilities of the pension systems in the major industrial countries'.[166] These suggestions are closely related to several theoretical studies that have pointed to the deficiencies of conventional cash-flow deficit measures in the assessment of fiscal impact and of budgetary sustainability. As to the latter, it has been suggested that, 'by relying on conventional accounting methods, budgetary authorities may not be provided with the means to adequately monitor and control the government's overall fiscal position'.[167]

In order to overcome these difficulties it has often been prescribed to resort to 'economic deficit' or 'government net worth'.[168] Both these solutions would require the inclusion of pensions in fiscal accounts when obligations are incurred rather than when the actual expenditure is made.[169] In order to evaluate economic deficit, contributions to PAYG schemes would have to be classified as a financing item, while pensions would be considered as a loan repayment or as an interest payment. Any change in the present value of pension liabilities would immediately influence government net worth.

Estimates of pension liabilities may represent a useful complement to conventional debt and deficit measures.[170] However, the ratio of accrued pension liabilities to GDP is not an indicator of pension schemes' sustainability.[171] A high liabilities to GDP ratio does not necessarily imply an imbalance in PAYG pension schemes. Nor does it imply that an imbalance will occur in the future. Any judgement about the sustainability of pension schemes and the pressure they exert on public budgets requires estimates about the resources available to pay for the accrued pensions, namely about the evolution of employment and per capita income. The sustainability issue should be addressed with other indicators, such as the pension expenditure to GDP ratio and the contribution rate that assures the cash balance of pension schemes.

Moreover, accrued pension rights differ in many ways from conventional public debt and there are practical as well as theoretical reasons for not including accrued pension liabilities in the deficit and debt statistics used in defining and evaluating current fiscal policy. Pension liabilities are uncertain and depend on the specific assumptions adopted for a variety of factors. Pension rights are not embodied in formal contracts and are not tradable (the debtor can modify both the timing and the amount of the payment even taking individual characteristics into account).

EMU Definitions

The definition of debt and deficit relevant for EMU's fiscal rules took into account the need to ensure comparability of national statistics and allowing a regular surveillance process. Methodological choices were therefore made with pragmatism. The sector of reference is general government, as defined in the European System of Accounts (ESA) under the responsibility of Eurostat. Debt and deficit are respectively defined as the total of gross general government liabilities at nominal (face) value[172] and as the balance of non-financial transactions (as defined in the ESA) of general government.

Reference to a common protocol is obviously helpful for international comparison. Using definitions in line with those adopted by Statistical Offices makes past data immediately available and allows forecasts to be based on the most detailed databases. The choice of a gross measure for debt also reflects data availability, since data on assets are not always available and their quality is often poor. However, these solutions come at a cost. The definitions adopted for debt and deficit are not mutually consistent with equation (7.1) as debt is defined in gross terms while the deficit does not take into account financial transactions in assets.[173] Applied work therefore has to take care of the reconciliation of the two measures.

For example, sales of shares of public corporations have played a relevant role in the recent reduction of debt to GDP ratios in some European countries (most notably in Italy). The evaluation of the potential further contribution to debt reduction via this channel is essential for a correct evaluation of the sustainability of a country's fiscal policy.

4. TESTING FOR THE PRESENT VALUE BUDGET CONSTRAINT

One strand of the literature is concerned with the statistical testing of the sustainability of past budgetary policies. The sustainability definition adopted in these studies is the second condition proposed by Blanchard *et al.* (1990), the one based on the intertemporal discounted budget constraint.

This constraint is a crucial tool in modelling Ricardian equivalence. These studies aim at verifying whether 'when a government runs a deficit, is it making an implicit promise to creditors that it will run offsetting surpluses in the future' (Hamilton and Flavin, 1986, p. 808). The answer to this question would shed light on the soundness of the hypothesis of Ricardian equivalence in macroeconomic modelling.

Aschauer (1985) and Seater and Mariano (1985) tested the hypothesis that governments' receipts must equal expenditures in present-value terms jointly with a permanent income hypothesis. Barro (1984) tested the hypothesis that government is subject to the present value budget constraint jointly with the assumption that taxation and deficit policies have historically been optimal. Hamilton and Flavin (1986) were probably the first to test the present value budget constraint *per se*. They used the absolute value version of equation (7.8):

$$\lim_{T\to\infty}(1+\rho)^{-T} D_T = D_0 + \lim_{T\to\infty} \sum_{t=1}^{T} P_t (1+\rho)^{-t} \qquad (7.11)$$

where D is the public debt and P is the primary balance. Their null hypothesis is therefore the absolute value version of equation (7.9):

$$\lim_{T\to\infty} (1+\rho)^{-T} D_T = 0 \qquad (7.12)$$

and to frame the alternative hypothesis they selected a class of unsustainable fiscal policies, in the sense that they did not meet constraint (7.11), so the discounted value of debt has a finite positive limit, that is:

$$\lim_{T\to\infty} D_T (1+\rho)^{-T} = A > 0 \qquad (7.13)$$

Substituting from (7.13) into (7.11) gives:

$$D_0 = -\lim_{T\to\infty} \sum_{t=1}^{T} P_t (1+\rho)^{-t} + A \tag{7.14}$$

And, finally:

$$D_t = -E_t \sum_{i=1}^{\infty} P_{t+i} (1+\rho)^{-i} + A(1+\rho)^t + \varepsilon_t \tag{7.15}$$

where E is the expectation operator and ε a regression disturbance. From (7.15) the null hypothesis $A=0$ can be put to test.

Hamilton and Flavin only consider the interest bearing share of the debt and measure it at market values in real terms. Strictly speaking, their debt measure is neither net nor gross as they take into account one category of government assets (gold holdings). The deficit measure is adjusted accordingly (mainly to include capital gains/losses and to get figures in real value terms). Based on these data, Hamilton and Flavin use a Dickey–Fuller test for unit roots to check for the stationarity of P_t. Having rejected non-stationarity, they note that for any stationary process for (ε_t, $E_t [\Sigma(1+\rho)^{-t}P_t]$), when $A=0$, D_t will be stationary, whereas for $A>0$, D_t will not be stationary, they apply the Dickey–Fuller test to D_t and reject the hypothesis of non-stationarity. They also run other tests based on the direct estimation of equation (7.15), making different assumptions about the information set underlying the formation of expectations about future surpluses. Also these tests point to consistency between the data and solvency as defined on the basis of a present-value budget constraint.

This exercise has three main drawbacks: (1) the use of a very small sample (annual data for the period 1960–84) is not suited for the implementation of the asymptotic tests used by the authors; (2) the assumption of a constant interest rate may imply a misspecification of the equation; and (3) the choice of a very specific alternative hypothesis to $\lim_{T\to\infty} (1+\rho)^{-T} D_T = 0$, namely non-stochastic violation of the solvency condition ($\lim_{T\to\infty} (1+\rho)^{-T} D_T = A$), may have a bearing on the results of the tests.

Concerning the first point, it must be noted that Haug (1990) reaches conclusions similar to those of Hamilton and Flavin using quarterly data for the period 1960–87. As to the other two points, however, Wilcox (1989), using the same data set as Hamilton and Flavin, shows that if the hypothesis of a constant interest rate is relaxed and if stochastic violations to the solvency condition are considered as well, then the hypothesis that the intertemporal budget constraint holds must be rejected.

Other similar studies show mixed results which seem to depend on the statistical procedures adopted[174] and on the data set used.[175] This variability of results is to be expected since the data samples are usually small[176] and the procedures applied have low power in this case, becoming especially sensitive to the specification of the hypotheses to be tested. It should also be considered that the profile of market value time series differs significantly from the one of nominal value data; this highlights further the relevance of the issue of data definition examined in the third section.

While certainly relevant and appropriate for the issue they explicitly address, from the point of view of policy evaluation, these studies have the obvious limitation that solvency within a sample period says nothing about solvency in the future. The prospective path of the debt ratio may be very different from the one already recorded, not only for regime changes, but also because exogenous factors (like demographic trends) may change the implication of current regimes for the public finances. Moreover, being based on equation (7.9), an ever rising debt (or debt to GDP ratio) may pass the tests proposed in these studies for the assessment of sustainability. The methodological difficulties encountered by a proper implementation of the tests further reduce the attractiveness of the approach.

5. LONG-TERM PROJECTIONS AND SYNTHETIC INDICATORS BASED ON NATIONAL ACCOUNTS

5.1 Long-term Projections

Long-term fiscal projections were carried out as early as in 1942 when a 30-year estimate of social expenditure in the UK was included in the Beveridge Report. However, it is since the mid-1980s, when it became apparent that western countries were experiencing major changes in their demographic structure, that an increasing number of studies have examined the long-term prospects for public budgets.

These studies usually focus on those public expenditure items which are particularly dependent on population age structure (such as pension, health, education) seeking to assess the likely change of their impact on GDP. Some studies go further and develop projections for the primary balance and estimates of the adjustments required to ensure budgetary sustainability in the sense of a stable undiscounted debt to GDP ratio. The stability of the ratio is to be achieved either at the level recorded at the beginning of the simulation period, in line with the first definition proposed by Blanchard *et al.* (1990), or at some other level. The latter solution is more in line with Domar's (1944) approach to the issue.

The most basic approach provides estimates of the effects of demographic changes on public expenditure under the assumption that age-related per capita expenditure levels remain constant in real terms or in per capita GDP terms at the initial level over the projection period. In other words, it is assumed that present standards of transfers and services are maintained for all population age groups and that there is no behavioural response from governments or households to demographic changes and their budgetary effects.

It should be stressed that estimates combining data on per capita expenditures for different age groups and for different budgetary items with demographic projections are only indicative measures of the likely effects of demographic change on public expenditure, since they do not take all relevant effects of demographic changes into account.[177] Mechanical estimates are based on the implicit assumption that the marginal cost of providing services to a smaller or a larger number of individuals in each age group in the future will be equal to the present average cost of these services.[178] In other words, it is assumed that there are no economies or diseconomies of scale in the production of public services. This assumption is surely implausible over relatively short periods, because of time-lags in the adjustment of inputs to changes in demand for public services.

Mechanical estimates implicitly assume that demographic changes do not modify present age-related per capita expenditure levels, while they can actually affect them through many different channels. Demographic changes can influence the cost of inputs used in services (e.g. a relative shortage of young workers may increase the cost of public services employing them)[179] and the demand for some services (e.g. a reduction in the number of children per household may, in the long run, increase the demand for elderly care).[180] They can also affect productivity trends, wage rates and saving ratios.[181]

Economies/diseconomies of scale and the effects of demographic changes on the level of age-related per capita expenditure are not usually taken into account in expenditure projections. While the failure to consider economies and diseconomies of scale may compromise short period estimates, that concerning system-wide effects may affect long period estimates. Moreover, it should be stressed that demographic change is just one of the several factors affecting public expenditure dynamics. The contribution of mechanical estimates of the effects of demographic changes to the assessment of the prospects for public expenditure is therefore necessarily limited.

Once non-demographic factors are taken into consideration, there is no reason why age-related per capita expenditure levels remain constant in real terms or in per capita GDP terms on the initial level over the projection period. Standards of transfers and services will change over time.

While several economic, political and social factors can obviously affect the dynamics of per capita transfers and services, the studies examining the prospects of age-related expenditure usually focus only on two rather specific factors: the effects of changes introduced in legislation, but not yet embodied in present expenditure profiles, and the continuation of structural expenditure trends. These two factors are considered because they are consistent with a constant policy approach, while there is usually no attempt to predict the effects of changes in behaviours and policies.

The effects of changes introduced in legislation, but not yet embodied in present expenditure profiles, are particularly relevant for pension expenditure projections, since pension eligibility and transfer ratios can change considerably over time due to the maturation of schemes, that is, the process of adjustment of all pensions to present retirement rules.[182] On the one hand, pension coverage extensions and benefit improvements usually only produce their full effects on the two ratios after many decades. On the other, quite often reforms curtailing pension benefits are implemented gradually and only display their full effects a long time later (OECD, 1988b). Therefore, the assumption that age-related per capita expenditure levels remain constant is not equivalent to a constant policy assumption. It implies that all the effects of changes introduced in legislation are reflected in present age-related per capita expenditure levels.

The continuation of structural expenditure trends (i.e. the assumption that some non-demographic factors relevant in the past will continue to affect expenditure dynamics in the future) is especially relevant for health care expenditure projections. In several countries the health sector has for long periods recorded a price deflator substantially higher than the GDP deflator and a tendency towards a continuous increase in per capita consumption.[183]

Projections integrating the mechanical effects of demographic changes with estimates of some additional factors influencing pension and health expenditure were produced by the IMF in 1986 for the seven main western economies (Heller *et al.*, 1986). The growth in the number of pensioners and the dynamics of the average pension were projected taking the maturity of the different systems into consideration. As to health expenditure, the study outlined a scenario in which average medical costs were rising more rapidly than productivity.

The overall impact of ageing populations on government budget was also examined in the studies carried out by OECD in 1995–96 (see Leibfritz *et al.*, 1995, Roseweare *et al.*, 1996 and OECD, 1996) and by the European Commission in 1997 (see Franco and Munzi, 1999). Growing awareness of population ageing has also led to a substantial increase in the resources devoted to national long-term public expenditure projections. However, projections for all the main public expenditure items are available for only some countries.[184]

The reliability of this type of estimates clearly depends on detailed and updated knowledge of the institutional setting of the countries examined. In this respect, the fact that national projections are not always available is regrettable. Furthermore, since these studies often rely on national accounts budgetary categories and on gross debt measures, they often leave unexplored the grey area between deficit estimates and debt dynamics deriving from changes in the asset side of general government balance sheets. Finally, given the partial equilibrium nature of the exercise, a larger role assigned to sensitivity analysis would be a welcome development in future exercises.

5.2 Synthetic Indicators

Synthetic indicators of the outcomes of long-term projections have been proposed to 'summarise their results through a single number which comes as a simple metric, allowing for a simple interpretation of the result' (Blanchard *et al.*, 1990, p. 32). In general such indicators are based on long-term projections and meet the same difficulties as the exercises already examined: their quality ultimately relies on the projections on which they are based.

Buiter (1985) suggests using the difference between the current primary deficit and the one (p^*) that would allow a constant net worth to GDP ratio (w):

$$p^* - p_t = [(\gamma - \rho)/(1+\gamma)]w_t - p_t \tag{7.16}$$

Apart from the difficulty of obtaining reliable data on net worth, the main problem with this indicator is that the value it takes at any given time says nothing regarding the implication of current policies for its future values. A negative (positive) value signalling a growing (decreasing) net worth ratio now may nevertheless be consistent with a prospective decrease (increase) of the ratio as the effects of current policies on deficits gradually unfold in the future.

A forward-looking perspective is taken by the tax-gap indicator proposed by Blanchard *et al.* (1990). This is based on their first condition for sustainability, which is that the debt ratio eventually comes back to its initial level over a period to be specified. Using projections of primary expenditure (G) and assuming constant interest and growth rates, a tax rate is computed (τ^*) that, if kept constant, allows this condition to be satisfied:

$$\tau_n^* = (\rho - \gamma)(1 - e^{-(\rho-\gamma)n})\int_0^n G_s e^{(\rho-\gamma)(-s)} ds + d_0 \tag{7.17}$$

The difference between such a tax rate and the current one ($\tau_n^* - \tau$) is the proposed sustainability index. A positive value indicates that a correction is needed to prevent the debt ratio from rising over the period considered. Higher values denote the need for larger corrections. The indicator has an intuitive interpretation and one which is in the spirit of Domar's approach (that sustainability is to be judged with respect to the tax rate implied by a given policy).[185]

The main shortcoming of the tax gap are in the arbitrary nature of the choices required about the time horizon (n) and the target debt to GDP ratio at the end of the period (d_0). Moreover, it should be considered that the simple and intuitive metric adopted by the tax gap does not immediately translate into policy indications. For example, a positive gap signals some budgetary pressures in the future, but says nothing about their timing. Over the period taken into consideration both the deficit and the debt ratios may experience 'unsustainable' peaks.

A synthetic indicator along the lines of the tax gap was also employed by Delbecque and Bogaert (1994) who carried out an analysis for Belgium for the period up to 2050 and calculated the 'recommended primary surplus', defined as the level of the primary surplus that would guarantee the long-term sustainability of fiscal policy, given the actual pension expenditure projections.[186] The recommended primary surplus allows pension expenditure increases to be fully offset by a decline in interest payments caused by a fast reduction in the debt to GDP ratio.

6. GENERATIONAL ACCOUNTS

'To assess the fiscal burden current generations are placing on future generations' (Auerbach *et al.*, 1991, p. 55), generational accounting uses long-term projections of the variables appearing in the present value budget constraint in absolute values:[187]

$$-D_t = \Sigma_{s=t+1,\infty} [P_s \Pi_{j=t+1,s} (1+r_j)^{-1}] \qquad (7.18)$$

Being based on long-term projections of budgetary items, generational accounts are subject to the same criticism as the methodologies examined in the previous section. In addition some problems specific to generational accounts can be identified.

In generational accounts the variables appearing in (7.18) are grouped in a different manner with respect to standard national accounts presentation. The primary surplus can be disaggregated into its components and there is no single way to operate. While the standard accounting convention is simply to distinguish between revenues and expenditures, other groupings may be preferred depending on the aim of the analysis. In generational accounts government consumption (C) is separated from the other components of the primary balance (O); the latter are then grouped according to the generation which pays them or benefits from them:

$$P_s = \Sigma_{i=0,M} O_{s,s-i} - C_s \tag{7.19}$$

where the terms $O_{s,s-i}$ represent the net payments to government made at time s by the generation born at time $s-i$; M is the maximum length of life so that payments made by all generations alive at time s are considered. By substituting (7.19) into (7.18) we get:

$$\begin{aligned} D_t &= \Sigma_{s=t+1,\infty} [(\Sigma_{i=0,M} O_{s,s-i} - C_s) \Pi_{j=t+1,s} (1+r_j)^{-1}] \\ &= \Sigma_{s=t+1,\infty} [(\Sigma_{i=0,M} O_{s,s-i}) \Pi_{j=t+1,s} (1+r_j)^{-1}] - \Sigma_{s=t+1,\infty} \\ &\quad [C_s \Pi_{j=t+1,s} (1+r_j)^{-1}] \end{aligned} \tag{7.20}$$

and, separating generations born prior to time t from those born thereafter:

$$\begin{aligned} D_t &= \Sigma_{i=0,M} [\Sigma_{s=t+1,t-i+M} O_{s,t-i} \Pi_{j=t+1,s} (1+r_j)^{-1}] + \Sigma_{i=1,\infty} [\Sigma_{s=t+i,t+i+M} \\ &\quad O_{s,t+i} \Pi_{j=t+1,s} (1+r_j)^{-1}] - \Sigma_{s=t+1,\infty} [C_s \Pi_{j=t+1,s} (1+r_j)^{-1}] \\ &= \Sigma_{i=0,M} N_{t,t-i} + \Sigma_{i=1,\infty} N_{t,t+i} - \Sigma_{s=t+1,\infty} [C_s \Pi_{j=t+1,s} (1+r_j)^{-1}] \end{aligned} \tag{7.21}$$

where $N_{t,k}$ represents the value at time t of the net payments to government to be made by a generation born at time k.

Equation (7.21) corresponds to the standard presentation of generational accounting (Auerbach *et al.*, 1991, 1992).[188] Given present debt (D_t), forecasts for future government consumption (the third term on the right-hand side (rhs)) and future net payments by existing generations based on current policies (the first term on the rhs), equation (7.19) can be solved for the present value of net payments required from future generations (the second term on the rhs). The amount that needs to be paid by each future generation is assumed constant up to an adjustment for real productivity growth. It is then compared with the amount projected to be paid by the generation born at time t (based on current policies) in order to signal a potential generational imbalance in fiscal policy.

The identification of the empirical counterparts of the theoretical variables appearing in equation (7.21) is a crucial issue. For example, in the standard presentation of generational accounts net wealth is used rather than gross debt and, since net wealth is measured by means of capitalized net interests, the problem of the appropriate treatment of non-interest bearing assets arises.

The quality of long-term projections is also essential. The current expenditure level for each generation remains stable in the future. This disregards the future effects of legislative changes already introduced, economies of scale in the production of public services, the likely effects of demographic developments on relative prices, and work, consumption and investment decisions. Moreover, as pointed out for standard long-term projections, the estimation of public expenditure attributed to each age group is problematic. Expenditure profiles can be estimated with reference to different age groups, budgetary items, and definitions of public sector. This may substantially limit the comparability of the results obtained for different countries.[189]

Another relevant issue concerns the grouping of primary balance components, the choice to classify non-age related expenditure as government consumption thus excluding the benefits (often delayed) they produce from the computation of net payments by each generation is not unquestionable.[190] The problem is made worse by the fact that different rules are used to produce future values of what is classified as government consumption and what is instead labelled as net payments.[191]

Moreover, generational grouping largely determines the result.[192] Suppose that the economic and demographic conditions are stable and that current policies have led to $D_t > 0$. Generational accounts apply the intertemporal budget constraint from time $t+1$; thus payments by generations alive from time $t+1$ on will have to be sufficient not only to repay past debt but also to balance new government consumption: such payments are split so that all those already alive prior to time $t+1$ will keep on paying according to previous rules (i.e. insufficiently to avoid new debt accumulation), while the others will have to pay the balance. By definition this is more than their fair share.

Summarizing, the main problem specific to generational accounting[193] is the upward bias its methodology induces in the assessment of the effort needed to ensure solvency. Given the existence of debt, the imposition of an intertemporal budget constraint implies it will have to be repaid. So we know from the start that an effort is needed for solvency. What is of relevance is an assessment of the effort needed. In generational accounts this assessment is problematic: (a) the special treatment of government consumption introduces an upward bias; (b) so do the different rules applying to present and future generations and especially the fact that future effects of legislative changes already introduced are not taken into account; and (c) the estimation of present net worth value is not unproblematic.

From a policy point of view, much as in the case of the tax gap, it is also relevant that the synthetic indicators derived from generational accounts do not provide information about the timing of the effects of demographic changes. Moreover, its results are not intuitive, which may hamper their use for policy objectives, and are very sensitive to assumptions about the determination of private consumption, productivity growth and discount rates.[194]

7. CONCLUSIONS

Our analysis has highlighted three main problems, respectively concerning the definition of sustainability, the choice of relevant variables, and the measurement of sustainability.

- *Definition of sustainability* – So far economic literature has not defined a unique benchmark against which to assess sustainability. Moreover, the definitions proposed are based on partial equilibrium analysis and therefore point to necessary but not sufficient conditions for sustainability. For example, in Domar's framework, in order to be sustainable the debt to GDP ratio must be stable, but not any stable level is necessarily sustainable. To assess the maximum sustainable debt level we should take the interaction of public finance and the economy into account.
- *Definition of variables* – The lack of a unique theoretical benchmark contributes to legitimating a multiplicity of statistical criteria for the definition of public debt and deficit. Furthermore, data availability constrains the degree to which the theoretical variables appearing in the models can be correctly measured or proxied in practice. Sometimes mutually inconsistent measures of debt and deficit are used.
- *Computation of sustainability indicators* – All indicators are based on long-term projections of budgetary trends which are necessarily uncertain and whose modelling is, moreover, still very simplistic. Long-term budgetary developments are determined by a multiplicity of interacting factors (e.g. changes in relative prices and family structure). However, existing projections usually take into account only demographic developments and rely on overly restrictive assumptions concerning the other factors (e.g. constant age-related expenditure profiles are projected to the future). Synthetic indicators have the additional disadvantage to provide measures of future imbalances that do not immediately translate into policy prescriptions. Moreover,

their computation may require arbitrary assumptions. These critiques particularly apply to generational accounting projections and summary measures. With respect to traditional techniques, however, generational accounting allows estimates of the distributive implications across generations of changes in budgetary policies and considers the effects of policy changes that do not affect the conventional deficit.

In devising fiscal rules for EMU, when confronted with these difficulties, European Union countries adopted a pragmatic approach. The Treaty of Maastricht defines sustainability as non-violation of arbitrarily predetermined parametric standards; it defines the relevant variables taking into account the need to ensure comparability of national statistics and to allow a regular surveillance process. However, the Treaty and the Stability and Growth Pact do not deal with the development of sustainability indicators. They introduce a complex procedure ensuring monitoring of budgetary trends over the medium term, but do not envisage any long-term control.

As pointed out in the second section, compliance with these rules and guidelines ensures sustainability. If EU countries stick to the close-to-balance guideline, they will converge to equilibrium low debt levels (significantly below the 60 per cent threshold). Some countries might even converge to negative debt levels. One may question whether a theory-based benchmark, if available, would have implied these results. However, this framework does not make sustainability indicators unnecessary. Even after the transition to the medium-term targets has been completed, compliance with the rules may require continuous policy action. Due to, *inter alia*, demographic changes, compliance over the medium term does not necessarily ensure compliance over the long term. There is a need for indicators highlighting prospectives deviations and measuring their size and timing.

The technique of long-term projections is still relatively new. As we pointed out in the fifth section, the first systematic attempts were produced in the 1980s. Although largely unsatisfactory from various respects, the available indicators have been extensively used by international organizations to highlight prospective budgetary risks and by national authorities to guide the adjustment of expenditure programmes to the new demographic conditions. In spite of a methodology which is still rather rough around the edges, the policy indications were broadly correct. They contributed to the significant reduction of prospective budgetary imbalances.

Further efforts are obviously needed to guide budgetary policy more effectively.

1. In order to improve the quality of projections, it is necessary to invest in better databases. The statistics underlying several studies are often inadequate both at the micro and the macro level. Age-related expenditure profiles should refer to detailed classifications of expenditure programmes and to microsimulation studies. The net asset position of general government needs to be more comprehensively assessed.
2. In spite of the unavoidable uncertainty of projections, indicators should consider long periods of time. This is necessary in order to avoid the risk of being confronted with the necessity to undertake large and abrupt adjustments which might turn out to be politically unsustainable.
3. Indicators should have a transparent interpretation in order to be viable as policy tools. This is also necessary to warrant the effectiveness of multilateral surveillance and peer pressure in fostering the adoption of needed corrections.
4. International institutions have largely contributed to the development of long-term budgetary indicators. However, accurate budgetary projections can be produced more easily at the national level, since the wealth of data and institutional knowledge available locally cannot be achieved by international studies. In order to ensure both the cross-country comparability of estimates and their quality, better cooperation is needed between national and international institutions. This is particularly relevant in the context of EMU.
5. Projections should be carried out on a regular basis. Experience shows that prospective imbalances can vary quite significantly over short periods due to policy changes and other factors. Revisions have a learning-by-doing advantage and may reduce the margins for creative accounting.
6. Policy makers should rely on more than one indicator. While standard long-term projections can provide indications about the size and the timing of prospective imbalances, generational accounting is more apt to evaluate the generational distribution of the ensuing burden.
7. Finally, indicators should be capable of considering different challenges. In addition to demographic trends, which have already been extensively considered, the risks related to high debt levels and unfavourable revenue developments should be taken into account.

Clearly, the higher the debt, the stronger the sensitivity of the budget balance to monetary shocks. The usual assumption of a constant interest rate overlooks the risk that a prolonged increase in rates may move public finances onto an unsustainable track. A more systematic use of sensitivity analysis, based on a distribution of interest rate shocks, would be useful.

With the abolition of tariffs and barriers, the increasing internationalization of markets and of the economies, direct taxation (personal, capital and financial taxation) and indirect taxation (goods and services) among European countries have come under the pressure of increasing competition. Tax bases are eroded as a result of their reallocation to other countries. Tax competition affects public finances also indirectly via its effects on investment, growth and employment. There is a risk that these developments may hamper the significance of available indicators which are based essentially on expenditure projections (revenues are usually assumed constant as a share of GDP). Greater research efforts are needed to integrate the revenue side of the budget in sustainability analyses.

8. Fiscal federalism*

1. INTRODUCTION

During the 1990s, the degree of fiscal decentralization in EU member states increased: a process to enlarge the responsibilities of local governments in the management of public expenditure and taxation was set in motion in countries not organized on a federal basis.[195] During the same years, budget rules aimed at guaranteeing the soundness of the public finances of EU member states and ensuring margins for counter-cyclical policies were defined and introduced at the European level. These rules are based on the consolidated budgets of general governments. The existence of different levels of government is not taken into account.

The interaction between these two developments has not yet been adequately examined. This chapter proposes a first analysis of the compatibility between the degree of decentralization decided at national level and the budget rules introduced at European level.

In highlighting the allocative advantages of local autonomy, traditional theories of fiscal federalism stress the need to guarantee both control of national public finances and the possibility of carrying out counter-cyclical policies at the national level. To that end, the introduction of limits on transfers from the central government and on recourse to market financing by local governments is necessary. These constraints must be flexible, in relation to cyclical events and to the need to spread the burden of public-sector investment over several generations.

These theoretical indications have been confirmed by the legislation adopted in many countries. When regulating the activities of local governments, it is unusual to rely solely on market action, that is, penalization in terms of higher interest rates, which would affect the most indebted governments. Variations of the so-called golden rule are often applied. Despite placing constraints on indebtedness, the possibility to compensate possible overshoots over several financial years is almost always permitted: on an annual basis the constraints apply *ex ante* but not *ex post*.

*Fabrizio Balassone and Daniele Franco, 'Fiscal Federalism and the Stability and Growth Pact: A Difficult Union', *Journal of Public Finance and Public Choice*, 1999, XVII (2–3): 135–63.

The launch of the Monetary Union posed a problem for fiscal regulation at the European level. The solutions adopted in several countries with federal structures are more flexible than the rules defined in the Maastricht Treaty and in the Stability and Growth Pact: the rules are defined in relation to numerical parameters that also have to be observed *ex post*; flexibility is envisaged only in connection with exceptional cyclical events or others beyond the control of governments; a monitoring procedure was introduced that provides for the formulation of multi-year financial programmes and the possibility formally to recommend corrective measures during the course of the year and to impose monetary sanctions in cases of default.

These rules apply to national states; there is no reference to local governments in the Union documents. Although the operations of all levels of government are relevant to compliance with the regulations, which refer to general government, in fact it is the central government that is responsible for compliance and for paying any penalties in the event of violation. Without suitable regulation, local governments that have the possibility to take on debt could free-ride on the back of central governments. More generally, a potential conflict exists between the constraints placed on national public finances and the flexibility allowed to decentralized public finances.

In those countries that are already organized on a federal basis and in those in which reforms are underway to increase the degree of decentralization, the need to make national rules conform to the new European context is strong. The level of domestic flexibility must be made compatible with the lower level envisaged in the Stability and Growth Pact; the asymmetry between the responsibilities assigned to the central government and those assigned to regional and local governments must be corrected.

The analysis conducted in this chapter demonstrates the difficulty of reconciling full enjoyment of the allocative benefits of fiscal decentralization with full utilization of the margins for counter-cyclical policies offered by compliance with the Pact. In considering possible solutions, particular attention is addressed to the solution outlined in Italy in the Domestic Stability Pact; it is pointed out that this solution will need to be improved.

The second section of this chapter briefly examines the propositions which have gained a wide consensus in the literature on fiscal federalism, comparing theoretical precepts with the practical solutions adopted in countries with federal structures. The third section first summarizes the European regulations on public-sector budgets and then examines their implications for regulating the relations among the various levels of government at national level. The fourth section analyses the solution adopted by Italy in the context of increasing decentralization of responsibility for expenditure and revenue.

2. FISCAL FEDERALISM AND BUDGET CONSTRAINTS

The current structure of national states is the result of a long process of aggregation and disaggregation of different jurisdictions, which over time have yielded some fiscal prerogatives while maintaining others. In recent decades a clear tendency to decentralize responsibility for expenditure and taxation has emerged in many countries (Ter-Minassian, 1997; Wildasin, 1997).

Economic theory also offers reasons favouring decentralized forms of government. Responsibility for the management of services should be entrusted to that level of government whose jurisdiction comes closer to the area in which the services are provided. In this way, supply could be adjusted to the needs and preferences of the citizens of each region, thus allowing closer monitoring of the conduct of elected representatives and competition among local governments to the benefit of citizens.[196] The expenditure functions assigned to each level of government affect the allocation of sources of tax receipts and financial relations between central and local governments.

This section examines the implications, in terms of instruments for controlling indebtedness in situations of decentralized finance, of two types of federation: the first type resembles a union of sovereign states (similar to the institutional structure of the European Union); the second is closer to the prescriptions of economic theories on fiscal federalism.[197] The solutions adopted by the leading federally structured countries are also analysed.

2.1 Budget Constraints in a Situation of Radical Federalism

Let us consider a situation in which local governments enjoy absolute autonomy in matters of public expenditure, taxation and recourse to debt. In this context, the stability of monetary and financial conditions represents a public good to which all local governments contribute by maintaining sustainable budget positions. There is an incentive for each local government to exploit the benefits accruing from the discipline of others without itself complying with the rules (free-riding). This creates a double cost for the other entities: the free-rider's excessive indebtedness can put pressure on interest rates to rise; it can also result in bankruptcies requiring bail-outs.[198] Before all else, we must ask if market regulations can avoid these kinds of situation. For regulations to be effective, certain conditions have to be met (Lane, 1993):

- no government body should have privileged access to the market;
- the market must have access to all the information necessary to evaluate the financial reliability of each body;
- the bailing-out of troubled bodies must not be allowed;
- mechanisms to ensure that entities react to market signals must exist.

These conditions are both very strict and unlikely to obtain simultaneously. In particular, the reaction times of decentralized fiscal authorities may be excessively long, for example when administrators work to short time horizons. It is also difficult to ensure absolute credibility of the ban on bail-outs. Finally, evaluation of the financial situation of a body could be hindered by 'creative accounting'.

Consequently, it may be useful to supplement market rules with the means to control the overall indebtedness of a federation's members. Excluding administrative controls, which require local governments to obtain prior approval of their financial strategies from central governments and which by their very nature are incompatible with a federal structure, two solutions may be considered: (1) collective management of indebtedness; and (2) the introduction of rules (balanced budget, prefixed ceiling for the total deficit, golden rule) and sanctions for non-compliance. With cooperative solutions, all levels of government must be involved in formulating the objectives of economic policy and be responsible for their attainment. However, these solutions do not eliminate the incentive for opportunistic behaviour. Moreover, cooperation may require protracted negotiations, especially when a large number of bodies is involved, to the detriment of the effectiveness of economic policy.

The introduction of rules also raises various problems, such as the credibility of their rigorous application, in particular for the management of bail-outs, and the possibility of efficient monitoring to avoid forms of 'creative accounting'. For these reasons an eclectic approach appears useful, one that combines rules with forms of cooperation based on peer pressure. Such an approach must in any case keep account of the need to allow margins of flexibility in order to offset cyclical effects on the budget without adopting pro-cyclical policies and to deal with exceptional circumstances that impact on the recourse to debt.[199]

Considerations of tax-smoothing and intergenerational equity may justify the funding of certain activities through limited recourse to debt.

The problem is especially acute in the case of public-sector investment. The realization of major projects requires a substantial temporary increase in total expenditure; without recourse to debt, this implies a peak in taxation, the intensity of which may lead to the projects being abandoned. In addition, since the benefits of the project may be spread over a long period of time, financing it through taxation would lead to an unfair division of the burden among generations.[200]

2.2 The Economic Theory of Fiscal Federalism

The literature on fiscal federalism is very extensive. A complete survey is beyond the scope of this chapter and we will therefore limit ourselves to summarizing the key propositions on which there seems to be broad agreement.

The main advantage of a federal structure is increased efficiency resulting from the decentralization of allocative functions. On the other hand, a central government can perform the functions of redistribution and macroeconomic stabilization more efficiently.[201]

The crucial element in the production of public goods is the territorial range of the benefits: each public service should be produced and financed according to the preferences of the citizens residing in the area that enjoys the benefits. This area may coincide with national boundaries or it may be limited to a particular region. The fact that political processes are needed to disclose the citizens' preferences justifies the existence of several administrative jurisdictions.[202] The redistribution function could also be interpreted as a local public good (Pauly, 1973), with each community being allowed to decide its own level. However, the analogy with the allocative function no longer holds if the effects on the citizens' choice of domicile are considered: where capital and labour are highly mobile, significant differences in redistribution levels may cause 'the rich to flee the poor and the poor to chase the rich' (Musgrave and Musgrave, 1984, p. 514).

A centralized authority for stabilization is justified by the risk that the impact of built-in stabilizers and expansionary or restrictive measures decided at local level may be diminished or annulled if jurisdictions are closely integrated in economic terms.[203] The coordination of decentralized stabilization policies may also be hindered by incentives for local authorities to behave as free-riders. By virtue of the functions assigned to it, central government should have access to the tax bases that are more mobile, more sensitive to cyclical factors and less uniformly distributed.

A rigorous interpretation of this criterion would allocate the lion's share of tax bases to central government. Progressive income tax, capital transfer and gift duties affect the distribution of income and wealth. Moreover, income tax is particularly sensitive to the cycle, as is sales tax. Finally, corporate income tax should be allocated to the central government so as to avoid distortions in choosing where to locate productive activities.[204] Local governments would retain only property tax and public utility charges:[205] the former affect tax bases that are not very mobile; the latter permit full application of the benefit principle. This implies that the revenue sources allocated to local governments may be insufficient to finance the expenditure relevant to the functions assigned to them. It may become necessary to make transfers to decentralized bodies or allow them a share of the central government's tax revenues. If qualitative and quantitative standards affecting the local production of public services are imposed at national level, the need for forms of financial support may increase.

Separating the responsibility for expenditure and its financing weakens the cost–benefit relationship associated with public services, reducing the allocative advantages of a decentralized system.[206] In addition, transfers not subject to predefined limits do not encourage efficient management;[207] central government's financial support to local administrations has often been cited as one of the factors underlying the excessive growth in public expenditure.[208] In some circumstances, increases in local government spending can jeopardize macroeconomic stabilization measures carried out by central governments.

Controls on the managerial efficiency of local authorities and limits on transfers and revenue-sharing are necessary. Just as controlling the indebtedness of local governments in conditions of 'radical federalism' cannot be rigid, nor can controls on transfers. There must be margins to offset the effects of cyclical swings or exceptional events on the budget and to permit tax-smoothing measures. One possibility is to allow recourse to debt, but this raises the problems already indicated.

2.3 Fiscal Federalism in Practice

Reference to western nations provides a wide range of arrangements for the allocation of expenditure and revenue functions and for controls on local government indebtedness. At the end of the 1980s, the share of central government outlays in total public-sector spending ranged from 41 per cent in Canada to 95 per cent in Paraguay (Ahmad *et al.*, 1997). The allocation of expenditure functions among the different levels of government partly reflects theoretical indications: in several cases the territorial range of the benefits seems to be the criterion (most countries assign defence, foreign affairs and international trade to central government but local transportation, firefighting and city police services to local governments.) Central governments are generally responsible for redistribution. However, responsibility for particularly important expenditure functions, such as health care and education, is not predominantly assigned to any given level of government.

The contribution of local governments' own revenues to total public-sector revenue also varies greatly: in the early 1990s, in the industrialized countries, it ranged from 3 per cent in the Netherlands to 49 per cent in Canada (Norregaard, 1997). The solutions adopted are often based on theoretical indications: in general, property taxes are assigned to local governments, while corporate taxation is assigned to central government (in relation to the different degree of mobility of the respective tax bases); income and sales taxes are assigned to central government, on account of their sensitivity to the cycle and of the redistributive function of income tax.

There are three means of covering any imbalances between local governments' revenues and spending: sharing in central governments' tax revenues; transfers; and indebtedness. The importance of controlling local government spending is confirmed by widespread dissatisfaction with the utilization of funds transferred from central governments (Ter-Minassian, 1997): varying kinds of organizational structures have been criticized, from 'conditional' transfers for health care and transportation utilized in Italy, to unconditional transfers for Medicaid and support of large families in the United States, to transfers based on full reimbursement of expenses for health care and higher education in Canada.

Recourse to debt is generally permitted. The industrialized countries rarely rely on market regulation alone; Canada is the only country that does not have provisions to limit the provinces' debt or other central government controls.[209] Brazil had relied on market regulation in the past, but in 1996 it introduced controls following the rapid accumulation of debt by local governments. The market model was also not effective in Argentina. In Australia and the Scandinavian countries, central and local governments cooperate in defining the objectives for national public finance. Predetermined regulations are in force in the United States, Spain and Switzerland. Germany utilizes a combination of rules and cooperation. The rules generally limit the total deficit, permit indebtedness for certain objectives only or set a ceiling on expenditure for interest payable. The constraints on indebtedness generally apply *ex ante*: possible overshoots may be compensated for in subsequent financial years.[210] Direct administrative controls are particularly widespread in non-federal states.

3. EUROPEAN TAX REGULATIONS AND THEIR IMPLICATIONS FOR NATIONAL LEGISLATION

3.1 European Balance Sheet Regulations

The model of European Union created by the Treaty of Maastricht is similar to the radical federalist system described above: member states have retained virtually total sovereignty in questions of expenditure and taxation.

A simple formalization of the no-rules risk

The risk of free-riding posed by a Monetary Union without budgetary rules[211] can be represented in terms of simple games such as 'prisoner's dilemma' or 'hawks and doves'.

For the sake of simplicity, let us suppose there are only two member states (I and J) and that the game is perfectly symmetrical. The tax regime of each state produces a benefit (B) and carries a cost (C) – with $B > C$– and the benefits are divided equally between the two states, so that the outcome for each is $B - C$ provided both are cooperative. If one country is not cooperative it will incur no costs but will continue to receive its part of the benefits produced by the other's cooperation (with the result $B/2$), while the other country will reap $B/2 - C$ only. If both countries are not cooperative, each will obtain D (Figure 8.1).

If the order of possible outcomes is $B/2 > B - C > D > B/2 - \text{C}$ the game is a prisoner's dilemma. If the order of possible outcomes is $B/2 > B - C > B/2 - C > D$ the game is hawks and doves.

In the prisoner's dilemma the uncooperative strategy wins over the cooperative strategy (by guaranteeing a better outcome regardless of the other player's strategy) so that both countries have an incentive to adopt it. An equilibrium is thus the result of both countries adopting an uncooperative strategy. In hawks and doves there is no dominant strategy (non-cooperation gives higher utility when the other player is cooperative but not

		Country I	
		disciplined	undisciplined
Country J	undisciplined	D D	$B/2$ $B/2 - C$
	disciplined	$B/2 - C$ $B/2$	$B - C$ $B - C$

[a] The outcome obtained by Country J is shown beneath the diagonal dotted lines; tha obtained by Country I is shown above.

Figure 8.1 A general game at EU level[a]

		Country I	
		undisciplined	disciplined
Country J	undisciplined	$D - S$; $D - S$	$B/2 - C$; $B/2 - S$
	disciplined	$B/2 - S$; $B/2 - C$	$B - C$; $B - C$

Figure 8.2 A sanction is introduced

when he is not); the game yields two equilibria in pure strategies; both imply the defection of one or the other players.

In this context sanctions (S) may change the result to make the cooperative strategy dominant (Figure 8.2). In the example given, the sanction must comply with the stricter of the two restrictions: $S > D - (B/2 - C)$ and $S > -(B/2 - C)$.

The solution adopted

The problem of potential incentives for fiscal disobedience has been addressed at the European level and a series of rules, procedures and sanctions has been identified. Specifically, the Treaty of Maastricht sets quantitative ceilings for the government deficit and the public debt (respectively, 3 and 60 per cent of GDP) and envisages sanctions for wayward states; the Stability and Growth Pact approved in Amsterdam in June 1997 spelled out the objectives, control procedures and sanctions in greater detail.[212]

The Pact commits member states to pursue the medium-term objective of 'a budget close to balance or in surplus'. The European Council later clarified that this objective should be achieved over the duration of the economic cycle.[213] The Pact may thus be considered as an attempt to reconcile counter-cyclical policies and sound public finances.

Each state must define a budgetary target for the neutral phase of the cycle. In practical terms this means defining a cyclically adjusted budget balance[214] around which the unadjusted balance fluctuates by virtue of built-in stabilizers and discretionary measures, if any. The further this balance lies below the 3 per cent ceiling, the greater is the margin available for counter-cyclical policies without incurring excessive deficits.[215]

The choice of a medium-term target for the neutral phase of the cycle is dictated mainly by three factors: (1) the depth of expected recessions;

(2) the elasticity of the budget in relation to the cycle;[216] and (3) the size of the discretionary measures that may be taken to enhance the impact of built-in stabilizers. Past experience suggests that in the majority of EU countries a cyclically adjusted deficit of between 0 and 1 per cent of GDP should make it possible for built-in stabilizers to become fully operative without incurring a risk of overshooting the 3 per cent ceiling.[217]

Any state with an excessive deficit is required to adopt corrective measures according to a fixed timetable. Failure to comply brings sanctions. Specifically, the country must pay a non-interest-bearing deposit equal to 0.2 per cent of GDP plus one-tenth of the difference between the 3 per cent ceiling and the actual deficit (up to a maximum of 0.5 per cent of GDP). For each successive year that the deficit is judged to be excessive only the variable component of the sanction must be paid.[218] Should the excessive deficit persist, the deposit is converted into a fine after two years.[219]

To the monetary costs of sanctions must be added their consequences in terms of loss of reputation, which could translate into the inclusion of a higher risk premium in yields on government securities. The approach taken is therefore actually less flexible than the solutions adopted in some federally structured countries:

- the rules are defined on the basis of established numerical parameters;
- *ex post* compliance with the parameters is required each year;
- margins of flexibility are envisaged only in connection with exceptional cyclical events (established *ex ante* as a decline in GDP) or in any case events beyond the governments' control;
- no margin of deficit is specifically reserved for investment expenditure;[220]
- monitoring procedures are envisaged, starting with an announcement of targets in special multi-year programmes (whose consistency with the rules is evaluated) and continuing with a mid-year examination of public finances and *ex post* verification of results;
- peer pressure is strengthened by the European Council's power to make formal representations to governments of the need to adopt corrective measures during the year;
- non-compliance triggers the application of pre-established monetary sanctions;
- overshoots must be rapidly dealt with; sanctions increase as situations of excessive deficit persist.

The public nature of the whole procedure can contribute to the efficacy of the control exerted by the market on governments' budgetary policies.

3.2 Implications of National Legislative Frameworks

These rules apply to national governments. More specifically, compliance with budgetary rules is evaluated in respect of general government as defined in the European System of Accounts (ESA), that is, including central government, local governments and social security funds.[221] EU documents do not assign specific responsibilities to local governments.

While compliance with the rules involves the behaviour of all levels of government, it is effectively the central government that is held responsible and that bears the costs of non-compliance. It is, in fact, the European Council that ensures coordination of the general economic policies of the member states and it is a representative of each member state at ministerial level, authorized to commit the government of that member state to sit in the Council.[222] Obviously, each member state is free to define the necessary procedures and regulations to ensure coordination between different levels of government.

To understand the consequences of this asymmetry in a scenario in which decentralized levels of government enjoy some measure of independence in their budgetary policies, another example based on games may be helpful. Let us suppose that there is only one local government agency (LG) and that fiscal compliance by both local (LG) and central (CG) governments produces a benefit B at cost C, which is split equally between the two levels of government. Let us then suppose that the same benefit can be produced by CG's fiscal compliance alone, in which case, while the benefit is split equally between CG and LG, the cost C is borne wholly by CG. Lastly, let us suppose that LG's compliance does not produce any benefit by itself (the cost C of this fruitless effort is borne entirely by LG) and that the outcome when CG is non-compliant is D.

The possible outcomes for this game are shown in Figure 8.3. LG's dominant strategy is undisciplined – this situation can be interpreted as an extreme example of the incentive problem encountered in a federation in which the responsibilities for expenditure and taxation are separated. According to the arrangement of outcomes, CG may find it expedient either to comply or not to comply (the outcomes of the two equilibria resulting from CG's choice are indicated in bold type): the general government may turn out undisciplined, or CG may ensure compliance while LG plays the free-rider. If $D < [(B/2) - (C/2)]$, in other words if CG achieves a better outcome when both governments are disciplined than it would by being uncooperative, the situation is one in which some form of control over local government deficits could usefully be introduced. The introduction of a sanction H ($H > C$) in the event of LG being undisciplined would alter the matrix, as shown in Figure 8.4, making cooperation

Central government \ Local government	undisciplined	disciplined
undisciplined	$\mathbf{D}$; $\mathbf{D}$	D ; $D - C$
disciplined	$\mathbf{B}/2 - C$; $\mathbf{B}/2$	$B/2 - C/2$; $B/2 - C/2$

Figure 8.3 The federal game at national level

Central government \ Local government	undisciplined	disciplined
undisciplined	D ; $D - H$	D ; $D - C$
disciplined	$B/2 - C$; $B/2 - H$	$\mathbf{B/2 - C/2}$; $\mathbf{B/2 - C/2}$

Figure 8.4 The effects of control over local deficits

LG's dominant strategy and shifting the equilibrium to one of full cooperation (in bold type).

Monetary Union introduces two modifications with respect to the matrices in Figures 8.3 and 8.4:

1. the cost of fiscal cooperation increases because the definition of cooperation is narrower than that used at the national level (in terms of both sanctions and the reference period for defining cooperation);
2. the pay-off of strategies changes, on account of the externality generated by the choices of other member states.

Let us suppose that the new cost level is K ($K > C$) and that the externality is such as to determine an expected increase in the outcome achieved by CG in the event of non-cooperation (from D to $D + E$), while leaving

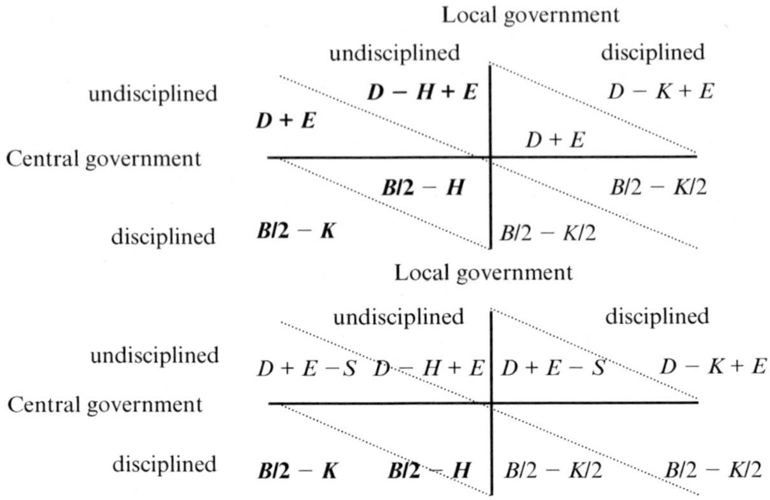

Figure 8.5 The federal game at national level after EMU (without 'European' sanctions)

unchanged the outcome achieved by CG in the event of cooperation.[223] The new game is shown in Figure 8.5.

In this environment the effect of national controls (the sanction H) may be cancelled by the higher cost of discipline (if $K>2H$, LG's dominant strategy becomes 'undisciplined'). Moreover, the combined effect of the higher cost of cooperation and of the changed outcome determined by externalities may render undisciplined the dominant strategy for CG too (if $D+E>B/2-K/2$). Again there are two possible equilibria (in bold type in Figure 8.5): general government may turn out to be undisciplined (a situation consistent with that described in Figure 8.1), or CG may ensure overall discipline while LG free-rides.

The sanctions envisaged in the Pact can be explained as a means of preventing some states (those where the equilibrium of the federal game at national level implies non-cooperation) from free-riding at the expense of others. If sanctions are borne only by CG, the prevention of free-riding at EU level will not solve the problem at national level: a review of national controls is also needed (sanction H). This outcome is shown in Figure 8.6, in which the sanction introduced in the Pact (S, $S>D+E+K-B/2$) affects only the outcome that can be achieved by CG, which is obliged to allow LG to free-ride in order to ensure overall cooperation.

To conclude, the Pact increases the need for mechanisms to control decentralized governments. If the constraints are not tightened the CG

		Local government	
		undisciplined	disciplined
Central government	undisciplined	$D + E - S$; $D - H + E$	$D + E - S$; $D - K + E$
	disciplined	$\mathbf{B/2 - K}$; $\mathbf{B/2 - H}$	$B/2 - K/2$; $B/2 - K/2$

Figure 8.6 The federal game at national level after EMU (with 'European' sanctions)

must offset LG's behaviour. Two considerations, in particular, could render national rules inadequate:

1. European regulations are generally speaking more restrictive than those adopted at national level; the resulting higher costs of cooperation could lead to national penalty systems becoming inadequate and to a conflict between the constraints on national public finances at the European level and the flexibility allowed to decentralized institutions at the national level. For example, the level of local government investment prior to the Pact in countries applying the *golden rule* may determine excessive deficits.
2. The allocation of responsibility for compliance with EMU fiscal rules among central and local governments and of the possible costs incurred because of non-compliance is asymmetrical; in the absence of adequate national rules, local governments that are able to contract debts could act as free-riders on the back of the central government.

3.3 Possible Solutions

In principle three strategies appear possible: the duplication of European rules at the national level; the amendment of existing legislative frameworks; and the introduction of a market for 'deficit permits'.

Extending the Stability and Growth Pact to the national level
This solution poses several problems:

- if the bodies to be disciplined are too small in economic terms, it could be difficult to measure GDP and in any case the meaningfulness of available data (with regard to mobility of factors of production, for example) would be affected;

- the high number of bodies involved could make monitoring particularly costly. The evaluations needed for the cyclical adjustment of budgetary data could be especially problematic, as could those necessary for a case-by-case examination of 'exceptional' circumstances to justify excessive deficits;
- the financing of local investment expenditure through local taxation could pose particular problems, especially where unusually costly projects could lead to expenditure peaks.

The extension of European rules to the larger decentralized governments only (i.e. in Italy, the Regions) could be a solution provided smaller decentralized governments have only limited autonomy; otherwise the cost of adjustment would merely be shifted from the central government to the larger local governments.

Adapting existing regulations at national level

This approach cannot take the form of an introduction of administrative controls on the indebtedness of decentralized governments. As stated earlier, this solution would be in clear conflict with the spirit of a federal set-up.

Amendments would have to be aimed at allowing recourse to debt financing for both structural reasons (e.g. public-sector investment) and cyclical reasons (e.g. the absorption of cyclical effects on the budget). Control systems in place in some states address these two aspects by setting flexible ceilings to the deficit: on the one hand the ceilings exclude capital expenditure (the golden rule); on the other hand they are applied only on an *ex ante* basis and if the deficit overshoots the ceiling the overshoot can be compensated in subsequent financial years: in some cases (e.g. some American states) the deficit overshoot must be financed through recourse to specially constituted 'rainy day funds', without recourse to the market.[224]

In the new scenario created by European regulations, these solutions appear most easily adaptable to structural aspects, in other words the financing of investment, while the cyclical aspect appears more complex. In both cases credible sanctions would have to be established to deal with non-compliance.

With regard to the structural aspect, adoption of the golden rule would have to be flanked by an overall ceiling on investment expenditure by local governments. When setting this limit, the need for the overall cyclically adjusted general government budget to be in balance or close to it would have to be taken into account: any deficits allowed to decentralized units would have to be compensated by a general government surplus with a generous enough margin to allow for the counter-cyclical measures. Moreover, rules would have to be drawn up to define the criteria for allocating among decentralized bodies the overall deficit allowed for investment programmes. To this end, given the difficulties of defining an adequate reference parameter (population, amount of infrastructure, overall receipts, etc.) a cooperative approach could be contemplated. By involving decentralized governments in the process of defining overall budgetary targets, they would acquire greater responsibility for behaving consistently with the pursuit of the targets set and reaching agreement on the allocation of resources. The peer-pressure incentive for compliance generated in a cooperative framework could be strengthened by allocating any sanctions handed down by the EU among those agencies responsible for overshooting.

With regard to the absorption of cyclical effects on the budget, the application of ceilings that are valid only *ex ante* is clearly in contrast with European legislation, which as we have seen is based on *ex post* limits. On the other hand, the introduction of strict budgetary constraints that are valid *ex post* is problematic, since it would distort the allocation of resources (to the detriment of the more flexible expenses) and force decentralized units to adopt pro-cyclical policies.

The establishment of rainy day funds could be a solution, though it would imply a review of the ESA accounting rules for calculating budgetary indicators. Under current rules transfers of resources to such funds are not included among the disbursements that comprise net indebtedness, nor is the use of such resources included among receipts; in neither case do movements of money through these funds alter the size of the deficit. The accumulation and use of these funds would have to be entered respectively under expenditure and receipts in the general government account; only in this way would their use avoid overshooting the 3 per cent threshold.[225]

A market in deficit permits

The thesis that the problems of externalities might be solved by creating appropriate ownership rights and allowing free trade in them was first put forward by Coase (1960). Casella (2001) suggested taking this approach to the question of fiscal discipline within the EMU (see also Chapter 11). Comparing the negative externality produced by members running excessive deficits to that of pollution, this article suggested using the machinery developed in environmental economics.[226] With reference to the Italian domestic stability pact (see later), the *Commissione Tecnica per la Spesa Pubblica* (an experts' committee on public expenditure) raised the possibility of introducing a system of deficit permits for local and regional governments in its 1998 paper.

Once the overall ceiling[227] on permits and their initial allotment has been set, market incentives would produce, through free trade, the most efficient allocation in relation to the financial needs of the various governments in any given year. The total volume of permits issued could be related to the national economic cycle, so as to allow both a 'structural' margin for investment and a variable margin to absorb the cyclical impact on the budget. Deficits above the amount fundable by the permits would result in a cut in the permits assigned the following year. The financial market could also be involved in the discipline by prohibiting borrowing or bond issues lacking debt permit coverage.

The system described is subject to three main difficulties. First, efficacy requires that the deficits of the various governments generate the same externality and are thus perfect substitutes. But the risk of triggering a financial crisis is not uniform across governments. If this risk were the function of a single variable, for example the level of debt, then one would merely have to make the value of the deficit permits of the governments inversely proportional to their stock of debt. However, the risk depends on a number of factors,[228] and determining the value of the permits held by each government is complicated. Second, the efficiency of the market in permits depends on how competitive it is. This makes the mechanism ill-suited to situations in which the number of governments is small (within the EMU there would be just 11 players, and vastly different in size at that).[229] Finally, there is no easy solution to the problem of determining the initial allotment of permits. The possible criteria (GDP, population, etc.) would produce greatly differing allocations. If the demand for permits exceeded the supply, then the countries with an allotment greater than their requirement would enjoy positional rents.

The first two objections appear more cogent for a permit market among member states at EMU level than for one among local governments within each country. Presumably the risk connected with each entity's deficit is more uniform within than between countries: the size of the governments is smaller, and in many cases they have only recently acquired the power to issue their own debt. The number of market operators would be vastly greater. Of course, so extensive a market could entail higher administrative costs. The third difficulty, which is strictly political, would be encountered at the national level as well. It would be compounded, at least initially, by local governments' problems in adapting to the new machinery for the allotment of resources.

Apart from these difficulties, the permit system seems better suited to financing investments than to buffering the budgetary effects of the business cycle. In the investment area, trading in permits could certainly contribute to greater efficiency in resource allocation. The financial needs connected with investment projects could be planned, and the realization of works modulated, as a function of available resources. As to the cyclical effects, however, the initial allotment would necessarily be based on forecasts of national economic developments; the emergence of a discrepancy in the course of the year could result in over demand for permits, which would penalize the governments of areas where cyclical performance was especially poor.

An overview

Each of the three solutions has drawbacks. Replicating the Stability Pact at national level is impeded by lack of the necessary data. Leaving room to buffer cyclical effects on local government budgets without compensating action by the central government (which would give local governments an incentive for opportunistic behaviour) requires solutions that are inconsistent with the ESA95 accounting rules. The formation of a deficit permit market faces the difficulty of finding an equitable criterion for the initial allotment of permits and that of the dubious ability of local governments to adapt to the new context. In light of these problems, a combination of actions could usefully be evaluated:

- A domestic stability pact would appear to be feasible for the larger local government bodies (in Italy, the Regions), for which the problem of lack of data is solvable.
- The need to spread investment costs over a number of years could be addressed (albeit with the difficulties recalled above) by recourse to either market mechanisms or the application of rules.
- To buffer cyclical effects, the best solution appears to be the institution of reserve funds. As noted, however, this would require the revision of the European rules for national accounts.

Italy: the Domestic Stability Pact

Some EU countries are faced with the necessity of adjusting relations between central and local government to the new European framework. Measures for budgetary coordination between the various levels of government are under study in Austria, Belgium and Germany.

Italy has taken a first step in this direction with the domestic stability pact introduced with the 1999 budget. This action was all the more necessary as a result of the decentralization begun in the early 1990s. Decentralization has brought a gradual transition from 'derived' regional finances, in which virtually the entire regional budget consisted of rigidly earmarked central government transfers, to fundamentally 'autonomous' financing, with revenues derived from regional taxes and percentage shares in certain central government taxes and their allocation increasingly left to regional decision.

The transition to more pronounced forms of decentralization has become a major political issue. The possibility of a federal reform of the Constitution has been broached by a number of observers.[230] Within this general framework, before the domestic stability pact, the limits on local authorities' borrowing were set by a 'golden rule' (borrowing to finance current expenditure was prohibited) with an indirect ceiling (debt service could not exceed 25 per cent of own revenues). Frequently, however, there was unlimited year-end coverage of deficits (in the health and transport sectors, for instance) by the central government. The emerging trend in institutional arrangements implied: (1) a comparatively high degree of decentralization; (2) high sensitivity of local government revenues to the economic cycle; and (3) relatively lax constraints on indebtedness. The analysis set forth earlier shows the risks that such arrangements entail for the observance of European budget rules.

The Domestic Stability Pact

The domestic stability pact is designed to involve the Regions and other local authorities in the effort to attain the objectives for general government budget under the European Stability and Growth Pact. The domestic pact requires local bodies to reduce deficits and their stock of debt.[231] The deficit referred to (DI) is the difference between total revenues (E) net of state transfers (T) and total expenditure (S) net of investment (K) and interest payments (I):[232]

$$DI = (E - T) - (S - K - I)$$

The definition differs widely from the European definition (DE), which is simply the difference between total revenue and total expenditure:

$$DE = E - S$$

The two definitions also differ in accounting rules. The domestic stability pact adopts a cash basis, while European rules, based on ESA95, refer to the accruals principle.

The target set for the first three years of the domestic pact, beginning in 1999, was an annual reduction in the total deficit of local governments equal to at least 0.1 per cent of GDP. In the absence of data on local GDP, the contribution of each district was set as proportional to the level of primary current expenditure ($S - K - I$).[233]

The local governments' accounts was monitored in the course of the year for consistency with the annual target. However, no sanctions for non-compliance were provided. The state–region and state–commune conferences were to decide on any corrective measures. In 1999 the only consequence of detection of a potential overshoot was the proposal to increase the size of the reduction planned for 2000.

If Italy is sanctioned under the excessive deficit procedure, the fines will be levied on the entities that failed to meet their targets, in proportion to the part of the overshoot for which they are responsible.

An evaluation

The domestic stability pact is essentially a rule imposing deficit reduction on local authorities. It is based on an extended version of the 'golden rule' (interest payments too are excluded from the deficit[234]) with an indirect ceiling (the previous law limited the deficit to a level that would produce debt service payments not exceeding 25 per cent of own revenue).[235] In practice, carrying annual deficits forward appears possible. The eventual correction of yearly budget overshoots is entrusted to a cooperative mechanism (the conferences).

This set of rules is marked by a series of inconsistencies and lacunae:

- While the objective is deficit reduction, each government's contribution is correlated not with the deficit but with primary current expenditure. Thus if one region's budget is balanced or in surplus while another's is in deficit but the primary expenditure of the former is greater than the latter's, it would paradoxically have to make a larger contribution to the adjustment.
- Ultimately, the aim of the pact is to contain the relevant deficit for European purposes (DE). Taking a different budget variable (DI) as an intermediate objective makes it impossible to estimate the implications of local government targets for observance of the European rules. Specifically, it could be that the difference between the two balances ($K+I-T$) records an increase that more than offsets the reduction in the pact's reference balance (DI).
- Usually the golden rule excludes only investment spending from the reference deficit. Interest expenditure always forms part of the balance, the aim being to amortize the cost of public works over a number of years and thus share the burden among the generations that enjoy the benefits.
- Though the pact sets the objective of reducing local government debt, it introduces no machinery to assure its attainment. Reduction of the pact's reference deficit (which excludes major budget items, including interest expenditure) does not actually guarantee that net new borrowing will diminish. Furthermore, the debt ceiling imposed

by the previous legislation based on the ratio between debt service and own revenue seems a weak instrument given increasing local taxation powers and relatively low interest rates.

- The pact divides a possible European sanction among the various government authorities in proportion to the share of the overshoot for which each is responsible. This formulation does strengthen the incentive for deficit reduction, but it also has certain undesirable characteristics. It would be better to impose sanctions for failure to achieve the deficit objective even if Italy is not fined at the European level. Apart from the fact that such conduct constitutes free-riding, failure to punish it could narrow the scope for national counter-cyclical measures within the 3 per cent ceiling. Moreover, if the overshoot is confined to a small number of governments, the size of the fine could be too large for credibility.

Certain features of the pact, moreover, appear ill-suited to strengthen Italian discipline consistently with the observance of European rules:

- even if recouped in the years following, any local government budget overshoots must be made good immediately by the central government;
- the problem of cyclical effects on local budgets is not dealt with (at a time when the devolution of tax base makes local government budgets more sensitive to macroeconomic conditions).

5. CONCLUSIONS

Our analysis underscores the problems inherent in the combination of increasing fiscal decentralization within the EU member states with rules set at European level to guarantee sound public finances at national level and leave scope for counter-cyclical policy measures.[236]

Specifically, we highlight the difficulty of reconciling full achievement of the allocative advantages of fiscal decentralization with full exploitation of the scope for counter-cyclical policy action offered by compliance with the Stability and Growth Pact.

We have noted: (1) the reduced flexibility of the European approach compared with solutions adopted in federally structured states; (2) the asymmetry between the responsibilities laid on national and local governments by European rules (compliance with the rules depends on the conduct of all levels of government, but *de facto* it is central government that is answerable to the EU and that must pay the price of non-compliance); (3) the consequent need for stricter controls over local governments to prevent free-riding; and (4) the difficulty of finding fully satisfactory solutions.

Devising appropriate solutions is hard for a number of reasons: (1) the mechanical extension of the Stability and Growth Pact is feasible only for the larger local bodies; (2) allowing local bodies to amortize investment expenditure over a number of years entails significant problems, whether market mechanisms or predetermined rules are used; and (3) the best way of buffering the effect of the economic cycle on local government budgets, that is, the use of a reserve fund, requires revision of the EU's rules for national accounts.

In the course of the 1990s, Italian institutional arrangements moved to a relatively high degree of decentralization, marked cyclical sensitivity of local government revenues and lax constraints on indebtedness. This set of arrangements could impede compliance with European budgetary rules. The domestic stability pact is a first step towards a solution. Essentially, it is a rule requiring local governments to reduce their deficits. Our examination has revealed a number of problems that require some fine-tuning of the mechanism:

- while the objective is deficit reduction, individual contributions are not correlated with that variable but with primary current expenditure;
- the adoption of a different budget variable as an intermediate objective precludes prior estimation of the implications of local government targets for the observance of European rules;
- the pact has an anomalous golden rule that excludes interest spending from the reference deficit;
- while setting the objective of reducing local government debt, the pact introduces no machinery to assure its attainment;
- a local authority's failure to achieve its objective is punished only if Italy is subjected to a European sanction, which could narrow the scope for counter-cyclical measures within the 3 per cent ceiling;
- local government budget overshoots, even if recouped in subsequent years, must be made good by central government in the year they are incurred;
- the problem of cyclical effects on local budgets is not addressed.

As recalled in Chapter 2, at the time of its introduction the Stability and Growth Pact gave rise to a wide debate. Many participants stressed that it provides no 'reward' for countries that are 'virtuous' during cyclical expansions, achieving budget balance or surplus. Bean (1998) observes that 'The problem with the pact as presently framed is that it is *all stick and no carrot*; rewarding good fiscal behaviour in booms rather than, or in addition to, punishing bad behaviour in slumps would surely make better sense' (p. 106). Paraphrasing this critique, one might say that Italy's domestic pact as it presently stands is 'neither stick nor carrot'.

9. Politics and the Pact*

1. INTRODUCTION

Europe's Economic and Monetary Union (EMU) is based on an original arrangement of public finance relations between member countries: fiscal policy remains decentralized, but is subject to rules which are meant to combine discipline and flexibility. The Stability and Growth Pact (SGP), which complements and tightens the fiscal provisions laid down in the Maastricht Treaty, is the backbone of fiscal discipline in EMU.

The SGP is unquestionably the most stringent supranational 'commitment technology' ever adopted by sovereign governments on a voluntary basis in the attempt to establish and maintain sound public finances. The SGP, if applied according to its letter and spirit, will have important implications for the behaviour of budgetary authorities in both the short term (cyclical stabilization, policy coordination) and the long term (sustainability of public finances).

The experience of the early years of EMU has, however, been disappointing. While many euro area countries continued the fiscal retrenchment, even moving into surplus, the three largest members – Germany, France and Italy – and Portugal remain trapped in high deficits.

This short chapter argues that failure to abide by the SGP's 'fiscal philosophy' can, at least in part, be traced back to resurrection of incentives – once EMU had been accomplished – to run politically motivated fiscal policies during important electoral episodes.

The chapter is organised as follows. The next section briefly reviews the budgetary developments in the early years of EMU and discusses the alleged asymmetric working of the Pact in bad times and good times. The third section provides a snapshot of the literature on electoral budget cycles. The fourth section presents a new indicator of discretionary fiscal policy. The indicator is then applied in the fifth section to the euro area countries in the years 1999–2002 to gauge the influence of elections on fiscal policy behaviour. The final section draws some policy conclusions.

* Marco Buti and Paul van den Noord, 'Fiscal Discretion and Elections in the Early Years of EMU', *Journal of Common Market Studies*, 2004, 39(4): 737–56.

2. FISCAL POLICY IN EMU'S INFANCY: A LONGER-THAN-HOPED-FOR TRANSITION

2.1 A Disappointing Fiscal Performance

According to the SGP, fiscal discipline would be enforced by establishing the 3 per cent of GDP deficit as a hard ceiling to be exceeded only in exceptional circumstances and maintaining the budget at around balance in normal times and letting automatic stabilizers play freely in downturns and upturns. An upper limit to the actual deficit combined with close-to-balance positions in normal times would ensure the gradual reabsorption of public debt which, in several countries, remains substantially higher than the 60 per cent of GDP reference value of the Treaty.

As many countries entered EMU with deficits close to 3 per cent of GDP, a further budgetary adjustment in the early years of EMU was required to move to close-to-balance positions. The determination of countries to continue the fiscal retrenchment in the early years of EMU came to be regarded as a test of whether EMU had brought about a genuine regime change and a political commitment to stability-oriented macroeconomic policy. Clearly, a number of euro area members have not lived up to such commitment.

Figure 9.1 shows the progress – or lack thereof – towards lower public deficits and debts made during the initial years of EMU.[237] It shows, for

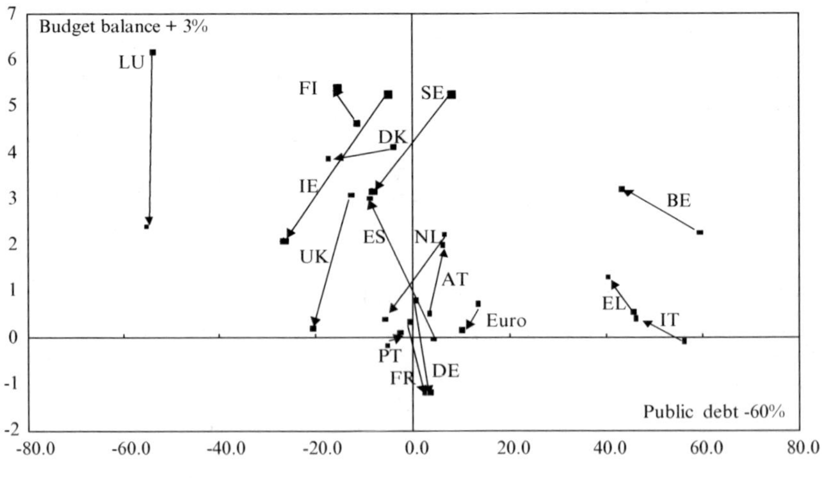

Source: Commission services.

Figure 9.1 Budgetary room for manoeuvre, 1998–2003

each country, on the horizontal axis the difference between the stock of public debt as a share of GDP and the 60 per cent Maastricht reference value, and on the vertical axis the difference between the budget deficit and the 3 per cent deficit ceiling. For both variables, the situation in 1998 and 2002 is pictured. A shift towards a safer territory is represented by a move down and to the left.

Several countries managed to move further away from the deficit threshold between 1998 and 2002 and achieved a reduction in public debt. However, the chart clearly shows that overall little progress has been accomplished on the way to budgetary consolidation, and in structural terms the picture is even bleaker. Indeed, as we show below, if one nets out the automatic effects of growth on the budget, countries on average relaxed their retrenchment efforts in the 1998–2002 period. In particular the three largest countries of the euro area – Germany, France, Italy – as well as Portugal – which has been the first country to have exceeded the 3 per cent of GDP deficit limit in 2001 followed by Germany in 2002 – did not behave according to the spirit (and the letter) of the SGP.

2.2. Fiscal Policy Incentives under the SGP

While the SGP is nominally very strict, it does not tackle a typical failure of fiscal policy behaviour in Europe, namely the tendency to run expansionary pro-cyclical policies in good times (see, e.g., European Commission, 2000b): while an excess over the 3 per cent of GDP deficit ceiling is sanctioned, there is no apparent reward for appropriate budgetary behaviour during cyclical upswings. Hence, the political temptation to 'spend the money when it comes in' may prove irresistible.

The fact that the SGP is 'all sticks and no carrots' (Bean, 1998) may entail a pro-cyclical bias in the conduct of budgetary policy. The implicit carrot for well-behaved participants, that they have room for the automatic stabilizers to operate unfettered during downturns without being hit by a stick, is apparently not 'tasty' enough. Figure 9.2, adapted from Buti and Martinot (2000), illustrates this case. It pictures the total and the cyclically adjusted budget balance against the output gap. The dotted lines represent budgetary behaviour consistent with the SGP philosophy, while the solid lines represent a 'surplus-resistant' fiscal behaviour. If governments remain trapped in the budgetary culture of the 1970s and 1980s, they will tend to offset the working of the automatic stabilizers for sufficiently large, positive output gaps. While the actual budget balance would remain broadly stable, the cyclically adjusted budget balance would worsen, adding to the risk of overheating.

These incorrect structures of incentives may be strengthened in electoral periods. While in the run up to EMU the incentives to stick to the

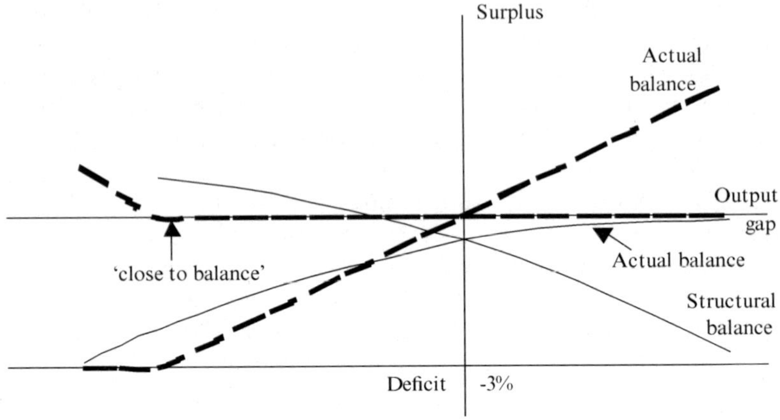

Notes:
Dotted line: SGP-compatible budgetary behaviour: symmetric operation of automatic stabilizers.
Solid line: pro-cyclical fiscal behaviour.

Figure 9.2 Budgetary behaviour under the SGP: symmetric and asymmetric behaviour

announced consolidation path were evident, at least for traditionally pro-European countries, things may be different once in EMU. Unlike the Maastricht convergence, sticking to the rules of the SGP may not pay politically. As argued by Buti and Giudice (2002), the reward for complying with Maastricht public finance requirements and the penalty for failing to do so were very clearly laid out. Meeting the convergence criteria would allow budgetary laggards to join the virtuous countries in the new policy regime. Conversely, failure carried the penalty of exclusion from the euro area. This was considered too hard a political sanction especially for countries traditionally at the forefront of the process of European integration. This may have temporarily affected also the political incentives to the extent that fiscal 'sacrifices' to join the euro area have a chance of being politically rewarded.

Once in EMU, however, the underlying political preferences may pop up again as the carrot of entry has been eaten while the stick of exclusion has been replaced by the threat of uncertain and delayed sanctions. If this is true one should be able to observe a reversal of fiscal behaviour to 'old habits' especially during electoral periods. This effect is compounded by a parallel break in some countries of the political consensus around fiscal consolidation between the government and the main opposition parties and the resurgence of ideological disputes. This has increased electoral polarization and therefore has also increased the incentives that incumbents face to manage the budget electorally.

The combination of a cyclical upturn and elections may strengthen the temptation to run pro-cyclical expansionary policies. As pointed out in Buti and Sapir (1998, 2002b) and Sapir and Sekkat (2002), the very success of the SGP in reducing the budget deficits would in fact rebuild the capacity of governments to pursue politically motivated fiscal actions.

3. THE LITERATURE ON ELECTORAL BUDGET CYCLES: A BIRD'S-EYE VIEW

The literature on politically motivated policies is vast. It started off with the seminal contributions by Nordhaus and Hibbs in the mid-1970s on political business cycles and was revived in the early 1990s by Alesina and others in models which incorporated political incentives with rational expectations (for a survey see Drazen, 2000). A strand of the literature has also analysed electoral budget cycles, with models of opportunistic electoral cycles (Rogoff and Sibert, 1988) and electoral accountability (Ferejohn, 1986). More recently, the new literature on 'political economics' has analysed the impact of different features of political systems on the running of fiscal policy (see Persson and Tabellini, 2002a and 2002b). The individual country model of opportunistic or partisan behaviour has been extended by Sapir and Sekkat (1999) to allow for cross-country spill-overs.

In essence, the predictions of the theoretical literature on fiscal behaviour in relation to elections can be summarized as follows: (1) opportunistic behaviour implies fiscal policy manipulations before the elections; (2) uncertainty about the electoral outcome and the degree of polarization induce governments to undertake short-sighted policies; (3) most models predict tax cuts before elections while the implications for spending are less clear-cut; (4) electoral rules shape fiscal behaviour, with majoritarian elections leading to larger fiscal activism focused on targeted programmes aimed at shifting votes in marginal districts, while proportional elections lead to increase in broad-based programmes. Recent empirical work has found support, though not unequivocal, for these predictions (see, e.g., Persson and Tabellini, 2002a and 2002b; Milesi-Ferretti *et al.*, 2002).[238]

Obviously, only four years into EMU, it is too early to carry out a systematic investigation of electoral manipulation of fiscal policy. Nonetheless, given the relatively large number of electoral episodes in the period 1999–2002 – all countries had either general elections as part of the regular electoral cycle, or early elections prompted by political crises, see

Table 9.1 Elections in euro area countries, 1999–2003

	1999	2000	2001	2002	2003
Austria	General elections	–	–	Early general elections	–
Belgium	General elections	–	–	Pre-election year	General elections
Finland	General elections	–	–	Pre-election year	General elections
France	–	–	Pre-election year	General elections	–
Germany	–	–	Pre-election year	General elections	–
Greece	Pre-election year	General elections	–	–	Pre-election year
Ireland	–	–	Pre-election year	General elections	–
Italy	–	Pre-election year	General elections	–	–
Netherlands	–	–	Pre-election year	General elections	Early general elections
Portugal	General elections	–	–	Early general elections	–
Spain	Pre-election year	General elections	–	–	Pre-election year
Number of election years	4	2	1	4	2
Number of early or pre-election years	2	1	4	4	3

Table 9.1 – we can provide some provisional evidence on incentives for politically motivated fiscal policies.

4. MEASURING DISCRETIONARY FISCAL POLICY

In order to explore the behaviour of fiscal policy in the early years of EMU we construct an indicator of discretionary fiscal policy – dubbed here DP. The indicator decomposes the primary fiscal balance into two components, a part that is consistent with a neutral stance of fiscal policy and the remainder that is attributable to fiscal stimulus or contraction.

A neutral fiscal stance is defined as a policy in which primary expenditure grows in line with potential GDP plus expected inflation, and tax revenue is a function of actual GDP. If in setting the budget a government adopts such rule, it can be said that it adopts a 'neutral' policy. Any deviation from there is considered 'discretionary'. Formally, neutral spending is written as follows:

$$g^* = \frac{G_{t-1}(1 + y^*\varepsilon_G + \pi^{ECB})}{Y_{t-1}(1 + y + \pi)} = g_{t-1}\frac{1 + y^*\varepsilon_G + \pi^{ECB}}{1 + y + \pi} \tag{9.1}$$

where G is nominal expenditure, Y is nominal GDP, g is the ratio between the two, π is inflation, y^* is trend growth and π^{ECB} is the inflation target of the ECB. In the case of some countries, Balassa-Samuelson effects can be considered. However, this possibility is ignored in the calculations below. Like Von Hagen (2002a), we adopt a unit elasticity for expenditure to potential output, the rationale being that a rise in potential output by x per cent allows to sustain a similar increase in spending. Hence ε_G is set equal to one.

Revenue growth is said to be neutral if it is in line with actual GDP, taking into account the elasticity of the various tax components:

$$\tau^* = \frac{T_{t-1}[1 + (y + \pi)\varepsilon_T]}{Y_{t-1}(1 + y + \pi)} = \tau_{t-1}\frac{1 + (y + \pi)\varepsilon_T}{1 + y + \pi} \tag{9.2}$$

where T is revenue and τ its ratio to GDP. The elasticity ε_T is set to the average tax elasticities reported in van den Noord (2002), hence is close to unity. As a result: (1) the neutral budget deficit (primary) is $d^* = g^* - \tau^*$;[239] and (2) actual expenditure can be written as:

$$g_t = g_{t-1}\frac{1 + y^e\varepsilon_G + \pi^e + \tilde{g}}{1 + y + \pi} \tag{9.3}$$

This is a crucial assumption in our approach. We assume that the government sets its spending plans on the basis of expected GDP growth, y^e, and expected inflation, π^e, plus discretionary spending changes, $\tilde{g}$. The relevance of this assumption on policy behaviour for our results will become clear below.

Actual revenue is written as:

$$\tau_t = \tau_{t-1}\frac{1 + (y + \pi)\varepsilon_T + \tilde{\tau}}{1 + y + \pi} \tag{9.4}$$

The rule for the tax revenue is the same as (9.2) supplemented by discretionary tax changes, $\tilde{\tau}$. Both spending and revenue are deflated by actual (*ex post*) nominal GDP growth. In the calculations, the expected variables are those in the country's stability programme. For trend growth, the OECD estimates published in the *Economic Outlook 72* that were published in late 2002 have been used. As to π^{ECB}, we used 1.5 per cent, which is consistent with the implicit inflation target of the ECB considering its 'first pillar' strategy.[240]

Given that the actual primary deficit is $d = g - \tau$, the indicator of discretionary policy is $DP = d - d^*$. After simple manipulations, DP can be written as follows:

$$DP = \frac{(g_{t-1}\tilde{g} - \tau_{t-1}\tilde{\tau}) + g_{t-1}\varepsilon_G(y^e - y^*) + g_{t-1}(\pi^e - \pi^{ECB})}{1 + y + \pi} \quad (9.5)$$

Hence discretionary fiscal policy can be broken down into three components:

- 'Genuine' or overt discretionary policy, that captures the impact of explicit discretionary fiscal policy on the primary balance, that is, the component that is funded directly through debt rather than through the projected growth or inflation 'dividend' (see below). This component is then split between discretionary expenditure changes and tax changes.
- A projected 'growth dividend' which, if positive ($y^e > y^*$), can be used by the government to fund extra expenditure. This growth dividend is computed by applying the tax and expenditure elasticities with respect to the output gap to the changes in the output gap that are implied by the growth projections underpinning the stability programmes.
- A projected 'inflation dividend' which is computed by applying the above elasticities to the inflation gap, that is, the difference between the officially projected rate of inflation and the rate of inflation that is consistent with normal capacity utilization. If $\pi^e > \pi^{ECB}$, the freed resources can be used for expenditure hikes.[241]

In practice, the second and the third components are computed first, while the 'genuine' component is obtained as a residual. Closer inspection of equation (9.5) shows that the same three-pronged breakdown can be applied to expenditure. However, this is not the case for revenues for which the growth and inflation dividends are zero by definition. The reason is that we associate 'neutral' revenue with the projected actual (as opposed to the structural) evolution of the tax base.

This indicator provides a different picture of discretionary policy compared to the change in the cyclically adjusted primary balance ($\Delta CAPB$).

This indicator of the fiscal stance (see, e.g., European Commission, 2002a, and Van den Noord, 2002) is usually taken as a gauge of the impact of fiscal policy on economic activity. By contrast, DP aims to capture the discretionary behaviour of the fiscal authorities against a benchmark of 'unchanged policy'. If nominal GDP growth collapses unexpectedly, the non-discretionary component of the expenditure ratio automatically increases because the allocation of resources is set on the basis of expected GDP growth. This is non-discretionary in DP while it is implicitly treated as discretionary in the fiscal stance measured $\Delta CAPB$. Moreover, unlike the $\Delta CAPB$, the indicator captures the effect of inflation.[242]

5. DISCRETIONARY FISCAL POLICIES IN EMU: DID ELECTIONS MATTER?

5.1 A Discretionary Loosening

The results of our calculations for DP are presented in Tables 9.2 to 9.4. A positive (negative) entry indicates a discretionary loosening (tightening). Table 9.2 shows that, on average for the area as a whole, fiscal policy has become easier over time.[243] Indeed, whereas in the first two sets of programmes there was a tightening bias, this turned into an easing bias in the last two vintages.[244] Interestingly, this is true also for the 'genuine' discretionary component (Table 9.3), suggesting that governments have indeed become less concerned with deficit financing and deliberately relaxed budget discipline in 2001 and 2002 beyond the 'unchanged policy' rule. The fiscal loosening started in 2000 in a number of countries and notably in Italy and Portugal, two of the countries currently trapped in high deficits.[245] The projected growth dividend was positive for 1999–2001, but negative for 2002–03. The inflation dividend was positive all along, but small.

Table 9.4 shows the breakdown of discretionary policy between expenditure and revenue. As the growth and inflation dividends only affect expenditure, they can be subtracted from the total discretionary spending to compute its 'genuine' component. The picture that emerges is mixed. The growth and inflation dividends 'swell' discretionary spending while genuine spending remained tight. The large loosening in 2001 and 2002 came from the revenue side which reversed a sizeable increase in the previous years.

5.2 Did Elections Matter?

The interesting question obviously is to what extent this behaviour can be related to the election cycle. The electoral business cycle will work

Table 9.2 Indicator of discretionary fiscal policy

	Discretionary policy					'Neutral' primary deficit					Actual primary deficit				
	1999	2000	2001	2002	2003	1999	2000	2001	2002	2003	1999	2000	2001	2002	2003
Austria	−0.8	−0.9	−3.2	−0.2	0.0	−0.1	−0.3	0.1	−2.0	−1.4	−0.8	−1.2	−3.2	−2.2	−1.4
Belgium	0.9	0.2	−0.3	0.5	0.5	−7.0	−6.8	−6.1	−6.2	−5.7	−6.2	−6.6	−6.4	−5.7	−5.2
Finland	−1.0	−2.2	2.2	0.6	1.5	−2.6	−5.8	−8.0	−5.4	−4.7	−3.6	−8.0	−5.8	−4.8	−3.2
France	−1.3	−0.4	−0.4	0.9	−0.7	0.2	−0.9	−0.7	−0.4	1.5	−1.1	−1.4	−1.1	0.5	0.8
Germany	−0.7	0.1	1.1	0.4	−0.8	−0.9	−1.6	−1.1	0.4	1.5	−1.6	−1.5	0.0	0.8	0.8
Greece	1.0	1.8	2.2	1.5	1.1	−6.4	−6.9	−6.6	−5.8	−5.4	−5.4	−5.1	−4.4	−4.3	−4.3
Ireland	1.7	−1.2	3.6	2.3	−0.1	−5.2	−4.2	−5.4	−2.0	0.7	−3.5	−5.4	−1.8	0.2	0.6
Italy	0.2	0.8	1.3	0.3	0.8	−4.6	−5.0	−4.5	−3.1	−3.0	−4.4	−4.1	−3.3	−2.9	−2.2
Netherlands	−0.9	0.6	2.6	1.0	0.6	−3.6	−5.4	−5.4	−2.5	−1.3	−4.5	−4.7	−2.8	−1.5	−0.7
Portugal	0.1	0.5	1.2	−1.4	0.3	−0.4	−0.5	−0.1	1.1	−0.1	−0.4	0.0	1.1	−0.4	0.1
Spain	0.0	1.1	0.2	0.8	0.7	−2.2	−3.2	−2.9	−3.4	−2.9	−2.2	−2.1	−2.7	−2.6	−2.2
Weighted average	−0.5	0.2	0.7	0.5	0.0	−2.1	−2.9	−2.5	−1.6	−0.7	−2.5	−2.6	−1.8	−1.0	−0.7
Unweighted average	−0.1	0.0	1.0	0.6	0.4	−3.0	−3.7	−3.7	−2.7	−1.9	−3.1	−3.6	−2.8	−2.1	−1.5

Table 9.3 *Discretionary fiscal policy: breakdown into 'genuine' discretionary policy, 'growth dividend' and 'inflation dividend'*

	'Genuine' discretionary policy					Projected 'growth dividend'					Projected 'inflation dividend'				
	1999	2000	2001	2002	2003	1999	2000	2001	2002	2003	1999	2000	2001	2002	2003
Austria	−0.8	−0.6	−3.4	0.0	0.2	0.2	0.0	0.1	−0.5	−0.3	−0.2	−0.3	0.1	0.3	0.0
Belgium	0.8	0.3	−0.2	0.5	0.4	0.1	0.1	0.0	−0.3	0.0	0.0	−0.2	−0.1	0.3	0.0
Finland	−1.6	−2.8	1.8	1.2	1.5	0.4	0.5	0.6	−0.5	0.1	0.2	0.0	−0.1	−0.2	−0.1
France	−1.4	−0.8	−0.7	0.6	−0.8	0.2	0.4	0.5	0.2	0.1	−0.1	0.0	−0.1	0.1	0.0
Germany	−0.7	0.2	0.6	0.6	−0.8	0.2	0.5	0.5	−0.3	0.0	−0.2	−0.2	0.0	0.0	0.0
Greece	0.4	1.3	1.2	0.8	0.5	0.2	0.3	0.8	0.2	0.1	0.3	0.2	0.3	0.5	0.6
Ireland	1.7	−1.8	2.4	2.2	−0.1	−0.3	0.2	0.5	−0.6	−0.6	0.3	0.4	0.8	0.6	0.6
Italy	−0.3	0.7	0.5	−0.3	0.4	0.3	0.1	0.4	0.2	0.2	0.2	0.1	0.4	0.4	0.2
Netherlands	−1.2	0.5	1.2	0.8	0.2	0.0	−0.2	0.5	−0.6	−0.6	0.3	0.4	0.9	0.7	0.9
Portugal	−0.3	0.2	0.3	−2.0	−0.4	0.1	0.0	0.1	−0.2	−0.1	0.3	0.3	0.8	0.7	0.7
Spain	−0.4	0.8	−0.2	0.5	0.2	0.3	0.2	0.2	−0.1	0.1	0.1	0.2	0.3	0.4	0.4
Weighted average	−0.7	0.0	0.1	0.4	−0.2	0.2	0.3	0.4	−0.1	0.0	0.0	0.0	0.1	0.2	0.2
Unweighted average	−0.3	−0.2	0.3	0.5	0.1	0.1	0.2	0.4	−0.2	−0.1	0.1	0.1	0.3	0.4	0.3

Table 9.4 Discretionary fiscal policy: breakdown into expenditure and revenue

	'Genuine' discretionary expenditure					Discretionary expenditure					Discretionary revenue				
	1999	2000	2001	2002	2003	1999	2000	2001	2002	2003	1999	2000	2001	2002	2003
Austria	−0.3	−0.8	−1.6	−0.6	0.4	−0.3	−1.1	−1.4	−0.8	0.1	0.5	−0.2	1.8	−0.6	0.1
Belgium	0.1	0.2	−0.2	0.9	0.0	0.2	0.1	−0.3	0.9	0.0	−0.7	−0.1	0.1	0.4	−0.4
Finland	−1.6	−1.6	−0.3	0.7	0.5	−1.0	−1.0	0.1	0.1	0.6	0.0	1.2	−2.1	−0.5	−0.9
France	−0.2	−0.7	−0.2	0.1	−0.1	−0.1	−0.3	0.2	0.6	0.0	1.2	0.1	0.6	−0.3	0.7
Germany	−0.1	−0.6	−1.0	0.1	−0.1	−0.1	−0.3	−0.4	−0.1	−0.1	0.6	−0.4	−1.5	−0.5	0.7
Greece	1.2	2.5	−0.5	0.0	−0.1	1.8	3.1	0.6	0.8	0.6	0.8	1.3	−1.6	−0.8	−0.6
Ireland	2.2	−1.0	1.5	2.0	0.1	2.2	−0.4	2.7	2.0	0.1	0.5	0.8	−0.9	−0.2	0.2
Italy	0.1	0.1	0.4	−1.0	−0.4	0.6	0.2	1.1	−0.5	0.0	0.4	−0.6	−0.1	−0.8	−0.7
Netherlands	0.2	0.5	0.4	0.6	0.1	0.4	0.7	1.8	0.8	0.5	1.3	0.0	−0.8	−0.2	0.0
Portugal	1.6	1.0	0.2	−0.4	−0.1	1.9	1.3	1.2	0.1	0.6	1.9	0.9	−0.1	1.5	0.3
Spain	0.2	0.9	−0.2	0.5	0.0	0.7	1.2	0.2	0.8	0.5	0.7	0.1	0.0	0.0	−0.2
Weighted average	0.1	−0.2	−0.3	0.0	−0.1	0.3	0.1	0.3	0.2	0.1	0.7	−0.1	−0.4	−0.4	0.1
Unweighted average	0.3	0.0	−0.1	0.3	0.0	0.6	0.3	0.5	0.4	0.3	0.7	0.3	−0.4	−0.2	−0.1

through the three channels of discretionary policy identified earlier, but their relative importance may change according to the type of electoral calendar. A priori we expect the 'genuine' discretionary policy as defined above to be easing in pre-election years (except if the elections are not anticipated) and in election years. The literature surveyed predicts that tax cuts should be observed in the run-up to elections. In principle, one could also expect a positive growth dividend justified by incumbents' optimism on growth prospects.

We have examined this by regressing the discretionary fiscal policy indicator and each of the computed components (i.e. expenditure, revenue, 'genuine' fiscal policy, 'growth dividend' and 'inflation dividend') that are reported in Tables 9.2–9.4 with dummies that represent the phase of the political cycle. We distinguish three phases: non-election years, pre- or early election years and full-blown election years. For each of these phases we compute the average and median fiscal stances.[246] The regression equation reads:

$$\begin{aligned} DP_t = {} & \lambda DP_{t-1} + \alpha_1(DEF_{t-1} - DEF^*_{t-1}) + \alpha_2 GAP_{t-1} + \alpha_3 PEE_t \\ & + \alpha_4 FBE_t + \alpha_5 \max(GAP_{t-1} \times PEE_t, 0) + \alpha_6 \max(GAP_{t-1} \\ & \times FBE_t, 0) + \alpha_7 + u_t \end{aligned} \qquad (9.6)$$

The rationale for this equation and the meaning of the mnemonics are as follows:

- The autoregressive term captures inertia in a fiscal policy setting. A country with a history of discretionary easing bias may be expected to continue this behaviour. The regression coefficient is expected to be zero or positive.[247]
- The first explanatory variable $DEF_{t-1} - DEF^*_{t-1}$ denotes the *deficit gap*, which is the gap between the actual deficit from which the programme jumps off, that is, the lagged deficit, and the deficit target embodied in the running stability programme (for which we take the projected deficit for the end-year of the programme).[248] This variable thus measures the required consolidation effort implied by the country's stability programme. The larger this required effort, the tighter discretionary policy will be; the sign of the regression coefficient should be negative.
- The second explanatory variable is the *output gap*, lagged by one period GAP_{t-1}. This is included to capture the impact of the cycle on DP through discretionary policy. A negative sign will emerge if the fiscal impulse is counter-cyclical and the reverse if it is pro-cyclical.
- To gauge where the country stands in its electoral cycle and the

Table 9.5 *Regression results*[a]

	Explanatory variables									
	DP_{t-1} (λ)	DEF_{t-1} DEF^*_{t-1} (α_1)	GAP_{t-1} (α_2)	PEE_t (α_3)	FBE_t (α_4)	max ($PEE_t \times GAP_{t-1}$, 0) (α_5)	max ($FBE_t \times GAP_{t-1}$, 0) (α_6)	R^2	R^2 *adj.*	*F-statistic*
Discretionary expenditure	0.47***	−0.12*	−0.18**	−0.13	0.47*	0.60***	0.14	*0.59*	*0.51*	*7.49*
t-statistic	*4.26*	*−1.78*	*−2.24*	*−0.48*	*1.61*	*4.62*	*0.95*			
Genuine discretionary expenditure	0.29***	−0.14**	−0.14*	0.02	0.66**	0.35***	0.23*	*0.48*	*0.38*	*4.77*
t-statistic	*2.60*	*−2.18*	*−1.76*	*0.08*	*2.23*	*2.66*	*1.59*			
Discretionary revenue	0.01	0.20***	0.13*	0.13	0.22	−0.22*	−0.08	*0.20*	*0.05*	*1.31*
t-statistic	*0.09*	*2.53*	*1.43*	*0.39*	*0.61*	*−1.46*	*−0.45*			
Total discretionary policy	0.24*	−0.27***	−0.25**	−0.30	0.28	0.77***	0.23	*0.42*	*0.31*	*3.79*
t-statistic	*1.74*	*−2.49*	*−1.97*	*−0.67*	*0.57*	*3.64*	*0.96*			
Genuine discretionary policy	0.14	−0.32***	−0.23**	−0.13	0.46	0.53***	0.30*	*0.44*	*0.33*	*4.01*
t-statistic	*1.06*	*−3.37*	*−2.05*	*−0.32*	*1.06*	*2.75*	*1.38*			
Growth dividend	0.36***	0.01	−0.06*	−0.27**	−0.15	0.18***	−0.08	*0.43*	*0.32*	*3.88*
t-statistic	*2.51*	*0.28*	*−1.62*	*−2.19*	*−1.10*	*3.02*	*−1.24*			
Inflation dividend	0.84***	0.02	0.04*	0.10	0.00	0.01	−0.04	*0.74*	*0.69*	*14.74*
t-statistic	*8.24*	*0.83*	*1.90*	*1.19*	*−0.05*	*0.28*	*−0.91*			

Note: [a]*, **, *** denote significance at the 10, 5 and 1 per cent levels.

degree to which this affects discretionary policy we have included two *dummy variables*, PEE_t and FBE_t. $PEE_t = 1$ in a pre- or early election year and zero otherwise and $FBE_t = 1$ in a full-blown election year and zero otherwise.

- We also want to test whether the impact of the electoral cycle on *DP* *interacts* with the business cycle. The interaction is captured by two explanatory variables that are the respective products of the election dummies and the lagged output gap, but only positive observations of the gap are included. This will tell us whether not only the level of *DP* but also the way it responds to the cycle is affected by electoral motives.

As usual u_t denotes the normally distributed residual. The total number of observations is 44, that is 11 countries times 4 years (we lose one year due to the autoregressive term). The method used is ordinary least squares. The equation is estimated not only for the total *DP* but also for its components (i.e. discretionary expenditure, 'genuine' discretionary expenditure, discretionary revenue, 'genuine' discretionary fiscal policy and the growth and inflation dividends).

Our findings are reported in Table 9.5.[249] In 'normal' years (no elections in either the current or next year), there is a bias towards fiscal tightening if the deficit target is lower than the actual deficit. In those years, moreover, the tightening is accentuated if the cyclical position of the economy is strong (and vice versa), suggesting a counter-cyclical bias of fiscal policy in the absence of elections. However, the prediction in the literature that expenditure is raised in election years is confirmed by our results. We also find evidence of fiscal easing in pre- or early election years if the cyclical position of the economy is strong (i.e. the output gap is positive). In that situation there is a bias towards expenditure hikes, but we also find evidence of tax cuts.

This implies that, in line with the SGP's fiscal philosophy, many countries did continue the fiscal retrenchment to attain safer budgetary positions, sufficiently far from the 3 per cent of GDP deficit ceiling. However, the fiscal stance moved towards easing in the pre-, early and full-blown election years. This basically confirms the predicted behaviour: in pre-election years, early election years and full-blown election years there is a bias towards easing 'genuine' discretionary fiscal policy.

One way to interpret the results is in terms of the political dynamics. In non-election years governments may want to build up a 'war chest' which shows up as tight fiscal policy, and then go into the election year with a subsequent easing of fiscal policy. The problem of course is that an insufficient safety margin was created in a number of countries, with the result that some of them dangerously approached or exceeded the 3 per cent of GDP deficit ceiling as soon as the economy slowed down.

The result for the growth dividend shows that countries systematically took out some of this dividend in pre- or early election years if the cyclical position of the economy was strong. The results for the inflation dividend suggest strong inertia, that is, countries consistently project inflation to be either above or below the ECB target rate. A link between the inflation dividend and the election cycle cannot be demonstrated.

In sum, our analysis suggests that the electoral budget cycle is alive and well in EMU. Electoral manipulation of fiscal policy in EU countries – evidence of which in the pre-EMU period is found by Hallerberg and Strauch (2002) – has not been curbed by EMU's fiscal policy rules.[250] While the period examined is short and the electoral episodes for each country are limited, one should be cautious in drawing firm conclusions. Nevertheless, a number of other papers support our empirical findings. Our results are consistent with those of Von Hagen (2002a) who uses a similar indicator of discretionary fiscal policy, but focuses only on pre-election years and does not distinguish between expenditure and revenue changes. He finds that the expansionary stance in the 1998–2001 period for years preceding the election has been twice as large as that in other years. They are also consistent with Buti (2002) who uses the change in the cyclically adjusted primary balance as a measure of discretionary policy. He compares, for each year since 1999, the target for the cyclically adjusted budget balance in the national stability programmes submitted two years earlier with the outturn for the same year. His conclusion is that, while most countries missed their targets, deviations from target appear larger and more systematic in elections years.

6. CONCLUSIONS

EMU's fiscal rules are undergoing a serious stress-test and are currently being contested. Evidence on the fiscal behaviour in the early years of EMU shows that several countries have failed to abide by the spirit of the SGP. We have documented that the discipline requirements of the SGP were insufficient to curb the temptation to run politically motivated fiscal policies when elections approached. In political economy terms, the short-term gains at the national level of higher deficits outweighed the systemic costs involved in violating the rules. This contributed to the erosion in the 'political ownership' of the discipline rules after the Maastricht convergence period (Buti and Giudice, 2002).

Tackling this double political bias (pro-cyclical loosening in good times and electoral manipulation of fiscal policy) will however be difficult. Suggestions – such as that of introducing 'rainy day' funds by allowing countries to set aside revenue in good times which could then be used in bad times[251] – may be helpful but are unlikely to curb politically motivated fiscal behaviour. A radical approach would be to harmonize the electoral cycles in EMU: Sapir and Sekkat (1999) show that, if spill-overs between countries are positive, adopting a single election day would reduce politically induced distortions and be welfare-enhancing. But this idea is unlikely to be considered in the foreseeable future.

In the end, we are left with the need to step up budgetary surveillance, as suggested in Chapter 3, focusing in particular on structural balances and using peer pressure and 'early warnings' to curb fiscal misbehaviour. If this succeeds in pushing countries to create sufficient room for manoeuvre in non-election periods, some systematic easing of fiscal policy in electoral periods may have to be accepted.

10. Fiscal rules and statistics*

1. INTRODUCTION

The pros and cons of fiscal rules have long been debated.[252] On the one hand, fiscal rules are seen as a prevention device against opportunistic behaviour by policy makers and sharp discontinuities in public policies. On the other hand, rules are seen as a source of unnecessary rigidity in the budgetary process leading to sub-optimal outcomes.[253]

From the debate a trade-off emerged between enforceability and flexibility. Enforceability increases with the simplicity of a rule whereas flexibility decreases with it. Neither extremely complex nor extremely simple rules are desirable. In principle, the former can minimize distortions but are difficult to enforce; the latter are easy to enforce but do not take into account all factors which are important to policy-making.

The effectiveness of rules crucially depends on the indicators they refer to. Not only has the indicator to be relevant in view of the purpose of the rule, it also has to be based on a transparent and unambiguous operational and statistical framework. This issue has not been adequately dealt with in the discussion on fiscal indicators, particularly in the EMU context.

A vast literature stresses that the evaluation of all aspects of fiscal policy (e.g. macroeconomic effects, size of discretionary policy measures, impact on national savings, fiscal sustainability) cannot be based on a single indicator. The analysis of each aspect of fiscal policy is best conducted with reference to a specific indicator.[254]

Experience highlights the possibility that policy-relevant indicators can be manipulated. It also points to the dangers inherent in statistical frameworks allowing for different interpretations of accounting rules.[255] The issue is especially relevant in the European context, where sovereign countries have agreed to a set of fiscal rules while retaining full responsibility for their fiscal policy. The experience of the large *ex post* revisions of budget deficit and debt in Greece in 2004 is a painful reminder of the crucial importance of effective statistical governance.

The chapter assesses the indicators adopted in the European context

* Fabrizio Balassone, Daniele Franco and Stefania Zotteri, 'Fiscal Rules: Indicators and Underlying Statistical Frameworks', paper presented at the IIPF congress, 2003, Prague.

with respect to the objectives of the fiscal rules applying to the monetary union (fiscal soundness and budgetary flexibility) and to the margins for interpretation allowed for by the underlying operational and statistical framework (transparency).

The next section briefly reviews the rationale for and the lay-out of EMU fiscal rules. The two following sections assess EMU's deficit and debt indicators with regard to the objectives of fiscal soundness and fiscal flexibility. The fifth section considers the margins for interpretation allowed for by the underlying operational and statistical framework, and the sixth section draws some preliminary conclusions.

2. EMU FISCAL RULES

EMU fiscal rules were first designed to keep a sound fiscal stance so as to preserve stable monetary and financial conditions within the Union. The need for a budgetary stabilization policy at the national level was later recognized and rules were supplemented so as to reconcile soundness and flexibility of public finances.[256]

Stability is a public good. It results from prudent budgetary policies by all member states. However, each country has an incentive to free ride by undertaking undisciplined policies while benefiting from the others' proper behaviour. Generalized free-riding would rapidly destroy monetary union. Free-riding by some member states may undermine the credibility of the central bank's commitment to maintain stable monetary conditions. Fiscal misbehaviour may induce pressure by high debt countries for both *ex ante* bail-out (refraining from raising interest rates under inflationary tensions) and *ex post* bail-out (debt relief through unanticipated inflation).[257]

According to the theory of fiscal federalism, stabilization policy should be run by the central government: were it to be run locally, it would lose effectiveness due to spill-over effects.[258] However, EMU has no federal government and the size of the Union's budget does not allow an effective stabilization policy.[259] Therefore, in EMU the responsibility for stabilization falls on national budgets. In the case of asymmetric shocks, greater margins may be needed than in a situation in which monetary policy is still a national responsibility.[260]

As explained in Chapter 2, the Maastricht Treaty stresses that a sound fiscal position is a necessary condition for a successful monetary union (article 121). Article 104 and the annexed Protocol on excessive deficits lay out the criteria for assessing budgetary positions: (1) general government deficit must not exceed 3 per cent of GDP (save for exceptional circumstances, for a limited period, and for a limited amount); (2) general government debt must not exceed 60 per cent of GDP or, if above this limit, it must be decreasing sufficiently and approaching the limit at a satisfactory pace.

As recalled in previous chapters, the Stability and Growth Pact (SGP) specifies that each country should aim for a medium-term objective of a budgetary position 'close to balance or in surplus'. According to the guidelines of the European Council,[261] compliance with the SGP should be assessed considering the cyclical position of the economy. Even though not explicitly phrased in these terms, EMU rules may therefore be interpreted as requiring that each member state choose a budgetary target in cyclically adjusted terms and let automatic stabilizers or discretionary action operate symmetrically around it without bringing the nominal deficit above the 3 per cent limit.

Each member state has to report officially to the Commission the yearly budgetary outcomes by 1 March of the following year. The Notification is then updated by 1 September. Moreover, member states must submit their medium-term budgetary targets (stability programmes). These are updated annually and are subject to a review by the European Commission, the Economic and Financial Committee and the Council. The programmes must state the fiscal targets, the measures intended to allow their achievement and the underlying macroeconomic assumptions. Violations of either the deficit or the debt rule determine a situation of 'excessive deficit' which triggers a procedure intended to induce the adoption of corrective measures. Lacking corrective measures or lacking correction of the excessive deficit within the deadlines specified by the Council, sanctions may be imposed.

The reference accounting framework for the definition of the general government deficit and debt is specified in the Protocol on the excessive deficit procedure. The deficit is identified as the net borrowing as defined in the European System of Integrated Economic Accounts (ESA).[262] The debt is defined as gross financial liabilities at nominal (face) value consolidated between and within the sectors of general government. Although the debt measure is not defined in ESA, the relevant financial instruments are those specified within that framework. ESA underwent revisions during the 1990s. With the switch from the 1979 to the 1995 version, both the criteria according to which general government units are identified and those determining the accounting method have been better specified. Regarding government accounts the most relevant change is the more prominent role assumed by the accrual principle. Eurostat oversees the correct implementation of definitions and computational criteria by national statistical institutes and releases explanatory notes concerning controversial issues.[263]

3. SOUNDNESS OF PUBLIC FINANCES

Fiscal soundness is the main objective of EMU rules. While the intuition is clear (a sound policy avoids bankruptcy), the analytical and operational definition of soundness is not straightforward: how is the equilibrium between unnecessary restraint and irresponsible excess to be defined? This difficulty is mirrored by the lengthy debate on the definition of fiscal sustainability.

Deficit finance has long been considered a danger for the soundness of public finances.[264] Up to the mid-twentieth century it still met opposition based on concerns that 'continuous government borrowing results in an ever rising public debt, the servicing of which will require higher and higher taxes; and that the latter will eventually destroy our economy or result in outright repudiation of the debt'.[265]

Addressing such concerns, Domar (1944) showed that, given interest and growth rates, a constant deficit to GDP ratio implies a constant debt ratio and therefore a constant tax ratio. However, Domar's model does not determine the maximum sustainable debt level.[266] Although *ad hoc* definitions have been proposed, whereby sustainable policies would be those capable of keeping the debt ratio at its current level, the problem is left unsolved.[267] To determine the maximum sustainable level of debt one would need to specify the equation governing the dynamics of the debt to GDP ratio as a function of budgetary variables and of their effects on macroeconomic variables. Unfortunately there is no agreed theory of the interactions between the public budget and the economy. Moreover, a constant deficit cannot just be assumed; rather the future implications of current policies need to be assessed.[268]

Difficulties arise also with respect to the definition of the deficit and debt concepts. First, the sector of reference is to be defined. In principle, the definition should include all the public bodies whose financial behaviour has an impact on government accounts. Second, since the focus of sustainability analysis is the tax rate needed to finance the activities of the public sector, a comprehensive deficit measure is needed, that is, one that takes into account all government outlays and revenues (financial and non-financial). Third, as the sustainability of a given tax revenue must be measured relative to the corresponding tax base, the deficit must be scaled somehow and GDP represents an obvious proxy. Fourth, the deficit definition should be consistent with the debt definition. Fifth, the valuation of liabilities, from the point of view of government solvency, should reflect the price to be paid when liabilities fall due.

It finally must be pointed out that sustainability analysis has a forward-looking nature and cannot be based on 'point indicators' which only depict the current budgetary situation.[269] The assessment of future developments can refer either to explicit medium- to long-term projections of traditional 'point indicators' or to summary indicators of these projections, such as the change in net worth.[270] However both solutions rely on strong assumptions, which can always be debated, and lead to results whose robustness has to be tested. Therefore, they do not lend themselves to be adopted as a reference for formal rules (see also the fifth section).

Against this background, EMU fiscal rules take a cautious approach. As practical reasons forced the adoption of 'point indicators' as opposed to more forward-looking measures, tighter ceilings than otherwise necessary were chosen for yearly outcomes.[271] While the ceiling to the deficit ratio is consistent with Domar's requirement for sustainability; the debt ceiling is intended to avoid convergence at high levels of debt.[272] The arbitrariness sometimes attributed to the choice of the actual thresholds appears to reflect ambiguities in the theory rather than poor design of the rules. The choice of a gross debt measure also appears consistent with the focus of sustainability analysis and with the reasonable degree of prudence that is to be used in assessing solvency, given the unavoidable arbitrariness involved in the valuation of financial assets and of their degree of liquidity.

However, it is worth emphasizing that the deficit measure is not comprehensive (in the computation of net lending/borrowing, transactions in financial assets are considered 'below the line'), so that the deficit and debt measures are not mutually consistent (i.e. that the ESA95 deficit is not the flow concept corresponding to changes in the stock of gross financial liabilities). Also, nominal (face) value does not always coincide with redemption value.[273] The difference between the change in the debt and the deficit measure chosen for EMU rules was by no means negligible over the 1990s; the yearly average for EU countries between 1992 and 2001 was almost 1 per cent of GDP.

Finally, it must be noted that within EMU the need for a forward-looking assessment of the budgetary situation is somehow taken into account in the SGP which foresees the submission by member states of multi-year programmes including medium- to long-term projections whose internal consistency, underlying assumption and, ultimately, attainability are also subject to scrutiny. Long-term projections are becoming increasingly important in the monitoring of budgetary trends.[274]

4. BUDGETARY FLEXIBILITY

EMU's deficit measure (a nominal one) may be criticized in relation to the flexibility objective. While reference to a nominal indicator is appropriate for coping with exceptional circumstances,[275] this is not the case once normal cyclical fluctuations are taken into account as the SGP does. In this case, the obvious candidate indicator would be a cyclically adjusted balance (CAB).

However, the CAB only takes into account the 'automatic' effects of the cycle on public finances, which depend on the budget size relative to GDP and on the elasticity of revenue and expenditure programmes with respect to changes in GDP. Reference to the CAB discriminates against discretionary policy intervention: temporary extra deficit, incurred to smooth the cycle, would be seen as of 'non-cyclical' origin. Therefore, countries with weak automatic stabilizers and traditionally strong reliance on discretionary intervention would be penalized.

Moreover, the CAB is not directly observable. Its measurement requires statistical estimation. This in turn may make it unfit as a reference indicator for a rule. First, the elasticity of each budgetary item to the cycle has to be estimated. This may be done through either econometric regressions or deterministic simulations based on the legal structure underlying each revenue and expenditure programme. Second, the trend value of GDP (or, according to some methods, the trend value of the relevant macro-variable) has to be estimated by using either statistical filters or structural macro-models ('production function' approach). Finally, the estimate of the budgetary elasticity and that of the macro-trends have to be combined to compute the CAB.

There clearly is source for endless controversy. There is no agreement on the most appropriate method either at the academic level or at the applied one.[276] Taking these problems into account, the CAB was not chosen as a reference indicator. However, as mentioned earlier, the medium-term objective of a budgetary position 'close to balance or in surplus' defined by the SGP can be interpreted as referring to a cyclically adjusted balance. The Council has specifically required the programmes submitted by member states to include all necessary information to assess their cyclically adjusted budgetary position consistent with the nominal targets.[277]

A second problem arises from the fact that reference to both a stock and a flow indicator may be problematic with respect to the reconciliation of budgetary flexibility with sound public finances. The SGP focused on supplementing the deficit rule. However, as the debt rule was not further specified, there is a risk that the Pact does not fully achieve such a reconciliation.[278] Running stabilization policy through the budget while ensuring a reduction of the debt ratio also during cyclical downturns may call for high structural surpluses. If countries with debt to GDP ratios greater than 60 per cent set less ambitious targets, they will not be able to make full use of the margins allowed by the 3 per cent threshold. During cyclical downturns these countries may have to take a pro-cyclical budgetary stance.

The conflict between the need to reduce the debt ratio and the need to allow margins for stabilization policies is strengthened by the methodological differences between the debt and deficit measures used: they refer to different transactions and to different accounting conventions.

A possible solution would be the explicit provision of exceptions to the debt rule. However, as debt dynamics depend, for a given deficit, on debt level, on GDP growth and on transactions not included in the deficit, the identification of the exceptions is not unproblematic. The abolition of the debt rule would not provide a satisfactory solution: given that the debt is affected by transactions not included in net lending/borrowing, reference to the deficit rule alone would not ensure control of debt dynamics. However, the degree of consistency between the deficit and the debt rule could be increased by defining the deficit to include all transactions affecting the stock of debt. No extra costs for the Excessive Deficit Procedure would arise, as all necessary information is already provided by member countries to the European Commission.[279]

5. TRANSPARENCY

The dangers of a non-transparent statistical framework are well summarized by Clarke commenting on public accounts in the UK at the turn of the nineteenth century: 'only an old Treasury hand could be expected to know the difference within this hybrid accounting framework . . . therefore, the simple moral imperative of balancing the budget was in practice wrapped in the esoteric conventions of the public accounts' (1998, p. 64). Although progress has been made since then, several issues arise with reference to the transparency of EMU fiscal rules.

First, while reference to a predetermined and independently defined protocol (ESA) represents a significant advantage in terms of transparency (especially in a context where international comparison is crucial), no protocol can be detailed enough to avoid the need to better specify the intended meaning of its provisions with respect to all circumstances. This implies that *ad hoc* decisions have to be reached when countries introduce new accounting operations. At times compromise solutions are introduced. This can be seen in the treatment of swap operations: in order to accommodate different views, the deficit definition valid for the Excessive Deficit Procedure is now different from the national accounts one, which excludes the effects of such operations. It can also be seen in the treatment of some liabilities with general government, which is not based on redemption value, but on face value. However, the need to adopt solutions with an *erga omnes* validity has contributed to limit the number of *ad hoc* exceptions and adaptations.

Second, the definition of general government units still allows margins for interpretation. In ESA95 the distinction between market and non-market units is based on the size of own revenues relative to costs regardless of the branch of economic activity (in ESA79 some branches were conventionally assumed to be non-market).[280] Still there can be borderline cases, especially when revenues of public enterprises come from general government, which implies the need to ascertain whether these flows are truly revenues rather than transfers. Different classification of units producing the same good in different countries may affect comparability and significance of data.[281]

Third, the inconsistency between EMU's deficit and debt measures complicates the assessment of the stability programmes submitted by member states, which is assigned to the European Commission. While the programmes have to include targets for both variables, the information required for assessing the coherence between the targets is not always provided. Moreover, the exclusion of transactions in financial assets from the computation of the deficit allows margins for window-dressing: deficit figures can be improved by exploiting the uncertainty concerning the proper classification of some transactions. This also introduces a bias in the budgetary decision process against non-financial outlays.[282]

Fourth, the reliance on accrual data may open excessive margins for discretion. While economically more significant than cash data, accrual data embody judgemental elements. There is a risk of a sort of Goodhart effect,[283] which may also undermine the significance of general government data from national accounts for economic analysis. Awareness of the potential problems linked with full reliance on accrual data is apparent in Eurostat's decision to specify that revenues computed in accrual terms should include only those items that are likely to be actually cashed in, and that over the medium term accrual and cash data should converge.[284] The relevance of the issue is witnessed by the recent revision of the 2001 Portuguese deficit by almost 2 percentage points of GDP, which was partly motivated by the expiration of the derogation allowing Portugal to provide accrual data without ensuring consistency with cash data.

Fifth, the complexity of the overall statistical framework (which, it should be recalled, was designed to support not the enforcement of rules but meaningful economic analysis) implies a lengthy assessment process and delayed decisions (a recent example is the decision concerning the treatment of the proceeds of general government securitizations), possibly reducing the effectiveness of rules. The problem is worsened by reference to the accrual principle. As accrual data are essentially estimates based, *inter alia*, on cash data, their production is more time-consuming than that of cash data. Accrual data are also more likely to be revised than cash data due to changes in the assumptions used in their estimation. This also affects the effectiveness of the monitoring process envisaged in the Excessive Deficit Procedure.

Further threats to transparency come from operational arrangements governing the actual implementation of the rules: both the definition of the medium-term objective introduced by the Stability and Growth Pact and the role of long-term projections need to be better specified.

The definition of the medium-term objective introduced by the SGP is problematic. First, the length of the economic cycle, to which the medium term is assimilated, is a somewhat ambiguous concept. Second, reference to a target to be attained over the length of the cycle poses the same problems that would have had to be faced if a CAB was chosen as the reference indicator in the first place. Third, the use of non-technical language in order to specify the meaning of the 'medium-term target' allows wider margins of interpretation of the SGP's provisions, thereby increasing the risk that the assessment of a country position could be tainted by political considerations.[285]

While long-term projections are not given the status of a reference indicator for the rules, forecasts are one of the elements of the assessment of member states' budgetary positions, so that current arrangements do not fully avoid the uncertainty, and the ensuing controversy, that accompanies any estimation procedure. It should be noted that summary indicators of the deficit and debt level including off-budget liabilities would not improve on current arrangements: not only are these measures based on long-term projections, but also, by collapsing all the information into a single figure they make the underlying assumptions less transparent.

6. CONCLUSIONS

A 'good rule' must be based on indicators that are relevant to the motivation underlying the rule and whose computation allows limited margins for interpretation. When dealing with budgetary rules it is hard to strike the fine balance between the Scylla of missed opportunities as a consequence of the constraint and the Charybdis of waste and instability caused by its removal.

The discussion here has highlighted a number of discrepancies between the solutions adopted for EMU and those that in principle ought to be preferred.

With respect to the targets of EMU fiscal rules, it has been noted that: (1) as far as sustainability analysis is concerned, EMU rules do not seem to take sufficiently into account its forward-looking nature; moreover, the deficit measure adopted is not comprehensive and is not consistent with the debt measure; (2) concerning flexibility, nominal values are not the most appropriate reference for allowing budgetary flexibility over the cycle; moreover, reference to both a stock and a flow indicator may be problematic.

As to transparency, the inconsistency between deficit and debt measures can be problematic. Most importantly, reliance on accrual data may widen margins for discretion. From an operational point of view, further issues are raised by the informal role played by long-term projections and by the ambiguity in the definition of the medium-term target introduced by the SGP.

The definitions of debt and deficit relevant for EMU's fiscal rules took into account the need to ensure comparability of national statistics and to allow regular surveillance. Methodological choices were made with pragmatism. ESA was in 1992 and still is nowadays the only statistical protocol contemporaneously implemented by all EMU member states.

However, it is not clear that the revision of ESA to strengthen the weight of the accrual principle was made bearing the impact on EMU rules in mind. Awareness of the potential problems linked to full reliance on accrual data is apparent from Eurostat's decision to specify that data computed in accrual terms should include only those revenues that are likely to be actually cashed in, and that over the medium term accrual and cash data should converge.

As pointed out in Chapter 11, an extensive reform of the EMU fiscal framework in order to better deal with the sustainability and flexibility issues appears problematic. The introduction of a more formal role for cyclically adjusted balances and for long-term projections would increase the margins for discussion of any decision concerning the implementation of the rules, possibly leading the whole control system to a standstill.

Some progress can be achieved with respect to the issue of transparency, perhaps the most pressing at present. Two changes could be considered, characterized by different degrees of complexity and by different impacts. The simpler change would be to refer to cash accounts when compiling the deficit measure presently adopted. This would increase transparency and timeliness of data, thereby improving the effectiveness of both the rules and the monitoring process, while leaving unaffected the other shortcomings of the current arrangements that this chapter has identified. While it must be recognized that cash data are not immune from window-dressing, for example by delaying payments to providers or to employees, it is also true that in these circumstances there would be somebody voicing against such practices (the providers and the employees) which is not the case for opportunistic accrual accounting.

The more complex change would be to redefine the reference deficit as the change in nominal debt. This would have further benefits in terms of timeliness and transparency. As to the former, data on financial liabilities are available more rapidly than data on real transactions and on transactions in financial assets (generally the information set for the general government is complete within a month after the end of the reference period); as to the latter, data are usually publicly available from market sources.[286]

This change would also imply the use of a comprehensive deficit measure, in line with the focus of sustainability analysis.[287] Moreover, it would increase the consistency of EMU's fiscal framework as it would amount to collapsing the two indicators currently used into one, with benefits also in terms of the rules' flexibility. By applying the new deficit definition to both the medium-term target of close to balance or in surplus and the 3 per cent threshold, debt dynamics would also be under control and occasional increases in the debt to GDP ratio during downturns may thus be tolerated.

Greater transparency may *de facto* imply a tightening of EMU rules at a time when this option does not seem to be extremely fashionable; indeed several requests for a loosening of the rules have been motivated by the current economic downturn. In this respect, the benefits in terms of flexibility of the switch to a deficit defined as the change in nominal debt should be emphasized.

11. Reforming EMU's fiscal rules*

1. INTRODUCTION

As recalled through this book, the Stability and Growth Pact (SGP) is one of the pillars of EMU. It is a discipline device aiming at ensuring sound budgetary balances and low public debts. While widely regarded as a major innovation (Artis, 2002), the Pact has been the subject of heated controversy ever since its inception. It has been extensively criticized by academics and opinion makers. Proposals for radical changes have been put forward and even the suppression of the Pact has been considered. This debate accelerated in 2002 under the influence of public finance developments in a number of euro area countries which called into question its effectiveness and wisdom.

In a way, these policy problems and debates are related to the success of EMU rules in curbing deficits. When the public finances in a number of EU countries appeared to be on an unsustainable path, the benefits of lower deficits were evident. Fiscal discipline was recognized as a pre-condition to lower interest rates and to use fiscal policy for cyclical stabilization (Chapter 2). The arbitrary nature of the 3 per cent deficit limit appeared acceptable in view of the need to enforce fiscal discipline. Now that deficits have been lowered, the issue of the proper balance between fiscal discipline and other targets has come to the fore.

Our analysis and proposals take as given the current preferences for political integration. This implies that fiscal policies stay decentralized and coordination continues to be mainly of the negative type (i.e. surveillance) reflecting an enduring mistrust among euro area members. Obviously, if the euro increases the taste for political integration towards a fully fledged federal structure a different public finance system could be devised.

The outline of the chapter is as follows. The next section analyses how the SGP qualifies against ideal standards to be met when designing a fiscal rule. The third section examines the main proposals put forward to replace or radically revise the Pact. In the fourth section we make some suggestions

*Marco Buti, Sylvester Eijffinger and Daniele Franco, 'Revisiting EMU's Stability Pact: A Pragmatic Way Forward', *Oxford Review of Economic Policy*, 2003, 19(1): 100–11.

for improving the functioning of the SGP which can be implemented within the current institutional setting. The fifth section concludes.

2. FISCAL RULES FOR A MONETARY UNION

The role of fiscal institutions and procedures in shaping budgetary outcomes has been increasingly recognized. While 'good rules' do not necessarily entail 'good policies', inadequate budgetary institutions and procedures may contribute to a lack of fiscal discipline.

In Buti *et al.* (2003), we have analysed the 'quality' of EU fiscal rules in terms of the criteria identified by Kopits and Symansky (1998) and Inman (1996) for the design, implementation and enforcement of a fiscal rule. A good fiscal rule should be well designed (clearly defined, simple, transparent, consistent and flexible), allow effective implementation (by entailing *ex ante* and *ex post* compliance and efficient monitoring) and be enforceable (in terms of decision, amendment and sanctions). Our conclusion is that the SGP has strong points – in particular with regard to simplicity and monitoring – and weak points – namely concerning enforcement. However, in order to pass judgement, one has to consider that the criteria discussed in the literature were devised for assessing the quality of domestic fiscal rules. With EMU for the first time fiscal rules had to be devised in a multinational context.

EMU fiscal rules reflect the interaction between the multinational nature of EMU and the lack of a political authority of federal rank (see Chapter 1). This has important implications. First, national sovereignty and subsidiarity concerns had to be respected. This implies that rules are to be as neutral as possible vis-à-vis the countries' social preferences which are quite heterogeneous in the EU. This prevented, for instance, the adoption of rules which entail a choice of the role and size of the public sector in the economy.

Second, in a supra-national context, *ex post* compliance is important, given the higher risks of moral hazard and the higher difficulty in monitoring *ex ante* policy announcements. Reputational effects, such as those of 'early warnings' and excessive deficit positions, are also important, while the implementation of formal sanctions remains under question because of the political difficulty of imposing them on sovereign countries.

Third, the multinational character influences the trade-offs between the various criteria in complex ways. Take the trade-off between simplicity and flexibility. On the one hand, there may be a preference for simplicity over flexibility to allow peer pressure and central monitoring, and to prevent moral hazard. On the other hand, a multiplicity of countries increases heterogeneity and dispersion of preferences with the consequence that a one-size-fits-all fiscal rule is likely to be sub-optimal.

The supra-national nature of the EU fiscal rules has to be kept in mind when considering their possible reform.

3. REVISITING THE SGP: MAIN PROPOSALS

According to its critics, the Pact has several shortcomings: it reduces budgetary flexibility, works asymmetrically, is too uniform, does not sanction politically motivated fiscal policies, discourages public investment, disregards the area fiscal stance, and disregards long-term sustainability. In the end, the Pact would hamper economic growth.

In this context several proposals have been put forward for replacing or modifying the Pact. One way or another, all the proposals draw on one or more of the above criticisms. They can be grouped in three categories: reforms of national budgetary procedures, coordination at the euro area level, and a shift to different numerical rules.

3.1 Reform National Procedures and Institutions

The first-best strategy in ensuring sound fiscal policies would be that of dealing directly with the factors leading to excessive deficits at the national level. This would avoid relying on numerical parameters which are necessarily arbitrary. Fiscal policy soundness would be ensured either by market discipline or by procedures assuring fiscal responsibility at the national level.

This strategy answers the criticism concerning the lack of budgetary flexibility. Budgetary flexibility is limited especially in the transition to broadly balanced budgets: in a situation of subdued growth, such transition requires pro-cyclical policies that may worsen the cyclical conditions. Moreover, pro-cyclical policies cannot be excluded in the future if the room for manoeuvre envisaged by the SGP turns out to be insufficient to cope with large-scale recessions and adverse shocks. Two sets of proposals come under this heading.

Procedural reforms

Procedural reforms impose changes on the rules concerning the presentation, adoption and execution of government budgets. Hierarchical procedures are more conducive to fiscal discipline than collegial procedures. At the national level, hierarchical rules attribute strong power to treasury ministers to overrule spending ministers during the intra-governmental preparation of the budget and limit the ability of the parliament to amend the government's budget proposals.

Replacing the numerical limits with procedures ensuring sound budgetary positions would raise two problems. First, there is still a need for transparent and rapid criteria for selecting new entrants to the euro area. Second, the adoption of harmonized budgetary procedures would raise problems from the point of view of national sovereignty and might conflict with national institutions and traditions. The alternative solution – country-specific procedures approved at EU level – would also be problematic. The *ex ante* effectiveness of these procedures would be very difficult to evaluate. Moreover, in case they did not prove effective in constraining deficits, the attribution of responsibility would be difficult as national governments might argue that they have implemented the agreed procedures.

In the end, while effective national budgetary procedures are important in ensuring sound fiscal policies at the national level, they do not appear at present to be a viable solution at the EU level. However, some procedural rules (such as common accounting conventions or the adoption of stability programmes) are called on to ensure compliance with the budget constraints.

Institutional reforms

The proposal to assign to a newly created independent body the role of setting fiscal targets draws on the experience of central banks running monetary policy. The independent body would aim at delivering both long-term stability/sustainability and flexible short-term stabilization. Setting up such institutions would imply a principal–agent solution for the fiscal discipline problem.

Wyplosz (2002) suggests allocating to a Fiscal Policy Committee (FPC) the responsibility for setting the budget balance on the basis of a debt sustainability constraint defined over a number of years. The constraint would either be expressed as an obligation to achieve budget balance over the cycle or to reduce or stabilize the debt ratio over a given horizon. The FPC would be accountable to Parliament. In order to replace the existing EU rules, each country would have to adopt a statute for the new body compatible with agreed norms. The FPC's statute would indicate its goals, powers and the conditions under which deviations from its goals are allowed.

While intellectually appealing, this proposal runs into serious feasibility problems. Fiscal policy is – differently from monetary policy – at the heart of the political decision-making process. The separation between setting a target for the budget balance (to be entrusted to the FPC) and the allocative and distribute functions (to remain the responsibility of government and parliament) may turn out to be difficult. Decisions about the budget balance affect the composition of expenditure and revenues. Politically, it is hard to conceive that a minister of finance would delegate part of fiscal policy authority to an independent agency.

3.2 Fiscal Policy Coordination at the Euro Area Level

A second category of reform proposals envisages fiscal coordination at the euro area level. In a currency union, only the aggregate fiscal stance is relevant for the policy mix at the euro area level and, as such, enters the reaction function of the central bank. Hence it is suggested to set a target for the euro area as a whole and then share it between member countries.

These solutions answer the allegation that SGP disregards the aggregate fiscal stance. Under the Pact, each country is responsible for national fiscal policies. However, the aggregation of nationally determined fiscal policies may not result in an optimal fiscal stance at the euro area level.

Fiscal coordination can be achieved either via community-level decisions indicating the desirable budget balance of each country or a market-based allocation of national deficit shares of the total euro area deficit.

Community allocation of deficit shares

A proposal for a coordination mechanism in the budgetary domain was submitted by the French Finance Minister at the informal Ecofin Council in April 1999. The proposal stressed that the aggregate policy stance at the EMU level must be examined on the basis of an aggregate stability programme. It pointed out that the objective to achieve an adequate policy stance for EMU as a whole should be taken into account when examining the national stability programmes.

A natural implication of this is that the 3 per cent of GDP deficit criterion would only apply to the average deficit for the euro area. Member states would be permitted to overshoot the 3 per cent deficit ceiling if there were other countries with deficits below that value. Since the amplitude of cyclical fluctuations is much smaller for the euro zone as a whole, the targets needed to prevent an overshooting of the aggregate deficit ceiling would be less stringent than those necessary for each member state individually.

However, in the present institutional set-up of EMU the deficit criterion applies to each member state individually. The Maastricht budgetary rules would thus have to be renegotiated in order to allow this interpretation to be implemented. Bureaucratic allocation of deficit shares would be highly controversial. Moreover, if the norm for budgetary behaviour in EMU is that of relying on automatic stabilizers, the likelihood that the aggregation of the national fiscal stances would give rise to an inappropriate stance at the aggregate level is negligible.

In sum, while a shift to numerical constraints applying to the euro area as a whole is politically unfeasible and probably economically undesirable, a move towards a framework which encompasses an assessment of the fiscal stance of the euro area as a whole prior to that of the individual members could be envisaged (see Chapter 12). However, steps in this direction should not lead to a relaxation of national fiscal responsibility.

Market allocation of deficit permits

Casella (2001) proposes to use market mechanisms in the allocation of 'deficit shares' in EMU. Having chosen an aggregate target for the Union and an initial distribution of tradable deficit permits, EMU countries could be allowed to trade rights to deficit creation. While this system keeps the aggregate area-wide deficit unchanged, it allows individual member states to deviate from the initial allowances in the case of idiosyncratic shocks. If a country is hit by a negative shock, it can use fiscal policy to counteract the shock by buying permits from surplus countries.

The mechanism would minimize the aggregate cost of compliance with the aggregate targets and provide rewards for countries running surpluses in favourable cyclical conditions, thereby tackling the issue of the asymmetric working of the Pact (Buti and Martinot, 2000). It would also reduce the room for political manipulation.

This scheme is subject to three main difficulties. First, efficacy requires that the deficits of the various governments generate the same externality and are thus perfect substitutes. But the risk of triggering a financial crisis is not uniform across governments. Second, the efficiency of the market in permits depends on how competitive it is. This makes the mechanism ill suited to situations in which the number of governments is small. Finally, there is no easy solution to the problem of determining the initial allotment of permits. The possible criteria (GDP, population, etc.) would produce greatly differing allocations. If the initial demand for permits exceeded the supply, then the countries with an allotment greater than their requirement would enjoy positional rents.

3.3 Alternative Numerical Rules: Factoring in the 'Quality' of Public Finances

Numerical constraints on domestic fiscal policy in terms of an indicator of overall fiscal performance are more suited to the multinational context of EMU, in which moral hazard issues are quite relevant, and to the need for rapid results. Compliance to numerical rules is somewhat simpler to evaluate.

Numerical rules can be divided into two groups. The first includes the rules of a *static* nature, concerning the level and composition of the public budget in a specific year. The second includes the rules of a more *dynamic* nature, referring to debt development and fiscal sustainability. The two categories are respectively examined in this part of the section and the next.

The SGP focuses on the yearly budget balance. However, a growing body of literature points out that the composition of public finances matters as well. The focus on quality has been translated into two proposals for reforming the SGP: shifting from a deficit target to (a) an *expenditure target/rule* or moving to (b) the so-called *golden rule* of deficit financing.

Expenditure rules

Focus on expenditure has the advantage of controllability because expenditure depends much less than revenue on the business cycle. Expenditure rules can link the annual budgetary process to a multi-annual policy framework. They refer to the budgetary items that governments can control and can be easily defined and monitored. Moreover, they allow stabilizers to work on the revenue side and may prevent expenditure relaxation in upturns.

Ideally, expenditure rules should use a comprehensive definition of public expenditure, including both discretionary items and entitlements, and apply to the different levels of government. They should require both *ex ante* and *ex post* compliance. Deviations in one year should be compensated in the following years.

The use of expenditure rules in a multinational context, however, appears problematic. First, uniform spending rules would *de facto* impose homogeneous social preferences to politically heterogeneous countries while country-specific rules would be difficult to enforce. Second, spending norms do not refer to the fiscal variables which can produce negative externalities. While a rising deficit or debt level in one country can create area-wide problems, a rising expenditure level as such does not have negative repercussions on other countries. Morever, expenditure rules cannot prevent deficit and debt increases stemming from tax cuts. Therefore, they would have to be complemented by a deficit or debt rule. Third, since no uniform expenditure to GDP ratio can be prescribed, countries would be required to indicate targets for the expenditure ratio consistent with the desired deficit ratio. Finally, the size of the budget typically reflects the political preferences of the government. A new government may want to renegotiate the commitments of its predecessor.

In sum, while expenditure rules may prove useful at the national level, they are more appropriate as complements to rather than substitutes of rules on deficits and debt.

The golden rule

A number of authors have suggested replacing the SGP by some form of golden rule (Blanchard and Giavazzi, 2004). Borrowing would be allowed to finance public investment. As already pointed out by Musgrave (1939), implementing the golden rule requires establishing a dual budget separating investment spending from current spending.

The golden rule would allow the burden of capital projects to be spread over the different generations of tax payers benefiting from them and would avoid the efficiency loss caused by distortionary taxation if the tax rate fluctuates over time. This would answer some criticisms expressed against the SGP. In fact, maintaining budget positions 'close to balance or in surplus' implies that capital expenditure will have to be funded from current revenues, which may in turn imply a disincentive to undertake projects producing deferred benefits. The disincentive is stronger during consolidation periods.

However, as pointed out in Chapter 6, there are a number of arguments against the introduction of the golden rule (see also Buiter, 2001). First, the alleged incompatibility between the SGP and a properly defined golden rule is questionable. In order to spread the burden of capital spending over the different generations of taxpayers, the rule would have to refer to net spending.[288] While commonly agreed estimates of amortization are not available, in developed countries in which infrastructures are partly developed by subjects not included in general government, the level of net investment seems limited and not necessarily inconsistent with the close-to-balance rule of the SGP.[289]

Second, if applied to gross public investment, the golden rule would be an obstacle to deficit and debt reduction. Given the ratio of public investment as a percentage of GDP, the long-run equilibrium level of government debt could be quite high, especially in an environment of low inflation.

Third, singling out public investment from other budget items makes little sense. What is important is overall capital accumulation in both private and public capital. For instance, a well-devised tax reform that, by lowering tax burden and distortions, leads to higher investment may be preferable to public investment. Moreover, there is no clear evidence in the empirical literature that investment in public infrastructure always leads to significant positive growth effects. Some studies suggest that government investment may be subject to rapidly decreasing returns (see, e.g., De la Fuente, 1997). From the standpoint of intergenerational equity, it is not clear that a combination of higher infrastructure investment and higher public debt would necessarily be preferable to lower investment *plus* lower debt. Moreover, a golden rule may distort expenditure decisions in favour of physical assets and against spending on intangibles that can make a relevant contribution to economic growth, for example those increasing human capital.

Finally, the golden rule would make the multilateral surveillance process more complex by providing leeway for opportunistic behaviour, since governments would have an incentive to classify current expenditure as capital spending.

3.4 Alternative Numerical Rules: Focus on Debt Level and Sustainability

The current EU rules do not focus on the issue of sustainability and disregard the fact that countries are different. This criticism has different nuances. First, the SGP focuses almost exclusively on short-term objectives for the budget deficit. As such, it provides incentives for creative accounting and one-off measures which blur the transparency of public accounts. Second, the stock of public debt does not enter the SGP and neither do the contingent liabilities of public pension systems. Hence, the Pact treats equally countries with different medium- and long-term prospects and different debt levels. Third, the Pact may prevent countries from implementing certain policies – such as pension reforms which improve long-term sustainability at the price of a short-term deficit worsening.[290]

Two solutions have been put forward in the literature: the first is to choose a medium-term target that ensures long-term sustainability while taking on board country specificities; the second is to give more weight to the public debt.

From the Maastricht parameters to tax smoothing

As catching-up countries are characterized by higher potential growth and higher inflation (the latter due to the Balassa–Samuelson effect), they can afford to have higher deficits without endangering the long-term sustainability of public finances. Hence the 3 per cent of GDP deficit ceiling and the close-to-balance rule are over-restrictive for these countries. Given the higher public investment needs of less mature economies, the current fiscal rules could harm the catching-up process.

Buiter and Grafe (2003) propose a Permanent Balance Rule which would ensure sustainability and fiscal prudence while taking into account country differences. Their rule is a strong form of tax smoothing: it requires that the inflation-and-real-growth-adjusted permanent government budget is in balance or surplus. The permanent budget balance is given by the difference between the constant long run average future values of tax revenue and government spending.

While the rule is theoretically appealing, its applicability appears doubtful (Pench, 2003). First, it requires estimation of the permanent value of tax and spending, thereby requiring to take into account future social and political preferences and make assumptions on future growth rates. This would probably violate the criteria of simplicity and enforceability discussed earlier. Second, nominal GDP growth can be higher in catching-up economies but also highly variable. This implies a potential conflict between discipline and stabilization. If a country which maintains a high structural deficit is hit by a shock, the automatic stabilizers may lead to very high deficits. While in principle these deficits are of a cyclical nature, the risk of spiralling debt and interest payments should not be disregarded. This risk is particularly high in accession countries which still suffer from limited creditworthiness and may see capital inflows dry up quickly.

More weight on the public debt

A way to overcome the uniformity of the Pact is to attribute more importance to public debt. Calmfors and Corsetti (2002) suggest making the deficit ceiling dependent on the stock of debt. The deficit ceiling of 3 per cent of GDP should apply only to countries with a debt ratio in excess of 55 per cent of GDP (see also EEAG, 2003). A higher ceiling would apply to countries with lower debt. For instance, a ceiling of 4 per cent of GDP would be set for countries with a stock of debt between 35 and 45 per cent.

This proposal respects the requirement of simplicity while improving incentives and country differentiation. It would be 'enlargement friendly' as most of the newcomers have a fairly low stock of debt. However, it would require a change in the Treaty. As we argue in the next section, a similar debt–deficit articulation could be obtained through a system of 'rainy day funds'.

Tackling the issue head on, Pisani-Ferry (2002) suggests giving countries the choice of opting out of the Excessive Deficit Procedure and embracing a Debt Sustainability Pact.[291] This Pact would allow countries that kept their debts below 50 per cent of GDP and published comprehensive fiscal accounts to be exempted from the standard excessive deficit procedure and sanctions. Fiscal accounts would provide estimates of the future impact of budgetary commitments, such as the financing needs of public pay-as-you-go pension schemes. Better fiscal accounting would provide more discipline by the financial markets.

The countries adopting the Debt Sustainability Pact would be required to submit a medium-term programme indicating a five-year target for the debt ratio, which would represent the benchmark for assessing their results. They would have greater flexibility in the short term. The focus of EU monitoring would shift from the year-by-year monitoring of the deficit to a medium-term perspective based on long-term fiscal sustainability.

This proposal, however, is also somewhat problematic. First, although targets for the debt ratio may install incentives for governments in the long term, there may be some room for manipulation, by, for example, sale-and-lease-back constructions. Moreover, the proposal is built on the assumption that deficits do not matter in EMU if debt levels are under control. This however is doubtful, especially from a policy mix standpoint. Second, while greater reference to the debt ratio does not raise measurement problems, reference to implicit liabilities is more problematic. Estimates are subject to considerable uncertainty related to the macroeconomic, demographic and behavioural scenarios.

Nonetheless, disregard of the issue of public debt is a clear limitation of the SGP. As argued below, this dimension could be reintegrated without overhauling the current fiscal rules.

4. REVISITING THE SGP: WORKABLE IMPROVEMENTS

4.1 Lessons from the Debate

Each of the proposals examined so far draws attention to one or more potentially serious problems with the design and implementation of the SGP. The suggestion to implement institutional and procedural reform highlights the need for an independent enforcer. The idea to move to a golden rule emphasizes the need to preserve the growth aspect of the SGP. A number of proposals highlight the excessive uniformity of the current rules. Taking into account the different levels of public debt points to the need to insert the sustainability dimension into the core of the SGP. The idea of an aggregate stability programme highlights the need to take into account the euro area dimension when assessing national budgetary policies. The proposal of establishing a market for deficit permits tackles the problem of the pro-cyclical bias in good times.

However, none of the proposals put forward in the literature represents a Pareto improvement. While appropriate for tackling some of the problems highlighted in the debate, each of them does not solve all problems and may even aggravate some of them. Also, 'first-best' solutions at the national level may end up being 'third-best' when transposed to a supra-national context. Finally, from a political perspective, attempting to rewrite the rules from scratch may lead to a vacuum in which the current rules are suspended while none of the alternative options is supported by a sufficiently large political constituency.

Our analysis of the SGP against desirable rules standards for design and compliance shows that the current EU fiscal rules fare reasonably well, especially if account is taken of their multinational character. Nonetheless, improvements can be achieved. In our view, key aspects are allowing a certain country specificity, rebalancing their sticks and carrots, and enhancing enforcement mechanisms.

4.2 A Pragmatic Way Forward

Our proposal involves a diversification of the medium-term targets, higher transparency and better monitoring, mechanisms to correct misbehaviour in good times and a non-partisan application of the rules.

A country-by-country articulation of the medium-term budgetary target

The close-to-balance rule interpreted as broadly balanced budgets in cyclically adjusted terms may lead to excessive uniformity between countries. It treats equally countries with different debt levels, contingent liabilities, and public investment needs. So far, countries are only differentiated in the variability of the cyclical component of the budget balance: economies subject to higher business cycle volatility and having larger automatic stabilizers require a larger cyclical safety margin in order to avoid breaching the 3 per cent of GDP deficit ceiling in normal cyclical circumstances (European Commission, 2002a).

The articulation of the medium-term budgetary targets could be extended to (a) the financial fragility of the country embodied in stock of public debt and (b) the threat to long-term sustainability given by the implicit liabilities of pension systems.

Countries with a relatively low stock of debt – that is, well below the 60 per cent of GDP reference value – and with relatively low estimated contingent liabilities could be allowed to have cyclically adjusted budget deficits up to their minimal benchmarks. This solution would be consistent, in most cases, with a prudent version of the golden rule.

Commonly agreed estimates of contingent liabilities in EU countries would have to be computed. Countries would have to provide transparent projections on a regular basis.[292] The possibility to have a small structural deficit could be limited to the countries for which expenditure trends do not imply a debt level rising above the 60 per cent threshold over a certain period of time.

The debt ratio in high debt countries and in countries with expected rising expenditure levels would decline fast, thereby contributing to offset the burden of ageing in the future, while in the other countries deficit levels would ensure the maintenance of a small public debt.

Improving transparency

An effort should be devoted to enhancing transparency in current and perspective fiscal accounts. In general, transparency can increase the credibility of rules by allowing better judgement of fiscal performance and by limiting the role of accounting creativity in meeting targets.

The current EMU fiscal framework has been criticized for its lack of transparency. This issue has different facets. First, in order to meet the short-term targets, countries have frequently adopted one-off, cash-raising measures instead of making the necessary structural adjustment. Second, under the current system of national accounts, monitoring is hampered by delays in data provision with the implication that the whistle is often blown far too late. Third, data on off-budget liabilities and budgetary prospects have generally been rather limited.

To remedy the first problem, compliance with the EU rules should distinguish between long-lasting and one-off measures (European Commission, 2002b). Given the current legislation and accounting conventions, the 3 per cent rule cannot be modified to allay this concern. However, in deciding whether or not to address an early warning to a deviant country, the existence of temporary measures should be ascertained.

The problem of early detection of deviations from targets was vividly exposed in the case of Portugal in 2001 and Greece in 2004. Moreover, one can see that public debt growth has frequently exceeded the deficit level. Stock-flow effects have systematically contributed to debt growth. A way to tackle this issue is to resurrect, in parallel with national accounts definitions, regular monitoring of cash flows (see Chapter 10). National authorities would be required to indicate *ex ante* cash figures broadly consistent with the ESA95 balance. Alternatively, changes in the debt level (net of the effects of exchange rate changes and privatization proceeds) could be monitored. If a significant departure from target is detected in financial flows, it would be up to them to explain this difference.

Finally, on the basis of an agreed and transparent framework, governments could be required to provide estimates of off-budget liabilities, of their net asset position and of long-term budgetary trends. Estimates should be revised every year, and changes should be explained.

Tackling misbehaviour in good time

It is widely recognized that the SGP does not provide sufficient incentives for countries to run prudent fiscal policies in good times. Within the boundaries of the current rules, a two-pronged approach could be the following: first, devise a sanction to punish early slippages in good times, and second, facilitate countries to behave prudently in periods of upturn.

In order to step up peer pressure, a possible solution could be that of using the early warning procedure of the SGP not only in bad times when the deficit approaches the 3 per cent ceiling, but also in good times when a significant divergence from structural targets is detected.

The introduction of rainy day funds may improve policies in good times. These are reserve funds that would be used in times of recession and replenished in upturns. Rainy day funds are used by several US states and Canadian provinces to buffer the effects of unexpected negative events and cyclical downturns (Knight and Levinson, 1999). These funds might increase the incentive for governments not to waste the surpluses in good times and increase the room for manoeuvre in bad times. They would also increase the role of public budgets in stabilizing the economy over the cycle. The possibility to accumulate such funds could be made a function of the country's level of public debt. For instance, it could be open only to countries with a stock of debt below a certain threshold and the allowed maximum size of accumulated funds could be increased the lower the stock of debt. This would *de facto* make the deficit ceiling a negative function of the debt ratio.

The establishment of rainy day funds would imply a review of the current ESA accounting rules for calculating budgetary indicators. Transfers of resources to and withdrawal from the fund would now be considered financial operations (below the line) and hence deficit-neutral. A revised interpretation should establish that transfer of resources to the fund in good times reduces the budget surplus while withdrawal from the fund in bad times is considered as additional revenue and thus reduces the deficit. There should be some rule to ensure that rainy day funds are used only in recessions.

The possibility to establish rainy day funds would obviously not tackle the root of the incentive problem that governments have in good times. However, the flexibility that they would provide would allow a tightening of sanctioning procedures for countries exceeding the 3 per cent limit. For instance, the payment of the non-interest bearing deposit could be accelerated and the closeness clause (the amount by which the 3 per cent limit can be exceeded) could be defined in a strict way.

Non-partisan implementation of the rules

A strong criticism of EMU rules is that enforcement is partisan: national authorities are supposed to apply the rules to themselves, thereby having incentives for collusion and horse-trading.

In order to move to a non-partisan implementation of the rules, one has to distinguish between three types of decisions which need to be taken in the implementation of the SGP: (1) technical decisions on the compliance with the rules; (2) political decisions on measures to be taken to prevent or correct an excessive deficit; and (3) implementation of sanctions.

The Commission should be entrusted with the implementation of decision (1). It should be entitled to deliver the first early warning, and to determine the existence of an excessive deficit. The Commission, without requiring approval by the Council, would also assess whether exceptional circumstances apply.

The Council should take decision (2) on the measures to be implemented to correct the fiscal imbalance. Hence, the Council should decide on the second early warning which has to specify the corrective measures. As prescribed by current rules, the decision would be taken by the Council on a qualified majority basis following a recommendation by the Commission.

Decision (3) on the application of sanctions is of both a technical and a political nature. Leaving it exclusively to the Commission alone would be unthinkable. A solution that would reduce the risk of a partisan (non) application of sanctions would be to move from a Commission *recommendation* to a Commission *proposal*. The difference is that the Council can move away from the Commission proposal only with unanimity and not with a qualified majority as in the case of a Commission recommendation. An alternative could be that countries in exessive deficit commit to abstain in the vote in EDP procedures concerning other countries (Buti and Pench, 2004).

These changes are consistent with the spirit of the current rules. However, in order to be implemented fully, a change in the Treaty would be required. If agreement on the principle is achieved, this could be enshrined in a European Council resolution which would state that, in the case of the technical decisions, the Council commits to reject the Commission recommendations only with unanimity. The crucial question is, of course, whether or not the Council is prepared to strengthen the authority of the Commission in the interest of the credibility of EU fiscal rules.

5. CONCLUSIONS

The SGP's aim is to balance fiscal discipline and fiscal stabilization in a multinational context in which countries ultimately remain responsible for fiscal policy. It tries to combine some flexibility for exceptional events with a need for predefining the necessary room for manoeuvre to smooth the business cycle.

While the Pact presents drawbacks – particularly in terms of investment financing, asymmetric incentives and lack of a long-term view – it is not evident that any alternative would be preferable on every account. Most of the benefits of alternative rules can be attained by an appropriate interpretation of the SGP provisions which would diversify countries' fiscal commitments according to their specific economic and public finance features.

Our basic tenet is that there are no miracle solutions to cure the Pact's weaknesses. Changes might obviously regard the specific values of the parameters, but not the underlying philosophy – that is, setting a prudent budgetary objective in normal times and a deficit ceiling in bad times.

Only five years into EMU, any radical change would be highly problematic from a political standpoint. The obvious risk is that of ending up in a vacuum in which the old rules are called into question while the agreement on a new set of rules fails to materialize. Venturing into an EMU without fiscal rules would be a leap in the dark. At the same time, given the current level of political integration, the conditions for a federal system of public finances do not seem to exist.

While we are sceptical of reopening the debate on the SGP, we think that its functioning can nonetheless be improved. Our main proposals concern redefining the medium-term budgetary targets, improving transparency, tackling the pro-cyclical fiscal bias in good times, moving towards non-partisan application of the rules and improving transparency in the data. This set of ideas can allow the achievement of both stronger discipline and higher flexibility and can be implemented without requiring major revision of the existing rules. An assessment of the aggregate fiscal position prior to the evaluation of the individual national policies can also be considered. It may help to achieve a coherent fiscal stance at the euro area level, but it should not weaken the current framework.

These proposals do not provide a recipe for tackling the problems encountered by countries still in transition towards lower deficits in the event of a cyclical slump. Nevertheless, if implemented, they would limit the type of behaviour which is largely responsible for the fiscal tensions experienced in the early years of EMU.

12. National budgets and the EU budget*

1. INTRODUCTION

As it stands today, the EU budget is a historical relic. Three failures are most evident. First, its spending composition is heavily tilted towards the support of a declining sector, agriculture; second, it is almost impossible to reallocate spending across time and across policies to reflect economic and political priorities; and third, its size bears no comparison to any of the budgets of EU countries and it is unrelated to the EU goals.

First, in terms of composition, the current EU budget still largely reflects a double deal: the EC-6's Common Market and the Single Act of 1985. The first deal entailed a large share of Community expenditure devoted to the Common Agricultural Policy (CAP) as a price to be paid for allowing Germany's industrial products to enter the French market. The second deal saw the rise of spending on cohesion and regional policies in the context of the Iberian enlargement as the price to be paid for compensating the possible losers of the 1992 Single Market project. Those two policies together represent some 85 per cent of the EU budget. The remaining 15 per cent is divided between third countries' policies (essentially development aid and growth-enhancing assistance), internal allocative policies (such as research, trans-European networks, etc.) and administrative expenditure. The EU does not finance a EU-wide welfare system and thus plays no role in explicit interpersonal redistribution. However, the CAP, which originally represented much of the allocative function of the EU budget by moving away from price support towards direct aid, increasingly contributes interpersonal redistribution. Equally the EU budget has no role in macroeconomic stabilization.

Second, the EU budget displays a degree of rigidity far exceeding that of national budgets both across time[293] and across budgetary headings. Both in the multi-annual programming and in the annual budgetary procedure, the transfer of money across budgetary headings is subject to cumbersome procedures, largely exceeding those at the national level.

*Marco Buti and Mario Nava, 'Towards a European Budgetary System', EUI Working Papers RSC, 2003/8.

Third, given its small size (1.05 per cent of GDP in 2003), the EU budget has practically no macroeconomic relevance. National budgets, measured as the average of public spending, amounted in 2002 to 48 per cent of GDP in the euro area and 47 per cent of GDP in the EU as a whole. The smallest national budget – that of Ireland – is almost 36 per cent of GDP. Moreover, the maximum size (1.27 per cent of EU GNP) of the EU budget is predetermined by a 1992 political agreement confirmed in 1999 and bears no relation to goals and objectives of the EU.

While highlighting these three failures, we do not deny two positive features of the EU budget compared to national budgets, namely simplicity and transparency. Nevertheless it is increasingly evident that the current EU budget is inconsistent with the present state and future prospects of European integration. While its historical and political roots are deep, the EU budget does not stand up to economic and political scrutiny: no federation (mature or not) around the world has a budget whose dominant share is devoted to supporting a declining sector, does not provide public goods typically featuring large economies of scale, and does not supply any stabilization in the case of idiosyncratic disturbances.

Starting from this initial assessment, two alternative approaches are possible. Either one considers that the current EU budget is a 'political equilibrium' whereby money is transferred across countries according to the logic of the *juste retour.*[294] Hence, any adjustment to the Budget can only be at the margin. Or, as we do in this chapter, one considers that the added value generated by EU expenditure should focus on the issue of 'who pays what' and therefore even a radical change of the functions of the EU budget is possible (and indeed desirable).

How can the weaknesses of the present budgetary arrangements be tackled? We propose to establish a vertical coordination between national and EU budgets by moving towards a European Budgetary System in which both the national and the EU budget 'play together'. At present, there is no coordination between the EU and national budgets, either on the spending or on the revenue side. The issue of coordination between EU and national budgets is an area left largely unexplored by the economic literature.

The chapter is organized as follows. The next section, after a bird's-eye view of the theory of multi-level finance, presents a conceptual framework for vertical coordination between the EU and the national budgets. The third section identifies the areas where EU finances should be reoriented and the fourth section deals with the issue of flexibility in the EU budget. The following two sections tackle the issue of coordination between the EU budget and the national budgets, with the fifth section putting forward the idea of a European Budgetary System, the main proposal of the chapter, and the sixth section spelling out how it could work in practice. The seventh section concludes.

2. RETHINKING THE FUNCTIONS OF THE EU BUDGET

2.1 The Old and New Theory of Multi-level Public Finance: A Bird's-eye View

Thinking of the future EU budgetary system raises the issue of the allocation of competencies between the Community and the member states. The classic theory of fiscal federalism and new political economy of multi-level government set a number of criteria for deciding how to allocate competencies between the central EU level and member states. Classic fiscal federalism emphasizes the need to:

1. *Internalize externalities*: if the positive effects of programmes on economic actors other than those financing them are not internalized, free-riding will lead to an under-supply of such programmes.
2. *Avoid internalities*: prevent beneficiaries of spending programmes from shifting their financing onto agents (usually tax payers in the same or in other jurisdictions) who do not benefit from those programmes.
3. *Exploit economies of scale*: increase the efficiency of supply arising from declining costs of production.
4. *Attain minimum size*: small countries or jurisdictions do not attain the critical mass to provide the minimum amount of certain types of public goods.
5. *Take into account heterogeneity of preferences*: when preferences between jurisdictions are heterogeneous, a decentralized provision of public goods is superior in comparison to a uniform supply at the central level.

While fiscal federalism focuses on competencies, a parallel can be drawn between these and spending allocations.[295] The theory implies that the functions of two of Musgraves' three branches of government – that is, income redistribution and cyclical stabilization – should be carried out at a sufficiently high level of government. In the public finance area, the allocation function deals with the provision of public goods either as pure public goods (non-rival and non-excludable), quasi-collective goods or merit goods (Moesen, 2002).

As shown by Alesina *et al.* (2001a, 2003), there exists a trade-off between the benefits of scale and the costs of heterogeneity: the EU should focus on policy areas where economies of scale and externalities are large, and delegate to national or lower-level governments the policy areas where heterogeneity of preferences is predominant relative to the benefits of scale.

Classic fiscal federalism is built on the assumption of a benevolent social planner. The new theory of fiscal federalism encompasses the political economy of the decision making process (see, e.g., Persson *et al.*, 1996; Tabellini, 2003).

Three aspects are emphasized. First, second-best considerations related to constraints in policy formation imply that the provision of a public good, at a level different from the optimal one, in the absence of such constraints, can still be welfare enhancing. Second, in order to foster political acceptability of provision of a certain programme, it is necessary to compensate the losers. For instance, 'giving something to everybody' may be inefficient (by entailing 'transfer churning'), but may enhance the political acceptability of redistribution.[296] Third, the fiscal federalism literature largely ignores decision-making costs (*ex ante*) and frustration costs (*ex post*) which are typical of large and heterogeneous groups.[297] The existence of such costs implies that the EU level should focus on medium-term or time-invariant priorities which do not require frequent renegotiations (see later).

Fiscal federalism, however, even if supplemented with the new political economy approach, does not encompass the EU political dimension of subsidiarity and proportionality enshrined in Article 5 TEU:[298] unless there is a clear case for carrying out a project at EU level, subsidiarity considerations would plead in favour of financing the project at national level. The burden of proof should be with the higher level.

3. A CONCEPTUAL FRAMEWORK FOR VERTICAL COORDINATION

At present, the EU and national budgets are almost completely separated. EU spending is practically fixed both in terms of size and composition, with its ceiling and structure set every seven years in the so-called Financial Perspectives. National budget priorities are set largely disregarding EU programmes, with the exceptions of agriculture and cohesion where EU intervention is sizeable. However, considerations on the relative effectiveness of EU and national spending are largely absent in determining how to carry out public policies. This is a source of inefficiency as it leads to lower-than-desirable provisions of public goods or higher-than-needed overall public spending.

For expository convenience, it is useful to think of any policy as a public good,[299] Y, which is being produced through two inputs, national spending, G_N, and EU spending, G_{EU}:[300]

$$Y = f(G_N, G_{EU}) \tag{12.1}$$

G_N and G_{EU} are characterized by a specific productivity, α and β, respectively. α and β should be seen as technical coefficients, reflecting the first four criteria ((1) to (4)) identified in the previous section.

Overall public spending plays the role of budget constraint and is indicated by G:

$$G = G_N + G_{EU} \tag{12.2}$$

However, in the case of some public goods (defence, redistribution) heterogeneity of preferences (criterion (5) in the previous section) may translate into a cap on the politically feasible amount of EU expenditure.

$$G_{EU} \leq \hat{G}, \tag{12.3}$$

where $\hat{G} \geq 0$.

This cap, which can be greater than or equal to zero depending on the heterogeneity of preferences, would introduce a kink in the linear formulation of equation (12.2), and would make the budget horizontal at the level of $G_{EU} = \hat{G}$.

Figures 12.1, 12.2 and 12.3 give a graphical representation of the model. The existing distribution of spending between the national and the EU level (E in all figures) most likely reflects current political and institutional constraints. E is clearly a sub-optimal position. Under no-capping, an optimizing benevolent policy maker, controlling both G_N and G_{EU} would, given the total amount of resources, choose the sharing of production between a national and an EU level of expenditure that maximizes the production of public goods, or, for a desired level of output, choose the optimal sharing of spending between an EU and a national level that allows G to be minimized. The sharing will be determined by the form of the production function $f(.)$, different productivity of the national and the EU expenditure and the form and level of the budget constraint.[301]

In Figure 12.1, we assume $\alpha > \beta$. An optimal allocation of spending between the EU and national budgets implies moving from E (reflecting the existing allocation between EU and national budgets) to either E^I (maximum Y) or E^{II} (minimum G).

The opposite holds in Figure 12.2, where $\beta > \alpha$. Hence, Y would be maximized for a given level of total spending if much of the financing took place at the Union level.[302]

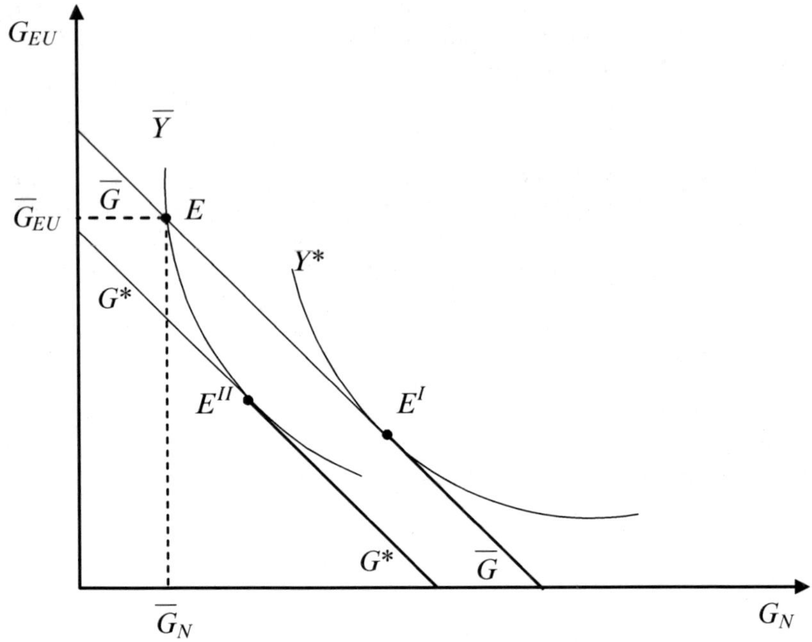

Figure 12.1 Higher productivity of national spending, $\alpha > \beta$

Figure 12.3 depicts the case where EU spending is more productive than national spending, but there is a ceiling on its amount (equation (12.3)). It means that for a particular policy the feasible amount of G_{EU} is constrained by heterogeneity of preferences, and therefore going beyond that level of EU expenditure proves politically unfeasible. Therefore, as the figure shows, the unconstrained optimum (E^I) cannot be achieved. Nonetheless, equilibrium E^{II} is still preferable to the initial distribution of spending between the two levels of government.

In Figures 12.1–12.3, jumping directly from the current sharing of spending to (unconstrained or constrained) optimal sharing may prove unfeasible. In particular, the decision-making process as well as rivalries between institutions and levels of governance may hinder reaching the first-best solution. Nonetheless, a gradual move towards the optimal composition of spending would still improve efficiency.

In essence, in order to reform public spending in the EU economy, one has to pass a judgement on the desired level of output, Y^*, on what type of production function is relevant for the production of any given public good,[303] on the relative values of α and β and on the possible political ceiling of

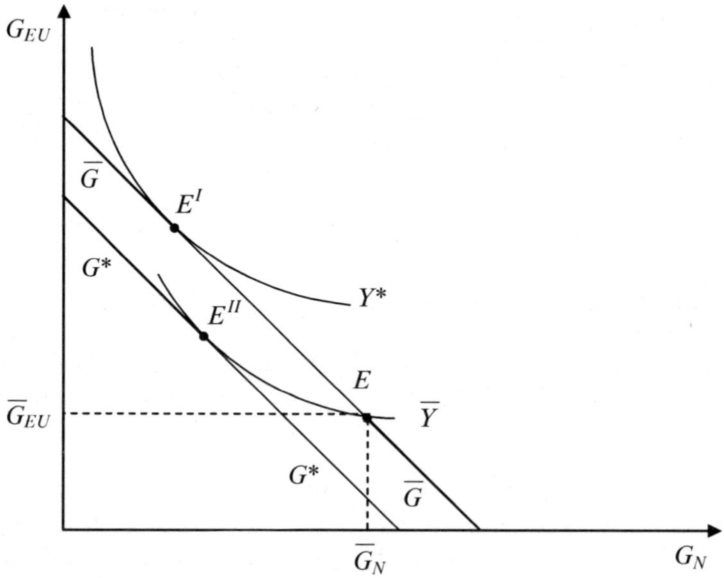

Figure 12.2 Higher productivity of EU spending, $\beta > \alpha$

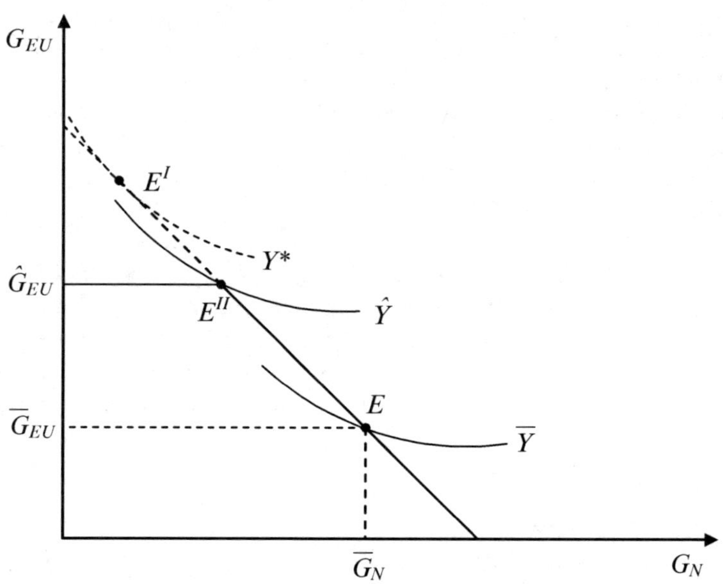

Figure 12.3 Constrained preference on EU spending, $\beta > \alpha$

EU spending, $\hat{G}$. As we will argue, an EU budgetary system should complement such an assessment with an overall budget constraint, G^*, thereby overcoming separate, and by definition sub-optimal, constraints on G_N and G_{EU}. This amounts to saying that the optimal amount of G_N and G_{EU} is endogenously determined and not set *a priori*.

4. WHAT SHOULD THE EU BUDGET DO?

4.1 Reorienting EU Spending

Even to the layman, it is apparent that the current EU budget hardly conforms to the normative implications of the theory of fiscal federalism, even taking into account the political economy constraints emphasized by the most recent literature.

As we argued in the introduction, the EU has a small central budget which is neither adequate in terms of composition to the new stage of economic and political integration, nor sufficiently flexible to adapt to changing circumstances and political priorities. Clearly, path dependency matters: it would be politically ingenuous to attempt to redesign the EU budget from scratch. Nonetheless, the contradictions of the current budget and, more broadly, the public finance arrangements within the EU (Community and member states' budgets) are becoming increasingly apparent as integration deepens among a subset of countries (those sharing monetary sovereignty) in a Union that, with enlargement, becomes more heterogeneous.

The discussion that follows is organized around the three Musgravian branches of government: allocation, redistribution and stabilization.[304]

Allocation

- *New EU public goods*. In the enlarged Europe, defence, internal security and external aid will have to be increasingly supplied at the central level. These are textbook examples of public goods to be provided centrally. Protection against organized crime and terrorism, border patrols, immigration policy, and aid to third countries are characterized by large economies of scale, strong externalities, relatively homogeneous preferences, the need to attain a minimum size and the risk of free riding. Moreover, as stressed by Tabellini (2003) and Berglöf *et al.* (2003), coordinating national policies is not enough as all these areas concern the executive power of governments and are executed by specific bureaucracies. Central provisioning will also strengthen the bargaining position of Europe on the world scene.

As to defence, several of the above criteria apply, but heterogeneity of preferences (e.g. political neutrality) persists. In the past, provisioning at the EU level has encountered political resistance, explained by the fact that centralized supply implies 'delegation' from national to European policy-making bodies of the authority to decide over 'sovereign-sensitive' goods (Persson *et al.*, 1996). This has imposed a close to zero cap on the defence expenditure made at EU level. To the extent that the EU moves towards political union, such reluctance should gradually be overcome. A solution could be to focus EU provisioning onto the relatively less controversial aspects of these policies (e.g. in defence, start with the Rapid Reaction Force) and dissociate direct participation from financing (all EU members would contribute to the financing via the EU budget, but the countries encountering political opposition would not be directly involved in execution).

- *Growth-enhancing expenditures.* The EU liberalization initiatives of the last decade have not translated into higher growth. The so-called Lisbon strategy, set out by the Lisbon European Council in Spring 2000, is set to transform the static efficiency gains of the Single Market into dynamic efficiency gains. Several of the components of the strategy do not have budgetary implications or, when they do, are to be carried out at national level. Nonetheless, some growth-enhancing policies with large externalities could be carried out at EU level. Examples of these are major R&D and innovation programmes and trans-European Networks, especially along East–West axes.
- *Other internal policies.* A larger heterogeneity of preferences in a wider Europe entails a strict application of the 'subsidiarity test'. Several existing spending programmes under the Internal Policies category do not pass this test. Future EU activities could focus on fostering citizens' Europe. Increased mobility across countries could be promoted by setting goals in education and language proficiency coupled with EU financing of minimum standards (Von Hagen, 2002b).[305]
- *Common Agricultural Policy.*[306] The reduction in agricultural spending is the *conditio sine qua non* to claim a stronger role of the EU budget in other, more suitable areas. The CAP hardly complies with any of the criteria identified in the second section, and can actually be taken as an example of optimization of internalities with perverse redistribution effects. The shift away from price support towards direct aid (supporting farmers' revenue) needs to continue. However, direct aid amounts to interpersonal redistribution of a specific class of citizens (workers in the agricultural sector): there is no justification to carry out these kinds of transfers via the EU budget. The need to

sharply reduce the share of the EU budget devoted to agriculture to make room for other priorities has long been recognized (e.g. Padoa-Schioppa, 1987). Boldness requires going beyond a very mild erosion of the CAP share in the budget – as decided in the Brussels European Council in October 2002 – and addressing head-on the issue of a radical reform of the CAP, including its partial renationalization (at least of direct aid).

Redistribution

Fiscal federalism suggests that income redistribution should be carried out at a sufficiently high level of government. This can be done both across individuals of a given country and across countries. So far, the bulk of EU involvement in redistribution has concentrated on income redistribution across countries. The interpersonal dimension, which is at the basis of the welfare state and the European Social Model has, up to now, remained within the remit of national governments. Interesting proposals for direct EU involvement in interpersonal redistribution have been made. However, although the idea of a EU-wide minimum social safety net has its merits,[307] political and feasibility constraints will most likely limit the main goal of EU redistribution to policies for regional or national convergence. This is consistent with the theory of fiscal federalism, with the heterogeneity of preferences towards redistribution and with the different information constraints faced by the EU and the national level. Indeed, 'the Community [. . .] is not well suited to executing distributive policies at the level of individual persons or small enterprises. Efficient income distribution requires detailed administration at the level of the individual, and coherence with features of income tax and social security systems, and the Community cannot assure this' (Padoa-Schioppa, 1987; p. 133).

The current design and implementation of the EU cohesion policy are such that EU transfers are very diffused across the EU territory. At present, all EU countries receive funds under the EU cohesion policy and only Luxembourg and Denmark (and Belgium and Netherlands from 2007) do not have at least one region assisted by the so-called Objective 1 intervention.[308]

In order to make the EU cohesion policy more effective, we argue in favour of redesigning EU it. Funds should focus on (1) fostering income convergence of poorer countries, and (2) reducing the social costs of factor reallocation. Hence, conceptually, one could therefore imagine a cohesion policy being implemented via two different funds, responding to the two needs of convergence and restructuring: 'Convergence Aid' funds devoted to helping backward countries and regions to catch up with richer countries; and 'Restructuring Aid' funds which are intended to facilitate the resource reallocation for those *entities* affected by shocks of exogenous nature (e.g. technological change, globalization, enlargement).

- *Convergence Aid funds* are intended as pure convergence policy in favour of less prosperous countries and should be used for two purposes: institution building and growth-enhancing expenditure (such as R&D, education and training, infrastructure, etc.). In order to be able to spend money efficiently, for growth-enhancing expenditure, a country needs a very efficient legal and administrative system in place. Building legal and administrative capacity is a top priority in any cohesion strategy across the EU, because of the contribution to growth that a high quality administrative and legal system makes. Several empirical studies show a positive correlation between income convergence in Europe and standard indicators of quality of administration.[309] Institution-building is particularly important for the new EU member states.
- *Restructuring Aid funds* should be available to those *entities*, in any country, affected by structural adjustment. Since resource reallocation affects people in different geographical locations and belonging to different industrial sectors, entities could be defined either as sectors or as territorial units, or as the combination of both (given sectors in given places). Restructuring funds may also play a stabilization role to a certain extent since it is very likely that shocks are uncorrelated across countries, regions and sectors.

A new design for the EU cohesion policy would help to address two directions for reform that are central to the ongoing debate on the future of EU cohesion policy: (1) geographical focus, and (2) earmarking of EU funds.

As for the first issue, several arguments have been put forward in the literature in favour of a shift from the current regional focus towards a country focus. First, efficiency may better be obtained by allocating money at country level and letting the country itself decide where to invest it, rather than the EU deciding which regions within a country deserve support (an argument paying respect to the subsidiarity principle). Second, the current regional focus may result in treating unequally, because of different regional imbalances, countries with otherwise similar levels of wealth (de la Fuente and Doménech, 2001). Third, EU cohesion and structural policy is only a part (often relatively small) of the regional (or sectoral) policy pursued at the national level using domestic funds. Fourth, enlargement will vastly increase national income disparities, but not regional income disparities.

Furthermore in the process of national income convergence, an increase in regional income imbalances is inevitable: it could be accommodated, but not impeded. Leaving to the countries, rather than to the regions, the task of deciding how to use EU funds would ensure greater coherence of the EU and national intervention and it would avoid the perverse implication of subsidizing those countries whose national regional policies are less effective. The on the ground management and use of the funds can obviously be made at the regional level.

The distinction between Convergence Aid and Restructuring Aid is important when assessing the relevance of these arguments. A country focus appears preferable in the case of Convergence Aid. This would imply that countries (as opposed to regions) would decide on the use of funds. Assignment of funds could still take into account to any chosen degree regional imbalances within a country (by looking at both the mean and dispersion of per capita income). However, a regional or a sectoral focus still seems justified in the case of Restructuring Aid, except perhaps for small and very specialized countries.

As for the second issue, earmarking EU funds makes sense only if two conditions are simultaneously reunited: (1) that 'Brussels' can effectively assess the need and monitor the outcome of the EU funds' use; and (2) that their 'specific use' is a central piece of a larger EU strategy. Building a high-quality legal and administrative system appears to meet those two conditions. Indeed, during the pre-accession period, the EU gained considerable experience in monitoring the quality of the national administrations and it set up a number of tools (financial assistance, but also twinning programmes between current and future EU member states) to improve that quality.

To strengthen the contribution of the convergence funds to EU growth, the key principle of 'conditionality' should be extended to both earmarked and non-earmarked funds. In particular one could make the disbursement of a significant part of the money, for the same or for the following financial period, dependent on reaching an agreed performance level in terms of results of the use of funds.[310] Conditionality has also an added benefit from a political economy viewpoint as imposing conditions on the use of resources may reassure countries which are net contributors to the EU budget. This argument may gain strength in an enlarged Europe.

Stabilization

EMU raises the issue of cyclical stabilization in the event of asymmetric shocks. Federations around the world typically have a large central budget and stabilizers, which automatically smooth idiosyncratic shocks. In principle, local budgets are subject to balance requirements and lending restriction while the federal budget is less so. The EU fiscal rules have an opposite logic. They imply that stabilization is carried out at the national level: countries should bring their budgets 'close to balance or in surplus' in normal times so as to have sufficient room for manoeuvre to absorb negative shocks without infringing the 3 per cent of GDP deficit limit. The Commission has recently stressed the importance of assessing the medium-term deficits targets in structural, rather than nominal terms (European Commission, 2002b). This is consistent with the absence of centralized stabilization.

While shock-absorption via national budgets will remain the norm in EMU, there is the question of risk sharing in the event of large idiosyncratic shocks. In such a case, a response by the EU budget could be welfare-enhancing. As either the setting of EU automatic stabilizers[311] or the possibility for the EU budget to run deficits or surpluses appears politically unfeasible, two options remain: an insurance instrument triggered by asymmetric disturbances (Italianer and Vanheukelen, 1993) or the possibility of raising funds in the market by the EU (extra-budget) and transferring them to the member country hit by the shock. The first option could be accommodated by creating a single, but 'universal' reserve which could be used for stabilization as well as other purposes. Such a reserve could be mobilized by the Commission via automatic rules, without passing through a cumbersome procedure, and possibly replenishing the reserve during the year by unused commitments.[312] An argument in favour of the second option is the fact that large country-specific shocks are rare and thus such a facility would be seldom activated.[313]

Summing up

The conceptual framework laid out in the second section allows us to summarize the challenges faced in rethinking the attribution of allocative tasks between the EU and the national budgets. The approach put forward amounts to 'endogenizing' the size of the EU budget so as to allow, in the steady state, the minimization of the total amount of public spending (national plus EU) for a given level of output.

Figure 12.4 illustrates the overall budget constraint (EU plus national spending) as the 45° straight line. The production schedules are the curves[314] going through *EB* in the case of higher efficiency of EU spending and the line going through *EC* in the case of higher efficiency of national spending.

According to the analysis in the previous section, the CAP should move from *E* towards *C*, implying a gradual renationalization of agricultural policy, coupled with, in perspective, lower support to the sector (shift to a lower level of *Y*). External aid, defence and internal security would be shifted along the *EA* line, representing a move from national to EU financing and,

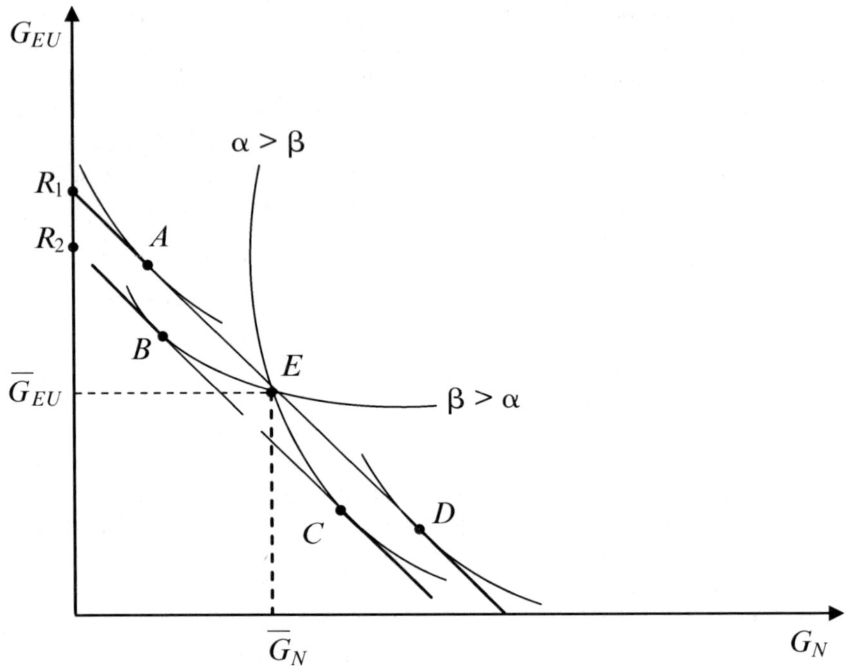

Figure 12.4 From the current to the future apportioning of spending across government levels

for some of the items, entailing also an overall rise in public spending. In line with the Lisbon strategy R&D, trans-European networks (TENs), European citizens' programmes (such as the Erasmus programme) and major innovation projects, would move from *E* towards *B* or *A*. Finally, most of the so-called 'other internal policies' in the current EU budget covering a host of smaller programmes would probably have to shift from *E* to *D* or *C*.

Redistribution programmes across countries are correctly undertaken at the EU level, that means along the *y*-axis. Whether the 'intensity' level should be at R_1 or R_2 is a political rather than a technical choice. As to stabilization, no centralized tool has been designed at the EU level and political constraints make any change unlikely in the foreseeable future.

4.2 Reorienting EU Revenues

This chapter deals mainly with the expenditure side of the EU budget. It pleads for a reassessment of the functions of the EU budget according to the generated added value of the EU and national expenditure. In other words it looks at the contribution of the EU expenditure to the EU aims rather than at the accounting logic of the *juste retour*.

Both the European Commission and academia have indicated that the current system of financing the EU budget is imperfect in several respects, namely, with respect to transparency, accountability vis-à-vis the EU citizens and citizens' perception of the financial autonomy of the EU institutions from member states.[315] By 2006, some 90 per cent[316] of the EU budget will be financed by national contributions linked to the GNP of any member state and only the remaining 10 per cent by direct levies on citizens. The GNP contribution, while having other positive facets, is at the root of the debate on the *juste retour*: this debate hampers a genuine discussion on the added value of any EU expenditure to emerge. Therefore, if the expenditure side of the EU budget were to evolve accordingly to the principles outlined above, the revenue side should also evolve consistently with them. This means that, while preserving the principle of budgetary equilibrium, those sources of funds having an obvious national identification (such as the GNP contributions) should be reduced in favour of new sources of funds having a natural EU base. Natural EU taxes are those sources of funds that have a clear rationale for accruing to the EU budget because their existence depends on EU policies, and that display a clear mismatch in the geographical pattern of tax collection and tax burden. That is the case, for example, with the profits of the ECB, which exist only because EMU exists and whose current national reapportioning is, from an economic standpoint, debatable.[317] It is also the case for other taxes, such as savings taxes, corporate taxes, stock exchange taxes, environmental taxes, and so on. Each of these taxes is suitable to a different degree depending on the different level of harmonization of the tax base. The size of the EU budget is so small that even a very partial accruing to the EU budget of one or more of the mentioned taxes would suffice to cover the financing needs. Further economic integration, in particular post-enlargement, is likely to only increase the number of natural EU taxes that could accrue (partially or totally) to the EU budget.

5. INCREASING THE FLEXIBILITY OF THE EU BUDGET

Looking at the EU budget in an historic perspective one observes, at the end of the 1980s, a change in the regularity of revenues and expenditure. Since 1988, the 'budgetary peace' between the Commission, the Council and the European Parliament, the three institutions involved in the EU budget procedure, has increased markedly.[318] This improvement in stability has gone hand in hand, however, with a reduction in the flexibility of the EU budget and an increase in the complexity of the rules governing it.[319]

There is a clear and well-understood trade-off between resource stability and financial peace, on the one hand, and margin of manoeuvre or flexibility, on the other hand. In 1988, with the adoption of the so-called Delors I package, which instituted the first Financial Perspectives (FP), a political choice had been made in favour of the former. Every seven years the FP set the ceilings for all budgetary headings and for certain sub-headings. Once the FP are set, member states have historically displayed stiff reluctance to shift resources across years and headings. At present, moving unused resources, even within the annual budgetary procedure, from one budgetary heading (or even sub-heading) to another, is difficult if not impossible altogether.

In the medium to long run, both the EU budget and the national budgets have to respect similar constraints in terms of deficits. The EU budget is subject to the strict requirement of equilibrium laid down in Art. 269 TEC, while national budgets are subject to the medium-term target of 'close to balance or in surplus' of the Stability and Growth Pact. The difference between the two conditions boils down to the fact that the EU budget must be balanced in each and every year, while national budgets have to be broadly balanced over the cycle, thus allowing for deficits (up to 3 per cent of GDP) to appear in recession years and surpluses in boom years.

A political choice in favour of stability at the expense of flexibility is not dissimilar from the one characterizing EMU. In the run-up to and in the early years of EMU, the trade-off between stability and flexibility of national finances was firmly resolved in favour of the former. Recently, however, the Commission has moved in the direction of taking account of flexibility (European Commission, 2002b) by accepting that countries with sound public finances (i.e. low stock of public debt, low implicit liabilities) could run small structural deficits without violating the requirements of the Pact. There is some ground to argue that a similar move should be undertaken in the EU finances.

In sum, while the FP have helped ensure orderly development of expenditure of the EU budget and guaranteed budgetary peace for the EU, it is increasingly evident that the current degree of flexibility is not compatible with the functions of a modern budget and does not permit the EU budget to react in a timely fashion to changing circumstances. More flexibility is a pre-condition for moving to a true European Budgetary System, as proposed next.

6. DESIGNING A EUROPEAN BUDGETARY SYSTEM

Rethinking the EU budgetary arrangements goes beyond rethinking at which level individual policies should be carried out and how to conduct an EU fiscal policy under the straitjacket of excessive rigidity and small and predetermined size. The basic tenet of this chapter is that introducing vertical coordination between the EU and national budgets can help to address the fiscal failures identified. Figure 12.5 sketches out the architecture of a European Budgetary System.

So far, the EU and national levels have remained separate. As exemplified in the top part of Figure 12.5, fiscal policy in the EU is the outcome of two non-coordinated sets of instruments: on the one hand the EU budget and on the other hand the national budgets of the 15 member states.[320] However, as the EU moves towards stronger fiscal policy coordination, such separation needs to be overcome. This has potentially profound implications for both the annual budget and the multiannual FP.

The bottom part of Figure 12.5 shows how a coherent EU budgetary system, which puts the EU budget in line with national budgets, could be articulated. The EU budget is to be looked at as a centralized (at EU level) fiscal policy subject to decentralized national constraints (EU budgetary resources are essentially member states' contributions). National budgets are to be looked at as a decentralized system of fiscal policies subject to centralized EU constraints (the Stability and Growth Pact and the Broad Economic Policy Guidelines, BEPGs).

In a medium-term framework (covering a time span of, say, five years), EU policy makers should elaborate an aggregate European Stability Programme which sets the spending priorities for the Union and the member states.[321] It would also decide how to allocate spending on individual items between the EU and the member states. The national stability programmes and a new EU-level stability programme – which would replace the current FP – would translate the common objectives into concrete medium-term spending programmes. The provisions of the Stability and Growth Pact – namely the medium-term target of 'close to balance or in surplus' and the 3 per cent of GDP deficit ceiling – would continue to apply to all EU countries.

The aggregate stability programme as well as its national and EU components would be rolled over and updated annually. This would mark a fundamental change compared to the existing situation where each national stability programme is decided on an individual basis and the FP are set every seven years and are fixed within such a period.

A similar process would take place on an annual basis. The EU budget and national budgets should form a coherent set, adhering to the strategic

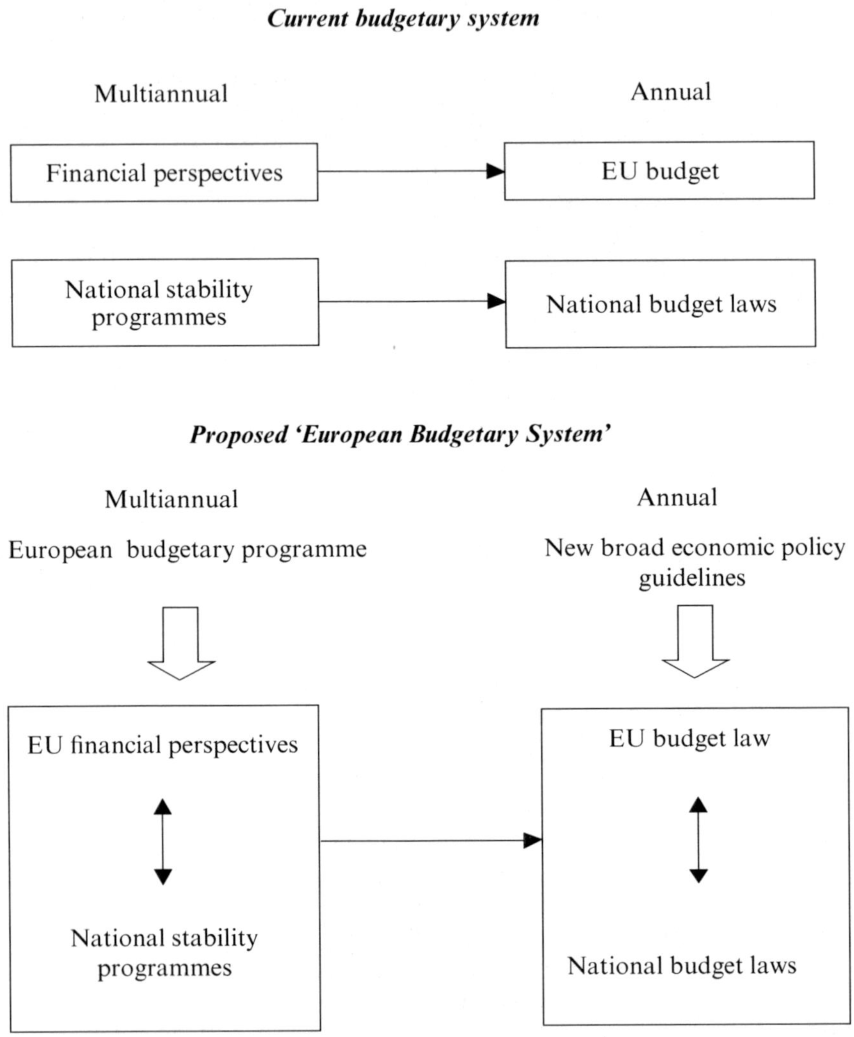

Figure 12.5 Towards a European Budgetary System

objectives of the BEPGs. This should be included in the 'new BEPGs', which should contain both recommendations for EU-level policies and country-tailored recommendations on national priorities. As mentioned earlier given the relatively high decision-making costs (*ex ante*) and frustration costs (*ex post*), at EU level, the annual process should mainly focus on fine-tuning multiannual priorities.

The upshot is that member states and EU institutions would decide together how to translate their common policy priorities into global budgetary commitments and how these commitments are shared between the national and the EU levels. This implies building vertical links between the EU and the national budgets. Clearly, fiscal discipline will need to be upheld: the reconsideration of the distribution across jurisdictions should not imply an overall increase in spending. In the past, the stress on the contradiction between (Maastricht-induced) national prudence and alleged EU 'largesse' has underpinned the refusal to reconsider EU budgetary responsibilities. However, as we move towards a EU budgetary system, such reluctance should be overcome. This reassessment would not necessarily imply a substantial rise in the EU budget. As we pointed out earlier, a rise in spending in certain areas would go hand in hand with a reduction in others. What this new approach would bring is more efficiency: to the extent that the existing distribution of spending between the national and the EU level is not optimal, the net effect would be a decrease in overall public expenditure.[322]

A couple of examples would help clarify this general statement. In September 2002 at the Johannesburg Summit on sustainable development, heads of state and government agreed to pledge 0.7 per cent of each country's GDP for development aid. The higher potential effectiveness of a centralized management of these resources calls for the assignment of such intervention prevalently at the EU level. The Lisbon growth strategy sets a target of investing 3 per cent of EU GDP in R&D in order to foster competitiveness. Criteria of efficiency and effectiveness should be the base for the split between private and public spending, and, within the latter, between the national level and the EU level. It makes sense, for instance, to carry out large research and innovation projects directly at the EU level.

The 2001 BEPGs showed an opening in this direction:

> Just like the member states, the Community should apply strict budgetary discipline. This must be applied to all categories of the Financial perspectives, while respecting the interinstitutional agreement on budget discipline *and the improvement of the budget procedure; a flexible allocation of Community resources should be exploited in order to enhance the economic impact of the EU Budget.* (emphasis added)

The Commission Communication on economic policy coordination of February 2001 (European Commission, 2001c) states that

> the establishment of guidelines and priorities in the EU budget should be embedded in a global vision encompassing both the guidelines and priorities in the budgets of the member states and the criteria established in the Broad

Economic Policy Guidelines in order to enable member states to take them into account in their budget laws.[323]

7. AN 'EU BUDGET LAW'

Consistent with the European Stability Programme, the annual EU budget should become a true 'EU Budget Law'. In order to achieve this aim, the current budgetary procedure (budget proposal, approval and implementation) would have to be overhauled. This would be possible only if a balance of 'sticks and carrots' is found to avoid conflicts among the Commission, the Council and the European Parliament (the last two being the two arms of the EU 'budgetary authority').

7.1 Phase 0: Multiannual Planning

Currently, the Council, acting on a proposal from the Commission and subject to majority approval in the European Parliament, fixes the FP which is then enshrined in the Inter Institutional Agreement. The FP establishes the maximum expenditure per annum, per budgetary heading and in certain cases per budgetary sub-heading (e.g. Cohesion and structural funds within the Structural action heading).

In its second Communication to the Convention (European Commission, 2002c), the Commission proposed that FP are adopted in co-decision between the Council and the European Parliament and that 'the Convention will have to look into the question of associating the national parliaments in this decision'. This goes in the direction we suggest. The multiannual planning of the EU should be in tune with national planning. Instead of being fixed for seven years, the FP would be rolling and linked with the BEPGs within a European Stability Programme.

7.2 Phase 1: Budget Proposal

Currently, this phase covers Internal (to the Commission) Budgetary Hearings. The Commission makes the arbitrages of the expenditure claims across its own departments while making sure that FP are respected. Before completing the draft budget the Council, Commission and Parliament hold a trilogue. By the end of April, the Commission submits the draft budget for the following year to the Budgetary Authority (Council and Parliament).

According to our proposal, the current budgetary hearings phase should be 'de-technicized' and 'opened to the outside'. This could become a political phase in tune with the debate taking place at the national level. The Commission would present (end January/early February), at a Jumbo Council (Ecofin plus Budget Councils) and the European Parliament, its budgetary proposal for the following year and listen to national priorities and to the national intentions for the different policies.[324] Budgetary hearings cease to be only internal, but become external, and more political, in order to coordinate EU budget and national political priorities. Following the Jumbo Council, individual Commissioners would go to specialized Councils to present the Commission's budget proposals. Commissioners and national ministers would check the coherence of their strategies – in line with the BEPG – and undertake to modify the initial proposal to achieve an overall consistent policy.

The Commission remains the *last authority* in the drafting phase and, as such, must ensure consistency between the EU budget and national budgets. The Council and the European Parliament, however, would get involved in a phase where their role is, so far, non-existent.

7.3 Phase 2: Budget Approval

Currently, the Council and European Parliament, in their capacity of budgetary authority, go through the first reading of the budget (approximately by September) and the second reading (between September and December). The Parliament finally adopts the budget in December. There is no formal role for the Commission during this phase.[325] This has facilitated the task of several lobbies attempting to influence the Parliament's *rapporteurs* to modify the appropriations of specific budget lines, with the result, in most cases, of increasing the proliferation of small programmes, entailing a misallocation of resources and reducing the overall coherence of the budget.

In our proposal, while the Council and the European Parliament would remain *the last authorities*, the Commission would play an active role, in particular making sure that, during the first and second readings, consistency between the EU and the national budgets is maintained.

7.4 Phase 3: Budget Implementation and Reporting

At present Article 274 lays down that '[t]he Commission executes the Budget under its own responsibility'. This has been criticized namely because, in economic terms, it does not always seem justified and in political terms it seems at odds with subsidiarity. If convergence policy were to be implemented via (conditional) block grants rather than the current earmarked funds, this legal provision would need to be changed in favour of joint responsibility of the Commission and the member states in executing the budget. Currently, the Commission implements the budget, but has a limited autonomous political role to play, even in the event of reallocation of the under-spending.

In our proposal, a parallel between the Commission and the EU member states would need also to be established in terms of reporting. Currently member states make their notifications known in March of each year (for the budget implementation of the previous year) and in September (for the budget implementation of the same year). A similar reporting should be established for the EU budget and an overall report should be sent to the Council and the European Parliament. Going beyond the purely financial dimension, the Implementation Report of the BEPG issued every February should be extended to the EU budget and policies. Finally, a critical issue is that of the mobilization of unused resources, in coordination with programmes and priorities of member states.

8. CONCLUSIONS

Due to its small size, historically determined rather than priority-oriented composition and lack of flexibility, the EU budget plays a modest role in the economic policy of the EU and the euro area. This translates into the fact that, at the central level, the EU is left, *de facto*, without one of the most powerful instruments of economic governance, the budget. Some take the view that this is because the EU budget is bent to satisfy national requests and nothing should be substantially changed otherwise the whole 'EU political equilibrium' would collapse. On the contrary, we have taken the 'benevolent' view that one can improve on the design and the structure of the EU budget.

The basic tenet of this chapter is that, as the EU moves towards a higher level of integration, it needs a more consistent system of public finances which encompasses both national and EU budgets. We propose moving towards a true European Budgetary System where EU and national budgetary processes are closely aligned and effective vertical coordination occurs in areas of common intervention. Implementation of this proposal would not require any change in the provisions of the Stability and Growth Pact. 'Endogenizing' the amount of public spending carried out at EU level would help reduce the political controversies surrounding the size of the EU budget.

The main objective of this proposal is to move towards economic governance of the EU where the community and national levels play together. The role of the EU budget would be valorized *in crescendo* with EU fiscal surveillance which is currently being extended from 'below the line' (budget balances) to 'above the line' (single items of expenditure and revenues), with a growing emphasis on the quality of public finances (European Commission, 2000a, 2002a).

It goes without saying that several aspects of the proposed system and its functioning need further reflection. For instance, it remains to be seen whether the aggregate stability programme and, *a fortiori*, the EU-level stability programme, should encompass non-euro area countries. Second, in order to make this proposal viable, one should study how to contain the transaction costs involved in the horizontal and vertical coordination processes. Third, in order to function effectively, the system would require some synchronization of budgetary procedures at the different levels of government (including regional ones in some member states). An interesting idea initially put forward originally by Jacques Delors (see Jacquet and Pisani-Ferry, 2001) is to separate the budgetary calendar between a first 'EU semester', in which EU priorities would be defined, and a 'national semester', in which such priorities are tailored to the national level. Such a proposal has been endorsed by the Sapir Report on relaunching growth in Europe (see Sapir *et al.*, 2003) and by the European Commission in its suggestions on reforming the Stability and Growth Pact in September 2004.

ANNEX THE DISTRIBUTION OF SPENDING BETWEEN NATIONAL AND EU BUDGET UNDER POLITICAL CONSTRAINTS: A SIMPLE MODEL

In the present circumstances, the decisions on how to allocate spending between national budgets and the EU budget are completely separated. Given the current institutional constraints, EU spending is practically fixed. At national level, fiscal discipline and political economy constraints make it costly to depart from the existing level of public spending.

In order to model the financing of a desired level of public good or service, we assume a linear 'production function':

$$Y = \alpha G_N + \beta G_{EU} \tag{12A.1}$$

where G_N is national spending, G_{EU} is community spending and α and β are their respective productivity.

As pointed out in the text, such a production function gives rise to corner solutions: if spending can be freely allocated between the EU and the national level, the whole financing would take place either at EU level (if $\beta > \alpha$) or at national level (if $\beta < \alpha$). We assume however that political or institutional constraints make it costly to move away from some EU and national spending levels (indicated by $\bar{G}_N$ and $\bar{G}_{EU}$) which are dictated by political/institutional constraints. In order to capture these constraints, we assume the following loss function:

$$L = (Y - Y^*)^2 + \theta(G_N - \bar{G}_N)^2 + \lambda(G_{EU} - \bar{G}_{EU})^2 \tag{12A.2}$$

where Y^* is the desired level of output.

Minimizing (12A.2) with respect to G_N and G_{EU} yields:

$$G_N^* = \frac{\theta(\beta^2 + \lambda)\bar{G}_N - \lambda\alpha\beta\bar{G}_{EU} + \lambda\alpha Y^*}{\lambda\alpha^2 + \theta(\beta^2 + \lambda)} \tag{12A.3}$$

$$G_{EU}^* = \frac{\lambda(\alpha^2 + \theta)\bar{G}_{EU} - \alpha\beta\theta\bar{G}_N + \beta\theta Y^*}{\lambda\alpha^2 + \theta(\beta^2 + \lambda)} \tag{12A.4}$$

The relationship between G_N and G_{EU} is represented in Figure 12A.1. A fall in $\bar{G}_N$ leads to a rise in G_{EU} and a higher Y^* implies a rise in both areas of spending. A fall in λ leads to a rise in both G_{EU} and G_N. As expected, higher and more productive EU spending leads to lower national spending.[326]

One can take the current situation as implying very high values of λ, implying that $G_{EU} = \bar{G}_{EU}$.[327] If the EU moves to a truly 'budgetary system', the constraints on G_N and G_{EU} will be lifted and the choice of financing will depend on the relative efficiency of each type of spending. Nevertheless, in

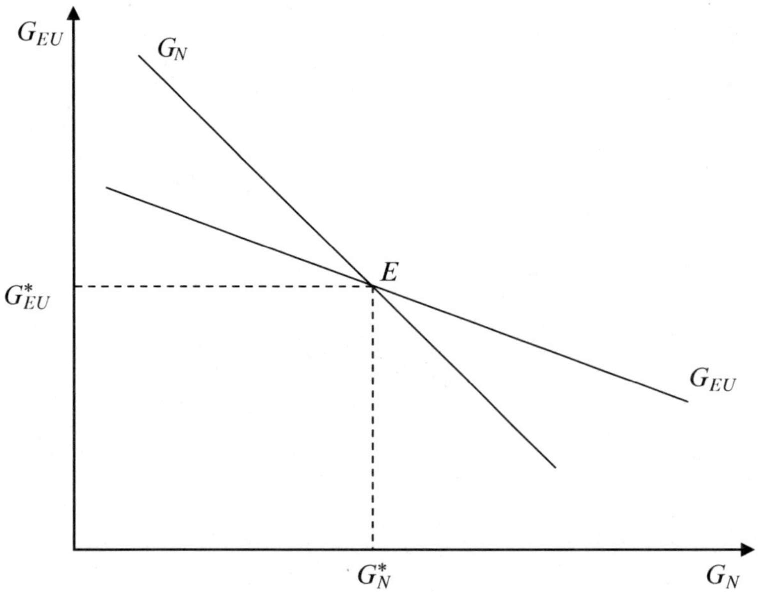

Figure 12A.1 EU and national spending under political constraints

the transition, the existing constraints may still play a role. The transition can be thought of as a gradual reduction in the value of λ and θ, with the former, which is very high today, coming down at a higher pace, together with a departure from the initial objectives of G_{EU} and G_N.

For analytical convenience, it is useful to take as a benchmark the case in which the desired level of output is equal or higher than that produced by allocating the total desired level of spending to the most efficient level of government. Formally:

$$Y^* \geq \alpha\bar{G} \quad \text{if } \alpha > \beta \quad \text{or} \quad Y^* \geq \beta\bar{G} \quad \text{if } \alpha < \beta.$$

Under such an assumption, and assuming that the current level of Y is lower than Y^*, it is easy to show that the current total level of spending is larger and the output is lower than the final equilibrium. Under $\alpha < \beta$ this occurs because, in order to shift Y towards Y^*, G_N is set higher than $\bar{G}_N$ even though it is less productive than G_{EU}. On the contrary, $\alpha > \beta$, the desired increase in G_N is not compensated by a corresponding reduction in G_{EU}. As pictured in Figures 12A.2 and 12A.3 (in the case of $Y^* = \beta G_{EU}$ and $Y^* = \alpha G_N$, respectively), the offsetting reduction in the least productive spending only takes place over time as the constraints on λ and θ are reduced. In the final equilibrium, the desired level of output is wholly financed via the most efficient spending.

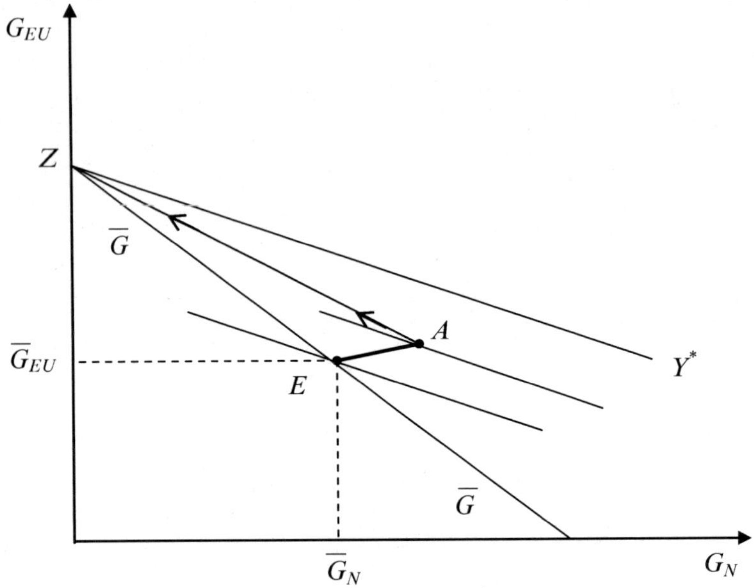

Figure 12A.2 More efficient EU spending

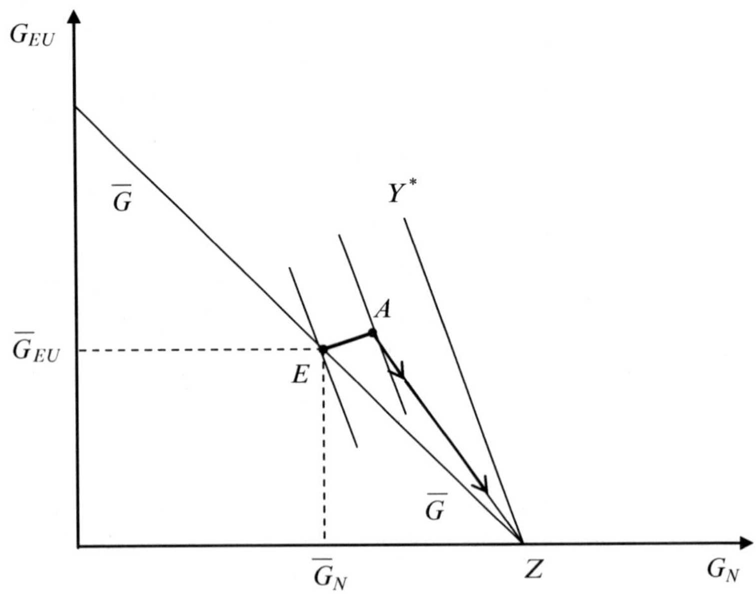

Figure 12A.3 More efficient national spending

13. Postscript: a new Stability and Growth Pact?

The Stability and Growth Pact (SGP) has been the most contentious element of EMU. There have been proposals to reform it ever since it was adopted by the Amsterdam European Council in June 1997. The debate accelerated in 2002 under the pressure of unfavourable budgetary developments in some euro-area countries. The insufficient fiscal consolidation of the previous years and the cyclical downturn pushed the deficits of several countries towards or above 3 per cent of GDP. In November 2002 the Commission issued a Communication on 'Strengthening the co-ordination of budgetary policies' which outlined some possible changes in interpretation, mostly focused on the issue of the medium-term budgetary targets. The ECOFIN Council decided to leave the rules unchanged while mentioning the need to put more emphasis on sustainability and the pace of debt reduction and stressing the need to avoid pro-cyclical policies, especially when growth conditions are favourable. The debate illustrated just how difficult it would be to reach agreement on any significant reform of the Pact.

The pace of events quickened in November 2003 when the ECOFIN Council decided not to follow the European Commission's recommendations to apply the excessive deficit procedure to France and Germany. However, the fact that several Member States supported the Commission threw the differences between the European institutions into sharp relief. The Commission took the case to the European Court of Justice which, in July 2004, annulled the ECOFIN Council conclusions. It also ruled, however, that the Council was free to decide whether or not to adopt proposals made by the Commission, thus making it perfectly clear that the EU fiscal rules can work smoothly only if the Council and the Commission co-operate.

While the debate in academic circles showed the depth of the divisions among economists as well as policy-makers, a certain consensus gradually emerged in the course of 2004 among the main policy players as to what changes were needed to the EMU fiscal framework. It was recognized that EMU needed numerical fiscal rules (since financial market discipline and national procedures were not deemed sufficient to ensure budgetary discipline) and that any radical changes to the rules introduced in 1992

(Maastricht Treaty) and 1997 (SGP) would be highly problematic. 'Internal adjustment' of the existing framework (as was dubbed in Buti *et al.*, 2003) rather than a radical overhaul of the rules came to be regarded as the only feasible way ahead. It was also acknowledged that complementary measures at the national level (such as better budgetary procedures and independent fiscal councils) would be highly desirable.

The common menu of internal reforms included action to improve fiscal policy in good times, more consideration of public debt and long-term sustainability in assessing Member States' budgetary positions, a greater focus on cyclical developments and more transparency in fiscal data. Other aspects were more controversial: these included changes to the excessive deficit procedure and a stronger role for the Commission as the enforcing agency. The risks involved in embarking on a reform process under the pressure of unfavourable fiscal developments were also highlighted in the debate: the credibility of the framework itself could be endangered and the reform process could prove very long and uncertain. It was also noted that if the problem was primarily one of adherence to the rules, the priority should be to ensure rigorous implementation of the existing rules rather than to change them. At the same time, it was widely recognized that simply attempting to apply the existing rules after the watershed of November 2003 was not a viable option. Re-establishing a sense of ownership of the fiscal rules by all parties would be the precondition for their effective enforcement.

At the request of the European Council, in September 2004, the Commission issued a Communication on 'Strengthening economic governance and clarifying the implementation of the Stability and Growth Pact'. Some of the proposals were taken over from those put forward in November 2002, but the Commission also suggested a number of more substantial innovations which would: aim at avoiding pro-cyclical policies, especially in good times; better define the medium-term objective by taking into account country-specific circumstances and reforms; give greater prominence to the debt criterion; modify the implementation of the excessive deficit procedure, in particular by allowing more time to correct an excessive deficit under certain circumstances; and improve governance and enforcement.

After a difficult and at times heated debate, an agreement was reached at the ECOFIN Council of March 2005. The guidelines of the reform were set out in a report on 'Improving the implementation of the Stability and Growth Pact', which envisaged changes to both the preventive and corrective arms of the Pact.

On the preventive side, medium-term budgetary objectives are now to be differentiated from one country to another on the basis of debt ratios and potential growth rates. Targets will be specified in cyclically adjusted terms and net of the effects of temporary measures and will range between a deficit of 1 per cent of GDP and a small surplus. The latter would apply to high-debt, slow-growth countries. Implicit liabilities will also be taken into account in the future, once the technical obstacles to doing so have been removed. Major structural reforms with long-term fiscal benefits will be taken into consideration both when defining the adjustment path towards the medium-term objective and when considering temporary deviations from the target.

On the corrective side, the Council modified the definition of the 'exceptional cyclical circumstances' which may justify the reference value for the deficit being exceeded. A breach of the threshold will now be considered exceptional if it results from a negative growth rate or an accumulated loss of output during a protracted period of very low growth relative to potential growth. When evaluating deficits exceeding the 3 per cent limit, the Commission will take into account a number of factors ranging from cyclical conditions to the implementation of the Lisbon agenda and policies to foster R&D and innovation, from debt sustainability to the overall quality of public finances, and from financial contributions to international solidarity to fiscal burdens related to European unification. However, any excess over the 3 per cent deficit threshold should remain limited and temporary. The implementation of pension reforms establishing a compulsory funded pillar will also be taken into consideration, especially when assessing whether an excessive deficit has been corrected. The Council was not able to agree on quantifying the minimum debt reduction requested from countries with debt ratios exceeding 60 per cent. While confirming that, as a rule, the deadline for the correction of an excessive deficit will remain the year after it is identified, the Council decided that the initial deadline could be set one year later if there were special circumstances, and could be revised at a later stage if unexpected adverse economic events with major unfavourable budgetary effects occurred.

The Council also outlined a number of steps to improve the governance of EU rules. It suggested closer co-operation between Member States, the Commission and the Council in the implementation of the Pact. It indicated the need to develop national budgetary rules and ensure that national parliaments are closely involved in the process. Finally, it called for reliable macroeconomic forecasts and budgetary statistics.

These suggestions have had a mixed reception. Some commentators argued that, given the host of exceptions to the 3 per cent rule, the Pact is *de facto* dead. Others considered the proposals to be an important step forward in achieving a better balance in the Pact between fiscal discipline and flexibility.

Some aspects of the reform of the Pact are in line with those that we considered in Chapter 11, notably the changes concerning the preventive arm of the Pact (the differentiation of medium-term targets, the emphasis on debt and sustainability and the treatment of one-off measures) and the issue of governance (in particular, improving transparency). On the other hand, the reform includes aspects which we did not consider (especially the changes to the corrective arm of the Pact) while excluding some of our proposals (in particular those aimed at non-partisan implementation of the rules and tackling fiscal misbehaviour in good times).

That said, can the reform be considered an improvement on the original Pact?

We can answer this either by comparing the new provisions with the old, or by considering the process which has lead to the new framework.

In the first case, having in mind Kopits and Symansky's (1998) criteria for an ideal fiscal rule, one can conclude that some elements of the reform improve the quality of the EU budgetary framework while others worsen it. Some innovations allow greater flexibility in dealing with special circumstances and country-specific problems. However, flexibility will remain bounded by the provision that any excess over 3 per cent of GDP has to remain temporary and limited, and no category of spending is excluded from the definition of the deficit. The steps being considered to improve fiscal transparency and enhance national budgetary institutions can reinforce the rules. The emphasis on long-term sustainability makes the fiscal rules less myopic, a criticism often levelled at the 'old' Pact. The revision of the exceptionality clause is probably positive in that it removes an excessively restrictive condition.

On the other hand, some changes may be more problematic. This is the case for the extended deadlines for correcting deficits which may risk becoming a moving target. The greater complexity of the new framework may lower the visibility of the fiscal targets and make monitoring less effective. As the literature stresses, complex and less clearly defined rules are more difficult to enforce. There are also a number of controversial technical issues that remain to be addressed, such as how sustainability is to be measured, how temporary measures are to be defined, how the quality of public finances is to be assessed, and how to account for the cost of European integration.

If we take the second approach to assessing the reform, the process that has led to the reform gives rise to certain unease, since the changes may be interpreted as having been designed to accommodate the specific fiscal difficulties of well identified countries. Clearly, the ideal would be to set or reform rules under a 'veil of ignorance', without knowing in advance who the winners and losers would be. However, the vacuum created by the *de facto* suspension of the rules following the ECOFIN decision of November 2003, demanded a policy response from the European institutions.

In the end, the success of the reform will depend on how effectively the new rules are implemented in the coming years and what actual efforts are made to curtail fiscal imbalances. The major weakness of the old Pact was poor enforcement mechanisms. Will the new rules be effectively enforced?

Here again, there are two views. Some make reference to the literature on rules versus discretion which suggests delegating the application of complex rules to an external agency. The fact that in the new Pact there is not only a greater margin for discretion but also no independent enforcer, may increase the incentives for collusion by the Council in subverting the implementation of the rules. In short, the new Pact makes the framework more complex but fails to strengthen the role of the Commission in ensuring a non-partisan implementation. According to this pessimistic view, countries in excessive deficit would be allowed to pick and choose the 'relevant factor' to appeal to and would be let off the hook provided that they loosely commit to correct the fiscal imbalances at some point in the future. In this context, in which the threat of sanctions appears very remote and limited and temporary breaches of the 3 per cent threshold can more easily be justified, one can also doubt the relevance of the medium-term objectives. Governments could end up paying lip service to these objectives and – *de facto* – target a higher deficit.

A second view stresses the perceived economic arbitrariness of the old Pact and its alleged 'obsession with the decimals' as one of the reasons for its lack of enforcement. To the extent that the economic rationale of the Pact is enhanced, there is a better chance that it becomes self-enforcing. Stronger national ownership of the EU rules, as foreseen by the Council report, would undoubtedly help implementation. According to such a view, the new Pact will allow going back to the original spirit of Maastricht in which the 3 per cent reference value – buttressed by the agreement that any excess over it should remain limited and temporary – served the double purpose of guideposts for domestic policies and genuine reference points for European surveillance.

Which view will eventually prevail? Whatever judgement is ultimately made regarding the revision of the Stability and Growth Pact, it would be wrong to assume that the Pact will become irrelevant. First, the reasons why fiscal rules were adopted in the monetary union of many sovereign countries in the first place are still valid. The future enlargement of the euro area to Central and Eastern European countries actually strengthens the need for a common fiscal framework. Second, as shown by the debate on the reform of the Pact, no viable alternative to a credible supranational rule emerged, since all the other potential solutions came up against serious criticism of one kind or another. Third, many countries need sound fiscal policies leading to a reduction in debt levels also for purely domestic reasons – particularly the demographic shock which lies around the corner: an external anchor may continue to be useful for many countries. Finally, it is likely that, as soon as serious imbalances emerge in some countries threatening the stability of the euro area, the other euro-area members will step up the pressure for rigorous implementation of the rules.

Therefore, in our view, the Stability and Growth Pact will not become yet another ineffective coordination process that, after a burst of attention, fades away and *de facto* be forgotten. This does not mean that with the agreement of March 2005 the controversy over the Pact will be laid to rest. On the contrary, as rules are necessary in a monetary union, but as such put a constraint on national choices, it can safely be predicted that the revised Pact will remain at the core of policy debate in Europe and that there will be no shortage of proposals for the 'reform of the reform'.

Notes

1. The actual definition of this medium-term objective requires several factors to be taken into account; see the first part of section 3.
2. Say (1853), p. 483.
3. *The Works and Correspondence of David Ricardo*, P. Sraffa, ed. (1952–73), vol. IV, p. 197.
4. *The Works and Correspondence of David Ricardo*, P. Sraffa, ed. (1952–73), vol. IV, pp. 247–8.
5. Premchand (1983), p. 4.
6. Charles Dickens, *David Copperfield.*
7. U. Hicks relates this view to the objective of reducing the debt and taxation, to the prevailing favourable economic conditions and also to some difficulties in managing the budget. She notes the growth of administrative expertise in budgeting contributed to the development of a different approach in the 1930s.
8. Schumacher, while reporting these views, did not share them.
9. De Viti de Marco goes on to justify deficit finance as a less painful alternative to extraordinary taxation which may penalize liquidity constrained taxpayers.
10. Sir F. Phillips, writing in 1936, quoted in Middleton (1985), p. 82.
11. Memorandum by Keynes for the National Debt Enquiry, 21 June 1945, in Keynes (1971–89), vol. XXVII, pp. 406–7. On the UK experience, Clarke (1998) also notes that 'in the best Gladstonian tradition . . . On the expenditure side, what mattered was expenditure above the famous "line" in the Exchequer accounts, dating from the Sinking Fund Act of 1875, broadly . . . distinguishing a revenue account from a capital account – but by no means unambiguously . . . Only an old Treasury hand could be expected to know the difference within this hybrid accounting framework . . . therefore, the simple moral imperative of balancing the budget was in practice wrapped in the esoteric conventions of the public accounts' (p. 64).
12. In Italy, in the late nineteenth century and the early twentieth century revenues and expenditures related to the construction of railways were included in a special balance sheet and separated from other ordinary and extraordinary items. Revenues were represented by the proceeds of the sale of bonds, expenditures by the outlays for investment projects (see Nitti, 1903). De facto, an item specific golden rule was implemented.
13. See the accounts in Premchand (1983) and Poterba (1995). For a recent discussion in the context of EMU, see Chapter 6.
14. For a discussion along these lines see also Steve (1972, pp. 163–5). Steve also notes that drawing the line between durable goods with direct and indirect revenue would pose similar problems.
15. Bastable (1927) already acknowledged the usefulness of non-remunerative expenditures such as those on education, improved housing and the like,

however he also pointed out that there is a 'difficulty of application. The results of expenditure of the kind are hard to trace or measure, and any statement respecting them must rest in a great degree of conjecture' (pp. 621–2).

16. 'Budgetary Policy', 15 May 1942, in Keynes (1971–89), vol. XXVII, pp. 277–8.
17. These developments reflected common problems but were to a large extent unrelated. On the relationship between Swedish fiscal policy and Keynesian theories see Lundberg (1996). He recalls that in 1929 Lindhal considered the use of fiscal policies to affect the level and composition of demand and that Myrdal was asked to write an appendix to the government budget proposal of January 1933 on the issue of the feasibility of active fiscal policies.
18. Middleton (1985) reviews the debate about budgetary policy in the United Kingdom in the 1930s. In 1933 the Treasury stressed the risks related to unbalanced budgets: 'Would not the ordinary taxpayer and the business man very soon begin to have a feeling of uneasiness and apprehension? After all people will realise that the bill must be paid if not this year next year or the year after. Uncertainty and apprehension about the future would very quickly cancel out any immediate psychological benefit which the reduction of taxation by unbalancing the Budget would promote' (1985, p. 88).
19. Neville Chamberlain (Chancellor of the Exchequer), quoted in Sabine (1970, p. 15).
20. Biehl, in summarizing several papers on fiscal policy issues, notes that 'It is strange to see that, e.g., the old-fashioned concept of the simple budget balance rule is still widely used in many countries and that . . . the full employment budget concept, the structural margin of fiscal impact concept, and the concept of the cyclically adjusted neutral budget . . . are only known to a small circle of specialists' (1973, p. 6).
21. See, for instance, Johansen (1965), in which the use of budgetary items for stabilization policy is unquestioned, the focus of the analysis being on the choice of the most appropriate instruments.
22. Steve stresses that the budget balance cannot be considered in isolation: the level and composition of public revenue and expenditure are extremely important.
23. Keynes's own views about active fiscal policy were rather prudent. He stressed the need to control inflation and retain appropriate market incentives. In evaluating the UK budget in 1940, he noted 'The importance of a war budget is not because it will "finance" the war. The goods ordered by the supply department will be financed anyway. Its importance is social: to prevent the social evils of inflation now and later; to do this in a way which satisfies the popular sense of social justice; whilst maintaining adequate incentives to work and economy' ('Notes on the Budget', 21 September 1940, in Keynes 1971–89, vol. XXII, p. 218).
24. The issue is extensively discussed in OECD (1999c). OECD notes that 'in the future governments should guard against the asymmetric use of automatic stabilisers, although this obviously does not preclude all discretionary action, particularly for structural reasons' (p. 145).
25. See European Commission (2001a), Kilpatrick (2001), Taylor (2000a) and Wren-Lewis (2000).
26. For a review of the justifications put forward for the Pact and for an analysis

of its potential macroeconomic implications see European Commission (1996), Artis and Winkler (1997) and Eichengreen and Wyplosz (1998).

27. Canzoneri and Diba (2001).
28. It was also noted that the multiplicity of fiscal authorities does not provide strong arguments in favour of permanent constraints on the deficit as it may actually dilute the pressure on the central bank. According to Canzoneri and Diba (2001), a more relevant reason to have fiscal rules is to underpin the 'functional', as opposed to the 'legal', independence of the central bank. Without a credible deficit criterion ensuring government fiscal solvency, the central bank would not be able to keep control of the price level.
29. See also Costello (2001).
30. See Kopits and Symansky (1998).
31. See, e.g., Roubini and Sachs (1989b), Alesina and Drazen (1991), Alt and Lowry (1994), Alesina and Perotti (1995a) and Balassone and Giordano (2001).
32. See, e.g., Von Hagen and Harden (1994) and the essays in Strauch and Von Hagen (2000).
33. See Buti and Sapir (1998) and Stark (2001).
34. A more detailed description of the rules is provided in Buti and Sapir (1998) and in Cabral (2001).
35. The three conditions make the 3 per cent threshold extremely binding (see Buti *et al.*, 1997).
36. Art. 104 of the Treaty says that when the ratio is above 60 per cent of GDP it must 'diminish sufficiently' and approach 60 per cent 'at a satisfactory pace'. If the ratio increases, the excessive deficit procedure begins. It should be noted that, while the Treaty allows exceptions to the 3 per cent deficit criterion, it does not for the criterion concerning the debt ratio. See Balassone and Monacelli (2000).
37. The choice of the medium-term fiscal target is examined in Artis and Buti (2001), Dalgaard and de Serres (1999) and Barrel and Dury (2001).
38. See Chapter 8.
39. The deficit ceiling, although arbitrary, is reminiscent of the results obtained by Domar (1944) in the analysis of fiscal sustainability assuming a constant deficit. Perhaps conscious of the partial equilibrium nature of Domar's results, the introduction of a debt ceiling as well avoids convergence at high levels of debt. See Chapter 7.
40. See Chapter 6.
41. EMU fiscal rules are targeted at national governments while many EMU member states have a federal or highly decentralized structure. A free-riding problem can re-emerge at national level. This problem is analysed in Chapter 8.
42. The risks clearly increase if member states are asymmetric in some relevant respect (e.g. accumulated public debt). These considerations are likely to have motivated the inclusion of a 'rule' concerning not only deficits but also debt.
43. For an in-depth analysis, see Chapter 4.
44. The unweighted average of the lowest negative output gaps in EU member states over the period 1960–97 is just above 4 per cent of trend GDP. Indicators for the country-specific cyclical fluctuations, such as the average volatility measured by the standard deviation or the largest negative gap recorded over the past decades, could also have been used for the calculations.

The results obtained with these alternative calculations are broadly similar to those given in the chapter.

45. In a retrospective application of the Pact to the post-war period, Buti *et al.* (1997) find that a cyclically adjusted balanced budget would have allowed to fend off the risk of moving into excessive deficit in 19 out of 20 cases of recessions entailing a fall in real GDP by at least 0.75 per cent.
46. On long-term sustainability, see Chapter 7.
47. Let us assume that the medium-term target is fixed so that the deficit equals the 3 per cent limit in the worst possible recession. Then, if such recession occurs, the debt ratio will start increasing in the countries with a debt ratio lower than 3 per cent divided by nominal GDP growth. If, as can be expected, nominal GDP growth is very low in those circumstances, there could be many countries which experience a rise in their debt ratio.
48. As the relative debt position of countries vis-à-vis the EU average is examined, member states can switch group during the period if their behaviour changes. Germany, Spain, France, Luxembourg and Finland always belong to the low-debt group, while Belgium, Ireland, Italy and the Netherlands are always classified as high-debt countries. The other countries switch position during the period. Although admittedly crude, this approach reflects the assumption that the fiscal behaviour of a country may differ over time depending on its level of government debt. Similar results as those presented in Figure 2.2 are obtained when the countries that switch groups are not taken into account in the analysis.
49. This section touches on a number of issues that are thoroughly explored in subsequent chapters.
50. As in De Grauwe (1996), if seignorage revenue, $(y + \pi)\, m$, in equation (2.2) is disregarded, the long run condition becomes vertical. Its position, however, will still depend on the size of the debt, so the conclusions here remain unaffected.
51. See also Chapter 6.
52. See Chapter 2 and European Commission (1999a).
53. In the seminal paper by Bertola and Drazen (1993), the element triggering the occurrence of non-Keynesian effects is the level of government spending.
54. Evidence of a positive interplay between fiscal discipline and fiscal stabilization is also found in Leeftink (2000).
55. In its simplest form, the Taylor rule (Taylor, 1993) posits that in setting the short-term interest rate, the central bank takes into account the difference between actual and target inflation and the gap between actual and potential output. A 'conservative' central banker will attribute a considerably larger weight to inflation than to the output gap. As pointed out by Svensson (1999), a positive weight on the output gap may signal that the central bank is concerned about future inflationary pressures rather than explicitly caring about output stabilization. For a model similar to that in Annex 1, but with a central bank minimizing a loss function featuring inflation and the output gap, see Artis and Buti (2001).
56. An important aspect not captured in this simple framework is the persistence of the shock. If, for instance, a long-lasting negative supply shock reduces output potential, taxes and spending will have to be adjusted on a structural basis. However, cyclical stabilizers may ease the adjustment process.
57. Broadly similar conclusions have been obtained by other studies using differ-

ent approaches (see, e.g., IMF, 1998a; OECD, 1997; Dalsgaard and de Serres, 1999; Dury and Pina, 2000; Barrell and Pina, 2000). The calculations above do not take into account that some of these large negative output gaps have occurred in periods of severe recession, which, according to the Pact rules, could have triggered the application of the exceptionality clause allowing countries to exceed the 3 per cent limit.

58. It is worth noting that, unless shocks are highly symmetric, such an effect is likely to be reduced in EMU as the ECB sets interest rates having in mind the euro area economy as a whole.
59. For a discussion of ageing and fiscal sustainability, see Chapter 7.
60. This does not imply, however, that the debt ratio decreases continuously. In periods of recession, as automatic stabilizers give rise to higher deficits, the debt may temporarily increase. This is likely to be the case especially for countries with a relatively low debt stock.
61. It could be argued that these results are on the high side of the spectrum, because the ageing estimates do not incorporate the effects of a number of reforms especially in the area of pensions introduced in some EU countries in the past years. As national estimates show, these reforms are expected to have substantial effects on public spending over a long run horizon. However it is common experience that national projections over the last years have proven too optimistic and have been systematically revised upwards.
62. See, e.g., Beetsma (2001) and Canzoneri and Diba (2001). See also the contributions in Buti *et al.* (2002a).
63. A later, more sophisticated, version of the 'unpleasant arithmetic' is provided by the so-called Fiscal Theory of the Price Level according to which monetary authorities would not be able to control the price level if fiscal plans do not satisfy the government budget constraint. For a policy oriented review, see Canzoneri and Diba (1998).
64. See Galí (1994), Rodrik (1998), Fatàs and Mihov (1999).
65. The model builds on that presented in Chapter 3. For a version of the model with optimizing fiscal and monetary authorities, see Chapter 5.
66. This implies that the part of the interest burden that is paid to compensate the public debt holder for the erosion of the real value of the debt due to inflation does not affect their consumption.
67. In order to keep the model simple, we do not consider the terms-of-trade effect. We also disregard the feedback effect on the domestic economy from the rest of the monetary union following a shock to the domestic economy. This seems an acceptable simplification in a currency area with many rather small economies.
68. ω is assumed to be independent of the size of automatic stabilizers. On the implications of relaxing this assumption, see Buti and van den Noord (2003, 2004).
69. The distinction between automatic stabilizers and discretionary fiscal policy is somewhat arbitrary. If a government pursues a counter-cyclical policy which is symmetric over the cycle, this behaviour will result in a larger α.
70. For a country retaining monetary independence, λ is obviously equal to one.
71. In this simple setting and given the assumed monetary rule, economic agents always expect inflation to be on target before the realization of shocks.
72. Formally, a higher ϕ_1 is output-stabilizing if $\alpha > b\beta$.
73. It is easy to show that this holds if the condition in the previous note is satisfied.

74. See Barrell and Pina (2000). Mélitz (1997b, 2002) and Wyplosz (1999) also find that the cyclical sensitivity of the budget to economic activity may be lower than normally estimated.
75. Among others, Blanchard and Perotti (2002), Perotti (2000), Fatàs and Mihov (2002).
76. The term 'fiscal multiplier' is used as a general indicator of the impact of 'fiscal expansions' and contractions on output.
77. In European Commission (2001a) an alternative method is also reported, in which the damping provided by a proportional tax system is directly calculated by comparing it to a system without proportional taxes (and where they are effectively replaced by lump-sum taxes). This gives generally much smaller estimates of smoothing of shocks, on average around 5 per cent in the model (see European Commission, 2001a, pp. 186–7).
78. See Roeger and in't Veld (1997).
79. As the single monetary policy reacts only to area-wide inflation, country-specific shocks in the euro area trigger monetary policy response only to the extent they affect area-wide inflation. Consequently, as was shown in the theoretical analysis in the second section, the role of monetary policy in stabilizing inflation and output is relatively modest in small euro area member countries compared with the large ones. The monetary policy assumption for countries not participating in EMU implies a somewhat tighter monetary stance, at least in the UK and Sweden, than in the euro area as in these countries the monetary policy reaction and the ensuing appreciation of the exchange rate offset more of the initial fiscal boost and as a result the GDP effect remains smaller than on average in the euro area.
80. The allowance of liquidity constrained consumers implies that Ricardian equivalence does not hold fully and thus, fiscal policy can have an impact on private consumption and aggregate demand.
81. Note that no quantitative assessment is given of the likelihood of different shocks occurring.
82. There are no large non-linearities in the model, hence the implicit assumption that the fiscal multipliers are unconditional on the state of the economy is acceptable in the model.
83. While this is the default assumption and applied in the simulations underlying the calculations reported here, this assumption can of course easily be relaxed in the model, for instance to analyse the effects of a more progressive income tax system.
84. While an expansion raises tax revenues, it also tends to raise government expenditure. According to Mélitz (1997b and 2002) this pro-cyclical discretionary policy had become systematic and in a sense quasi-automatic. Hence the distinction between 'pure' automatic stabilization and discretionary policy reactions may not be as clear-cut as often assumed.
85. See European Commission (2000a).
86. Differences in the average OECD elasticities are to a large extent driven by the different estimates of the output elasticity of primary current expenditure (high for the Netherlands and Denmark, low for most other countries, see Van den Noord, 2002).
87. In fact, it is assumed that the fiscal expansion is followed in the medium term by a fiscal contraction, such that there is no autonomous increase in government indebtedness (and no increase in future tax liabilities).

88. This is partly due to the way GDP is measured, with GDP defined as the sum of private GDP and the government wage bill. An increase in the latter raises potential GDP automatically.
89. In a pure optimizing model, temporary tax changes that are later reversed should not have any effect on spending. The reason temporary income tax multipliers are positive in the model is because some consumers and firms are assumed to finance their spending out of current disposable income and profits respectively, due to liquidity constraints.
90. In the model these differences are reflected in the indexation of unemployment benefits to gross/net wages.
91. These results cannot directly be compared to the results found in the VAR-based literature (Blanchard and Perotti, 2002; Perotti, 2000; CEPS, 2002), as these are temporary fiscal shocks, while the fiscal innovations in the VAR studies tend to have a stronger persistence. But on the whole, VAR-based studies show extremely large confidence intervals and the effects are often zero or insignificant.
92. However, the focus on impact effects may mask deeper imbalances building up over the longer run in the case of permanent shocks. In a dynamic perspective, the 'direct' adverse implications of income smoothing have to be weighted against the possibly favourable effect of income support in fostering real wage flexibility and labour mobility. On the other hand, welfare systems which give rise to benefit dependency may harm structural flexibility. The interplay between replacement rates and benefit duration is crucial in delivering the appropriate balance between stabilization and flexibility.
93. Some terminological confusion exists in the literature. Such fiscal behaviour is dubbed 'active' by Sims (1999), following the original contribution by Leeper (1991), or 'Ricardian' according to Woodford (1995), whereas Leith and Wren-Lewis (2000) call such a reaction function 'passive'.
94. One should, however, make a distinction between the 'level' and the 'direction' of the monetary stance. While monetary policy loosened over the retrenchment period, it remained basically cautious as confirmed by looking at the difference between actual and 'Taylor' interest rates (see OECD, 1999c).
95. However, this is not true for all countries. As shown in European Commission (1999b), tighter monetary policy has gone hand in hand with tight fiscal policy in Italy. This complementarity between the two policies is probably explained by the 'double convergence' – on budget deficit and inflation – that Italy had to accomplish to meet the Maastricht requirements.
96. As indicated in Chapter 3, mainstream estimates indicate that the value of α is around 0.5 for the EU and EMU as a whole. However, it varies between 0.3–0.4 for the Mediterranean countries to 0.8–0.9 for the Nordic countries. See also European Commission (2000a) and Van den Noord (2000). However, other studies (Mélitz, 1997b and 2002; and Wyplosz, 1999) find much smaller stabilizers (between 0.1 and 0.2).
97. The instrument of fiscal authorities is the cyclically adjusted budget balance. This formulation implies that, when interest rates move, there occurs an internal compensation between the interest burden and the primary balance. This specification of the fiscal policy rule simplifies considerably the algebra, but misses a potentially important channel of interaction between monetary and fiscal policy via the effect of monetary decisions on interest payments. This effect is quantitatively limited if the stock of public debt is low and/or its

maturity is relatively long. It also implies that, in the jargon of the FTPL, that fiscal policy is 'active', that is it reacts to a change in monetary policy.

98. A positive output gap target in *L(FP)* may also reflect the shorter time horizon of the governments relative to that of the central bank.
99. This implies that fiscal authorities set a medium-term target which is able to withstand all shocks – regardless of their severity – without exceeding the deficit ceiling. This approach is behind the calculations of the so-called 'minimal benchmarks' which, on the basis of past business cycle experience, allow a sufficient safety margin under the 3 per cent of GDP deficit ceiling. See European Commission (1999a, 2000a) and Chapter 3.
100. For a summary of the evidence, see Clarida *et al.* (1999) and Favero and Rovelli (2000).
101. A number of empirical analyses find that the weight of output stabilization in the reaction function of central banks in Europe is very low.
102. This implies that the central bank behaviour is output destabilizing in the case of supply shocks. However, it has been pointed out (see, e.g., Smets, 2000) that, in the event of permanent shocks affecting potential output, inflation stabilization implies output stabilization around the 'new' level of potential output. In such a case, fiscal behaviour which aims at smoothing the path of actual output (as in our model) may lead to a rise in the 'true' output gap. On the undesirability of output stabilization in the event of supply shocks, see Chapter 4.
103. The expressions of the slope of FP and CB are, respectively:

$$\frac{(1+\phi_1\alpha)^2+\theta\phi_1^2}{\theta\phi_1\phi_2} \quad \text{and} \quad \frac{\phi_1\phi_2}{\beta\omega^2(1+\phi_1\alpha)^2+\phi_2^2}$$

The difference between the two slopes is always positive. This implies that an expansionary fiscal policy coupled with a restrictive monetary policy results in a higher budget deficit and a higher interest rate (instead of the opposite, as would be the case if CB were steeper than FP).

104. Notice that a deficit bias does not imply a time inconsistent fiscal policy. If the economy starts with a zero stock of public debt, following the fiscal impulse (say, via higher primary spending) the debt will start growing and stabilize at a positive level. A constant, positive deficit implies that the initial rise in spending is eventually reversed to make room for the interest payments.
105. If y appears explicitly in the CB's loss function, demand shocks are still fully offset. However, supply shocks will imply a deviation of inflation and output gap from the target values reflecting the conflicting objectives of price and income stabilization. See Artis and Buti (2001).
106. This can be obtained by replacing the solution for the y, π, d_s and i (equations (5.4), (5.5), (5.8) and (5.9)) in the FP and CB loss functions (equations (5.6) and (5.7), respectively) and cross-differentiating for the monetary and fiscal parameters.
107. The conclusions are less straightforward if the government aims at a positive output gap ($y' > 0$). The above results apply in the case of negative shocks and large positive shocks. However, as shown by Buti *et al.* (2001a), in the case of positive but small shocks, the government would benefit from a weak response by the central bank because this will allow the output gap to remain in the neighbourhood of y'.

108. For the analysis of the extreme cases of cooperation, 'fiscal dominance' ($\eta = 1$) and 'monetary dominance' ($\eta = 0$), see Buti *et al.* (2001a).
109. Notice that FP's reaction function is not directly affected by the supply shock. This implies that the original equilibrium under no shocks (E in Figure 5.3) remains the preferred position for the fiscal authority. Under more general assumptions on the IS equation or FP preferences (including an inflation term), FP's reaction function would shift to the right and so would the new Nash equilibrium. Obviously, the conclusions in the text remain unchanged.
110. See Bennett and Loayza (2000).
111. For a description of the basic structure of the model and its parameter values, see Roeger *et al.* (2001). The version used here allows for overlapping wage contracts and sluggishness in prices with firms facing quadratic price adjustment costs per unit of output (see Roeger, 1999).
112. For more details see Buti *et al.* (2001a). Note that here we deviate from the theoretical model by explicitly specifying a debt rule which guarantees fiscal solvency. This is a mild form of the SGP and captures the 'close-to-balance' rule. However, the debt rule as specified in this chapter will not automatically guarantee that fiscal policy will meet the deficit target for all shocks. In cases where the deficit target is violated in the experiments conducted, we will both look at an unconstrained as well as a constrained optimization problem.
113. Notice, since all variables in the model are defined in efficiency units, the growth rate of y must be interpreted as deviation from its long run trend as defined by the growth rate of TFP and population.
114. Notice, monetary policy does not target output at all.
115. As shown in Buti *et al.* (2001a), the SGP constrained optimum lies far to the left of the Nash solution with a lower fiscal response to the shock and also a slightly lower monetary response. The implied output gap in the constrained case is larger than under the Nash (FP loss exceeds that under the Nash) while inflation is lower (CB loss smaller). In terms of welfare losses, CB gains a lot from the deficit constraint and the CB loss is reduced to a quarter of that under the Nash solution, while the additional loss of FP is relatively small.
116. These conclusions are in line with those of Bini Smaghi and Casini (2000).
117. This point of view is taken by Modigliani *et al.* (1998). Opinions in favour of some kind of golden rule have also been expressed by former European Commissioner Mario Monti. It should be noted that when defining an 'excessive deficit' the Treaty does not discriminate between current and capital outlays; however, it provides for the Commission's Report on Excessive Deficits to take into account a list of relevant factors and, among those, 'whether government deficit exceeds government investment expenditure' (article 104(3)).
118. The idea that investment is reduced more than other items during fiscal consolidations is largely shared in the literature. For example, Oxley and Martin (1991) point to 'the political reality that it is easier to cut back or postpone investment spending than it is to cut current expenditure' (p. 161); De Haan *et al.* (1996) argue that investment '[is] the least rigid component of expenditure' (p. 68).
119. Let us express all variables in real terms and assume that the deficit is equal to investment expenditure (I) and constant as a ratio to GDP (Y): $It/Yt = it = i\,\forall t$. If i is such that the debt (D) to GDP ratio converges (i.e. if $i = (g/1+g)\,d$, where $d = dt = Dt/Yt\,\forall t$ and g is the growth rate of GDP), then since taxes (T) must equal interest outlays ($rDt-1$, where r is the interest rate) plus primary current

expenditure (C) we have $Tt/Yt = rDt-1/Yt + Ct/Yt = rDt-1/(1+g)Yt-1 + Ct/Yt = (r/1+g)\ d + ct\ \forall t$; where $ct = Ct/Yt$. If the same level of i were to be financed by taxes, we would have $Tt/Yt = i + ct = (g/1+g)d + ct$. The difference between the two cases once the debt ratio is stable would then be negligible if $r \cong g$ (i.e. if the real interest rate were close to the real GDP growth).

120. See Kitterer (1994) for an analysis based on an overlapping generations-general equilibrium model. The Central Planning Bureau of the Netherlands estimates that the shift from deficit to tax finance would entail a welfare loss for current generations equal to 34 per cent of GDP (van Ewijk, 1997).
121. If capital expenditures were reduced, the burden of transition would be shifted onto future generations who would suffer from the lower accumulated stock of public capital.
122. Budgetary problems involved in this second transition are analysed in Holzmann (1999).
123. By 'lasting and significant improvement' we mean a reduction of the deficit ratio for at least two years and by at least 1.5 percentage points of GDP. Luxembourg is not included in the analysis. Similar evidence is also reported by Roubini and Sachs (1989a) and by De Haan *et al.* (1996) with reference to different time spans and using a sample of OECD countries.
124. The implications of deficit financing of public investment also raise doubts from a theoretical point of view. Among the relevant issues, the possibility of crowding out should be mentioned. A review of the theory is provided by Dalamagas (1995).
125. Cost function estimations have also been used (see the references in Dalenberg *et al.*, 1998). In Dalenberg *et al.* (1998) the analysis focuses on the relationship between public infrastructure and private employment using a labour demand function: 'public highway capital is significantly related to state employment growth in all specifications' (p. 46). Also the effects of public investment on private investment have been investigated; Erenburg (1993) finds a significant positive relationship between the two variables at state level for the USA. Overall the results are ambiguous.
126. The production function method is based on an aggregate production function where public capital (G) is a factor of production (Q) together with private capital (K) and labour (L):

$$Q = MFP * f(K, L, G)$$

where MFP (multifactor productivity) is the residual after subtracting from the growth in total output the direct contributions from capital and labour. Subsequent to the specification of the function (usually a Cobb–Douglas) and of the error term (a typical structure for a panel would be $\varepsilon it = fi + gt + mit$; where f is a country-specific effect, g is a time-specific component and m is an identically and independently distributed error), a regression analysis is conducted to check whether the coefficient of G is positive and significant. The literature shows that the results of the analysis are strongly dependent on the assumptions concerning f and g; specifically the presence of significant productivity effects from public capital seems to depend on the hypothesis that $f = 0\ \forall i$.
127. Comparative analyses show that the stock of infrastructure in Italy is currently 10 per cent lower than the EU average; a similar gap was estimated for the mid-1980s. See, for example, Pontolillo (1998).

128. De la Fuente (1997), using a sample of OECD countries, finds that the elasticity of GDP with respect to investment expenditure decreases rapidly as outlays increase and can even assume negative values as a consequence of distortions and crowding out induced by public intervention.
129. Proposals to exclude capital outlays from the operating budget and to include depreciation of government capital stock date back at least to Musgrave (1939). The issue is reviewed, for example, in Goode and Birnbaum (1955), Steve (1972), Premchand (1983), Poterba (1995) and Robinson (1998, 1999b).
130. The inclusion in the capital account (which can be debt-financed) of all expenditures contributing to human capital accumulation would imply high levels of deficits and pose serious classification problems. One should also take into account that part of expenditures replaces existing capital. Modigliani and Padoa Schioppa Kostoris (1998) estimate that in Italy gross public expenditure for 'development' amounts to 15 per cent of GDP; the corresponding net figure would be 5 per cent.
131. We follow the definitions of the IMF, the OECD and the European Commission: structural is synonymous with cyclically adjusted, and only automatic reactions to the cycle (i.e. those induced by existing legislation) are considered (see Banca d'Italia, 1999, for a review of methodologies and practices). It is common in the literature to term 'elasticity' rather than 'semi-elasticity' the relation between point changes in the deficit to GDP ratio and percentage changes in output.
132. Art. 104 of the Treaty says that when the ratio is above 60 per cent of GDP it must 'diminish sufficiently' and approach 60 per cent 'at a satisfactory pace'. If the ratio increases, the excessive deficit procedure begins. It should be noted that, while the Treaty allows exceptions to the 3 per cent deficit criterion, it does not for the criterion concerning the debt ratio. The implications for stabilization policy of the interaction between the deficit and the debt rule are analysed in Balassone and Monacelli (2000). Other relevant issues concerning the stabilization function of fiscal policy in EMU are discussed in Buti and Sapir (1998) and Chapter 4.
133. 'Borrowing cannot exceed the total investment expenditure in the budget; exceptions are only allowed to avoid disturbances to the overall economic equilibrium.'
134. On this, see HM Treasury (1998).
135. For example: how would one distinguish between maintenance and new investment?
136. In the procedure, investment is defined as 'gross fixed capital formation'.
137. It would be different if all capital expenditure were excluded from the deficit. Among these expenditures payments aimed at covering current deficits of public enterprises or at settling past debts would be included.
138. In several countries general government accounts are only available on a yearly basis. Monitoring of overall balances is often based on more readily available financial data (e.g. borrowing requirement), which do not provide indications concerning the composition of balances and, more specifically, investment expenditure.
139. In Figure 6.4b fluctuation margins are always equal to 2 percentage points of GDP.
140. In the UK net investment to GDP is probably below 1 per cent (the gross ratio is just above 1 per cent).

141. In HM Treasury (1997) a safeguard clause is included for the stability of the debt to GDP ratio over the economic cycle.
142. These problems become more relevant when referring to the overall contribution of public sector outlays to human and physical capital accumulation. Estimates by Modigliani and Padoa Schioppa Kostoris (1998) clearly show how high the deficit could reach and the complexity of evaluating that contribution; the latter would be further compounded at the EU level.
143. It has been suggested that the effects of expansionary policies diminish with the level of debt and that an increase in deficit may even have restrictive effects. See, for example, Bertola and Drazen (1993) and Giavazzi and Pagano (1990 and 1996).
144. See, respectively, Domar (1944) and Blanchard *et al.* (1990).
145. The policy stance implied by these parameters may often be tighter than that needed for sustainability by any definition adopted; see, e.g., Pasinetti (1997), Kinnunen and Kuoppamaki (1998), Balassone and Monacelli (2000).
146. The economic rationale of the parameters has indeed been questioned, see, e.g., Buiter *et al.* (1993) and Eichengreen and Von Hagen (1996) for a discussion.
147. See Shaviro (1997) for a summary of the early debate.
148. See Sraffa (1952–73) vol. IV, pp. 187–8 and vol. I, p. 247. See also Shoup (1960). Also Smith discussed fiscal illusion and the merit of expenditures to be deficit-financed.
149. See, for example, Griziotti (1917), De Viti de Marco (1934) and Puviani (1903).
150. The so-called 'utility view' elaborated a different argument by shifting the focus of the analysis from social to individual costs. According to this view, the burden of the debt falls onto future generations independently of the effects of debt on capital accumulation. Bond-holders have voluntarily given up resources now to have them back in the future so that their utility is not reduced; future tax payers, on the other hand, will be forced to transfer (via the tax bill) resources to the bond-holders so that their utility will be reduced (see, e.g., Buchanan, 1958). It may be argued that there is no contrast between the 'real resource view' and the 'utility view' as they attach different meanings to the same label (see Scitovsky, 1961, and West, 1975).
151. The theory of functional finance also develops in these years. Lerner (1943) argues in favour of debt financing to boost aggregate demand during recessions and suggests compensating for those deficits by corresponding budget surpluses during expansions.
152. See Premchand (1983). Poterba (1995) points out that in the USA proposals to exclude capital outlays from the operating budget and to include depreciation of government capital stock date back at least to Musgrave (1939).
153. The debate on the golden rule is still ongoing. See Chapter 6.
154. There is of course the risk that when the size of roll-overs grows, public finances become exposed to financial markets turbulence.
155. The limits of the approach were of course clearly perceived: 'the issue rather is how interest service will affect the economy' (Musgrave and Musgrave, 1984, p. 689); 'the problem of the debt burden is a problem of an expanding national income. How can a rapidly rising income be achieved?' (Domar, 1944, p. 817).
156. The burden of debt can also be measured in terms of primary balances. In

Domar's model, given a constant overall deficit, the primary balance will have to adjust to compensate for growing interest payments. The primary balance is defined as $p_t = b - \rho[d_{t-1}/(1+\gamma)]$ so that also convergence of p to a finite value requires convergence of d. Using equation (7.3) in the text, we see that p converges to a surplus: $\lim_{t\to\infty} p_t = b[(\gamma - \rho)/\gamma]$.

157. International economic organizations largely contributed to developing long term projections. See, for example, OECD (1985) and the IMF study by Heller *et al.* (1986).
158. The definition of a precise benchmark is functional to the computation of the synthetic indicators of sustainability proposed by Blanchard *et al.* (1990). See the fifth section of this chapter.
159. Compliance with EMU rules is clearly consistent with the second definition proposed by Blanchard *et al.* (1990): a debt ratio converging below a finite threshold implies a discounted debt ratio converging to zero.
160. On problems related to the measurement of net worth and its changes see Blejer and Cheasty (1991).
161. If a net measure of debt is used, symmetry would require that assets be valued in the same way as liabilities. However, an argument for market valuation of assets in any case could be made, based on the consideration that they can only be sold at market prices.
162. To obtain a measure consistent with gross debt changes, national account deficit data should be corrected for transactions in assets (obtaining a measure of borrowing requirement).
163. Concerning the first aspect, the nominal value of liabilities affects the debt while it is the price actually paid by the creditor that corresponds to the deficit. Concerning the second aspect, foreign currency debt is converted in domestic currency values based on end-of-period exchange rates, while the value of the transaction corresponding to the deficit is the one computed on the basis of the exchange rate at the time of the transaction.
164. See Van den Noord and Herd (1993 and 1994), Kuné *et al.* (1993), Hagemann and Nicoletti (1989), Hills (1984), Castellino (1985), Beltrametti (1993) and Rostagno (1995).
165. See Van den Noord and Herd (1993), IMF (1993), Hoffman (1993) and Castellino (1985).
166. IMF (1993, p. 56). The IMF refers to the estimates presented in Van den Noord and Herd (1993).
167. Towe (1991, p. 110).
168. See, respectively, Kotlikoff (1984) and Buiter (1983). For a critique see Mackenzie (1989). For a survey, see Towe (1991) and Blejer and Cheasty (1991).
169. The same methodology would be applied to all 'contingent liabilities'. A contingent liability can be defined as a public sector action that determines a cash expenditure only if and when a certain event takes place.
170. They provide a measure of the cost of terminating PAYG pension schemes when complying fully with present benefits rules.
171. See Franco (1995).
172. The list of financial instruments to be considered in the compilation of debt figures is also defined with reference to the ESA.
173. Moreover, with the adoption of the 1995 version of the European System of Accounts (ESA95) the deficit figures are based on accrual accounting.

174. See Artis and Marcellino (1998) for a review.
175. The data definitions adopted by Hamilton and Flavin and by Wilcox are not used in all other studies. In some cases the national accounts figures for debt to GDP ratios have been used (e.g. in Ucktum and Wickens, 1997).
176. One exception is Ahmed and Rogers (1995) who use a sample period of 200 and 300 years respectively for the US (1792–1992) and the UK (1692–1992).
177. This point is made in OECD (1988a, pp. 27–8).
178. See also the several criticisms expressed in Pearson *et al.* (1989).
179. This point is stressed in Pearson *et al.* (1989).
180. Elderly people without children are more likely to demand public services (Pearson *et al.*, 1989).
181. The use of current per capita age profiles to project expenditure levels is particularly problematic for health care. Several studies noted that a sizeable share of health expenditure occurs in the final part of life. This implies that the number of deaths occurring each year also affects expenditure. It also implies that an increase in life expectancy may have limited effects on lifetime health expenditure. See Zweifel *et al.* (1995).
182. The maturation of pension schemes is examined in Franco and Munzi (1996).
183. OECD (1993c) decomposed nominal health care expenditure growth over the period 1980–90 for the OECD area (11.8 per cent per year) into the effects of general inflation (8 per cent), medical specific inflation (0.7 per cent), and the increase in volume of services (2.9 per cent, of which 2.4 per cent was attributed to the increase in per capita services and only 0.3 per cent was due to the ageing process).
184. See Ministry of Finance of Denmark (1995), Ministry of Social Affairs and Health of Finland (1994), State General Accounting Office, Ministry of Treasury of Italy (1997), Shoven *et al.* (1994), for the USA and Englert *et al.* (1994), for Belgium.
185. Blanchard *et al.* (1990) estimated a long-term tax gap for 18 countries over a 40-year horizon taking long-term projections of pension and health care expenditure into account. They also estimated a short- and a medium-term tax gap which are not affected by demographic changes: the former is computed on a one-year time horizon and does not require projections; the latter relies on five-year projections of economic activity and public spending and considers expected cyclical effects. OECD (1996) estimated short-term tax gaps from the year 2000 onwards in order to evaluate the increase in tax rates which, in each year, would offset the increase in public expenditure determined by ageing.
186. In a first stage, they computed the 'required minimum primary surplus', defined as the level of the primary surplus that could be maintained forever without giving rise to an explosion of the public debt. This is similar to the computation of Buiter's (1985) indicator. As pointed out in the text, the main drawback of this exercise is that it says nothing regarding whether current policies allow the actual primary balance to remain in line with the one required for a stable debt to GDP ratio.
187. Generational accounting was first applied in the United States by Auerbach *et al.* (1991). In the United States and Norway it has also been introduced in official budget documents. Estimates have since been produced for several European countries (see Raffelhüschen, 1999 for a review).
188. There are a couple of differences: (a) in our formulation gross debt is used rather

than net wealth; and (b) the terms $O_{i,j}$ are already adjusted for the size of the generations whereas in the standard presentation the adjustment is made explicit.

189. For a comparison of the age-related expenditure profiles underlying some studies referring to European countries see Franco and Munzi (1999).
190. The point is especially relevant for investment expenditures.
191. This point is made by Robinson (1999a) who shows that the 'equity norm' implicit in GA is arbitrary since while it requires that net payment be constant across generations as a share of generation's income, concerning government consumption it demands that it be constant in per capita terms.
192. See, e.g., Haveman (1994) and Robinson (1999a).
193. For a critical assessment of generational accounting, see, e.g., Buiter (1995) and Haveman (1994).
194. On this issue, see Hagemann and John (1995) and IMF (1996).
195. In this chapter, the term 'federalism' has been attributed a broad meaning. With regard to the significance of the term federalism and the classification of the various institutional structures that can be defined federal, see for example Brosio (1996), Forte and Cerioni (1996) and Patrizi (1998).
196. For a critical analysis of these indications, see Fausto (1999).
197. The distinction made in this chapter is comparable to the more common one between confederations and federations.
198. Somewhat similar problems arise in regard to regulating taxation policies so as to avoid fiscal competition; in other words, the introduction of preferential tax treatment in order to attract tax bases. On this subject, see for example Smith (1996).
199. The solution adopted by the European Union includes these features (see the first part of the next section).
200. See Balassone and Franco (1999) and the references therein. For an analysis of the problems connected with public sector investment within the framework of the Stability and Growth Pact, see Chapter 6.
201. The principal bibliographical reference is Musgrave (1959). For an updated discussion of the problem of the allocation of expenditure functions, see Ter-Minassian (1997).
202. One difficulty arises from the fact that it is rare for public services to coincide with territorial divisions: theoretically, it could be necessary to provide as many jurisdictions as there are services to be produced. There are also problems in relation to free-riding and the difficulty of expressing preferences (see Olson, 1965, and Arrow, 1951). Solutions to these problems have been suggested (for example, Tiebout's 'voting with the feet', 1956). The classic reference on the optimal size of jurisdictions is Buchanan (1965); for an updated analysis, see Cornes and Sandler (1995).
203. The importance of these considerations for the allocation of stabilization functions in the European Union tends to increase as the markets gradually become more closely integrated.
204. The assigning of mobile tax bases to decentralized governments also risks encouraging fiscal competition (see, for example, Smith, 1996).
205. The difficulty of evading taxes on natural resources makes them suitable for decentralized levels of government. However, the fact that the central government is responsible for their allocation among the different jurisdictions argues in favour of their attribution to the latter.
206. See, for example, Buchanan (1967) and Oates (1972).

207. The structuring of transfers so as to provide useful incentives is one of the most complex elements in the theory of fiscal federalism. Cullis and Jones (1992) offer a review of the budget constraints determined by different types of transfer. Garcia-Milá *et al.* (1999) stress the risks associated with heavy reliance on central government grants, especially when institutions make it difficult for central government to avoid regional government's expectation of higher future grants in response to increased borrowing.
208. King (1984) examines explanations of the so-called 'fly-paper effect' (i.e. the fact that an increase in central government transfers causes an increase in local public-sector expenditure that is greater than that which would result from an equivalent increase in personal income); see also Oates (1979). For the implications of programmes in which the benefits are geographically concentrated and financing is met by general taxation, see Weingast *et al.* (1981).
209. The Canadian experience seems to suggest that there are large lags in the effects of market controls: despite a significant deterioration in its rating and a subsequent increase in risk premium, the debt of the Canadian provinces consistently increased for years before corrective budget policies were introduced (Ter-Minassian and Craig, 1997).
210. This, for example, is the case of the United States; for a detailed analysis, see McGranahan (1999).
211. For references to this risk, see among others: Canzoneri and Diba (1991), Allsopp and Vines (1996), Artis and Winkler (1998), Eichengreen and Wyplosz (1998) and Flandreau *et al.* (1998).
212. For a review of the reasons adduced for introducing the Pact and an analysis of its potential macroeconomic implications, see Buti and Sapir (1998), Artis and Winkler (1997) and Eichengreen and Wyplosz (1998).
213. This interpretation is supported by the Resolution of the European Council of 16–17 June 1997, in Council Regulation No. 1466/97 of 7 July 1997 and in the Opinion of the Monetary Committee of 12 October 1998, later adopted by the Council.
214. We use the definitions given by the IMF, the OECD and the European Commission: budget corrections apply only to automatic reactions (i.e. those determined by current legislation). For a methodological review of the methods for estimating structural balances, see Banca d'Italia (1999).
215. The Treaty establishes that the deficit may not exceed 3 per cent of GDP unless (a) exceptional circumstances obtain (these may include a recession leading to a reduction in real GDP of at least 2 per cent; (b) it is close to 3 per cent; (c) the overshoot is absorbed in the short term. These three conditions render the 3 per cent ceiling particularly strict (see Buti *et al.*, 1997).
216. The term 'elasticity' is commonly used in preference to the term 'semi-elasticity' to indicate the ratio between the absolute change in the deficit/GDP ratio and the percentage change in GDP.
217. As explained in Chapter 3 these figures are based on European Commission estimates for the period 1960–1997 (a maximum output gap averaging 4 percentage points; average budget elasticity equal to 0.6). The choice of medium-term target should reflect the need to cover adverse circumstances other than those connected with the economic cycle (e.g. increases in interest rates), to reduce the public debt and to deflect pressures on spending generated by demographic trends. On this point, see the Opinion of the Monetary Committee of 12 October 1998, later adopted by the European Council.

218. The fixed component is intended to discourage excessive deficits, while the variable component is an incentive to limit their amount. The German Finance Minister, Theo Waigel, had initially proposed a deposit equal to 0.25 per cent of GDP for each point – or fraction thereof – between the actual deficit and the 3 per cent ceiling. This would have produced discontinuities in the application of sanctions and could, furthermore, have pushed the latter to politically unacceptable heights.
219. If no corrective measures are adopted, the sanctions can be applied in the same year in which the deficit is judged to be excessive.
220. No distinction is made in the Treaty between current and capital expenditure for the purposes of determining the deficit. The volume of capital expenditure is included only among the relevant factors to be borne in mind when deciding whether there is excessive debt.
221. See Article 2 of the Protocol on procedures for excessive debt.
222. See Articles 145 and 146 of the Treaty establishing the European Community, as amended by the Treaty on European Union of 7 February 1992.
223. In other words it is assumed that an uncooperative state will benefit from other states' cooperation while not being penalized by their defection, whereas a cooperative state will not only benefit from other states' cooperation but also bear the cost of other states' defection.
224. See McGranahan (1999) for the US experience.
225. These operations would nevertheless have to be excluded when evaluating cyclically adjusted budgetary positions.
226. Creating a market in pollution permits was first suggested by Crocker (1966) and Dales (1968). This original contribution generated a vast literature; for a discussion of the benefits and limitations of the approach see Baumol and Oates (1988).
227. The ceiling is needed to prevent the sort of problems cited earlier in relation to the possibility that financial markets can prevent excessive build-up of debt.
228. For instance, the degree of exposure of the banking system, the degree of international openness, and so on. See among others Eichengreen and Portes (1986), Kharas (1984), Hernandez-Trillo (1995), Cantor and Packer (1996).
229. The problem could be attenuated by a continuous double auction market (a system used in many financial markets); see Friedman and Rust (1993).
230. See for example Buglione (1998), Forte and Cerioni (1996) and Giarda (1996).
231. Pica (1999) notes 'the anomalous use of the word "pact": the word assumes the existence of a forum in which local governments can agree (have the power to agree) on their conduct, bargaining with the central government. [Actually, however] . . . state law . . . constitutes [a] concrete means of coercion in the desired direction, not consent freely decided' (pp. 1–2; our translation).
232. Revenues are net of the proceeds of sales of financial assets and gross of the proceeds of sales of real estate assets. The same standard is used to calculate the deficit for European purposes.
233. The total correction, estimated at about 2.2 trillion lire, was divided among levels of government in proportion to total expenditure (*S*). The resulting targets for the individual categories of government were translated into specific objectives for each entity. For the Regions, the reduction was set at 1 per cent of primary current expenditure in 1998. For municipalities and provinces it was put at the larger between 1.1 per cent of primary current expenditure in 1998 and 3 per cent of the current programmes deficit for the year. The

latter was calculated by each government body by augmenting the 1998 deficit by 80 per cent of the nominal GDP growth forecast for 1999.

234. However, the rule restricting market borrowing to cover only investment spending remains; consistency between the two rules would have to be ensured by state transfers.
235. Another limit is implied by the need to reduce the stock of debt. But no sanctions are provided if the debt increases. Moreover, the relevant definition of debt is not sufficiently well defined, increasing the scope for 'creative accounting'.
236. Balassone *et al.* (2004) further examine the issue also on the basis of the solutions adopted in other European countries.
237. Due to lack of or erratic data hindering the analysis in the next sections, Luxembourg is not considered.
238. Maroto and Mulas-Granados (2002) find election year is an insignificant predictor of the probability of ending a consolidation episode when consolidation is defined as a change in the cyclically adjusted primary balance >0 per cent <1 per cent. Only when the definition of consolidation is made stronger (changes >1 per cent, as in most of the literature), then election year becomes significant, and political variables such as coalition size, cabinet size, and elections become stronger predictors than economic variables regarding the probability of ending the adjustment. These results indicate that governments worry about elections when the required consolidation is important enough to be visible to the electorate.
239. Interestingly, Coricelli and Ercolani (2002) posit a similar rule as a possible reform of the Stability and Growth Pact in the context of EU enlargement. Their proposal implies balancing the structural budget and then running a 'neutral' policy according to the behavioural rules set out in equations (9.1) and (9.2). For a similar approach, see Larch and Salto (2003).
240. The implicit assumption is that governments adopt the ECB target as their benchmark for 'equilibrium' rate of inflation, which may or may not be true, but any other assumption risks introducing an arbitrary element. Moreover, the results in this chapter are relatively robust with respect to the inflation assumption (see Note 241).
241. Note that the size of the inflation dividend and the total DP depend on the assumed target inflation rate (here 1.5 per cent). However, the size of the other two components is invariant with respect to this assumption.
242. It can easily be shown that $DP = \Delta CAPB$ if the following conditions hold: $y = y^*$ (actual growth is equal to trend growth), $\pi = \pi^e$ (no inflation expectational error), and $\varepsilon_G = \varepsilon_T = 1$.
243. Note that the numbers presented are excluding receipts from UMTS licences, which were substantial in some countries notably in 2000 and 2001. However, the numbers are not corrected for the impact of securitizations which in some countries have been used to mask underlying fiscal easing. As a result, the true easing may have been larger than shown here.
244. The tightening bias in 1999 and 2000 (including in Germany and France) may seem surprising in view of the quite different results reported elsewhere based on the traditional measure of fiscal stance, namely the change in the cyclically adjusted budget balance (CAPB). However, this different assessment stems from the fact that the DP treats expenditure hikes in upswings as 'neutral' to the extent these are in line with growth in (nominal) potential GDP whereas the CAPB would treat these partly as 'discretionary'.

245. Using the change in the CAPB, Buti and Sapir (2002b) show that budgetary consolidation in Germany, France and Italy – three of the countries which did not meet the close-to-balance rule of the SGP – was considerably worse than the already timid efforts which were planned in their stability programme. This contrasts sharply with other euro area members whose budgetary outturn was better than planned.
246. Note that for simplicity we ignore the timing of elections during the year (the most extreme example is that elections in January are treated the same way as elections in December of the same year). However, this choice may also be justified by the annual frequency of budgets.
247. An alternative estimation strategy would be to include country dummies that capture to a large extent the same effect. See Buti and van den Noord (2004).
248. All variables are expressed as a percentage of GDP.
249. The constant term is not shown. The results are similar to those reported in Buti and van den Noord (2004). In that study the autoregressive term was omitted and replaced with a vector of country dummies.
250. Since our analysis focuses on the period since the start of EMU, the results point to the existence of an electoral cycle in the first years of EMU, but do not document what changed due to the creation of the euro area and the establishment of the SGP. In order to ascertain possible changes via DP, one would have to trace back the fiscal policy intentions of the governments in their convergence programmes in EMU's stage two. This extension is part of our future research agenda.
251. See Chapter 11.
252. See Kopits and Symansky (1998) and the papers in Banca d'Italia (2001).
253. Blinder and Solow (1974) forcefully support this view. See also Steve (1972), Kopits (2001) and references therein.
254. See, for example, Blanchard (1990), Blanchard *et al.* (1990) and Blejer and Cheasty (1991 and 1993).
255. See Chapter 6.
256. The rationale for EMU rules is discussed, e.g., in Buti and Sapir (1998) and in Brunila *et al.* (2001).
257. See Chapter 2 and references therein. Direct bail-out is ruled out by the Treaty.
258. A classical reference is Musgrave and Musgrave (1984).
259. See Goodhart and Smith (1993) and Majocchi and Rey (1993).
260. See Lindh and Ohlsson (2002), Buti and Sapir (1998), and Chapter 3.
261. See: Council Resolution on the SGP, 17 June 1997; Council Regulation no. 1466/97; Council Declaration, 1 May 1998; Opinions of the Monetary Committee, 12 October 1998 and of the Economic and Financial Committee, 27 June 2001, as endorsed by the Council.
262. Eurostat (1979 and 1995).
263. The definitions and computational criteria for the two indicators are collected in a guidebook (Eurostat, 2000).
264. See Chapter 7 and Banca d'Italia (2000).
265. Domar (1944, p. 799).
266. The limits of the approach were of course clearly perceived: 'the problem of the debt burden is a problem of an expanding national income. How can a rapidly rising income be achieved?' (Domar, 1944, p. 817); 'the issue rather is how interest service will affect the economy' (Musgrave and Musgrave, 1984, p. 689).

267. See, e.g., Buiter (1985) and Blanchard *et al.* (1990). As Blanchard *et al.* (1990) acknowledge, 'the justification for the ratio to eventually return to its initial level as opposed say to zero, or to a higher but stable level, is, however, much less evident' (p. 11). Blanchard *et al.* (1990) suggest another *ad hoc* definition based on the intertemporal discounted budget constraint, whereby a sustainable policy implies that the discounted value of the debt ratio tends to zero. This definition, however, is consistent with the undiscounted debt ratio converging to any finite level or even diverging, though at a rate lower than the difference between the interest rate and the rate of growth of GDP; 'this is because of discounting, which implies that things far in the future do not matter much for today' (p. 14).
268. This became increasingly clear during the 1980s when, in connection with the growth of the public sector and the unfavourable demographic trends, estimates started to point to substantial prospective increases in welfare expenditure. International economic organization largely contributed to developing long-term projections. See for example, OECD (1985) and the IMF study by Heller *et al.* (1986).
269. In this context, whether the deficit is measured in cash or in accrual terms (à la ESA95) is not crucial given that over the medium term the two measures should not differ significantly.
270. Several studies have stressed the shortcomings of conventional 'point indicators' in the assessment of budgetary sustainability. Some authors have prescribed to resort to either 'economic deficit' (Kotlikoff, 1984) or to 'government net worth' (Buiter, 1983); these solutions would require, *inter alia*, the inclusion of pensions in fiscal accounts when obligations are incurred rather than when the actual expenditure is made. For a survey see Towe (1991) and Blejer and Cheasty (1991); for a critique see Mackenzie (1989). It has been suggested that pension liabilities should be taken into account when evaluating the state and perspectives of public finances (e.g. Van den Noord and Herd, 1993; IMF, 1993; Hoffman, 1993; Castellino, 1985). However, while estimates of such liabilities may represent a useful complement to conventional debt measures in that they provide a measure of the cost of terminating pay-as-you-go pension schemes when complying fully with present benefits rules, they are not an indicator of pension schemes' sustainability whose assessment instead requires estimates of the resources available to pay for the accrued pensions. Moreover, accrued pension rights differ in many ways from conventional public debt and there are practical and theoretical reasons for keeping the two apart (Franco, 1995).
271. See Chapter 1.
272. The target was set close to the European average at the time of the Treaty.
273. One example is the valuation of Italian Post Office Deposit Certificates whose nominal (face) value does not include accrued interest which will have to be paid at withdrawal of funds (similar bonds are issued in Portugal). Market valuation (the criterion adopted in ESA95) would not represent a satisfactory solution. Market valuation refers to the sum the government would be asked to pay if it were to buy back its debt before it falls due, but the government has no obligation to do so. Furthermore, reference to market values would make the debt measure extremely volatile.
274. See the Opinion of the Economic and Financial Committee, 27 June 2001, as endorsed by the Council.

275. Flexibility with respect to the deficit in exceptional circumstances was already allowed for by the Treaty.
276. For a discussion of the issues involved, see the papers in Banca d'Italia (1999). As far as estimates of the effect of the cycle on the budget are concerned, the European Commission, the IMF and the OECD refer directly to GDP (see, respectively, European Commission, 2002a; Hagemann, 1999; Van den Noord, 2000); on the contrary, the European System of Central Banks (ESCB) and Banca d'Italia refer to the macroeconomic variable relevant to each revenue and expenditure item (see, respectively, Bouthevillain *et al.*, 2001; Momigliano and Staderini, 1999). The latter method ensures that the composition effects arising from unbalanced growth are taken into account. As far as the estimation of trend values is concerned, the IMF and the OECD adopt a production function approach, whereas the ESCB and Banca d'Italia use the Hodrick–Prescott (HP) filter. The European Commission, which had been using the HP filter, recently also adopted the production function approach, a decision endorsed by the Ecofin Council.
277. See the Opinion of the Economic and Financial Committee, 27 June 2001, as endorsed by the Council.
278. See Balassone and Monacelli (2000).
279. It may be objected that this would allow transitory effects, such as those of privatization, to enter the definition of deficit. While the new definition would also include transitory effects with the opposite sign, it should be noted that also the present definition includes transitory items (e.g. the so-called 'Euro tax' in Italy). Controlling for this type of measures seems appropriate in any case. The treatment of valuation effects, such as those concerning bonds issued below/above par and foreign currency denominated debt, should also be reconsidered.
280. See Malizia (2000).
281. The case of public enterprises involved in public investment or in the sale of public assets has recently come to the fore with reforms in Austria and Italy as compared to the current arrangements in Germany.
282. Recent proposals in favour of the adoption of the golden rule (i.e., the exclusion of net investment in real assets from the deficit) would obviously increase margins for opportunistic accounting (the evaluation of amortization is but one example). Moreover, the golden rule would only partly remove the bias against non-financial outlays embodied in present rules, while introducing new biases (e.g., against investment in human capital). Interestingly Article 104 of the Treaty includes gross investment expenditure among the elements to be taken into account when assessing governments' fiscal positions but does not make explicit reference to the golden rule. For a discussion of the golden rule and of the feasibility of its implementation in the framework of EMU fiscal rules see Chapter 6.
283. See Goodhart (1984).
284. See Eurostat (2000) and EU Regulations 2516/2000 and 995/2001.
285. An example of the risks determined by these ambiguities is given by the Council decision that member states' budgets ought to be close-to-balance or in surplus by 2000 (a deadline already revised twice), which induced some confusion: first, as to what applied during the transition towards the attainment of the medium-term target and what applied afterwards; second, as to whether the attainment of the target ought to be judged in nominal terms or not (i.e. in cyclically adjusted terms).

286. Or, at worst, they are available not only from government sources but also from the counterparts of the underlying financial transactions.
287. The change would imply the inclusion in the deficit measure of the difference between the nominal value of bonds and their price at issuance, which, as argued earlier, is fine within the context of sustainability analysis. On the contrary, the change in nominal debt ought to be measured net of the effects of exchange rate movements via foreign currency denominated government bonds (which are not under government's control). However, the opportunity and necessity of using this kind of financial instruments may also need to be reassessed.
288. Indeed, it is only the net addition to public capital that should be financed via borrowing while the part that covers depreciation should remain tax-financed. See Blanchard and Giavazzi (2004), HM Treasury (1998) and Kilpatrick (2001).
289. For Germany, see Wendorff (2001).
290. For a theoretical model, see Razin and Sadka (2002).
291. See also Coeré and Pisani-Ferry (2003). Gros (2003) proposes to set a debt target for each country coupled with a commitment to reduce the distance between their existing debt ratio and that target by one-twentieth each year.
292. It would also be useful to attribute the responsibility for projections to independent authorities or to competing institutions. See Franco and Marino (2002).
293. Article 269 TEC constrains the EU budget to equilibrium in each and every budgetary year.
294. In EU jargon, the *juste retour* (or the net balance) approach is the issue of 'who pays what'. This approach epitomized by Margaret Thatcher's famous sentence 'I want my money back', consists in a rather crude calculation of the accounting difference between estimated payments from and expenditure to any given member states of the EU. Economic added value generated by the EU expenditure, externalities of the EU expenditure and revenues (which by definition are very large), the economic significance and reliability of the accounting evidence are totally disregarded by the net balance approach.
295. Clearly, the relation between competencies and spending is complex. Competencies allocated to the EU, disregarding whether exclusive or shared, may generate four types of spending: (1) only EU spending (e.g. CAP); (2) EU and national spending (e.g. structural actions); (3) only national spending (e.g. environmental regulation); (4) no spending at all (e.g. competition policies).
296. This applies also at the national level to the welfare state where the willingness of relatively well-off income earners to finance the social programmes has been eased by the fact that they themselves benefited from such programmes. See Buti *et al.* (1999a).
297. See Teutemann (1992). A possible political reaction could be the shift, in the case of certain public goods, to clubs within the EU, making use of the 'reinforced cooperation' procedure foreseen in the Nice Treaty.
298. 'The Community shall act within the limits of the powers conferred upon it by this Treaty and of the objectives assigned to it therein. In areas which do not fall within its exclusive competence, the Community shall take action, in accordance with the principle of subsidiarity, only if and insofar as the objectives of the proposed action cannot be sufficiently achieved by the member States and can therefore, by reason of scale or effects of the proposed action,

be better achieved by the Community. Any action by the Community shall not go beyond what is necessary to achieve the objectives of this Treaty.'

299. This applies naturally to the allocation function of public spending, but also equity and stabilization can be thought of as public goods supplied by the national and the EU level. Clearly, in the case of equity, cross-country redistribution can only be carried out at supranational level.
300. For simplicity, in what follows G_N and G_{EU} are treated as a single value. However G_N should be thought of as a matrix (the spending items per line and the countries per column) and G_{EU} as a vector.
301. Equation (12.2) implies a 45-degree budget constraint. However the expression could be generalized by attaching to G_N and G_{EU} their specific 'prices' which would capture the distortions due to taxation. Today, the EU Budget is mostly financed by national contributions, which are financed by national taxes: the financing of G_N and G_{EU} generates, therefore, the same distortion. In the future, if the EU budget were to be financed by a particular subset of national taxes, the distortions generated by the two sets of taxes (and hence the coefficients of G_N and G_{EU} in (12.2)) could be different, thereby changing the slope to the budget constraint. While this would affect the location of the optimal point, the qualitative conclusions of our analysis do not change. We are indebted to Wilhelm Kohler for this intuition.
302. While in Figures 12.1 and 12.2 we have an internal solution (i.e. a certain public good is produced optimally by a combination of EU and national spending), it cannot be excluded that efficiency is optimized by allocating spending on a certain public good totally at the EU or at the national level. This must be the case for a host of public services of purely national or local interest, see next section.
303. For instance, a linear production function associated with a linear budget constraint will deliver only corner solutions: that is, policies which ought to be run totally either at the national level or at the EU level depending on which level the productivity is the greatest. In the Annex, we develop a simple model based on the linear setting where we analyse the problem of spending allocation between the national and the EU level and we also take into account institutional or political constraints.
304. The scope of the following discussion (and of the chapter in general) is not to determine the values of α and β for any type of policy, but rather to show how competencies could be reorganized on the basis of the implicit values of α and β which have emerged from the most recent literature on fiscal federalism. Several of the issues discussed in this section were dealt with at the beginning of the 1990s in the report 'Stable Money, Sound Finances', see European Commission (1993).
305. As pointed out by Von Hagen (2002b), increasing mobility could also be seen as a way of lessening the costs of EMU.
306. The nature of CAP as an allocative or redistributive policy is much disputed (see Nava, 2000). As a redistributive policy, one of the many reasons why the CAP is widely criticized is due to the fact that its redistribution function depends more on the work title (e.g. producer of a given product) and it is positively correlated with the potential income of the beneficiary.
307. See, Bertola (1999), Bertola *et al.* (2000a), and Boeri and Terrell (2002).
308. Objective 1 regions are those where residents have a per capita income of less than 75 per cent of Community average. This is the result, *inter alia*, of the

predominant regional focus of EU cohesion expenditure and of cohesion negotiations driven by net balance considerations. Net balance considerations find their natural humus in the EU cohesion policy, because the Council needs unanimity to agree on this policy, which gives each and every country a *de facto* veto. National political constraints mean each country worries more about being able to flag 'a negotiation success' than about being sure that funds are spent in those policies having a higher Community added value.

309. See, e.g., Mairate and Hall (2000) and Hallet (2002).
310. This would be an improvement on the current mechanism of the 'performance reserve' which triggers a 4 per cent increase in the funds in the case of good performance.
311. For instance, Von Hagen (2002b) has suggested that minimum unemployment benefits for a limited period (say six months) could be paid by the EU. An idea along similar lines was first put forward in the Marjolin report in the 1970s (European Commission, 1975).
312. As a precedent, for the first time in August 2002, following the flooding in Central Europe (especially the Czech Republic and Germany), the resources for the emergency funds were taken from the unused commitments for the structural policy.
313. However, the literature has pointed out that, even leaving aside political and moral hazard constraints, constructing such an automatic mechanism is not easy. See, e.g., Von Hagen and Hammond (1996).
314. For those policies where optimal production takes place fully at the national level or at the EU level, the outcome would be either a move towards total renationalization or a move towards total centralization at the EU level.
315. See European Commission (2002c), section 1.4., Goulard and Nava (2002) and Tabellini (2003).
316. GNP contributions plus that part of the VAT contributions calculated via the GNP keys.
317. Article 33 of the ECB's Statute provides for a transfer from the ECB to the national central banks using a key equal to the arithmetic average of population and GNP (Article 29 of the Statute). This is the subject of much controversy, see Sinn and Feist (1997) and European Central Bank (2001).
318. Since 1988 the EU budget has always been adopted on time and complaints to the Court of Justice by one or the other Institutions have nearly disappeared. In the period 1975–88, preceding the FP, the adoption of the EU budget was delayed in 6 years out of 13 and the EU institutions complained to the Court of Justice on three occasions.
319. For a lucid overview of the issue of flexibility in the EU Budget, see Montagnon (2002).
320. In line with the Presidency Conclusions of the Copenhagen European Council of December 2002, the number of EU members rose to 25 on 1 May 2004, and is planned to become 27 from 2007.
321. This chapter focuses mainly on allocative policies. A proposal for a budgetary coordination mechanism putting the emphasis on stabilization was submitted by the then French Finance Minister, Dominique Strauss-Khan, at the informal Ecofin Council in Dresden in April 1999. The French proposal stressed that the aggregate policy stance at the EMU level must be examined on the basis of an aggregate stability programme. The proposal pointed out that the

objective to achieve an adequate policy stance for the EMU as a whole should be taken into account when examining the national stability programmes. For a discussion see Buti *et al.* (2003). A similar proposal has been presented by the vice president of the EU Convention, Giuliano Amato, see Amato (2002). On similar lines, see Collignon (2003) and Majocchi (2002).

322. We show in the Annex, that, in certain circumstances, the current budgetary arrangements imply a higher overall spending and a lower supply of public goods than what would be implied by the optimal allocation of spending between the two levels of government.
323. An even more ambitious objective would be to discuss, when establishing the priorities in the EU budget, also those policies which have little financial impact for the EU budget, but a great financial impact on national budgets (for example, Community fiscal directives, environmental directives, etc.). This would allow national policy makers to take account of community inputs and embody them into their national policies. Von Hagen (2002b) strongly supports the view of making 'law making' compatible with 'money spending' and more generally of assessing the financial impact, for the EU system, of 'law making'.
324. If the more ambitious approach mentioned in Note 323 is chosen, the Commission may also be expected to discuss those regulatory policies that have an impact on national budgets.
325. However, on average the changes with respect to the draft budget are minute (often less than 1 per cent of the total budget, 0.32 per cent in 2003).
326. However, the resulting level of output will correspond to the desired level only if $\bar{Y} = Y^*$, where $\bar{Y} = G_{EU}$.
327. If so, the level of national spending becomes: $G_N^* = \frac{\alpha Y^* + \theta \bar{G}_N - \alpha\beta \bar{G}_{EU}}{\alpha^2 + \theta}$.

Bibliography

Ackrill, R. and D. Garrat (1997), 'Rules versus Discretion: Why EMU Needs a Stability Pact', University of Leicester Discussion Papers, 97/3.

Agell, J., L. Calmfors and G. Jonsson (1996), 'Fiscal Policy when Monetary Policy is Tied to the Mast', *European Economic Review*, 40: 1413–40.

Ahmad, E., D. Hewitt and E. Ruggiero (1997), 'Assigning Expenditure Responsibilities', in T. Ter-Minassian (ed.), *Fiscal Federalism in Theory and Practice*, Washington: IMF.

Ahmed, S. and J.H. Rogers (1995), 'Government Budget Deficits and Trade Deficits. Are Present Value Constraints Satisfied in Long-term Data?', *Journal of Monetary Economics*, 36: 351–74.

Alesina, A., I. Angeloni and F. Etro (2001a), 'The Political Economy of International Unions', CEPR Discussion Papers, 3117.

—— (2003), 'International Unions', mimeo, March.

Alesina, A. and S. Ardagna (1998), 'Tales of Fiscal Adjustment', *Economic Policy*, 27: 489–545.

Alesina, A., O. Blanchard, J. Galí, F. Giavazzi and H. Uhlig (2001b), *Defining a Macroeconomic Framework for the Euro Area*, CEPR, MECB, 3.

Alesina, A. and A. Drazen (1991), 'Why are Stabilizations Delayed?', *American Economic Review*, 82: 1170–88.

Alesina, A. and R. Perotti (1995a), 'The Political Economy of Budget Deficits', *IMF Staff Papers*, 42: 1–31.

—— (1995b), 'Fiscal Expansions and Adjustments in OECD Countries', *Economic Policy*, 21.

—— (1996a), 'Budget Deficits and Budget Institutions', IMF Working Papers, 52.

—— (1996b), 'Fiscal Discipline and the Budget Process', *American Economic Review*, AEA Papers and Proceedings, 86: 401–7.

Alesina, A. and G. Tabellini (1987), 'Rules versus Discretion with Non-coordinated Monetary and Fiscal Policies', *Economic Inquiry*, 25(4): 619–30.

Aliber, R.Z. (ed.) (1974), *National Monetary Policies and the International Financial System*, Chicago: University of Chicago Press.

Allsopp, C. and D. Vines (1996), 'Fiscal Policy and EMU', *National Institute Economic Review*, 158: 91–107.

Allsopp, C., W. McKibbin and D. Vines (1999), 'Fiscal Consolidation in

Europe: Some Empirical Issues', in A.J. Hughes Hallett, M.M. Hutchison and S.E. Hougaard Jensen (eds), *Fiscal Aspects of European Monetary Integration*, Cambridge: Cambridge University Press.

Alt, J.E. and R.C. Lowry (1994), 'Divided Government and Budget Deficits: Evidence from the States', *American Political Science Review*, 88: 811–28.

Amato, G. (2002), 'Verso un DPEF europeo?', *Nuova Economia Nuova Società*.

Amtenbrink, F., J. de Haan and O.C.H.M. Sleijpen (1997), 'Stability and Growth Pact: Placebo or Panacea?', *European Business Law Review*, 202–10 and 223–38.

Andersson, A.E., B. Harsman and J.M. Quigley (eds) (1997), *Government for the Future – Unification, Fragmentation and Regionalism*, Amsterdam: Elsevier Science BV.

Arachi, G. and A. Zanardi (2000), 'Il federalismo fiscale regionale: opportunità e limiti', in L. Bernardi (ed.), *La finanza pubblica italiana – Rapporto 1999*, Bologna: Il Mulino.

Arrow, K.J. (1951), *Social Choice and Individual Values*, New York: Wiley.

Artis, M.J. (2002), 'The Stability and Growth Pact: Fiscal Policy in the EMU', in F. Breuss, G. Fink and S. Griller (eds), *Institutional, Legal and Economic Aspects of the EMU*, Wien/New York: Springer.

Artis, M.J. and M. Buti (2001), 'Setting Medium-term Fiscal Targets in EMU', in A. Brunila, M. Buti and D. Franco (eds), *The Stability and Growth Pact – The Architecture of Fiscal Policy in EMU*, Basingstoke: Palgrave.

Artis, M.J. and M. Marcellino (1998), 'Fiscal Solvency and Fiscal Forecasting in Europe', EUI Working Papers, ECO. 98/2; also CEPR Discussion Papers, 1836.

—— (1999), 'Fiscal Forecasting: The Track Record of the IMF, OECD and EC', CEPR Discussion Papers, 2206.

—— (2000), 'The Solvency of Government Finances in Europe', in Banca d'Italia, *Fiscal Sustainability*, Proceedings of the Banca d'Italia Workshop on Public Finance, Perugia, 20–22 January, Rome.

Artis, M.J. and B. Winkler (1997), 'The Stability Pact: Safeguarding the Credibility of the European Central Bank', CEPR Discussion Papers, 1688.

—— (1998), 'The Stability Pact: Trading-off Flexibility for Credibility?', in A.J. Hughes Hallett, M.M. Hutchinson and S.E. Hougaard Jensen (eds), *Fiscal Aspects of European Monetary Integration*, Cambridge: Cambridge University Press.

Aschauer, D.A. (1985), 'Fiscal Policy and Aggregate Demand', *American Economic Review*, 75: 117–27.

Aschauer, D.A. (1989), 'Is Public Expenditure Productive?', *Journal of Monetary Economics*, 23: 177–200.

Auerbach, A.J. and D. Feenberg (2000), 'The Significance of Federal Taxes as Automatic Stabilizers', *Journal of Economic Perspectives*, 14(3): 37–56.

Auerbach, A.J., J. Gokhale and L.J. Kotlikoff (1991), 'Generational Accounts: A Meaningful Alternative to Deficit Accounting', in D. Bradford (ed.), *Tax Policy and the Economy*, Vol. 5, Cambridge, MA: MIT Press, pp. 55–110.

—— (1992), 'Generational Accounting: A New Approach for Understanding the Effects of Fiscal Policy on Saving', *Scandinavian Journal of Economics*, 94: 303–18.

Auerbach, A.J., L.J. Kotlikoff and W. Leibfritz (1997), *Generational Accounting – Worldwide*, NBER Series, Cambridge: Cambridge University Press.

Austrian Federal Ministry of Finance (2000), *Austrian Stability Programme: Update for the Period 2000–04*, December.

Balassone, F. and D. Franco (1999), 'Public investment in the Stability Pact Framework', in M. Bordignon and D. da Empoli (eds), *Concorrenza fiscale in un'economia internazionale integrata*, Milano: Franco Angeli.

Balassone, F., D. Franco and S. Zotteri (2004), 'Fiscal Rules for Subnational Governments: Lessons from EMU Countries', in G. Kopits (ed.), *Rules-based Fiscal Policy in Emerging Markets: Background, Analysis and Prospects*, Basingstoke: Macmillan.

Balassone, F. and R. Giordano (2001), 'Budget Deficits and Coalition Governments', *Public Choice*, 06: 327–49.

Balassone, F. and D. Monacelli (2000), 'EMU Fiscal Rules: Is There a Gap?', *Temi di Discussione*, 375.

Baldwin, R., D. Cohen, A. Sapir and A. Venables (eds) (1999), *Market Integration, Regionalism and the Global Economy*, Cambridge: Cambridge University Press.

Ballabriga, F. and C. Martinez-Mongay (2003), 'Has EMU Shifted Monetary and Fiscal Policies?', in M. Buti, *Monetary and Fiscal Policies in EMU: Interactions and Coordination*, Cambridge: Cambridge University Press.

Banca d'Italia (1999), *Indicators of Structural Budget Balances*, Proceedings of the Banca d'Italia Workshop on Public Finance held in Perugia, 26–28 November 1998, Rome.

—— (2000), *Fiscal Sustainability*, Proceedings of the Banca d'Italia Workshop on Public Finance held in Perugia, 20–22 January 2000, Rome.

—— (2001), *Fiscal Rules*, Proceedings of the Banca d'Italia Workshop on Public Finance held in Perugia, 1–3 February 2001, Rome.

Banca d'Italia (2002), *The Impact of Fiscal Policy*, Proceedings of the

Banca d'Italia Workshop on Public Finance held in Perugia, 21–23 March 2002, Rome.
Banco de España (2002), *Boletín Economico*, January.
Barrel, R. and K. Dury (2001), 'Will the SGP Ever Be Breached?', in A. Brunila, M. Buti and D. Franco (eds), *The Stability and Growth Pact – The Architecture of Fiscal Policy in EMU*, Basingstoke: Palgrave.
Barrell, R. and A. Pina (2000), 'How Important are Automatic Stabilisers in Europe?', EUI Working Papers, ECO. 2000/2.
Barro, R.J. (1974), 'Are Government Bonds Net Wealth?', *Journal of Political Economy*, 82: 1095–117.
—— (1979), 'On the Determination of Public Debt', *Journal of Political Economy*, 87: 940–71.
—— (1984), 'The Behaviour of U.S. Deficits', NBER Working Papers, 1309.
Barro, R.J. and D.B. Gordon (1983), 'Rules, Discretion and Reputation in a Model of Monetary Policy', *Journal of Monetary Economics*, 12: 101–21.
Bastable, C.F. (1927), *Public Finance*, London: Macmillan.
Baumol, W.J. and W.E. Oates (1988), *The Theory of Environmental Policy*, Cambridge: Cambridge University Press.
Bayoumi, T. and B. Eichengreen (1995), 'Restraining Yourself: The Implications of Fiscal Rules for Economic Stabilization', *IMF Staff Papers*, 42: 32–48.
Bean, C.R. (1998), 'Discussion', *Economic Policy*, 26: 104–7.
Beetsma, R. (2001), 'Does EMU Need a Stability Pact?', in A. Brunila, M. Buti and D. Franco (eds), *The Stability and Growth Pact – The Architecture of Fiscal Policy in EMU*, Basingstoke: Palgrave.
Beetsma, R. and A.L. Bovenberg (1998), 'Monetary Union without Fiscal Coordination May Discipline Policymakers', *Journal of International Economics*, 45: 239–58.
Beetsma, R., X. Debrun and F. Klaassen (2001), 'Is Fiscal Policy Coordination in EMU Desirable?', *Swedish Economic Policy Review*, 8(1): 57–97.
Beetsma, R. and H. Uhlig (1999), 'An Analysis of the Stability and Growth Pact', *Economic Journal*, 109: 546–71.
Beltrametti, L. (1993), 'Una stima della ricchezza pensionistica per l'Italia (1951–1991)', *Rivista Internazionale di Scienze Sociali*, 1: 3–15.
Bennett, H. and N. Loayza (2000), 'Policy Biases when the Monetary and Fiscal Authorities Have Different Objectives', Central Bank of Chile Working Papers, 66.
Berglöf, E., B. Eichengreen, G. Roland, G. Tabellini and C. Wyplosz (2003), *Built to Last: A Political Architecture for Europe*, CEPR, MEI, 12.

Bertola, G. (1999), 'Convergence: An Overview', in R. Baldwin *et al.* (eds), *Market Integration, Regionalism and the Global Economy*, Cambridge: Cambridge University Press.

Bertola, G., T. Boeri and G. Nicoletti (2000a), *Welfare and Employment in a United Europe*, Cambridge, MA: MIT Press.

Bertola, G. and Drazen, A. (1993), 'Trigger Points and Budgetary Cuts: Explaining the Effects of Fiscal Austerity', *American Economic Review*, 38(1): 11–26.

Bertola, G., J.F. Jimeno, R. Marimón and C. Pissarides (2000b), 'Welfare Systems and Labour Markets in Europe: What Convergence Before and After EMU?', in G. Bertola, T. Boeri and G. Nicoletti (eds), *Welfare and Employment in a United Europe*, Cambridge, MA: MIT Press.

Bhandari, J.S. and B.H. Putnam (eds) (1983), *Economic Interdependence and Flexible Exchange Rates*, Cambridge, MA: MIT Press.

Biehl, D. (1973), 'Introduction of Round Table Discussion', in H. Giersch (ed.), *Fiscal Policy and Demand Management*, Tubingen: JCB Mohr.

Bini Smaghi, L. and C. Casini (2000), 'Monetary and Fiscal Policy Cooperation: Institutions and Procedures in EMU', *Journal of Common Market Studies*, 38(3): 375–91.

Blanchard, O. (1984), 'Current and Anticipated Deficits, Interest Rates and Economic Activity', *European Economic Review*, 25(1): 7–28.

—— (1990), 'Suggestions for a New Set of Fiscal Indicators', *OECD* Department of Economics and Statistics Working Papers, 79.

—— (2000), 'Commentary', in 'Fiscal Policy in an Era of Surpluses: Economic and Financial Implications', Federal Reserve Bank of New York, *Economic Policy Review*, 6(1): 69–74.

Blanchard, O., J.C. Chouraqui, R.P. Hagemann and N. Sartor (1990), 'The Sustainability of Fiscal Policy: New Answers to an Old Question', *Economic Studies*, OECD, 15: 7–36.

Blanchard, O.J. and F. Giavazzi (2004), 'Reforms that Can Be Done: Improving the SGP through a Proper Accounting of Public Investment', CEPR Discussion Papers, 4220.

Blanchard, O. and R. Perotti (2002), 'An Empirical Characterization of the Dynamic Effects of Changes in Government Spending and Taxes on Output', *Quarterly Journal of Economics*, 117(4): 1329–68.

Blejer, M.I. and A. Cheasty (1991), 'The Measurement of Fiscal Deficits: Analytical and Methodological Issues', *Journal of Economic Literature*, 29(4): 1644–78.

—— (eds) (1993), *How to Measure the Fiscal Deficit, Analytical and Methodological Issues*, Washington, DC: IMF.

Blinder, A.S. (1982), 'Issues in the Coordination of Monetary and Fiscal Policy', NBER Working Papers, 982.

—— (2002), 'Discussion of Canzoneri, Cumby and Diba', Symposium Proceedings, *Rethinking Stabilization Policy*, FRB of Kansas City, August.

Blinder, A. and R.M. Solow (1974), *The Economics of Public Finance*, Washington: The Brookings Institution.

—— (1973), 'Does Fiscal Policy Matter?', *Journal of Public Economics*, 2: 319–37.

Boeri, T. and K. Terrell (2002), 'Institutional Determinants of Labour Reallocation in Transition', *Journal of Economic Perspectives*, 16(1): 51–76.

Bouthevillain, C., P. Cour-Thimann, G. Van Den Dool, P. Hernandez de Cos, G. Langenus, M. Mohr, S. Momigliano and M. Tujula (2001), 'Cyclically Adjusted Budget Balances: An Alternative Approach', ECB Working Paper Series, 77.

Bradford, D. (ed.) (1991), *Tax Policy and the Economy*, Vol. 5, Cambridge, MA: MIT Press, 55–110.

Bredenkamp, H. (1988), 'The Cyclically Adjusted Deficit as a Measure of Fiscal Stance', HM Treasury, GES Working Paper, 102.

Breuss, F., G. Fink and S. Griller (2002), *Institutional, Legal and Economic Aspects of the EMU*, Wien/New York: Springer.

Brosio, G. (1996), 'Federalismo politico e federalismo fiscale', in E. Giardina, F. Osculati and M. Rey (eds), *Federalismo*, Milan: Franco Angeli.

Brunila, A. (2000), 'Public Finances in the XXI Century: Limitations, Challenges and Directions of Reforms in Finland', in Banca d'Italia, *Fiscal Sustainability*, Proceedings of the Banca d'Italia Workshop on Public Finance, Perugia, 20–22 January, Rome.

—— (2002), 'Fiscal Policy: Coordination, Discipline and Stabilisation', paper prepared for a meeting of the Group of Policy Advisers of the European Commission, April.

Brunila, A., M. Buti and D. Franco (eds) (2001), *The Stability and Growth Pact – The Architecture of Fiscal Policy in EMU*, Basingstoke: Palgrave.

Brunila, A. and C. Martinez-Mongay (2002), 'Fiscal Policy in the Early Years of EMU', in M. Buti and A. Sapir (eds), *EMU and Economic Policy in Europe – Challenges of the Early Years*, Cheltenham, UK and Northampton, MA, USA: Edward Elgar.

Buchanan, J.M. (1958), *Public Principles of Public Debt*, Homewood, IL: Richard D. Irwin.

—— (1965), 'An Economic Theory of Clubs', *Economica*, 2(125): 1–14.

—— (1967), *Public Finance in Democratic Process*, Chapel Hill: University of Carolina Press.

Buchanan, J.M. (1997), 'The Balanced Budget Amendment: Clarifying the Arguments', *Public Choice*, 90: 117–38.

Buchanan, J.M., R.E. Wagner and J. Burton (1978), 'The Consequences of Mr. Keynes', Hobart Paper, 78, Institute of Economic Affairs, London.
Buglione, E. (1998), 'Istituzioni e autonomia finanziaria in Italia', in E. Buglione and V. Patrizii (eds), *Governo e governi*, Milan: Giuffrè Editore.
Buglione, E. and V. Patrizii (eds), *Governo e governi*, Milan: Giuffrè Editore.
Buiter, W.H. (1983), 'Measurement of the Public Sector Deficit and Its Implication for Policy Evaluation and Design', *IMF Staff Papers*, 30(2): 306–49.
—— (1985), 'A Guide to Public Sector Debt and Deficits', *Economic Policy*, 1: 612–35.
—— (1995), 'What Do Generational Accounts Tell Us about the Effects of the Budget on Intergenerational Distribution and Saving Behaviour?', Conference Paper, S. 111, Centre for Economic Performance, Seminar, Cambridge.
—— (1999), 'The Fallacy of the Fiscal Theory of the Price Level', CEPR Discussion Papers, 2205.
—— (2001), 'Notes on a "Code for Fiscal Stability"', *Oxford Economic Papers*, 53(1): 1–19.
—— (2003), 'Ten Commandments for a Fiscal Rule in E(M)U', *Oxford Review of Economic Policy*, 19(1): 84–99.
Buiter, W.H., G. Corsetti and N. Roubini (1993), 'Excessive Deficits: Sense and Nonsense in the Treaty of Maastricht', *Economic Policy*, 16: 57–100.
Buiter, W.H. and C. Grafe (2003), 'Reforming EMU's Fiscal Policy Rules – Some Suggestions for Enhancing Fiscal Sustainability and Macroeconomic Stability in an Enlarged European Union', in M. Buti (ed.), *Monetary and Fiscal Policies in EMU: Interactions and Coordination*, Cambridge: Cambridge University Press.
Burchardt, F.A. (1944), *The Economics of Full Employment*, Oxford: Basil Blackwell.
Burkhead, J. (1954), 'The Balanced Budget', *Quarterly Journal of Economics*, LXVIII: 191–216.
Buti, M. (2000), 'Comment', in Banca d'Italia, *Fiscal Sustainability*, Proceedings of the Banca d'Italia Workshop on Public Finance, Perugia, 20–22 January, Rome.
—— (2002), 'Public Finances in the Early Years of EMU: Adjusting to the New Policy Regime', paper presented at a workshop organized by the Foundation for the Modernisation of Spain, October.
—— (2003a), *Monetary and Fiscal Policies in EMU: Interactions and Coordination*, Cambridge: Cambridge University Press.
Buti, M. (2003b), 'Interactions and Coordination between Monetary and Fiscal Policies in EMU: What Are the Issues?', in M. Buti (2003).

Monetary and Fiscal Policies in EMU: Interactions and Coordination, Cambridge: Cambridge University Press.

Buti, M. and G. Giudice (2002), 'Maastricht Fiscal Rules at Ten: An Assessment', *Journal of Common Market Studies*, 40(5): 823–47.

—— (2004), 'EMU's Fiscal Rules: What Can and Cannot Be Exported', in G. Kopits (ed.), *Rules-based Fiscal Policy in Emerging Markets: Background, Analysis and Prospects*, Basingstoke: Macmillan.

Buti, M. and B. Martinot (2000), 'Open Issues in the Implementation of the Stability and Growth Pact', *National Institute Economic Review*, 174: 92–104.

Buti, M. and L.R. Pench (2004), 'Why do Large Countries Flout the Stability Pact? And What can be Done About it?', *Journal of Common Market Studies*, 42(5): 1025–32.

Buti, M. and A. Sapir (eds) (1998), *Economic Policy in EMU: A Study by the European Commission Services*, Oxford: Oxford University Press.

—— (2002a), 'EMU in the Early Years: Differences and Credibility', in M. Buti and A. Sapir (eds), *EMU and Economic Policy in Europe – Challenges of the Early Years*, Cheltenham, UK and Northampton, MA, USA: Edward Elgar.

—— (eds) (2002b), *EMU and Economic Policy in Europe – Challenges of the Early Years*, Cheltenham, UK and Northampton, MA, USA: Edward Elgar.

Buti, M. and M. Suardi (2000), 'Cyclical Convergence or Differentiation? Insights from the First Year of EMU', *Revue de la Banque*, 2–3: 164–72.

Buti, M. and P. van den Noord (2003), 'What is the Impact of Tax and Welfare Reforms on Fiscal Stabilisers? A Simple Model and an Application to EMU', *European Economy – Economic Papers*, 187.

—— (2004), 'Fiscal Policy in EMU: Rules, Discretion and Political Incentives', *Moneda y Crédito*, 218: 261–304.

Buti, M., S. Eijffinger and D. Franco (2003), 'Revisiting the Stability and Growth Pact: Grand Design or Internal Adjustment?', CEPR Discussion Papers, 3692.

Buti, M., D. Franco and H. Ongena (1997), 'Budgetary Policies during Recessions – Retrospective Application of the Stability and Growth Pact to the Post-war Period', *Recherches Economiques de Louvain*, 63(4): 321–66.

Buti, M., D. Franco and L. Pench (eds) (1999a), *The Welfare State in Europe: Challenges and Reforms*, Cheltenham, UK and Northampton, MA, USA: Edward Elgar.

Buti, M., L.R. Pench and P. Sestito (1999b), 'European Unemployment: Contending Theories and Institutional Complexities. A Summary of the Policy Arguments', in C. Lucifora and W. Salverda (eds), *Policies for Low Wage Employment and Social Exclusion*, Milan: Franco Angeli.

Buti, M., W. Roeger and J. in't Veld (2001a), 'Monetary and Fiscal Policy Interactions Under a Stability Pact', EUI Working Papers, ECO, 8.

Buti, M., P. Sestito and H. Wijkander (eds) (2001b), *Taxation, Welfare and the Crisis of Unemployment in Europe*, Cheltenham, UK and Northampton, MA, USA: Edward Elgar.

Buti, M., J. Von Hagen and C. Martinez-Mongay (eds) (2002a), *The Behaviour of Fiscal Authorities – Stabilisation, Growth and Institutions*, Basingstoke: Palgrave.

Buti, M., C. Martinez-Mongay, K. Sekkat and P. van den Noord (2002b), 'Automatic Stabilisers and Market Flexibility in EMU: Is There a Trade-off?', OECD Economic Department Working Papers, 21.

—— (2003b), 'Automatic Stabilisers in EMU: A Conflict between Efficiency and Stabilisation?', *CES-Ifo Economic Studies*, 49(1): 123–39.

Cabral, A.J. (2001), 'Main Aspects of the Working of the Stability and Growth Pact', in A. Brunila, M. Buti and D. Franco (eds), *The Stability and Growth Pact – The Architecture of Fiscal Policy in EMU*, Basingstoke: Palgrave.

Calmfors, L. and G. Corsetti (2002), 'How to Reform Europe's Fiscal Policy Framework', *World Economics*, 4(1): 109–16.

Calvo, G., R. Dornbusch and M. Obstfeld (eds) (2000), *Money, Capital Mobility and Trade, Essays in Honor of Robert Mundell*, Cambridge, MA: MIT Press.

Canova, F. (1993), 'Detrending and Business Cycle Facts', CEPR Discussion Papers, 782.

Cantor, R. and F. Packer, (1996), 'Determinants and Impact of Sovereign Credit Ratings', *Federal Reserve Bank of New York Economic Policy Review*, 2(2): 37–53.

Canzoneri, M.B. and B.T. Diba (1991), 'Fiscal Deficits, Financial Integration and a Central Bank for Europe', *Journal of Japanese and International Economies*, 5: 381–403.

—— (1996), 'Fiscal Constraints on Central Bank Independence and Price Stability', CEPR Discussion Papers, 1463.

Canzoneri, M.B. and B.T. Diba (1998), 'Is the Price Level Determined by the Needs of Fiscal Solvency?', NBER Working Paper, 6471.

—— (2001), 'The Stability and Growth Pact: A Delicate Balance or an Albatross?', in A. Brunila, M. Buti and D. Franco (eds), *The Stability and Growth Pact – The Architecture of Fiscal Policy in EMU*, Basingstoke: Palgrave.

Carone, G. and A. Salomäki (2001), 'Reforms in Tax-Benefit Systems in Order to Increase Employment Incentives in the EU', European Commission Economic Papers, 160.

Casella, A. (2001), 'Tradable Deficit Permits', in A. Brunila, M. Buti and D. Franco (eds), *The Stability and Growth Pact – The Architecture of Fiscal Policy in EMU*, Basingstoke: Palgrave.

Castellino, O. (1985), 'C'è un secondo debito pubblico (più grande del primo)?', *Moneta e credito*, 149: 21–30.

Catenaro, M. and P. Tirelli (2000), 'Reconsidering the Pros and Cons of Fiscal Policy Coordination in a Monetary Union: Should We Set Public Expenditure Targets?', mimeo, University of Milano-Bicocca.

Centre for European Policy Studies (CEPS) (2002), *Fiscal and Monetary Policy for a Low-Speed Europe*, 4th Annual Report of the CEPS Macroeconomic Policy Group, Brussels, June.

Chalk, N. and R. Hemming (2000), 'Assessing Fiscal Sustainability in Theory and Practice', in Banca d'Italia, *Fiscal Sustainability*, Proceedings of the Banca d'Italia Workshop on Public Finance, Perugia, 20–22 January, Rome.

Chari, V.V. and H. Cole (1993), 'A Contribution to the Theory of "Pork Barrel" Spending', Federal Reserve Bank of Minneapolis Discussion Papers, 156.

Chari, V.V. and P.J. Kehoe (1998), 'On the Need for Fiscal Constraints in a Monetary Union', Federal Reserve Bank of Minnesota Working Papers, 589.

Chase, S. (1943), *Where's the Money Coming From?*, New York: Twentieth Century Fund.

Clarida, R., J. Galí and M. Gertler (1998), 'Monetary Policy Rules and Macroeconomic Stability: Evidence and Some Theory', NBER Working Papers, 6642.

—— (1999), 'The Science of Monetary Policy: A New Keynesian Perspective', *Journal of Economic Literature*, 37(4): 1661–707.

Clarke, P. (1998), 'Keynes, Buchanan and the Balanced Budget Doctrine', in J. Maloney (ed.), *Debt and Deficits*, Cheltenham, UK and Northampton, MA, USA: Edward Elgar.

Coase, R. (1960), 'The Problem of Social Costs', *Journal of Law and Economics*, 3: 1–44.

Coeré, B. and J. Pisani-Ferry (2003), 'A Sustainability Pact for the Eurozone', paper presented at HM Treasury's 'Keynes Seminar', February.

Cohn, G. (1895), *The Science of Finance*, Chicago: University of Chicago Press.

Collignon, S. (2003), *The European Republic*, London: The Federal Trust for Education and Research and Bertelsmann Foundation.

Colm, G. and P. Wagner (1963), 'Some Observations on the Budget Concept', *Review of Economic Studies*, 45: 122–6.

Commissione Tecnica per la Spesa Pubblica (1998), *Razionalizzazione e semplificazione dei documenti e delle procedure contabili*, Documento No. 3, ottobre.

Conseil Superieur des Finances (1998), *Rapport annuel*, June, Brussels.

—— (1999), *Avis relatif a l'execution du nouveau programme de convergence en 1998*, March, Brussels.

Cooper, R.N. (1985), 'Economic Interdependence and Coordination of Economic Policies', in R.W. Jones and P.B. Kenen (eds), *Handbook of International Economics*, Vol. II, Amsterdam: North-Holland.

Cooper, R. and H. Kempf (2000), 'Designing Stabilisation Policy in a Monetary Union', NBER Working Papers, 7607.

Coricelli, F. and V. Ercolani (2002), 'Cyclical and Structural Deficits on the Road to Accession: Fiscal Rules for an Enlarged European Union', CEPR Discussion Papers, 3672.

Cornes, R. and T. Sandler (1995), *The Theory of Externalities, Public Goods, and Club Goods*, Cambridge: Cambridge University Press.

Corsetti, G. and N. Roubini (1992), 'Tax Smoothing Discretion versus Balanced Budget Rules in the Presence of Politically Motivated Fiscal Deficits: The Design of Optimal Fiscal Rules for Europe after 1992', CEPR Discussion Papers, 682.

—— (1996), 'European versus American Perspectives on Balanced-budget Rules', *American Economic Review, Papers and Proceedings*, 86(2): 408–13.

Costello, D. (2001), 'The SGP: How Did We Get There', in A. Brunila, M. Buti and D. Franco (eds), *The Stability and Growth Pact – The Architecture of Fiscal Policy in EMU*, Basingstoke: Palgrave.

Crocker, T.D. (1966), 'The Structuring of Atmospheric Pollution Control Systems', in H. Wolozin (ed.), *The Economics of Air Pollution*, New York: W.W. Norton & Co, 61–86.

Cronin, D. and D. McCoy (2000), 'Fiscal Sustainability when Time is on Your Side', in Banca d'Italia, *Fiscal Sustainability*, Proceedings of the Banca d'Italia Workshop on Public Finance, Perugia, 20–22 January, Rome.

Cullis, J. and P. Jones (1992), *Public Finance and Public Choice Analytical Perspectives*, London: McGraw-Hill.

Daban, T., E. Detragiache, G.M. Milesi Ferretti and S. Dymansky (2003), 'Rules-based Fiscal Policy and the Fiscal Framework in France, Germany, Italy and Spain', IMF Occasional Papers, 225.

Dalamagas, B. (1995), 'Growth, Public Investment and Deficit Financing', *Australian Economic Papers*, 65: 244–62.

Dalenberg, D.R., M.D. Partridge and D.S. Rickman (1998), 'Public Infrastructure: Pork or Jobs Creator?', *Public Finance Review*, 1: 24–52.

Dales, J. (1968), *Pollution, Property and Prices*, Toronto: Toronto University Press.

Dalsgaard, T. and A. de Serres (1999), 'Estimating Prudent Budgetary Margins for 11 EU Countries: A Simulated SVAR Model Approach', OECD Economics Department Working Papers, 216.

Dalton, H., T. Brinley, J.N. Reednam, T.J. Hughes and W.J. Leaning (1934), *Unbalanced Budgets – A Study of the Financial Crisis in Fifteen Countries*, London: George Routledge & Sons.

Daveri, F. and G. Tabellini (2000), 'Unemployment, Growth and Taxation in Industrial Countries', *Economic Policy*, 30: 47–104.

Dawes, M. and M. Hurst (1992), 'The Effects of the Cycle on Public Expenditure', UK Treasury, mimeo.

De Callataу, E. and R. Savage (1998), 'Fedéralisme et choix budgétaires', *Reflects et Perspéctives*, XXXVII (2): 101–21.

De Grauwe, P. (1996), 'The Economics of Convergence Towards Monetary Union in Europe', *Weltwirtschaftliches Archiv*, 132(1): 1–27.

—— (2000), 'The Challenge of Monetary Policy in Euroland', in H. Ooghe *et al.* (eds), *EMU, Dé Uitdaging*, Gent: Vereniging voor Economie/Voseko.

—— (2002), 'Europe's Instability Pact', *Financial Times*, 25 July.

De Haan, J., C.G.M. Sterks and C.A. de Kam (1992), 'Towards Budget Discipline: An Economic Assessment of the Possibilities for Reducing National Deficits in the Run-up to EMU', Economic Papers, European Commission, 99.

De Haan, J., J.E. Sturm and B.J. Sikken (1996), 'Government Capital Expenditure: Explaining the Decline', *Review of World Economics*, 132: 55–74.

De la Fuente, A. (1997), 'Fiscal Policy and Growth in the OECD', CEPR Discussion Papers, 1755.

De la Fuente, A. and R. Doménech (2001), 'The Redistributive Effects of the EU Budget: An Analysis and Proposal for Reform', *Journal of Common Market Studies*, 39(2): 307–30.

De Viti de Marco, A. (1934), *Principi di economia finanziaria*, Torino: Einaudi.

Delbecque, B. and H. Bogaert (1994), 'L'incidence de la dette publique et du viellissement démographique sur la conduite de la politique budgétaire: une étude théorique appliquée au cas de la Belgique', Bureau du Plan – Planning Papers, 70.

Delors, J. (1989), *Report on Economic and Monetary Union in the European Community*, Committee for the Study of Economic and Monetary Union, Brussels.

Demertzis, M., A.J. Hughes Hallett and N. Viegi (1999), 'An Independent Central Bank Faced with Elected Governments', CEPR Discussion Papers, 2219.

Deroose, S. and S. Langedijk (2002), 'Economic Policy Coordination in EMU: Accomplishments and Challenges', in M. Buti and A. Sapir (eds), *EMU and Economic Policy in Europe – Challenges of the Early Years*, Cheltenham, UK and Northampton, MA, USA: Edward Elgar.

Dixit, A. (2000), 'Games of Monetary and Fiscal Interactions in the EMU', Working Paper, Princeton, August.

—— (2001), 'Games of Monetary and Fiscal Interactions in the EMU', *European Economic Review*, 45: 589–613.

Dixit, A. and L. Lambertini (2000a), 'Symbiosis of Monetary and Fiscal Policies in a Monetary Union', Princeton and UCLA Working Papers, March.

—— (2000b), 'Fiscal Discretion Destroys Monetary Commitment', Princeton and UCLA Working Papers, August.

—— (2000c), 'Monetary–Fiscal Policy Interactions and Commitments Versus Deiscretion in a Monetary Union', Working Paper, Princeton/UCLA, August.

—— (2001), 'Monetary–Fiscal Policy Interactions and Commitment Versus Discretion in a Monetary Union', *European Economic Review*, 45: 977–87.

Domar, E.D. (1944), 'The Burden of the Debt and the National Income', *American Economic Review*, 34: 798–827.

Drazen, A. (2000), 'The Political Business Cycle After 25 Years', *NBER Macroeconomic Annual.*

Drees, W. Jr (1955), *On the Level of Government Expenditure in the Netherlands after the War*, Leiden: Stenfert Kroese.

Durrell, A.J.V. (1917), *The Principle and Practice of the System of Control over Parliamentary Grants*, London: Gieves Publishing House.

Dury, K. and A. Pina (2000), 'European Fiscal Policy after EMU: Simulating the Operation of the Stability Pact', EUI Working Papers, ECO, No 2000/3.

Easterly, W. and S. Rebelo (1993), 'Fiscal Policy and Economic Growth: An Empirical Investigation', *Journal of Monetary Economics*, 32(3): 417–58.

Eberts, R. (1990), 'Public Infrastructure and Regional Economic Development', *Economic Review of the Federal Reserve Bank of Cleveland*, 26: 15–28.

EEAG (2003), *Report on the European Economy 2003*, CES Ifo, February.

Eichengreen, B. (1993), 'Fiscal Policy and EMU', in B. Eichengreen and

J. Frieden (eds), *The Political Economy of European Monetary Integration*, Boulder, CO: Westview Press.
—— (1996), 'Saving Europe's Automatic Stabilisers', *National Institute Economic Review*, 159: 92–8.
—— (1997), *European Monetary Unification: Theory, Practice and Analysis*, Cambridge, MA: MIT Press.
Eichengreen B. and J. Frieden (eds) (1993), *The Political Economy of European Monetary Integration*, Boulder, CO: Westview Press.
Eichengreen, B. and R. Portes (1986), 'Debt and Default in the 1930s: Causes and Consequences', *European Economic Review*, 30(3): 599–640.
Eichengreen, B. and J. Von Hagen (1996), 'Fiscal Policy and Monetary Union: Federalism, Fiscal Restrictions, and the No-bailout Rule', in H. Siebert (ed.), *Monetary Policy in an Integrated World Economy – Symposium 1995*, Tubingen: Mohr.
Eichengreen, B. and C. Wyplosz (1998), 'The Stability Pact: More than a Minor Nuisance?', *Economic Policy*, 26: 65–115.
Eijffinger, S.C.W. and J. De Haan (2000), *European Monetary and Fiscal Policy*, Oxford: Oxford University Press.
Einaudi, L. (1948), *Princìpi di scienza della finanza*, Torino: Boringhieri.
Englert, M., N. Fasquelle and S. Weemaes (1994), 'Les perspectives d'évolution à très long terme de la Sécurité sociale (1991–2050)', Bureau du Plan – Planning Papers, 66, Brussels.
Erenburg, S.J. (1993), 'The Real Effects of Public Investment on Private Investment', *Applied Economics*, 25: 831–7.
Eschenbach, F. and L. Schuknecht (2002), 'Asset Prices and Fiscal Balances', European Central Bank Working Papers, 141.
European Central Bank (2001), 'Decisions on the Issue of Euro Banknotes and on the Allocation of Monetary Income', Press Release, December.
European Commission (1975), *Report of the Study Group on Economic and Monetary Union 1980 (Marjolin Report)*, Brussels, March.
—— (1990), 'One Market, One Money', *European Economy*, 40.
—— (1993), 'Stable Money – Sound Finances: Community Public Finance in the Perspective of EMU', *European Economy*, 53.
—— (1996), 'Stability Pact for Ensuring Budgetary Discipline in Stage Three of EMU', *Explanatory Memorandum to the Commission Proposal for a Council Regulation on the Strengthening of the Surveillance and Coordination of Budgetary Positions and on Speeding up and Clarifying the Implementation of the Excessive Deficit Procedure*, Document COM(96) 496, October.
—— (1998), *Euro 1999 – Report on Progress Towards Convergence and*

Recommendation with a View to the Transition to the Third Stage of Economic and Monetary Union, March.
—— (1999a), 'Budgetary Surveillance in EMU: The New Stability and Convergence Programmes', *European Economy*, Supplement A, 2/3.
—— (1999b), 'Italy's Slow Growth in the 1990s: Facts, Explanations and Prospects', *European Economy – Reports and Studies*, 5.
—— (2000a), 'Public Finances in EMU – 2000', *European Economy – Reports and Studies*, 3.
—— (2000b), 'The Contribution of Public Finances to Growth and Employment: Improving Quality and Sustainability', COM(2000) 846, Brussels.
—— (2001a), 'Public Finances in EMU – 2001', *European Economy, Reports and Studies*, 3.
—— (2001b), *Spring Forecasts*, Brussels.
—— (2001c), 'Strengthening Economic Policy Coordination Within the Euro Area', COM (2001), 82, February.
—— (2002a), 'Public Finances in EMU – 2002', *European Economy*, 3.
—— (2002b), 'Strengthening the Coordination of Budgetary Policies', COM (2002) 668, Brussels.
—— (2002c), 'For the European Union – Peace, Freedom, Solidarity', COM (2002) 728, Brussels.
Eurostat (1979), *European System of Accounts*, Luxembourg.
—— (1995), *European System of Accounts*, Luxembourg.
—— (1997), *The Government Sector in the European Union – A Long-term Analysis of Receipts and Expenditures*, Luxembourg.
—— (2000), *ESA Manual on Deficit and Debt*, Luxembourg.
Evans, P. and G. Karras (1994), 'Is Government Capital Productive? Evidence from a Panel of Seven Countries', *Journal of Macroeconomics*, 16: 271–9.
Fatàs, A. and I. Mihov (1999), 'Government Size and Automatic Stabilisers: International and Intranational Evidence', CEPR Discussion Papers, 2259.
—— (2002), 'Fiscal Policy and EMU: Challenges of the Early Years', in M. Buti and A. Sapir (eds), *EMU and Economic Policy in Europe – Challenges of the Early Years*, Cheltenham, UK and Northampton, MA, USA: Edward Elgar.
Fausto, D. (1999), 'Note sulla teoria economica del federalismo fiscale', *Rivista Economica del Mezzogiorno*, 3–4: 457–80.
Favero, C. (2003), 'How Do European Monetary and Fiscal Authorities Behave?', in M. Buti, *Monetary and Fiscal Policies in EMU: Interactions and Coordination*, Cambridge: Cambridge University Press.
Favero, C. and R. Rovelli (2000), 'Modelling and Identifying Central Banks' Preferences', CEPR Discussion Papers, 2178.

Fazio, A. (2001), *Fact-finding with regard to the Effects on the Legal System of the Amendments to Title V of Part II of the Constitution*, Rome: Banca d'Italia.

Ferejohn, J. (1986), 'Incumbent Performance and Electoral Control', *Public Choice*, 50: 50–65.

Fernandez, F. and P. de Cos (2000), 'On the Sustainability of the Spanish Public Budget Performance', in Banca d'Italia, *Fiscal Sustainability*, Proceedings of the Banca d'Italia Workshop on Public Finance, 20–22 January, Rome.

Fischer, J. (2001), 'National and EU Budgetary Rules and Procedures: An Evolving Interaction', in Banca d'Italia, *Fiscal Rules*, Proceedings of the Banca d'Italia Workshop on Public Finance, 1–3 February, Rome.

Fischer, J. and G. Giudice (2001), 'The Stability and Convergence Programmes', in A. Brunila, M. Buti and D. Franco (eds), *The Stability and Growth Pact – The Architecture of Fiscal Policy in EMU*, Basingstoke: Palgrave.

Flandreau, M., J. Le Cacheux and F. Zumer (1998), 'Stability Without a Pact? Lessons from the European Gold Standard, 1880–1914', CEPR Discussion Papers, 1872.

Forte, F. and E. Cerioni (1996), 'Proposte teoriche ed operative per il federalismo fiscale in Italia', in Giardina *et al.* (eds), *Federalismo*, Milan: Franco Angeli.

Fossati, A. and G. Panella (eds) (1999), *Fiscal Federalism in the European Union*, London: Routledge.

Franco, D. (1995), 'Pension Liabilities – Their Use and Misuse in the Assessment of Fiscal Policies', European Commission Economic Papers, 110.

Franco, D. and M.R. Marino (2002), 'The Role of Forecasts in Social Security Policy', *Giornale degli Economisti*, 61(2): 215–65.

Franco, D. and T. Munzi (1996), 'Public Pension Expenditure Prospects in the European Union: A Survey of National Projections', *European Economy – Reports and Studies*, 3.

—— (1999), 'Ageing and Fiscal Policies in the European Union', in M. Buti, D. Franco and L. Pench (eds), *The Welfare State in Europe: Challenges and Reforms*, Cheltenham, UK and Northampton, MA, USA: Edward Elgar.

Fredriksen, N.K. (2000), 'Fiscal Sustainability and Tax Smoothing: A Preliminary Analysis of the Case of Denmark', in Banca d'Italia, *Fiscal Sustainability*, Proceedings of the Banca d'Italia Workshop on Public Finance, 20–22 January, Rome.

Friedman, D. and J. Rust (eds) (1993), *The Double Auction Market: Institutions, Theories and Evidence*, New York: Addison-Wesley.

Galí, J. (1994), 'Government Size and Macroeconomic Stability', *European Economic Review*, 38: 117–32.

Garcia-Milá, T., T.J. Goodspeed and T.J. McGuire (1999), 'Fiscal Decentralization Policies and Sub-national Government Debt in Evolving Federations', Universitat Pompeu Fabra, Department of Economics and Business Economics Working Papers, 549.

Garcia-Milá T., T.J. McGuire and R.H. Porter (1996), 'The Effect of Public Capital in State-level Production Functions Reconsidered', *Review of Economics and Statistics*, 78: 177–80.

Giarda, P. (1996), 'Alcune proprietà di un sistema di federalismo fiscale', in E. Giardina, F. Osculati and M. Rey (eds), *Federalismo*, Milan: Franco Angeli.

Giardina, E., F. Osculati and M. Rey (eds) (1996), *Federalismo*, Milan: Franco Angeli.

Giavazzi, F. and M. Pagano (1990), 'Can Severe Fiscal Contractions be Expansionary? Tales of Two Small European Countries', CEPR Discussion Papers, 417.

—— (1996), 'Non-Keynesian Effects of Fiscal Policy Change: International Evidence and the Swedish Experience', *Swedish Economic Policy Review*, 3(1): 67–105.

Giavazzi, F., T. Jappelli and M. Pagano (1998), 'Searching for Non-Keynesian Effects of Fiscal Policy?', IGIER Working Paper, 136, October.

Giersch, H. (1973), *Fiscal Policy and Demand Management*, Tubingen: J.C.B. Mohr.

Giorno, Cl., P. Richardson, D. Roseveare and P. van den Noord (1995), 'Estimating Potential Output, Output Gaps and Structural Budget Balances', OECD Economics Department Working Papers, 152.

Girard, J., H. Gruber and C. Hurst (1994), 'A Discussion of the Role of Public Investment in Economic Growth', *Cahiers BEI-EIB Papers*, 23: 39–55.

Girard, J., H. Gruber and C. Hurst (1995), 'Increasing Public Investment in Europe: Some Practical Consideration', *European Economic Review*, 39: 731–8.

Girard, J. and C. Hurst (1994), 'Investment and Growth: Quality versus Quantity', *Cahiers BEI-EIB Papers*, 23: 13–19.

Goode, R. and E.A. Birnbaum (1955), *Government Capital Budgets*, Washington, DC: International Monetary Fund.

Goodhart, C.A.E. (1984), *Monetary Theory and Practice: The UK Experience*, Basingstoke: Macmillan.

Goodhart, C.A.E. and S. Smith (1993), 'Stabilisation', *European Economy – Reports and Studies*, 5.

Gordo, L. and P. Hernandez de Cos (2001), 'The Financing Arrangements for the Regional (Autonomous) Governments for the Period 1997–2001', Banco de Espana – Servicio de Estudios, Documento de Trabajo, 30.

Goulard, S. and M. Nava (2002), 'Vers un financement plus démocratique de l'Union européenne', *Revue Française des Finances Publiques*, 80: 31.

Gramlich, E.M. (1994), 'Infrastructure Investment: A Review Essay', *Journal of Economic Literature*, 32: 1147–75.

Grilli, V., D. Masciandaro and G. Tabellini (1991), 'Political and Monetary Institutions and Public Financial Policies in the Industrial Countries', *Economic Policy*, 13: 341–92.

Griziotti, G. (1917), 'La diversa pressione tributaria del prestito e dell'imposta', *Giornale degli Economisti*, 193–261.

Gros, D. (2003), 'A Stability Pact for Public Debt?', CEPS Policy Brief, 30.

Gros, D. and C. Hefeker (2000), 'One Size Must Fit All National Divergences in a Monetary Union', CESifo Working Papers, 326.

Hagemann, R. (1999), 'The Structural Budget Balance: The IMF's Methodology', in Banca d'Italia, *Indicators of Structural Budget Balances*, Proceedings of the Banca d'Italia Workshop on Public Finances, 26–28 November, 1998, Rome.

Hagemann, R.P. and C. John (1995), 'The Fiscal Stance in Sweden: A Generational Accounting Perspective', IMF Working Papers, 105.

Hagemann, R.P. and G. Nicoletti (1989), 'Ageing Populations: Economic Effects and Implications for Public Finance', OECD Department of Economics and Statistics Working Papers, 61.

Hahm, S.D., M.S. Kamletand and D.C. Mowery (1995), 'Influence on Deficit Spending in Industrialized Countries', *Journal of Public Policy*, 15.

Hairault, J.O. and F. Portier (1993), 'Money, New-Keynesian Macroeconomics and the Business Cycle', *European Economic Review*, 37: 1533–68.

Hairault, J.O., F. Langot and F. Portier (2001), 'Efficiency and Stabilization: Reducing Harberger Triangles and Okun Gaps', *Economics Letters*, 70: 209–14.

Hallenberg, M., R. Strauch and J. Von Hagen (2001), *The Use and Effectiveness of Budgetary Rules and Norms in EU Member States – Report Prepared for the Dutch Ministry of Finance*, The Hague: Dutch Ministry of Finance.

Hallerberg, M. and R. Strauch (2002), 'On the Cyclicality of Public Finances in Europe', *Empirica*, 29: 183–207.

Hallet, M. (2002), 'Convergencia de renta y políticas regionales en Europa: Resultados y retos para el futuro', *Papeles de Economía Española*, 93: 38–50.

Hamada, K. (1974), 'Alternative Exchange Rate Systems and the Interdependence of Monetary Policies', in R.Z. Aliber (ed.), *National Monetary Policies and the International Financial System*, Chicago: University of Chicago Press.

—— (1976), 'A Strategic Analysis of Monetary Interdependence', *Journal of Political Economy*, 84(4): 677–701.

Hamilton, J.D. and M.A. Flavin (1986), 'On the Limitations of Government Borrowing: A Framework for Empirical Testing', *American Economic Review*, 76(4): 808–19.

Hansen, A.H. (1941), *Fiscal Policy and the Business Cycle*, New York: Norton & Co.

Haug, A.A. (1990), 'Cointegration and Government Borrowing Constraints: Evidence for the United States', *Journal of Business and Economic Statistics*, 9: 97–101.

Hautala, U. and J. Tuukkanen (2000), 'Towards a Sustainable and Job-oriented Pension System in Finland', in Banca d'Italia, *Fiscal Sustainability*, Proceedings of the Banca d'Italia Workshop on Public Finance, 20–22 January, Rome.

Haveman, R. (1994), 'Should Generational Accounts Replace Public Budgets and Deficits?', *Journal of Economic Perspectives*, 8(1): 95–111.

Heeringa, W. and Y. Lindh (2001), 'Dutch versus Swedish Budgetary Rules: A Comparison', in Banca d'Italia, *Fiscal Rules*, Proceedings of the Banca d'Italia Workshop on Public Finance, 1–3 February, Rome.

Heller, P.S., R. Hemming and P. Kohnert (1986), 'Ageing and Social Expenditures in the Major Industrialized Countries, 1980–2025', IMF Occasional Papers, 47.

Hemming, R. and M. Kell (2001), 'Promoting Fiscal Responsibility: Transparency, Rules and Independent Fiscal Authorities', in Banca d'Italia, *Fiscal Rules*, Proceedings of the Banca d'Italia Workshop on Public Finance, 1–3 February, Rome.

Hernandez-Trillo, F. (1995), 'A Model-based Estimation of the Probability of Default in Sovereign Credit Markets', *Journal of Development Economics*, 46(1): 163–79.

Hicks, K. (1953), 'The Budget as an Instrument of Policy, 1837–1953', *The Three Banks Review*, 16–34.

Hills, J. (1984), 'What is the Public Sector Worth?', *Fiscal Studies*, 5(1): 18–31.

HM Treasury (1997), *A Code for Fiscal Stability*, London.

—— (1998), *The Public Sector Balance Sheet*, London.

—— (1999), *Fiscal Policy: Public Finances and the Cycle*, London.

Hoeller, P., C. Giorno and C. de la Maisonneuve (2002), 'Overheating in Small Euro Area Economies: Should Fiscal Policy React?', OECD Economics Department Working Papers, 323.

Hoffman, J. (1993), *The Remaking of Europe – Employment and the Hidden Debt*, Boston, MA: CS First Boston.
Holtz-Eakin, D. (1994), 'Public Sector Capital and the Productivity Puzzle', *Review of Economics and Statistics*, 76: 12–21.
Holzmann, R. (1999), 'On Economic Benefits and Fiscal Requirements of Moving from Unfunded to Funded Pensions', in M. Buti, D. Franco and L. Pench (eds), *The Welfare State in Europe – Challenges and Reforms*, Cheltenham, UK and Northampton, MA, USA: Edward Elgar.
Hughes Hallett, A.J., M.M. Hutchison and S.E. Hougaard Jensen (eds) (1999), *Fiscal Aspects of European Monetary Integration*, Cambridge: Cambridge, University Press.
Hughes Hallett, A.J. and P. McAdam (1999), 'Implications of the Stability and Growth Pact: Why the "Growth" Element Is Important', in A.J. Hughes Hallett, M.M. Hutchison and S.E. Hougaard Jensen (eds), *Fiscal Aspects of European Monetary Integration*, Cambridge: Cambridge University Press.
Hughes Hallett, A.J. and N. Viegi (2000), Central Bank Independence, Political Uncertainty and the Assignment of Instruments to Targets', mimeo, November.
—— (2002), 'Central Bank Independence, Political Uncertainty and the Assignment of Instruments to Targets', in M. Buti, J. Von Hagen and C. Martinez-Mongay (eds), *The Behaviour of Fiscal Authorities – Stabilisation, Growth and Institutions*, Basingstoke: Palgrave.
Hurst, C. (1994), 'Infrastructure and Growth: A Literature Review', *Cahiers BEI-EIB Papers*, 23, 57–66.
IMF (1993), 'Structural Budget Indicators for the Major Industrial Countries', *World Economic Outlook*, October.
—— (1996), *World Economic Outlook*, May, Washington.
—— (1998a), *World Economic Outlook*, April, Washington.
—— (1998b), *World Economic Outlook*, October, Washington.
—— (2000), *Government Finance Statistics Yearbook*, Washington.
—— (2001), *Fiscal Policy and Macroeconomic Stability*, May, Washington.
Inman, R.P. (1996), 'Do Balanced Budget Rules Work? U.S. Experience and Possible Lessons for the EMU', NBER Working Papers, 5838.
Inman, R.P. and H. Bohn (1996), 'Balanced Budget Rules and Public Deficits: Evidence from the U.S. States', NBER Working Papers, 5533.
Issing, O. (2000), 'How to Achieve a Durable Macro-economic Policy Mix Favourable to Growth and Employment?', speech at the Conference on 'Growth and Employment in Europe', European Commission, Brussels, May.
—— (2002), 'On Macroeconomic Policy Coordination in EMU', *Journal of Common Market Studies*, 40(2): 345–58.

Issing, O., I. Angeloni, V. Gaspar and O. Tristani (2001), *Monetary Policy in the Euro Area: Strategy and Decision-Making at the European Central Bank*, Cambridge: Cambridge University Press.

Italianer, A. (1999), 'The Euro and International Economic Policy Coordination', *Empirica*, 26: 201–16.

Italianer, A. and M. Vanheukelen (1993), 'Proposals for Community Stabilisation Mechanisms: Some Historical Applications', *European Economy – Reports and Studies*, 5.

Jacquet, P. and J. Pisani-Ferry (2001), 'Economic Policy Coordination in the Euro Zone. What has been Achieved? What Should Be Done?', Centre for European Reform, January.

Jensen, H. (1996), 'The Advantage of International Fiscal Cooperation Under Alternative Monetary Regimes', *European Journal of Political Economy*, 12: 485–504.

—— (2001), 'New Zealand's Fiscal Policy Framework: Experience and Evolution', in Banca d'Italia, *Fiscal Rules*, Proceedings of the Banca d'Italia Workshop on Public Finance, 1–3 February, Rome.

Johansen, L. (1965), *Public Economics*, Amsterdam: North-Holland.

Jones, R.W. and P.B. Kenen (eds) (1985), *Handbook of International Economics*, Vol. II, Amsterdam: North-Holland.

Keereman, F. (1999), 'The Track Record of the Commission Forecasts', *European Economy – Economic Papers*, 137.

Kelejian, H.H. and D.P. Robinson (1997), 'Infrastructure Productivity Estimation and its Underlying Econometric Specification: A Sensitivity Analysis', *Papers in Regional Science*, 72: 297–312.

Kell, M. (2001), 'An Assessment of Fiscal Rules in the United Kingdom', IMF Working Papers, 91.

Keynes, J.M. (1971–89), *The Collected Writings of John Maynard Keynes*, D. Moggridge and A. Robinson (eds), Basingstoke: Macmillan.

Kharas, H. (1984), 'The Long-run Creditworthiness of Developing Countries: Theory and Practice', *Quarterly Journal of Economics*, 3: 415–39.

Kilpatrick, A. (2001), 'Transparent Frameworks, Fiscal Rules and Policy-making Under Uncertainty', in Banca d'Italia, *Fiscal Rules*, Proceedings of the Banca d'Italia Workshop on Public Finance, 1–3 February, Rome.

King, D. (1984), *Fiscal Tiers: The Economics of Multi-level Government*, London: Allen & Unwin.

King, M. (1995), 'Comment on J.B. Taylor', Symposium Proceedings, *Budget Deficits and Debt: Issues and Options*, Kansas: FRB of Kansas City.

Kinnunen, H. and P. Kuoppamaki (1998), 'Sustainability of Public Finances in Finland and in the Four Largest Euro-area Economies', Bank of Finland Discussion Papers, 25.

Kitterer, W. (1994), 'Tax- versus Debt-financing of Public Investment: A Dynamic Simulation Analysis', *Kredit und Kapital*, 2: 163–87.

Kneller, R., M.F. Bleaney and N. Gemmell (1999), 'Fiscal Policy and Growth: Evidence from OECD Countries', *Journal of Public Economics*, 74: 171–90.

Knight, B. and A. Levinson (1999), 'Rainy Day Funds and State Government Savings', *National Tax Journal*, LII, 3: 459–72.

Kopits, G. (2001), 'Fiscal Rules: Useful Policy Framework or Unnecessary Ornament?', in Banca d'Italia, *Fiscal Rules*, Proceedings of the Banca d'Italia Workshop on Public Finance, 1–3 February, Rome.

—— (ed.) (2004), *Rules-based Fiscal Policy in Emerging Markets: Background, Analysis and Prospects*, Basingstoke: Macmillan.

Kopits, G. and S. Symansky (1998), 'Fiscal Policy Rules', IMF Occasional Papers, 162.

Korkman, S. (2001), 'Fiscal Policy Coordination in EMU: Should it Go Beyond the SGP?', in A. Brunila, M. Buti and D. Franco (eds), *The Stability and Growth Pact – The Architecture of Fiscal Policy in EMU*, Basingstoke: Palgrave.

Kotlikoff, L.J. (1984), 'Economic Impact of Deficit Financing', *IMF Staff Papers*, 33: 549–81.

Kuné, J.B., W.F.M. Petit and A.J.H. Pinxt (1993), 'The Hidden Liabilities of Basic Pension Systems in the European Community', CEPS Working Document, 80.

Lambrecht, M., N. Fasquelle and S. Weemaes (1994), 'L'évolution démographique de long-terme et son incidence isolée sur quelques grandeurs socio-économiques (1992–2050)', Bureau du Plan – Planning Papers, 68.

Lane, T. (1993), 'Market Discipline', *IMF Staff Papers*, 40: 53–88.

Larch, M. and M. Salto (2003), 'Fiscal Rules, Inertia and Discretionary Fiscal Policy', *European Economy – Economic Papers*, 194.

Layard, R. (1997), 'Preventing Long-term Unemployment', in D.J. Snower and G. de la Dehesa (eds), *Unemployment Policy. Government Options for the Labour Market*, Cambridge: Cambridge University Press.

Leeftink, B. (2000), 'Rules versus Flexibility: Does the Stability Pact Limit Budgetary Flexibility?', in Banca d'Italia, *Fiscal Sustainability*, Proceedings of the Banca d'Italia Workshop on Public Finance, 20–22 January, Rome.

Leeper, E.M. (1991), 'Equilibrium under Active and Passive Monetary and Fiscal Policies', *Journal of Monetary Economics*, 27(1): 129–47.

Leibfritz, W. (2000), 'Generational Accounting Around the World', in Banca d'Italia, *Fiscal Sustainability*, Proceedings of the Banca d'Italia Workshop on Public Finance, 20–22 January, Rome.

Leibfritz W., D. Roseweare and P. van den Noord (1994), 'Fiscal Policy, Government Debt and Economic Performance', OECD Economic Department Working Papers, 144.

Leibfritz, W., D. Roseweare, D. Fore and E. Wurzel (1995), 'Ageing Populations, Pension Systems and Government Budgets: How Do They Affect Saving?', OECD Economic Department Working Papers, 156.

Leigh, C. and S. Wren-Lewis (2000), 'Interaction between Monetary and Fiscal Policy Rules', *Economic Journal*, 110(462): 94–108.

Leitmo, K. (2000), 'Strategic Interactions between the Fiscal and Monetary Authorities under Inflation Targeting', mimeo.

Lerner, A.P. (1943), 'Functional Finance and the Federal Debt', *Social Research*, 10: 38–51.

Levine, J.H. (1983), 'A Model of Stabilization Policy in a Jointly Floating Currency Area', in J.S. Bhandari and B.H. Putnam (eds), *Economic Interdependence and Flexible Exchange Rates*, Cambridge, MA: MIT Press.

Levine, P. and A. Brochiner (1994), 'Fiscal Policy Coordination and EMU', *Journal of Economic Dynamics and Control*, 18: 699–729.

Lindbeck, A. (1968), 'Theories and Problems in Swedish Economic Policy in the Post-war Period', *American Economic Review*, June Supplement: 1–87.

Lindh, Y. and H. Ohlsson (2000), 'Long-term Developments of Swedish Public Finances – Can "Straight Jackets" Reverse the Trends?', in Banca d'Italia, *Fiscal Sustainability*, Proceedings of the Banca d'Italia Workshop on Public Finance, 20–22 January, Rome.

—— (2002), 'Fiscal Policy in a Currency Union – Instruments and Implementation', in Banca d'Italia, *The Impact of Fiscal Policy*, Proceedings of the Banca d'Italia Workshop on Public Finance, 21–23 March, Rome.

Lucas, R.E. (1987), *Models of Business Cycles*, Oxford: Basil Blackwell.

Lucas, R.E. and T.J. Sargent (eds) (1981), *Rational Expectations and Econometric Practice*, London: George Allen and Unwin.

Lucifora, C. and W. Salverda (eds) (1999), *Policies for Low Wage Employment and Social Exclusion*, LoWER, Milan: Franco Angeli.

Lundberg, E.F. (1996), *The Development of Swedish and Keynesian Macroeconomic Theory and its Impact on Economic Policy*, Raffaele Mattioli Foundation, Cambridge: Cambridge University Press.

McGranahan, L. (1999), 'State Budgets and the Business Cycle: Implications for the Federal Balanced Budget Amendment Debate', Federal Reserve Bank of Chicago, *Economic Perspectives*, 3: 3–17.

Mackenzie, G.A. (1989), 'Are All Summary Indicators of the Stance of Fiscal Policy Misleading?', *IMF Staff Papers*, 36(4): 743–70.

McKinnon, R.I. (1994), 'A Common Monetary Standard or a Common

Currency for Europe? Fiscal Lessons from the United States', *Scottish Journal of Political Economy*, 41, November: 337–57.

—— (1997), 'EMU as a Device for Collective Fiscal Retrenchment', *American Economic Review, Papers and Proceedings*, 87: 211–33.

McMorrow, K. and W. Roeger (1999), 'The Economic Consequences of Ageing Populations', European Commission, Economic Papers, 138.

Mairate, A. and R. Hall (2000), 'Structural Policies', in L. Tsoukalis (ed.), *Competitiveness and Cohesion*, Oxford: Oxford University Press.

Majocchi, A. (2002), 'Beyond the Single Currency: Does Europe Need a Single Government of the Economy?', paper presented at University of Trento, October.

Majocchi, A. and M. Rey (1993), 'A Special Financial Support Scheme in Economic and Monetary Union: Need and Nature', in *European Economy – Reports and Studies*, 5.

Malizia, R. (2000), 'Il nuovo conto delle amministrazioni pubbliche', mimeo, Istat, Rome.

Maloney, J. (1998), *Debt and Deficits*, Cheltenham, UK and Lyme, USA: Edward Elgar.

Maroto Illera, R. and C. Mulas-Granandos (2002), 'Duration of Fiscal Budgetary Consolidations in the European Union', European Economy Group Working Papers, 18.

Martinez-Mongay, C. (2000), 'Effective Tax Rates Based on AMECO Data. Updating of March 2000', European Commission, Economic Papers, 146.

—— (2002), 'Fiscal Policy and the Size of Governments', in M. Buti, J. Von Hagen and C. Martinez-Mongay (eds), *The Behaviour of Fiscal Authorities – Stabilisation, Growth and Institutions*, Basingstoke: Palgrave.

Martinot, B. (2000), 'Pacte de stabilité et efficacité de la politique budgétaire', Document de travail, Ministère de l'économie, des finances et de l'industrie.

Masson, P. (1996), 'Fiscal Dimensions of EMU', *Economic Journal*, 106: 996–1004.

Mélitz J. (1997a), 'The Evidence about the Costs and Benefits of EMU', report to the Swedish Government Commission on Monetary Union, *Swedish Economic Policy Review*, 4(2): 359–410.

Mélitz J. (1997b), 'Some Cross-country Evidence about Debt, Deficits, and the Behaviour of Monetary and Fiscal Authorities', CEPR Discussion Papers, 1653.

—— (2000), 'Some Cross-country Evidence about Fiscal Policy Behaviour and Consequences for EMU', *European Economy Reports and Studies*, 2: 3–21.

—— (2002), 'Some Cross-country Evidence about Fiscal Policy Behaviour and Consequences for EMU', in M. Buti, J. Von Hagen and C. Martinez-Mongay (eds), *The Behaviour of Fiscal Authorities – Stabilisation, Growth and Institutions*, Basingstoke: Palgrave.

Mera, K. (1973), 'Production Functions and Social Overhead Capital: An Analysis of the Japanese Case', *Regional and Urban Economics*, 3: 297–312.

Middleton, R. (1985), *Towards the Managed Economy: Keynes, the Treasury and the Fiscal Policy Debate of the 1930*, London: Methuen.

Mieszkowski, P. and W.H. Oakland (eds), *Fiscal Federalism and Grants in Aid*, Coupe Papers in Public Economics, Washington, DC: Urban Institute.

Milesi-Ferretti, G.M., R. Perotti and M. Rostagno (2002), 'Electoral Systems and the Composition of Public Spending', *Quarterly Journal of Economics*, 117: 609–57.

Mills, P. and A. Quinet (2001), 'The Case for Spending Rules', in Banca d'Italia, *Fiscal Rules*, Proceedings of the Banca d'Italia Workshop on Public Finance, 1–3 February, Rome.

Ministry of Finance of Denmark – Finansministeriet (1995), 'Policy Implications of the Ageing Population in Denmark', Working Papers, 4.

Ministry of Social Affairs and Health (1994), 'Sociaalimenotoimikunnan Mietintö' (Social Expenditure Committee), Helsinki.

Missale, A. (2000), 'Optimal Debt Management with a Stability and Growth Pact', *Public Finance and Management*, 1(1): 1–3.

Modigliani F., J.P. Fitoussi, B. Moro, D. Snower, R. Solow, A. Steinherr and P. Sylos Labini (1998), 'Manifesto contro la disoccupazione nell'Unione Europea', *Moneta e Credito*, LI (203): 375–412.

Modigliani, F. and F. Padoa Schioppa Kostoris (1998), *Sostenibilità e solvibilità del debito pubblico in Italia*, Bologna: Il Mulino.

Moesen, W. (2002), 'Enhanced Community Role in Resource Allocation', presentation at the Commission Workshop on The Future of the EU Budget, October.

Momigliano, S. and A. Staderini (1999), 'A New Method of Assessing the Structural Budget Balance: Results for the Years 1995–2000', in Banca d'Italia, *Indicators of Structural Budget Balances*, Proceedings of the Banca d'Italia Workshop on Public Finance, 26–28 November 1998, Rome.

Monasterio Escudero, C., I. Sánchez Alvarez and F. Blanco Angel (1999), *Controles Internos del Edeudamiento versus Racionamiento del Credito. Estudio Especial del Caso de las Comunidades Autonomas Españolas*, Madrid: Fondación BBV.

Montagnon, A. (2002), 'Flexibility for the Next Financial Perspectives', mimeo, Brussels, November.

Munnel, A.H. (1992), 'Infrastructure Investment and Economic Growth', *Journal of Economic Perspectives*, 6: 189–98.

Musgrave, R.A. (1939), 'The Nature of Budgetary Balance and the Case for a Capital Budget', *American Economic Review*, 29: 260–71.

—— (1959), *The Theory of Public Finance: A Study in Public Economy*, New York: McGraw-Hill.

Musgrave, R.A. and P.B. Musgrave (1984), *Public Finance in Theory and Practice*, New York: McGraw-Hill.

Naess-Schmidt, H.S. (2002), 'Progression in Taxation of Earned Income, Wage Formation and Labour Market Performance', Danish Ministry of Finance Working Papers, Copenhagen.

Nava, M. (2000), *La finanza europea*, Roma: Carocci.

Nitti, F.S. (1903), *Principi di Scienza delle Finanze*, Napoli: Luigi Pierro.

Nordhaus, W. (1994), 'Policy Games: Coordination and Independence in Monetary and Fiscal Policies', Brooking Papers on Economic Activity, 25(2): 139–216.

Norregaard, J. (1997), 'Tax Assignment', in T. Ter-Minassian (ed.), *Fiscal Federalism in Theory and Practice*, Washington, DC: IMF.

Oates, W. (1972), *Fiscal Federalism*, New York: Harcourt Brace Jovanovich.

—— (1979), 'Lump-sum Intergovernmental Grants Have Price Effects', in P. Mieszkowski and W.H. Oakland (eds), *Fiscal Federalism and Grants in Aid*, Coupe Papers in Public Economics, Washington, DC: Urban Institute.

OECD (1977), *Economic Surveys – Austria*, Paris.

—— (1978), *Economic Surveys – Austria*, Paris.

—— (1985), *Social Expenditure 1960–1990 – Problems of Growth and Control*, Paris.

—— (1988a), *Ageing Populations – The Social Policy Implications*, Paris.

—— (1988b), *Reforming Public Pensions*, Paris.

—— (1993a), 'Automatic Stabilisers: Their Extent and Role', *OECD Economic Outlook*: 37–44, June.

—— (1993b), *Economic Surveys – Spain*, Paris.

OECD (1993c), 'OECD Health Systems – Facts and Trends 1960–1991 – Vol. 1', *Health Policy Studies*, 3.

—— (1996), 'Ageing in OECD Countries – A Critical Policy Challenge', *Social Policy Studies*, 20.

OECD (1997), *OECD Economic Outlook*, December, Paris.

—— (1998), *Fiscal Policy Issues in the Euro Area*, Paris.

—— (1999a), *Economic Outlook*, 66, Paris.

—— (1999b), *Economic Surveys – Austria*, Paris.

—— (1999c), *EMU – Facts, Challenges and Policies*, Paris.

—— (1999d), *Implementing the OECD's Jobs Strategy: Assessing Performance and Policy*, Paris.

—— (2000a), 'Links between Policy and Growth: Cross-country Evidence', *Economic Outlook*, 68.
—— (2000b), *Revenue Statistics*, Paris.
—— (2002), 'Tax and the Economy: A Comparative Assessment of OECD Countries', OECD *Tax Policy Studies*, 6.
Olson, M. (1965), *The Logic of Collective Action*, Cambridge, MA: Harvard University Press.
Onrubia-Fernandez, J. and J. Sanchez-Revenga (2002), 'Estabilidad Presupuestaria en España: un análisis económico-institucional del marco legal', paper prepared for the Conference on 'Rules-based Macroeconomic Policies in Emerging Market Economies', IMF-World Bank, Oaxaca, Mexico, February.
Ooghe, H., F. Heylen and R. Vander Vennet (eds) (2000), *EMU, Dé Uitdaging*, Gent: Vereniging voor Economie/Voseko.
Oxley, H. and J.P. Martin (1991), 'Controlling Government Spending and Deficits: Trends in the 80s and Prospects for the 90s', *OECD Economic Studies*, 17: 145–89.
Padoa-Schioppa, T. (1987), *Efficiency, Stability and Equity – A Strategy for the Evolution of the Economic System of the European Community*, Oxford: Oxford University Press.
Pasinetti, L. (1997), 'European Union at the end of 1997: Who is Within the Public Finance "Sustainability" Zone?', Lezione Lincea 'Luigi Einaudi'.
Patrizi, V. (1998), 'Rappresentanza ed efficienza in un sistema di governo a più livelli', in E. Buglione and V. Patrizii (eds), *Governo e governi*, Milan: Giuffré Editore.
Pauly, M. (1973), 'Income Redistribution as a Local Public Good', *Journal of Public Economics*, 1 (February): 35–58.
Pearson, M., S. Smith and S. White (1989), 'Demographic Influences on Public Spending', *Fiscal Studies*, 2: 48–65.
Pench, L.R. (2003), 'Comment on Buiter and Grafe', in M. Buti, *Monetary and Fiscal Policies in EMU: Interactions and Coordination*, Cambridge: Cambridge University Press.
Perotti, R. (1996), 'Fiscal Consolidation in Europe: Composition Matters', *American Economic Review, Papers and Proceedings*, 86: 105–10.
Perotti, R. (1999), 'Fiscal Policy in Good Times and Bad', *Quarterly Journal of Economics*, 114: 1399–436.
—— (2000), 'What Do We Know About the Effects of Fiscal Policy?', XII Riunione scientifica, 'Politica fiscale, flessibilità dei mercati e crescita', Pavia, Collegio Ghislieri, October.
Perotti, R., R. Strauch and J. Von Hagen (1997), 'Sustainability of Public Finances', CEPR Discussion Papers, 1781.

Persson, T. and G. Tabellini (2002a), 'Do Electoral Cycles Differ across Political Systems?', IGIER Working Papers, Bocconi University, 232.
—— (2002b), 'Political Institutions and Policy Outcomes: What Are the Stylised Facts?', CESifo Working Papers, 459.
Persson, T., G. Roland and G. Tabellini (1996), 'The Theory of Fiscal Federalism: What Does It Mean for Europe?', IGIER Working Papers, Bocconi University, 101.
Pica, F. (1999), 'Fatti ed opinioni in materia di federalismo fiscale italiano', mimeo.
Pigou, A.C. (1927), *Public Finance*, London: Macmillan.
—— (1929), *A Study in Public Finance*, 2nd revised edn, London: Macmillan.
Pisani-Ferry, J. (1996), 'Fiscal Policy under EMU', CEPII Newsletter, No. 6, 2nd semester, Paris, pp. 1–2.
—— (2002), 'Fiscal Discipline and Policy Coordination in the Eurozone: Assessment and Proposals', Group of Economic Advisers of the European Commission.
Pissarides, C.A. (1998), 'The Impact of Employment Tax Cuts on Unemployment and Wages; The Role of Unemployment Benefits and Tax Structure', *European Economic Review*, 42(1): 155–83.
Pola G., G. France and R. Levaggi (eds) (1996), *Developments in Local Government Finance*, Cheltenham, UK and Brookfield, USA: Edward Elgar.
Pontolillo, V. (1998), 'Aspetti economico-istituzionali del project financing. Problematiche ed esperienze in Italia', *Documenti*, 589, Banca d'Italia.
Poterba, J.M. (1995), 'Capital Budgets, Borrowing Rules and State Capital Spending', *Journal of Public Economics*, 56: 165–87.
Premchand, A. (1983), *Government Budgeting and Expenditure Controls: Theory and Practice*, Washington, DC: IMF.
Puviani, A. (1903), *Teoria dell'illusione fiscale*, reprinted by F. Volpi (1973), Milan: ISEDI.
Raffelhüschen, B. (1999), 'Generational Accounting in Europe', *American Economic Review*, 89(2): 167–70.
Ratner, J.B. (1983), 'Government Capital and the Production Function for U.S. Private Output', *Economics Letters*, 13: 213–17.
Razin, A. and E. Sadka (2002), 'The Stability and Growth Pact as an Impediment to Privatizing Social Security', CEPR Discussion Papers, 3621.
Reynolds, A. (2001), 'The Fiscal–Monetary Policy Mix', *Cato Journal*, 21(2): 263–75.
Robinson, M. (1998), 'Measuring Compliance with the Golden Rule', *Fiscal Studies*, 19(4): 447–62.

—— (1999a), 'Intergenerational Equity, Deficits and Generational Accounting', Queensland University of Technology, Brisbane, mimeo.

—— (1999b), 'The Role and Nature of Public Sector Balance Sheets', *Queensland University of Technology Discussion Papers in Economics, Finance and International Competitiveness*, 49.

—— (2001) 'National and State Fiscal Rules in Australia: An Outline and Critical Analysis', in Banca d'Italia, *Fiscal Rules*, Proceedings of the Banca d'Italia Workshop on Public Finance, 1–3 February, Rome.

Rodrick, D. (1998), 'Why Do More Open Economies Have Bigger Governments?', *Journal of Political Economy*, 106: 997–1032.

Roeger, W. (1999), 'Output, Prices and Interest Rates over the Business Cycle', *Zeitschrift fur Wirtschafts und Sozialwissenschaften*, 19: 57–98.

Roeger, W. and J. in't Veld (1997), 'QUEST II: A Multi Country Business Cycle and Growth Model', European Economy, Economic Papers, 123.

Roeger, W., J. in't Veld and D.I.A. Woehrmann (2001), 'Some Equity and Efficiency Considerations of International Tax Competition', *International Tax and Public Finance*, 9(1): 7–31.

Rogoff, K. (1985), 'Can International Monetary Policy Cooperation Be Counterproductive?', *Journal of International Economics*, 18: 199–217.

Rogoff, K. and A. Sibert (1988), 'Elections and Macroeconomic Policy Cycles', *Review of Economic Studies*, 55: 1–16.

Rose, A. (1999), 'One Money, One Market', *Economic Policy*, 30: 7–46.

Roseweare, D., W. Leibfritz, D. Fore and E. Wurzel (1996), 'Ageing Populations, Pension Systems and Government Budgets: Simulations for 20 OECD Countries', OECD Economics Department Working Papers, 168.

Ross, K. and A. Ubide (2002), 'Mind the Gap: What is the Best Measure of Slack in the Euro Area', IMF Working Papers, 203.

Rostagno, M. (1995), 'Il debito previdenziale italiano – Il Fondo Pensioni Lavoratori Dipendenti', mimeo.

Rotemberg, J.J. (1982), 'Sticky Prices in the United States', *Journal of Political Economy*, 90: 1187–211.

—— (1996), 'Prices, Output and Hours: An Empirical Analysis Based on a Sticky Price Model', *Journal of Monetary Economics*, 37: 505–33.

Roubini, N. and J.D. Sachs (1989a), 'Government Spending and Budget Deficits in the Industrial Countries', *Economic Policy*, 8: 99–132.

—— (1989b), 'Political and Economic Determinants of Budget Deficits in the Industrial Democracies', *European Economic Review*, 33: 903–38.

Sabine, B.E.V. (1970), *British Budgets in Peace and War. 1932–45*, London: Allen and Unwin.

Sapir, A. and K. Sekkat (1999), 'Optimum Electoral Areas: Should Europe Adopt a Single Election Day?', *European Economic Review*, 43: 1595–619.

—— (2002), 'Political Cycles, Fiscal Deficits, and Output Spillovers in Europe', *Public Choice*, 111: 195–202.

Sapir, A. *et al.* (2003), *An Agenda for a Growing Europe: Making the EU System Deliver*, Oxford: Oxford University Press.

Sargent, T. and N. Wallace (1981), 'Some Unpleasant Monetarist Arithmetic', *Quarterly Review of Minneapolis Federal Reserve Bank*, 5: 1–17.

Sartor, N. (ed.) (1998), *Il risanamento mancato – La politica di bilancio italiana: 1986–90*, Rome: Carocci.

Say, J.B. (1853), *A Treatise on Political Economy*, trans. from French 4th edn, Philadelphia: Lippincott, Grambo & Co.

Schumacher, E.F. (1944), 'Public Finance – Its Relation to Full Employment', in F.A. Burchardt (ed.), *The Economics of Full Employment*, Oxford: Basil Blackwell.

Scitovsky, T. (1961), 'The Burden of the Debt: Comment', *American Economic Review*, 137–8.

Seater, J.J. and R.S. Mariano (1985), 'New Tests of the Life Cycle and Tax Discounting Hypotheses', *Journal of Monetary Economics*, 15: 195–215.

Shaviro, D. (1997), *Do Deficits Matter?*, Chicago: University of Chicago Press.

Shoup, C.S. (1960), *Ricardo on Taxation*, New York: Columbia University Press.

Shoven, J.B., M.D. Topper and D.A. Wise (1994), 'The Impact of the Demographic Transition on Government Spending', in D.A. Wise (ed.), *Studies in the Economics of Aging*, Chicago: University of Chicago Press, 13–40.

Sibert, A. (1992), 'Government Finance in a Common Currency Area', *Journal of International Money and Finance*, 11: 567–78.

Siebert H. (ed.) (1996), *Monetary Policy in an Integrated World Economy – Symposium 1995*, Tubingen: Mohr.

Sims, C.A. (1999), 'The Precarious Fiscal Foundations of EMU', *De Economist*, 147(4): 415–36.

Sinn, H.W. and H. Feist (1997), 'Eurowinners and Eurolosers: The Distribution of Seignorage Wealth in EMU', NBER Working Paper, 6072.

Smets, F. (2000), 'The First Year of the Eurosystem', in H. Ooghe *et al.* (eds), *EMU, Dé Uitdaging*, Gent: Vereniging voor Economie/Voseko.

Smith, S. (1996), 'European Integration and Local Government Finance', in G. Pola, G. France and R. Levaggi (eds), *Developments in Local*

Government Finance, Cheltenham, UK and Brookfield, USA: Edward Elgar.

Smithies, A. (1960), 'The Balanced Budget', *American Economic Review*, L(2): 301–9.

Snower, D.J. and G. de la Dehesa (eds) (1997), *Unemployment Policy. Government Options for the Labour Market*, Cambridge: Cambridge University Press.

Solow, R.M. (2002), 'Is Fiscal Policy Possible? Is it Desirable?', MIT Press, mimeo.

Spahn, P.B. and W. Föttinger (1997), 'Germany', in T. Ter-Minassian (ed.), *Fiscal Federalism in Theory and Practice*, Washington, DC: IMF.

Spinnoy, C. (1998), 'Le financement des communautés et des régions', *Reflects et Perspèctives*, XXXVII(2): 7–32.

Sraffa, P. (ed.) (1952–73), *The Works and Correspondence of David Ricardo*, Cambridge: Cambridge University Press.

Stark, J. (2001), 'Where Did the Pact Come From? Genesis of a Pact', in A. Brunila, M. Buti and D. Franco (eds), *The Stability and Growth Pact – The Architecture of Fiscal Policy in EMU*, Basingstoke: Palgrave.

State General Accounting Office – Ministry of Treasury of Italy (1997), 'Sanità, scuola e pensioni – Le nuove previsioni basate sugli scenari demografici ISTAT', *Quaderno Monografico di Conti Pubblici e Congiuntura Economica*, 13.

Steve, S. (1972), *Lezioni di scienza delle finanze*, Padova: Cedam.

Strauch, R. and J. Von Hagen (eds) (2000), *Institutions, Politics and Fiscal Policy*, Dordrecht: Kluwer Academic Publishers.

Sutherland, A. (1997), 'Fiscal Crisis and Aggregate Demand: Can High Public Debt Reverse the Effects of Fiscal Policy?', *Journal of Public Economics*, 65: 147–62.

Svensson, L. (1999), 'Monetary Policy Issues for the Euro-system', Carnegie-Rochester Conference Series on Public Policy.

Tabellini, G. (2003), 'Principles of Policymaking in the European Union: An Economic Perspective', *CES Ifo Economic Studies*, 49(1): 49–75.

Tanzi, V. and D. Fanizza (1995), 'Fiscal Deficit and Public Debt in Industrial Countries, 1970–1994', IMF Working Papers, 49.

Taylor, J.B. (1993), 'Discretion versus Policy Rules in Practice', *Carnegie-Rochester Conference Series on Public Policy*, 39: 195–214.

—— (2000a), 'Reassessing Discretionary Fiscal Policy', *Journal of Economic Perspectives*, 14(3): 21–36.

—— (2000b), 'The Policy Rule Mix: A Macroeconomic Policy Evaluation', in G. Calvo, R. Dornbusch and M. Obstfeld (eds), *Money, Capital*

Mobility and Trade, Essays in Honor of Robert Mundell, Cambridge, MA: MIT Press.

Ter-Minassian, T. (ed.) (1997), *Fiscal Federalism in Theory and Practice*, Washington, DC: IMF.

Ter-Minassian, T. and J. Craig (1997), 'Control of Sub-national Borrowing Requirement', in T. Ter-Minassian (ed.), *Fiscal Federalism in Theory and Practice*, Washington, DC: IMF.

Teutemann, M. (1992), 'Rational Distribution of Competencies in the Process of European Integration', PhD thesis (in German with English summary), Berlin.

Thoni, E. (1999), 'Fiscal Federalism in Austria: Facts and New Developments', in A. Fossati and G. Panella (eds), *Fiscal Federalism in the European Union*, London: Routledge.

Tiebout, C.M. (1956), 'A Pure Theory of Local Government Expenditures', *Journal of Political Economy*, 64(5): 416–24.

Todman, L.C. (1997), 'The Decentralisation of the Belgian Government', in A.E. Andersson, B. Harsman and J.M. Quigley (eds), *Government for the Future – Unification, Fragmentation and Regionalism*, Amsterdam: Elsevier Science.

Towe, C.M. (1991), 'The Budgetary Control and Fiscal Impact of Government Contingent Liabilities', IMF Staff Papers, 38(1).

Truman, H.S. (1951), 'The Economic Report of the President', U.S. Government Printing Office, 12 January.

Tsoukalis, L. (ed.) (2000), *Competitiveness and Cohesion*, Oxford: Oxford University Press, 245–76.

Ucktum, M. and M. Wickens (1997), 'Debt and Deficit Ceilings, and Sustainability of Fiscal Policies: An Intertemporal Analysis', CEPR Discussion Papers, 1612.

Uhlig, H. (2003), 'One Money, but Many Fiscal Policies in Europe: What Are the Consequences?', in M. Buti, *Monetary and Fiscal Policies in EMU – Interactions and Coordination*, Cambridge: Cambridge University Press.

United Nations (1951), *Budgetary Structure and Classification of Government Accounts*, New York.

van Aarle, B., J. Engwerda and J. Plasmans (2001), 'Monetary and Fiscal Policy Interaction in EMU: A Dynamic Game Approach', CESifo Working Papers, 437.

van Aarle, B., J.C. Engwerda, J.E.J. Plasmans and A. Weeren (2000), 'Monetary and Fiscal Policy Design under EMU: A Dynamic Game Approach', CESifo Working Papers, 262.

Van den Noord, P. (2000), 'The Size and Role of Automatic Stabilizers in the 1990s and Beyond', OECD Economic Department, revised version in M. Buti, J. Von Hagen and C. Martinez-Mongay (eds), *The Behaviour of Fiscal Authorities*, Basingstoke: Palgrave.

—— (2002), 'Automatic Stabilizers in the 1990s and Beyond', in M. Buti, J. Von Hagen and C. Martinez-Mongay (eds), *The Behaviour of Fiscal Authorities – Stabilisation Growth and Institutions*, Basingstoke: Palgrave.

—— (2003), 'Tax Incentives and House Price Volatility in the Euro Area: Theory and Evidence', OECD Economics Department Working Papers, 356.

Van den Noord, P. and C. Heady (2001), 'Surveillance of Tax Policies: A Synthesis of Findings in Economic Surveys', OECD Economics Department Working Papers, 303.

Van den Noord, P. and R. Herd (1993), 'Pension Liabilities in the Seven Major Economies', OECD Economics Department Working Papers, 142.

—— (1994), 'Estimating pension liabilities: A methodological framework', OECD, *Economic Studies*, 23, Winter, pp. 131–66.

van Ewijk, C. (1997), 'Infrastructure, Intergenerational Conflict and the *Golden Rule* of Finance', *De Economist*, 145(3): 447–60.

van Meerhaeghe, M.A.G. (1995), 'Belgian Federalism. An Appraisal', *Journal of Public Finance and Public Choice*, 1: 71–6.

Vanston, N. (2000), 'Comment', in Banca d'Italia, *Fiscal Sustainability*, Proceedings of the Banca d'Italia Workshop on Public Finance, 20–22 January, Rome.

Von Hagen, J. (1992), 'Budgeting Procedures and Fiscal Performance in the EC', European Economy, Economic Papers, 96.

—— (2002a), 'More Growth for Stability – Reflections on Fiscal Policy in Euroland', University of Bonn, EMU Monitor Background Papers ZEI.

—— (2002b), 'Is There a Need/Rationale for Rethinking Existing Community Allocative and Redistributive Competencies?', presentation at the Commission Workshop on The Future of the EU Budget, October.

Von Hagen, J. and M. Brückner (2001), 'Monetary Policy in Unknown Territory: The European Central Bank in the Early Years', ZEI Working Papers, B 18.

Von Hagen, J. and G.W. Hammond (1996), 'Insurance against Asymmetric Shocks in a European Monetary Union', in CEPREMAP, *Should We Rebuild Built-in Stabilisers?*, Paris: CEPREMAP.

Von Hagen, J. and I. Harden (1994), 'National Budget Processes and Fiscal Performance', *European Economy Reports and Studies*, 3: 311–418.

Von Hagen, J., A. Hughes Hallett and R. Strauch (2001), 'Budgetary Consolidation in EMU', European Economy – Economic Papers, 148.

Von Hagen, J. and S. Mundshenk (2002), 'The Functioning of Economic Policy Coordination', in M. Buti and A. Sapir (eds), *EMU and Economic Policy in Europe – Challenges of the Early Years*, Cheltenham, UK and Northampton, MA, USA: Edward Elgar.

Weingast, B.R., K.A. Shepsle and C. Johnsen (1981), 'The Political Economy of Benefits and Costs: A Neoclassical Approach to Distribution Politics', *Journal of Political Economy*, 89(4): 642–64.

Wendorff, K. (2001), 'The Discussion of a National Stability Pact in Germany', in Banca d'Italia, *Fiscal Rules*, Proceedings of the Banca d'Italia Workshop on Public Finance, 1–3 February, Rome.

West, E.G. (1975), 'Public Debt Burden and Cost Theory', *Economic Inquiry*, 13: 179–90.

Wijkander, H. and W. Roeger (2002), 'Fiscal Policy in EMU: The Stabilisation Aspect', in M. Buti, J. Von Hagen, and C. Martinez-Mongay (eds), *The Behaviour of Fiscal Authorities – Stabilisation, Growth and Institutions*, Basingstoke: Palgrave.

Wilcox, D. (1989), 'The Sustainability of Government Deficits: Implications of the Present Value Borrowing Constraint', *Journal of Money, Credit and Banking*, 21: 291–306.

Wildasin, D.E. (ed.) (1997), *Fiscal Aspects of Evolving Federations*, Cambridge: Cambridge University Press.

Woodford, M. (1995), 'Price Level Determinacy Without Control of a Monetary Aggregate', *Carnegie-Rochester Conference Series on Public Policy*, 43: 1–46

—— (2001), 'Fiscal Requirements for Price Stability', *Journal of Money, Credit and Banking*, 33: 669–728.

Woodward, B. (2000), *Maestro – Greenspan's Fed and the Americam Boom*, New York: Simon & Schuster.

Wren-Lewis, S. (2000), 'The Limits to Discretionary Fiscal Stabilisation Policy', *Oxford Review of Economic Policy*, 16(4): 92–105.

Wren-Lewis, S. (2002), 'Fiscal Policy, Inflation and Stabilisation in EMU', in M. Buti, *Monetary and Fiscal Policies in EMU: Interactions and Coordination*, Cambridge: Cambridge University Press.

Wyplosz, C. (1999), 'Economic Policy Coordination in EMU: Strategies and Institutions', CEPII Working Papers, 99–04.

—— (2001), 'Fiscal Policy: Institutions vs. Rules', Report prepared for the Swedish Government's Committee on Stabilisation Policy in EMU, December.

Wyplosz, C. (2002), 'Fiscal Discipline in EMU: Rules or Institution?', EVROPAEVM Lecture, 22 November, available at http://www.oxford.ac.uk.

Zimmermann, H. (1999), 'Experiences with German Fiscal Federalism:

How to Preserve the Decentral Content?', in A. Fossati and G. Panella (eds), *Fiscal Federalism in the European Union*, London: Routledge.

Zweifel, P., S. Felder and M. Meier (1995), 'Ageing of Population and Health Care Expenditure: A Red Herring?', presented at the International Conference on Ageing and Old-Age Econometrics, Health Care Econometrics – IX, University of Athens, May.

Index